The European Union and
the regulation of media markets

MANCHESTER
1824

Manchester University Press

European Policy Research Unit Series

Series Editors: *Simon Bulmer, Peter Humphreys* and *Mick Moran*

The European Policy Research Unit Series aims to provide advanced textbooks and thematic studies of key public policy issues in Europe. They concentrate, in particular, on comparing patterns of national policy content, but pay due attention to the European Union dimension. The thematic studies are guided by the +character of the policy issue under examination.

The European Policy Research Unit (EPRU) was set up in 1989 within the University of Manchester's Department of Government to promote research on European politics and public policy. The series is part of EPRU's effort to facilitate intellectual exchange and substantive debate on the key policy issues confronting the European states and the European Union.

The European Union and the regulation of media markets

Alison Harcourt

Manchester University Press
Manchester and New York

distributed exclusively in the USA by Palgrave

Published by Manchester University Press
Oxford Road, Manchester M13 9NR, UK
and Room 400, 175 Fifth Avenue, New York, NY 10010, USA
www.manchesteruniversitypress.co.uk

Distributed exclusively in the USA by
Palgrave, 175 Fifth Avenue, New York,
NY 10010, USA

Distributed exclusively in Canada by
UBC Press, University of British Columbia, 2029 West Mall
Vancouver, BC, Canada V6T 1Z2

British Library Cataloguing-in-Publication Data
A catalogue record for this book is available from the British Library

Library of Congress Cataloging-in-Publication Data applied for

EAN 978 0 7190 6644 3 *hardback*
EAN 978 0 7190 6645 0 *paperback*

First published in paperback 2006

14 13 12 11 10 09 08 07 06   10 9 8 7 6 5 4 3 2 1

Typeset in Sabon
by SNP Best-set Typesetter Ltd., Hong Kong
Printed in Great Britain
by Biddles Ltd, King's Lynn

For my children

Contents

Tables and figures

Tables

Figures

Acknowledgements

I would like to acknowledge the funding bodies which made the research for this book possible: research took place during my two-year employment on the ESRC project 'Regulating for Media Pluralism: Issues in Competition and Ownership' at the Department of Government, University of Manchester (reference no: L126251009), my fellowship at Programme for Comparative Media Law and Policy (PCMLP) at the University of Oxford, and my Jean Monnet fellowship at the Robert Schuman Center, European University Institute (EUI). Travel grants were provided by the British Academy. Completion of the book would not have been possible without support from colleagues. In particular, I much appreciate the comments made on individual chapters by the following persons: Monica Arino, Esteban Arribas, Tom Gibbons, Tourya Guaaybess, Peter Humphreys, Roberto Mastroianni, Claudio Radaelli, Runar Woldt, and the external reviewer. A heartfelt thank you goes to Peter Humphreys for his expert advice on media policy and warm encouragement throughout. Gratitude goes to my mother who pre-copy-edited the text. I would also like to thank the following for comments on presentations leading up to this work: Giuliano Amato, Simon Bulmer, Adrienne Heritier, John Horgan, Carles Llorens-Maluquer, Ad Van Loon, Tony Prosser, Jeremy Richardson, Philip Schmitter, Stefaan Verhulst, and members of the Working Group on Media Law and Policy at the EUI. I would like to thank the editor Tony Mason, editorial controllers, Rachael Bolden and Rachel Armstrong at Manchester University Press and my copy editor, Anne Rix, who did a terrific job.

Likewise I am grateful to the many interviewees in the European Institutions, media companies, national authorities, unions and associations. I would also like to thank support staff at the EU institution libraries, the Fondation Universitaire, the European Audio-visual Observatory, the Manchester Business School library, and European University Institute. In particular, I would like to thank Andrew Baylis at the EUI for his skill in translating my hand-scribbled chart into the coherent figure on European media ownership, in Chapter 6 of the book.

I am also truly indebted to my childminders without whom this book would never have been realised: to Adrianna Cocchi for her kindness and resolute joie de vie; likewise to Donatella and Ilaria at the excellent state nursery (asilo nido) in the town of Fiesole (a Tuscan regional policy which should be a prime target for transfer).

Abbreviations

3G	Third generation mobile telephones
ADSL	asymmetric digital subscriber line
API	application programming interface
CA	conditional access
CFI	Court of First Instance
CoE	Council of Europe
COREPER	Committee of Permanent Representatives to the European Union
CULT	European Parliament Committee on Culture, Youth, Education and the Media
DAB	digital audio broadcasting
DBEG	Digital Broadcasting Expert Group
DECT	digital European cordless telecommunications
DG	Directorate General of the European Commission
DG EAC	DG Education and Culture
DTT	digital terrestrial television
DVB	Digital Video Broadcasting Group
DVB-C	DVB standard for cable transmission
DVB – CSA	Common Scrambling Algorithm (European standard)
DVB-S	DVB standard for satellite
DVB-T	DVB standard for terrestrial
EBU	European Broadcasting Union
EC	European Commission
ECJ	European Court of Justice
ECOSOC	Economic and Social Committee
ECTRA	European Committee for Telecommunications Regulatory Affairs
EP	European Parliament
EPG	Electronic programming guide
ERC	European Radiocommunications Committee
ERG	European Regulators Group

ERMES	European Radio Messaging System
ESC	Economic and Social Committe
HDTV	High definition television
IGC	Intergovernmental Conference
IPTS	Institute for Prospective Technological Stuides
Ipv6	Internet Protocol Version 6
IRG	Independent Regulators Group
ITU	International Telecommunications Union
MEDIA	Measures to improve the development of the European audio-visual industry
MTF	European Commission Merger Task force
MUDIA	MultiMedia in the Digital Age project (Seville)
NRAs	National regulatory authorities
OMC	Open method of co-ordination
ONP	Open Network Provision
PBS	public service broadcaster
SMP	Single Market project
SNP	Significant market power
TEU	Treaty on European Union (Maastricht)
TWF	Television Without Frontiers
WTO	World Trade Organisation

Introduction

The generation of Single Market initiatives are increasingly experiencing political obstacles.[1] As Wallace points out European integration was deemed in the mid-1990s to have 'hit a critical threshold beyond which it would need to be a fully fledged polity and not only an accepted arena for some shared policy regimes'. (1996: 1) Limits to European integration are encountered through the politicisation of policy areas which overstep the boundaries of the European Union (EU) as a 'regulatory state'.[2] Following the Lisbon Council Summit, the focus has shifted to the potential for 'new' or 'soft' governance to overcome these impasses (Heritier, 2001; De La Porte, 2002; Scott and Trubek, 2002). Many authors conclude that these measures, which bypass European Parliament approval (and therefore the electorate), lack democratic input and legitimacy, thereby laying bare the fragile bones of the EU polity (Radaelli, 2003; Cram, 2001; Wincott, 2001). However, others have argued that 'spaces rarely emerge and institutionalize without a concomitant development of organizations' (Stone, Sweet, Sandholtz and Fligstein, 2001: 19).

This book sheds light on to the academic debate on European governance with a case study of a borderline space: media market regulation. Since media regulation bridges concerns of both democratic governance and industrial policy, it has represented a frontier test for EU policy-making. The book asks whether media market regulation is pushing forward European integration by challenging the boundaries of the regulatory state by requiring changes to the composition of the EU polity.

In addressing this question, the book investigates the processes through which the EU has become a major actor in regulating the media sector. Media regulation presents an excellent case for the observation of European governance as communications is one of the EU's most successful policy areas. The book explains how the EU, as a constrained political system, is able to innovate new approaches to regulating this legally and politically challenging sector. It argues that, although media regulation has represented significant impasses to policy-making at various points in time, the EU has found other ways to push its agenda forward: through the initiation of European-level consortia and fora, the decentralisation of decision-making bodies, presenting 'best-practice' solutions to domestic policy problems, in combination with implementation of its policy agenda through the direct action of the competition law and jurisprudence. This combination of 'soft' and 'hard' law has driven policy convergence across Europe.

The book's finding is that even though the European institutions have been successful in regulating media markets, they have thus far been overly reliant on a policy framework dependent upon technocratic solutions to policy problems based upon economic arguments. These were ill matched to the policy impasses faced by the European Union, which were due to the democratic significance of media regulation at national levels. Conservative interpretations of the Treaties by the European Court of Justice (ECJ), the failure of the *media ownership* Directive and the success of the *convergence* Directives further embedded the EU's dependence on economic instruments. The way forward for the Commission was further market liberalisation or a resort to soft governance – without taking on board proposals geared towards protection of the public interest and democratic principles (which are stated aims of national media legislation). Hence, the EU has been unable to expand its regulatory space with an even hand to encompass democratic objectives, such as media pluralism.

Scharpf has argued that the EU bias towards regulatory policy is producing 'negative' integration based on an overemphasis on economic competition. He states that once the doctrines of the Common Market were accepted (free movement of goods, services, capital and workers) and later reinforced by the Single European Act, 'the Commission and the Court of Justice had the opportunity to continuously expand the scope of negative integration' (1996: 1). This book questions the ability of the EU institutions to forever extend the field of market regulation. Although the book finds that ECJ rulings in the media field have not strayed far from Treaty obligations, this is not always true of the European Commission (EC). Directorate Generals of the European Commission (DGs) Competition and Market have shown leanings towards 'positive' regulation (as Scharpf might define it), as they have not only regulated on the basis of furthering the Single Market, but have also shown concern for media pluralism.

Whether these leanings can actually translate into institutional change is the subject of inquiry. A number of opportunities in this respect present themselves at the time of writing: the creation of the European Constitution, EU enlargement under the Treaty of Nice, the intake of a new Commission in 2004 and the revision of the Television Without Frontiers Directive. It remains to be seen as to whether the EU can continue to bypass policy-making relevant to public interest goals or whether a 'critical threshold' has been reached whereby a change must be made to the institutional make-up of the EU.

Existing literature

The book builds upon existing work in the field. Some books have provided comparative studies of national- and European-level media policies (e.g. Ostergaard, 1997; Humphreys, 1996a). Others have looked specifically at EU policy-making (Levy, 1999; Collins, 1994b; Krebber, 2001; Ward, 2002). Many studies have concentrated on the important role of Member States in formulating EU policy across many sectors. Analogous to inter-governmentalist scholars of European integration, Levy (1999) and Krebber (2001) generally argue that the EU media policy is an arena for interstate bargaining in which France, Germany and the UK are dominant actors. EU regulation is often seen as a response to national initiatives. Levy's work in particular focuses on the continuing importance of cultural and political factors in shaping national legislation. He argues that widely differing policy styles continue to persist at the national level, due to diverse regulatory traditions, despite Commission attempts at harmonisation. Levy challenges conventional belief that technological change is promoting deregulation at the national level, arguing that Member States will continue to hold jurisdiction over this very sensitive policy area of the broadcasting industry. Other authors (e.g. Humphreys, 1996) have argued that policy convergence is occurring but is heavily influenced by other non-EU factors, such as technological change and globalisation. The EU is seen as a shield against wider global forces.

This book offers a fresh approach. It argues that although Member State governments have played a significant role in European policy-making, the EU is not just an arena where one can plot the interaction between different national actors and find a result. The same can be stated of globalisation and technological change, which are salient, but not dominant factors. The book argues that the policy process is more dynamic and that EU institutions can be pro-active and make a difference. It is argued that there has been rather a high occurrence of convergence rather than divergence in media policy, not only between the larger Member State countries, but also across the European Union. It will show how the policies of the European Union have had a substantial effect upon policy convergence. There is an increasing shift in the quest for solutions to policy problems from the national level to the international level. This shift is clear in the rising number of competition and court cases dealing with media markets. In these cases, national actors (companies, courts, governments, etc.) have directly requested that the European institutions intervene in national decision-making. Less apparent is the interaction of national interest groups and key market stakeholders, which choose to lobby at the European level in addition to the national level. The book shall detail the interplay between national and European factors with particular attention paid to the direct effect institutional decision-making has upon national policy-making.

Book layout

The book proceeds as follows: Chapter 1, 'The Evolution of EU media market regulation', details the progression of EU media policy to date, focusing upon the limits to regulation encountered by the European Union over the years. The chapter explains how the European institutions have acted upon a pro-active basis and thereby have been able to overcome hurdles to policy-making.

Chapter 2, 'Governing by judges', investigates the approach of the European Court of Justice to the regulation of media markets. The Court's developing policy on the media sector is detailed with an examination of cases dating from 1974 to the present. The chapter illustrates how the Court has played an active role in steering national media policies. In particular, it shows how, when faced with efforts by Member States to by-pass many requirements of EU Directives, the diligence of the ECJ has enforced implementation throughout EU Member States, changing forever the course of media regulation at national levels.

Chapter 3, 'Competition law, beyond the boundaries of the politically possible', explains how the EC competition directorate has taken an increasingly active role in determining the development of media markets in Europe. The competition authority will be shown to have adopted a hands-on approach to governing media mergers and acquisitions, even those made entirely within a national context. In many cases, the decisions of the competition authority have ridden roughshod over political choices made at the domestic level, regardless of national claims of subsidiarity. Thus competition law has furthered EU governance in an area, media policy, which is increasingly politically difficult to legislate through other EU regulatory instruments, such as Directives and Regulations. The chapter shows how the EC competition authority has gradually taken on considerations of media pluralism and the public interest in contrast to the ECJ in its rulings, but shows how these are not tenable without further legal basis.

Chapter 4, 'The Commission, the Parliament and media market regulation', considers the difficulties the EC faces in regulating media markets, focusing on its initiatives on media ownership and convergence. It shows how obstacles to policy-making were encountered due to limitations in the EU Treaties and inconsistencies between approaches of the different DGs in media market definition. Reasons for the failure of the media ownership Directive and the success of the convergence Directive are illustrated, and how these have reaffirmed the EC's technocratic approach to regulation. The chapter shows how the European Parliament (EP) brought the EU into wider debates about democracy through public discussion of these initiatives. The failure of the EP to influence EU policy-making, even, in one case, with a large majority of amending votes, starkly draws attention to the lack of democratic legitimacy in the EU. The chapter examines whether this has created momentum for the EU to progress towards a democratic polity.

Chapter 5, 'Interest group participation in the policy process', shows the substantial involvement of interest groups in policy processes. During the media ownership initiative, wider public consultation was used by the Commission to build support for its proposal. This move away from the closed-door policy-making style of the Commission resulted in increased politicisation. As a result, the Commission lost the support of large industry and became increasingly reliant on an advocacy coalition of smaller companies, public service broadcasters, unions and the EP. As a result of democratic enquiry, the draft Directive became increasingly detailed and restrictive, mirroring national media legislations. This approach failed, as it was essentially politically unsuccessful given the institutional arrangements of EU policy-making. The Directive may have failed, but it produced a change in the Commission technocratic policy style towards a more consensual style of decision-making. This spread to other initiatives, which had significance for the public interest (e.g. convergence, electronic commerce, data protection and parental control). However, public consultation is producing insurmountable political obstacles in Commission decision-making, which may be enforcing the trend towards less democratic forms of policy-making, such as self-regulation.

Chapter 6, 'Whither a European media market?', summarises the effect of EU policy-making on actual market development. It reviews the state of play of national media markets, pin-pointing how EU policy has restructured markets over the years. It shows that EU policy thus far appears be supporting the growth of large European groups with media interests in many Member States, but preventing further concentration in national markets. The EU is also found to prefer horizontal to vertical concentration. This differs to national approaches, which have traditionally favoured vertical over horizontal concentration. The chapter demonstrates how a key weakness in EU policy, lack of internal co-ordination within the European Commission, may be contributing to market failure at the national level. An example is internal EC discordance over standard requirements. The collapse of pay television platforms has effected most media operators in Europe, as investment largely came from existing broadcasting and publishing companies. This may have been prevented had the different DGs agreed internally on a standard-setting policy. The lack of a consistent EU approach comes from the absence of clear political guidelines.

Chapter 7, 'Engineering Europeanisation at the national level', analyses the effect that the Commission's initiatives have had at the national level, by examining the changes dictated to national media laws. In particular, the chapter will analyse the extent to which the institutions of the EU, in particular, the European Commission Merger Task Force (MTF) and ECJ, have promoted sector liberalisation and between them engineered a process of Europeanisation. It will be shown that gradually regulatory convergence is occurring between the Member States as a result. Detailed examination of regulatory overhauls of national policies occur around the mid-1980s, the early and late 1990s. At the beginning of the twenty-first century, the latest stage of regulatory convergence is occurring with national initiatives on the convergence of media and telecommunications markets following the Commission's lead.

Chapter 8 presents the book's conclusions. It summarises the empirical evidence presented in the book and its significance for the academic debate on European governance. The conclusion is that the somewhat grandiose plans for good governance introduced in the White Paper on Governance and the European Convention remain largely unfulfilled in this policy area. The chapter will add to the theoretical discussion on new governance and its problematic links with the quest for legitimacy and transparency in the EU and the debate on the future of EU regulation. The book concludes that EU media market regulation provides *potential* for the expansion of the boundaries of the EU as a regulatory state, but it essentially lacks the necessary political will from Member States to do so. The EC remains constrained by its reliance on economic arguments with which it is unable to regulate for the public interest. The conclusion points to the inherent fragility of EC media policy, due to the economic rationales upon which is based.

Notes

1   Single market policy-making began as a direct result of the Single European Act in 1986. At this time a compromise was sought in the Council of Europe over decades of stalemate in policy-making and qualified majority voting was introduced for the first time. Qualified majority voting was limited to Single Market issues governed by certain articles (e.g. 100a, 67).

2   Majone, in his 1996 work *Regulating Europe*, drew upon the earlier US literature on the rationales for regulatory policy with the aim of proposing a characterisation of the EU as a 'regulatory' political system. Majone starts with the observation that the EU – at least so far – has not followed the typical political development of western European states (Majone, 1992, 1993, 1994, 1996). The main difference has to do with policy types. Nation states developed around distributive and redistributive policies (in brief, welfare and extractive policies, such as taxation). By contrast, the EU, Majone argues, has grown disproportionately in its regulatory dimension. The limited Community budget has prevented the growth of a EU welfare state. Tax powers attributed to the EU have not gone much further than an embryonic direct tax system and harmonisation of value added tax. There is no such thing as EU income tax co-ordination or

EU corporate tax that could resemble the US federal corporation tax. However, the EU has excelled in the production of *regulation* (as a distinct policy type). Relevant examples of this are the regulation of telecommunications, HDTV and cross-border broadcasting.

1

The evolution of EU media market regulation

EU media market regulation is part of an umbrella regulatory framework for communications. Significantly, the EU's framework for the communication sector is rooted in industrial policy. Principal concerns have been the drive for capital investment and correction of the trade imbalance with the United States. The policy itself has been locked into a discourse of 'job growth'. The communications industry has been portrayed by the EC as a panacea solution to the long-term loss of jobs in manufacturing industries, as domestic companies move offshore. The 'convergence' Green Paper of the European Commission (1997a) predicted that 'market growth can be transformed into jobs to bring the number of people employed in the industry in Europe (1.8 million) closer to the level in the United States (2.6 million)' (IPTS, 2000; CEC, 1998a). Consecutive EU policy documents have built up a communal faith by governments in the capacity of the communications industries to ease the very serious problem of growing unemployment in Europe.[1]

●Two landmark Directives, Television Without Frontiers and Open Network Provision, together form the backbone of the EU communications policy regime. The 1989 'Television without frontiers' (TWF) Directive provided a framework for capital mobility within the EU for services which were previously confined to national markets – television and radio signals. The goal was chiefly to encourage (via national deregulation) the exploitation of new technologies (initially cable and satellite). By defining television signals as services entitled to free movement within the internal market, TWF paved the way for cross-border transmission via satellite and cable. According to TWF, a broadcaster could only be regulated by the country of origin and not by the country of reception – a principle that was derived from the EJC rulings in the 1970s and early 1980s. The 1990 Open Network Provision (ONP) Directive provided open access to telecommunications services and networks based upon the principle of non-discrimination and the elimination of exclusive rights. Two streams of Directives were adopted in parallel: the liberalisation Directives under

Article 86 (competition law) and the ONP Directives under Article 95 (internal market). As Thatcher (1999) and Natalicchi (2002) have explained, the telecommunications liberalisation Directives are unique as they were based upon competition law, specifically Article 90.3 (now 86.3) of the Treaty of Rome.[2] The TWF and ONP Directives together paved the way for a series of subsequent Directives in the field (Appendix 1).

In the 1990s, technological innovation began to blur the boundaries between the traditional telecommunications and media sectors. Digital technology suddenly made it possible to compress data, visual image and sound into digital bytes which can be sent down fixed lines (e.g. telephone, cable, Asymmetric Digital Subscriber Lines (ADSL), powerline systems, broadband cable) or wireless systems (e.g. satellite, mobile telephony) to television sets, home computers and new generation mobile telephones.[3] Digital compression put an end to spectrum scarcity. Broadband cable, whether copper or the more advanced fibre-optic, can carry so much capacity that it facilitates the broadcast of digital television and radio.[4] This makes it possible for even national terrestrial broadcasters to broadcast abroad. Broadband can carry two-way communication, which facilitates interactive television and interactive advertising. Digital technology enables television channels to be received in many languages simultaneously. New services such as video-on-demand, near video-on-demand, multi-angle broadcasting, interactive television, telebanking, gaming (including interactive game shows) and computer telephony are becoming or have already become possible. New technology has also led to a proliferation in new advertising techniques: split-screen advertising, virtual advertising, T-commerce (television-commerce), e-commerce (electronic commerce), self-promotion, teleshopping, infomercials, telepromotions, etc. Companies that traditionally operated in separate markets (e.g. terrestrial broadcasters, satellite broadcasters, cable operators, long-distance telephone companies, local exchange carriers, personal computer manufacturers, software developers, content producers, internet service providers) are able to cross over to adjacent markets. The regulatory implications are enormous. This is particularly the case for the various stages of transmission: bundling, decoder technology, delivery system technology, scrambling, conditional access systems, common interfaces, application programming interfaces (APIs), electronic programming guides (EPGs), smart cards, etc.

The EC embraced the advent of new technologies with a series of 'White Papers' in the 1990s in which it presented policy recommendations to the European Council. Technological convergence became central to arguments for market liberalisation. The Commission viewed the concentration of financial capital as indispensable for the exploitation of new technologies. The papers focused heavily on the potential of technological growth for job creation (Collins and Murroni, 1996: 1–3). The 1993 Delors White Paper on 'Growth, competitiveness and employment' identified the media market as one of only three sectors expected to produce future job growth (Appendix 1). The 1994 Bangemann White Paper on 'Europe and the global information society' hones in on the importance of the sector for both job growth and international trade.[5] It was in this paper that the term 'information society' was first coined and used from this point onwards to frame communications policy debates.[6] The paper states that national media regulations 'are a patchwork of inconsistency which tend to distort and fragment the market. They impede companies from taking advantage of the opportunities offered by the internal market, especially in multimedia, and could put them in jeopardy *vis-à-vis* non-European competitors.' This discourse was endorsed politically at the 1998 Birmingham European Audio-visual Conference; Jacques Santer predicted a 70 per cent global growth rate in the industry to take place within the subsequent decade.

Forwarding the policy agenda

The Commission sought to advance liberalisation in the field with two initiatives: *media ownership* and *convergence*. The chief concern in the first 1992 Green Paper, 'Pluralism and media concentration in the internal market' (CEC, 1992a), is the negative effect of national media legislation upon internal market growth. As a precursor to the Bangemann Report, it argues that Europe's media industry was hindered by extensively different ownership rules in each Member State. The main argument throughout the paper is for the harmonisation of Member States' media ownership rules, the 'disparity' of which were seen to 'brake structural adjustment' in the internal market. The draft Directive proposed the common market measure that no owner could dominate over 30 per cent audience share in a multi-media market. Multi-media at this point in time meant the traditional media markets of newspapers, radio and television (excluding new services). This measure was designed to allow for three large players and one small player at national levels. The second Green Paper, 'Convergence of the telecommunications, media and information technology sectors, and the implications for regulation', (CEC, 1997b), proposed to break down national regulatory boundaries between internet, telecommunications and television with a policy framework which encompassed all communication technologies and sought to eradicate inconsistencies between policies in different communications sectors. It recommends expansion of large communications conglomerates, which it envisions would compete with each other in many different countries in different markets. The market measure suggested in the Green Paper on convergence was that no player could own more than 30 per cent of market share. But the definition of the 'market' was to include traditional media markets, telecommunications markets and new services markets, which would allow for the possibility to create larger players.

The EC was presented with significant impasses to these policy proposals. Firstly, the Commission had come to the end of its Single Market programme. Single Market implementation was planned for a limited period of time only. It began as a direct result of the Single European Act in 1987 and ended with the completion of the Single Market in 1992 (Wessels and Weidenfeld, 1997). Its implementation had enabled a surge in regulatory growth during the 1980s. The fact that 1992 had come and gone, and the increased realisation by Member States of implementation costs, inevitably slowed regulatory growth. At the end of the Single Market programme, at the European Council Edinburgh summit in 1992, Member States formally agreed to slow the growth in policy by limiting the number of initiatives per year. The political emphasis turned to subsidiarity and flexibility as was formalised by the Maastricht Treaty in 1992. By 1997, only seven new Directives were passed by the European Council in a single year. A second factor hindering the introduction of further single market initiatives was that implementation of existing Directives was proving unsatisfactory. This was recognised in the Sutherland Reports which set up a programme to accelerate the implementation of Single Market policies (CEC, 1992b, 1992c, 1993b, 1993c). Satisfactory progress was not achieved. Consequently, the Commission established the 'Action plan for the Single Market', which was endorsed by the Amsterdam European Council in 1997 (CEC, 1997d). The plan manifested itself in a bi-annual implementation scoreboard, which the Commission submits to the Internal Market Council of the European Council.

Despite the slow-down in regulatory growth, the EU was able to push forward its agenda during the 1990s through other instruments, namely competition law and jurisprudence. Through these two powerful instruments, EU institutions were able to override the many political obstacles presented to the Commission's liberalising policy framework. The TWF and ONP Directives were enforced under competition law. In media markets, the MTF became particularly active in moulding emerging digital television markets. When faced with efforts by Member States to bypass European legislation, the diligence of the ECJ over a ten year period enforced implementation at the national level.

To complement actions of the ECJ and the MTF, the EC simultaneously practiced a 'softer' approach to furthering its policy agenda through the suggestion of best practices, models and solutions to the problem of regulating media markets. This was done specifically through the promotion of regulatory instruments in Commission Reports, Green Papers and Draft Directives. Consultation with national administrations and interest groups enabled the dissemination of suggested policy instruments and recommendations at the national level. In its 1994 Green Paper on ownership (CEC, 1994a) and two studies (GAH, 1993, 1994), the Commission suggested a new policy instrument, the measurement of media markets by audience share. This model was adopted by the UK and Germany in 1996 and later by other countries. In its 1997 Convergence Green Paper, the Commission recommended a new joint authority for both media and telecommunications (1997a). Spain (1997), Italy (1998), Switzerland (2000), Slovenia (2001) and the UK (2003) subsequently adopted the model for a joint regulatory authority at the national level. The embracement of European policy recommendations by national legislators legitimised the EC policy agenda.

This combination of 'soft' and 'hard' approaches to regulating media markets enabled the EC to move the policy process forward. The next step was to attain consensus on the direction of policy-making through the initiation of and dialogue with industrial consortia. In the media field, these were, specifically, the Bangemann Group and the Digital Video Broadcasting (DVB) Group. The first Bangemann Group of 20 European industry leaders was set up in 1994, the second group in 1995. Dialogue over standard setting was initiated with the DVB Group. DVB was originally established in 1993 as the European Launching Group. It evolved into an industry-led consortium of with over 300 members.[8]

These initiatives proved highly successful. The Bangemann Group attained industry consensus on the 'convergence' initiative. A follow-up to the Convergence Green Paper was published in 1999, 'The convergence of the telecommunications, media and information technology sectors, and the implications for regulation: results of the public consultation on the Green Paper' (CEC, 1999b). This led to the 2002 'regulatory framework for electronic communications and services'.[9] The DVB Group agreed on delivery standards for digital television and data services. It accorded a number of standard agreements on the transmission of satellite services (DVB-S), cable (DVB-C), terrestrial (DVB-T), service information (DVB-SI), and videotext (DVB-TXT) for European markets. DAB (Digital Audio Broadcasting) was the standard established for radio broadcasting. The standard for compression for digital television is DVB-MPEG 2. For scrambling, it is the DVB – CSA (Common Scrambling Algorithm).[10] The DVB Group established two standards for decoders (used in set-top boxes): multicrypt and simultcrypt. The Commission plans to enforce these agreements by developing co-ordination mechanisms at the European level.

The new ('convergence') regulatory framework consists of six Directives: a 'framework' Directive and five accompanying Directives ('Authorisation' Directive, 'Access' Directive, 'Universal Service' Directive, 'Data Protection' Directive and the 'Liberalisation' Directive) (Appendix 1). Also included in the package was a Commission Decision on Radio Spectrum (the 'Spectrum Decision'), a Market Recommendation and Guidelines for SMP.[11] The plan is to 'roll back' regulation as competition becomes effective in relevant markets (CEC, 2002a: 8). The European Commission wants assurances in national laws that national legal systems allow for appeals on national regulatory decisions. In order to guide implementation, the EC has set up the

Communications Committee, which operates in addition to the pre-existing Open Network Provision Committee and Licensing Committee. In addition there is the internal Digital Broadcasting Expert Group (DBEG) which was established by the ONP Committee in October 2000.

This regulatory framework seeks to regulate both traditional media and telecommunications networks together. Specifically, 'networks and services used for the transmission of radio and television broadcast content, such as satellite broadcasting networks, terrestrial broadcasting networks or cable television networks, will be subject to the general authorisation regime provided in the Authorisation Directive' (CEC, 2002a: 8). The 'Authorisation' Directive therefore has a number of implications for traditional broadcasting markets. According to Article 3 (2), communications operators (including television and radio) 'can no longer be subject to an individual licence'. It adds 'Member States *may* be permitted to attach conditions' to communications operators outlined in Part A of the Annex of the Authorisation Directive, and 'additional conditions relating to content' found in national broadcasting law and TWF. Significantly, the Directive states, 'The separation between the regulation of transmission and the regulation of content does not prejudice the taking into account of the links existing between them, in particular in order to guarantee media pluralism, cultural diversity and consumer protection.'

The Authorisation *permits* Member States to require 'must-carry rules'[12] on certain broadcasters but only 'where a significant number of end-users of such networks use them as their principal means to receive radio and television broadcasts' (e.g. presently the UK, Belgium and Germany have 'must-carry' rules platforms to carry national public service broadcasters). The must-carry rule was an original plan of the European Commission, but with a compensation obligation. Compensation for must-carry requirements was removed during the consultation period for the Directive. Nascient broadcast operators carrying content cannot be obligated to must-carry rules, meaning that telecommunications operators, broadband and 3G mobile networks are exempt.

The regulatory framework included the establishment of a new European forum: the European Regulators Group (ERG). The ERG was established by a Commission Decision (Appendix 1). Its establishment is the result of a new regulatory trend of legitimising European regulatory fora in Commission Decisions. (CEC, 1997a)[13] The ERG acts as a forum for national regulatory authorities (NRAs) of both telecommunications and media markets. It is based upon the model outlined in the Commission's 1997 Green Paper on Convergence. The ERG is to establish

'co-operation and co-ordination of national regulatory authorities, in order to promote the development of the internal market or electronic communications networks and services, and to seek to achieve consistent application, in all Member States, of the provisions set out in this directive and the Specific directives, in particular in areas where national law implementing Community law gives national regulatory authorities considerable discretionary powers in application of the relevant rules'. (Recital 36 of the Framework Directive)

The Commission's role in the ERG is to 'produce Guidelines to assist NRAs with market analysis and the assessment of significant market power'. The ERG operates in parallel to the pre-existing regulatory fora in the separate fields: the European Platform of Regulatory Authorities (EPRA) (of regulatory authorities in the broadcasting field), the European Radiocommunications Committee (ERC), the European Committee for Telecommunications Regulatory Affairs (ECTRA),[14] the Independent Regulators Group (IRG) (for telecommunications).[15] As stated, ERG is the only forum, in the communications field, legitimised by a Commission Decision and the only one to have formalised consultation rules. This empowers ERG *vis-à-vis* existing regulatory fora. Similar to fora in other fields,[16] EPRA is a *voluntary* forum for national regulatory authorities, which functions on the exchange of information only and does not have the power to accord agreements or best-practice guidelines. Although EPRA is (financially) endorsed by the EC, it was not established by the EC and is not acknowledged in any EC Decision or other document.

In addition, the Framework Directive recommends a number of standards agreed in consultation with industrial consortia. For example, it recommends the SCART/Peritel connector as the standard for open interface sockets on analogue and digital television sets. The Directive demands that 'such sockets have to be standardised by a recognised European Standards Organisation'. It also recommends the DVB common interface for conditional access and interactive television services; the 16:9 aspect ratio standard for wide-screen services; and the DVB-MHP standard for interoperability in interactive television.[17]

The move towards soft governance

In March 2000, the European Council established its 'Open method of co-ordination' (OMC), which was announced in the conclusions of the Lisbon Council summit (European Council, 2002). Although made official at Lisbon, OMC was used before Lisbon in economic and employment policies. The OMC is essentially a method for the agreement of policy guidelines for the EU through exchange of information, benchmarking, emulation of best practice, target-setting, monitoring and peer review. It proceeds on an annual review process (De La Porte, 2002). The method is exceptional as it is to be executed within the European Council effectively bypassing approval by the Commission and European Parliament.[18] The announcement of OMC came clothed in the customary rhetoric of job creation and reiterated the faith that new technologies would conjure up jobs that had not existed before. The Lisbon summit promised the creation of a most dynamic 'knowledge-based economy with more and better employment and social cohesion' – the deadline for implementation is 2010. The Lisbon meeting set up the 'Information Society Project', which aims to take advantage of new technologies and services. Some potentially hot political issues are named, such as e-government, e-democracy, e-voting, e-learning, e-culture, e-health, e-banking, e-education, e-media, e-security, e-banking, e-business, e-commerce and so on.[19] The idea for the e-initiatives had actually come from the European Commission, which was preparing the ground for the launch of its eEurope initiative.[20] The policy areas covered by the OMC are detailed more specifically in an explanatory note following the Lisbon meeting. Six policy areas are designated[21] the first of which is notably the 'information society' under which communications and media policy fall (European Council, 2000: 4).

Many authors see the OMC as a new form of governance created as a solution to a failure in traditional policy-making methods (Heritier, 2001; Trubeck and Mosher, 2002; Scott and Trubeck, 2002).[22] This explanation does not hold up well in communications policy – where arguably the EC has been quite successful compared with other policy areas. More plausible is that the OMC method reflects an institutional struggle for power between the Commission and the Council. In the communications field (labelled 'information society' by the Council and Commission alike), it is clear that the OMC is an attempt by national governments to retain policy-making competence within the jurisdiction of national institutions. The OMC may serve as a political counterweight to the newer generation of EC initiatives, which have relied heavily on agreement between key private actors. Importantly, it gives the Council the power of initiative, a power formerly maintained by the EC.

The Commission responded to the Lisbon Summit with its White Paper on 'European Governance' (CEC, 2001b) in the summer of 2001. The White Paper was more or less a defensive reaction to the proposals of the Council. It recognises the difficulties with traditional EC policy-making methods but insists on the continued use of the community method, which has proved essential for European integration. If an alternative method is used, however, it should be chiefly the Commission, not the Council, which should advance new approaches to governance. In particular, it objects to the use of OMC in areas already covered by the *acquis communitaire,* which would include communications policy. Despite Commission opposition, the Council has been very vocal in the field of media policy and has acted as a forum for Member States to have a more direct say in Commission agenda setting. For example, in June 2000, the Council recommended the need for Europe to expand its use of digital, broadband and IPv6. The Commission's DG for Information Society responded to the call with the inclusion of the

Council's suggestions in its eEurope Action Plan[23] as established in an EC Communication.[24] The Council idea is for increased public–private co-operation in new markets and the establishment of digital platforms. The Council's influence over Commission policy-making has been felt further with its resistance to the expansion of the TWF Directive, in its 2003–4 review. This comes from both the Ministers for Education, Youth and Culture[25] and the Ministers of Telecommunications. TWF revision has also been highlighted by the Italian presidency of the EU in a number of 'informal' Council meetings.[26]

The Commission, of course, has long engaged in soft approaches to governance. Examples of these in the media field are the 1995 Data Protection Directive and the 2000 Electronic Commerce[27] Directive (Appendix 1) which outline Codes of Conduct for national governments. Another example is found in the Annex of the 1998 Council 'Recommendation on the protection of minors and human dignity', which stipulates, 'Indicative guidelines for the implementation, at national level, of a self-regulation framework for the protection of minors and human dignity in on-line audio-visual and information services.' The guidelines contain legal recommendations and codes of conduct and monitoring mechanisms. Another example is the EC 'Action plan on safer use of the internet.' The Commission is advancing these initiatives through regular reviews and progress reports.

The White Paper on Governance provides some political legitimacy to the *expansion* of these types of initiatives. The Commission is rapidly enlarging its soft governance sphere in the media field with 'self-regulation', 'self-monitoring', and 'co-regulation'.[28] It seeks to legitimise existing self-regulatory bodies and to cement them at the European level, and to establish new bodies, perhaps based upon national models. The search is on for existing self-regulatory bodies. The European Commission (under the Internet Action Plan – IAP) is presently funding a three-year study (IAPCODE) at the University of Oxford[29] which is tracking down 'self-regulatory codes of conduct across national, EU and international boundaries covering a wide range of media from Internet, film, video (games), (digital) television to mobile communications'. The project offers self-regulatory bodies assistance in the development and implementation of codes of conduct.

National bodies have long been involved in self-regulatory practice in the media field. Emulative examples recommended by a 2003 Council of Europe study are the Freiwillige Selbstkontrolle Fernsehesn (FSF) and Nederlands Instituut voor de Classificatie van Audiovisuele Media (NICAM). FSF is a body for the self-regulation of content in television in Germany whose board contains one-third representation from broadcasters and two-thirds field experts and civil society representatives. NICAM is an example of co-regulation. An industry consortium classifies content on television, video, film and games, which is then legitimised by the Dutch government. An example of a *European* level self-regulatory body is the European Advertising Standards Alliance (EASA). EASA is a European association of national advertising association members, which adopted an agreement on 'Self-regulation – A Statement of Common Principles and Operating Standards of Best Practice' in June 2002. Within this framework, EASA has established a committee for cross-border advertising complaints.

This move towards self-regulation through European fora and industry consortia is flanked by the creation and decentralisation of European-level agencies. An example is the European Union Satellite Centre,[30] which was established by a 'joint action' of the European Council in 2001[31] in Madrid. A second example is the Joint Research Centre (JRC) of the European Commission. JRC is actually an entire Directorate General of the European Commission which is split into seven 'institutes' located in five different EU Member States. The Institute for Prospective Technological Studies (IPTS)[32] conducts research and projects on media markets and is located in Seville. It hosts the MUDIA MultiMedia in the Digital Age (MUDIA) project[33] which collects data and consumption patterns of European media industries.

Conclusion

This chapter has shown how the EU has advanced its policy agenda when presented with political limitations to integration. This was through a combination of 'soft' and 'hard' instruments of European governance. However, this approach is only furthering economic integration while bypassing and often overriding public interest regulation. The following chapters will flesh out how exactly EU policies have side stepped the public interest in the interest of greater European integration. In doing so, the book seeks to assess whether this method of regulatory policy-making is straining the capacity of the EU as a regulatory state, thereby forcing a change in the EU polity.

Notes

1 This has mirrored similar debates in the US. The 1993 National Information Infrastructure (NII) Agenda for Action states 'An advanced information infrastructure will enable US firms to compete and win in the global economy, generating good jobs for the American people and economic growth for the nation'. See McKenna (2000) for discussion. Similar claims are evident in latter US debates leading to the 1996 Communications Act and recent legislation (2003) removing media ownership rules.

2 This is important as EC competition law does not require approval by the Council of Ministers or the European Parliament and is only subject to review by the European Court of Justice. Under the 1989 Luxembourg compromise, the Commission agreed to use competition law in agreement with the council.

3 The transmission of digital television to home computers and mobile telephones through the Internet Protocol is called IP datacasting. The standard the European Commission is promoting for this is IPv6. IPv6 is an abbreviation of 'Internet Protocol Version 6'. IPv6 is the 'next generation' protocol designed by the Internet Engineering Task Force (IETF) to replace the current version Internet Protocol, IP Version 4 ('IPv4').

4 Scheuer and Knopp estimate that whereas digital terrestrial television can carry up to 100 programmes, broadband cable can carry up to 1,000 (2003: 15).

5 The Bangemann report (CEC, 1994d) was a report of the (Bangemann chaired) Council of Ministers Higher Level Group, entitled 'Europe and the global information society' as the submitted to the European Council for its meeting in Corfu on 24–25 June 1994.

6 Bangemann's 'Information society' was a direct (European) response to the US 'information superhighway' project announced by Al Gore in January 1994, which began under the National Information Infrastructure in 1993. In 1994, Al Gore stated that the United States would drop restrictions limiting foreign investment in telecommunications services in order to force other countries to open up their markets.

7 Similarly, agreement in the telecommunications sector was sought through consultation with the industria consortia, the European Telecommunications Platform (ETP) and European Telecommunications Network Operators' Association.

8 DVB is a group of manufacturers, network operators, software developers, regulatory bodies and others. www.dvb.org/.

9 The 2002 'Regulatory framework for electronic communications and services' consisted of five Directives and one Decision: the Framework Directive, Authorisation Directive, Access Directive, Universal Service Directive, Data Protection Directive and the Radio Spectrum Decision (Appendix 1).

10 Scrambling means that the sequence of the data stream for a programme or service is sorted according to a mathematical rule (see Scheuer and Kropp for detail).

11 The guidelines are on market analysis and the calculation of 'significant market power' (SMP), which set out (in Article 13 of the Directive) the principles for use by NRAs in analysing effective competition. Market players designated as having SMP may be subject to obligations under other Directives in the regulatory package. The draft Guidelines are based on the relevant jurisprudence of the Court of First Instance and the Court of Justice cases in addition to EC competition policy in defining relevant market and collective dominant position. The draft Guidelines are available at http://europa.eu.int/ispo/infosoc/telecompolicy.

12 'Must-carry' rules require platform operators (e.g. cable, satellite) to carry broadcasting channels or packages as stipulated by regulatory authorities. The system was firstly introduced in the USA as a congressional amendment to the Communications Act in 1992. It required cable systems to allocate up to one-third of their capacity to carry broadcast signals and the broadcast of non-commercial stations.

13 The Committee of European Securities Regulators (CESR) was the first of these fora established by the European Commission Decision of June 2001. This

decision was taken in the light of the recommendation of the Report of the EC Committee of Wise Men on the Regulation of European Securities Markets (CESR) (Lamfalussy Report), as endorsed by the European Union (Stockholm, 23 March 2001). CESR is an independent Committee regrouping senior representatives from national public authorities competent in the field of securities.

14 ECTRA is based in Copenhagen where it has established the European Telecommunications Office (ETO).

15 The Independent Regulators Group (IRG) was established in 1997 as a voluntary group of European National Telecommunications Regulatory Authorities (NRAs) to share information. Hills and Michalis suggests that this group was established in reaction to the Commission's proposals on convergence (Hills and Michalis, 2000: 458).

16 E.g. the Electricity Regulatory Forum, the Gas Regulatory Forum and the European Union Satellite Center. See Eberlein (2003) for discussion of regulatory fora in utilities sectors.

17 The standard is called Multimedia Home Platform (DVB-MHP) and is based on the Java system developed by the company Sun Microsystems. MHP was officially recognised by the European Telecommunications Standards Institute on 12 July 2000.

18 As a number of authors have noted, the objectives of the OMC are hazy at best and change year to year (Radaelli, 2003; Cram, 2001; Wincott, 2001; Trubeck and Mosher, 2002; Scott and Trubeck, 2002). De La Porte details the Council's creeping competence of initiative through its Broad Economic Policy Guidelines (BEPG) review, which began exclusively as a plan for the co-ordination of economic policy, but is now encompassing other policy areas. BEPG is reviewed yearly in March at Spring Summit of the European Council.

19 On e-voting see Kies, 2002. For e-learning see Noam (1995; 1998).

20 The Presidency conclusions of the Lisbon Council gave recognition to the eEurope proposal.

21 These are the information society, research and development (R&D), enterprises, economic reforms, education, employment and social inclusion.

22 In the traditional 'Community method', the Commission has a monopoly over the right of initiative, the Council of Ministers and European Parliament adopt proposals, Member States implement under observation of the Commission that may refer a State to the ECJ. Under the OMC method, the European Council initiates, the national strategies of each Member State are implemented by the State, and the Commission can only co-ordinate and make recommendations to the Member State.

23 http://europa.eu.int/information_society/eeurope/index_en.htm. This includes a number of e-initiatives such as the eEBO (eContent Exposure and Business Opportunities) and eContent initiatives.

24 European Council and European Commission (2000), *'eEurope 2002: an information society for all'* – Action plan prepared for the European Council of Feira, 19–20 June 2000. http://europa.eu.int/information_society/eeurope/action_plan/actionplantext/index_en.htm.

25 Press release 8430/03 (Presse 114) of the 2503rd Council meeting on Education, Youth and Culture, Brussels, 5–6 May 2003.

26 Informal Council of Audiovisual Ministries Siracusa 12–14 September 2003.
27 Directive 2000/31/EC of 8 June 2000 on certain legal aspects of information society services, in particular electronic commerce, in the Internal Market OJL 178, 17 July 2000.
28 For definitions of 'self-monitoring', 'self-regulation', 'co-regulation' see Palzer (2003).
29 Carried out by the Programme in Comparative Media Law and Policy at the centre for Socio-Legal Studies at Oxford University. www.selfregulation.info/.
30 www.eusc.org/.
31 Council Joint Action of 20 July 2001 on the establishment of a European Union Satellite Centre (2001/555/CFSP).
32 www.jrc.es/welcome.html.
33 The MUDIA project was launched in May 2001 (www.mudia.org). It is based in Seville at IPTS with the following partners: (1) Institute for Infonomics, Maastricht (co-ordinator); (2) World Association of Newspapers (WAN), Paris; (3) News World International Limited, London; (4) Institute for Prospective Technological Studies (IPTS), Sevilla; (5) Comtec, Dublin City University.

2

Governing by judges

Introduction

Europeanisation of the policy domain began during the 1970s with the first ECJ decisions on the media market, following which the ECJ has made over 50 decisions in the sector. ECJ decisions provided the European Commission (EC) with a basis for a number of initiatives during the 1980s which affected the media market, the most significant of which is the 1989 Television Without Frontiers (TWF) Directive. This chapter explores the development of the ECJ approach to media market regulation with an examination of cases dating from 1974 to 2003. The chapter illustrates how the Court has played a decisive role in steering national media policies. In particular it shows how the ECJ has interpreted the TWF Directive for national courts. However, it has paid strict attention to TWF's provisions on market liberalisation (e.g. cross-border broadcasting), whilst ignoring those relating to public interest goals (e.g. restriction of advertising time, content quotas) and sometimes overriding them (e.g. protection of minors). This has eroded the national capacity to regulate media markets and created a situation of regulatory arbitrage in Europe.

For the purposes of this chapter, it is useful to consider the literature on the role of the ECJ as a political actor in the EU policy process. The function of the ECJ, according to Article 164 [220] of the Treaty of Rome, is to make sure that the 'law is observed' when interpreting the Treaties. It does this by reviewing Community legislation, monitoring Member State compliance and ruling on cases brought before it (Chalmers, 1998: 136). The legal foundation for all ECJ decisions is found in the EU treaties.[1] As national compliance with international treaties has proven historically weak, the creation and tenacity of the EU as a political system has been heralded by academic lawyers as a major achievement. It has been much agreed upon that the establishment and evolution of the EU into its present state has largely been determined by the ECJ. Academic lawyers have claimed that the ECJ has taken the founding EU treaties and transformed them into a constitution (Shapiro, 1980; Weiler, 1993; Wincott, 1993; Dehousse, 1998). Through strengthening its own role, the ECJ has 'acted as a catalyst in the integration process, through the innovations it is exerted on the legislature' (Dehousse, 1998: 71).

Authors have pointed to the Court's role as a policy-maker. Bulmer (1994) and Cini and McGowen (1999) gave the example of the Court's role as an agenda setter in EC competition policy. Other authors have looked at the Court's role in policy-making areas such as the Single Market and social policy (Volcansek, 1992; Allen, 1996; Leibfried and Pierson, 1996). Dehousse (1998: 82) outlines the ways in which the Court can influence policy at each stage of the policy process:

• it can suggest new avenues to be explored
• it can legitimate certain choices and delegitimate others
• it can provoke Community legislative intervention
• its existence affects the relationships between the various actors involved in policy debates
• it plays a central role in the implementation of common decisions.

This framework is useful when examining the effect of ECJ case law on EC media policy. Indeed, the evidence presented in this chapter confirms the ECJ's assertive action in all stages of the policy process listed above. However, it should be noted that the Court, due to the limitations of the Treaties, has a tendency towards economic rather than political integration in its decisions. Dehousse indicates that the Court recognises its own propensity towards negative integration (1998: 80) and compensates for this by increasing the number of exceptions to the principle of freedom of movement to compensate for Member State national polices in 'positive' policy areas (Dehousse gives examples of environmental policy, consumer protection and health and safety of works). However, as Shapiro has remarked, when dealing with areas that have 'political dimensions [the Court's] progress [has] been painfully slow' (Dehousse, 1998: ix). This is certainly true for the public interest aspects of media regulation, as will be shown. The majority of ECJ rulings in the media sector have the tendency to further market integration, rather than the defence of national laws geared towards the protection of pluralism. The chapter recognises that the Court has been overwhelmingly important in its role of agenda setting and harmonising national laws. However, later chapters will show that it has been left up to the other institutions of the EU (most notably the Commission and European Parliament) to inject aspects of public interest regulation into the EU's overall media policy.

It shall be shown that a series of ECJ and Court of First Instance (CFI) rulings have gradually weaned media policy away from the domain of the Member State and placed it in the realm of the Single Market. This had the effect of enabling other EU institutions to take an increasingly active approach towards governing media markets. In many cases, the ECJ decisions ran roughshod over the cultural considerations of the Member States in the goal of implementing the Single Market. There is no doubt that these Court decisions have had a direct effect upon the development of national media legislation.

This chapter examines chronologically ECJ decisions relating to media markets with detail on cases of significance. Broadcasting market cases will be discussed first, followed by press market cases. The effects of the ECJ rulings *vis-à-vis* the policies of the Commission and Member States are commented upon. The chapter concludes with a discussion on how ECJ decisions have contributed generally to the EU's regulatory framework for the media.

ECJ decisions in broadcasting markets

The first significant ECJ case dealing with the media industry is the *Sacchi* case in 1974 (Appendix 2). The case was brought by the cable operator, Giuseppe Sacchi, to the tribunal court of the small Italian town of Biella. Sacchi claimed that the national Italian Public Service Broadcaster (PSB) Radio Audizioni Italiane (RAI) could not continue its monopoly over advertising revenue as it prevented obstacles to the sale of goods from other Member States, which should be sold through cable television as well as through the national PSB. The Biella Court referred the case first to the Italian Constitutional Court in 1974, which upheld that RAI could indeed hold a national monopoly. The Biella Court then referred the case directly to the ECJ. It asked specifically whether the movement of *goods* within the common market applied to television signals. The Court did not find that RAI's monopoly restricted the trade of *goods* within the EC, neither did it object to the fact that RAI was acting in the capacity of a monopoly as this was justified under national cultural policy. However, the case gave it the opportunity to define broadcasting signals as an economic activity, thereby coming under the jurisdiction of the Treaty of Rome. The ECJ ruled that 'in the absence of express provision to the contrary in the treaty, a television signal must, by reason of its nature, be regarded *a provision of services*'. It added that 'trade in material, sound recordings, films, apparatus and other products used for the diffusion of television signals are subject to the rules relating to freedom of movement for *goods*'.

The second case of such importance was the 1980 *Debauve* case 1980 (Appendix 2), which established that any discrimination by a Member State against a broadcasting signal due to national origin is illegal. The case dealt with the cable company Coditel, which was receiving terrestrial broadcasts from abroad and retransmitting to Belgian customers via cable. Belgium legislation at the time banned the transmission of commercial advertising.[2] Because Coditel was transmitting advertising to cable subscribers in Belgium, the company was prosecuted. The Belgian court referred the case to the ECJ. The ECJ stated 'in the absence of harmonisation of the rules applicable in the matter of television broadcasting, all Member States are competent to regulate, restrain or prohibit advertising messages, for reasons of general interest and without discrimination'. This ruling gave impetus for the TWF initiative of the EC, which sought to break down restrictions on cross-national broadcasting. The judgement restates the *Sacchi* ruling that broadcasting should be considered as an economic service.

The *Sacchi* and *Debauve* rulings were extremely significant for the future development of EU media policy. The *Sacchi* case declared that broadcasting be considered a tradable service.[3] Therewith the sector was established as ripe for the single market policy-making. Both *Sacchi* and *Debauve* provided a legal basis for the 1989 TWF Directive.

The next ECJ case dealing with cross-national broadcasting was *Coditel SA v. Cinévog Films* (Appendix 2). In this case, an exclusive licence for showing the film 'La Boucher' was granted to Cinévog, a Belgian company, for use in Belgium and Luxembourg. The film could be shown on television after 40 months of cinema release. Across the border, the German cable company Coditel had bought rights to broadcast the film from a German company, which could show the film in Germany after only 12 months of general release. As Coditel also showed the film to its subscribers in Belgium and Luxembourg it was ruled to be infringing upon Cinévog's copyright. Cinévog's copyright was upheld in this case, but the Court stated that each exclusive rights case must be examined in the context of the relevant market.

In contrast to the Cinévog ruling, in its next case on exclusive rights, the ECJ ruled that an infringement of European law had occurred. This was the first of the *Magill* cases that handled the appeal for the annulment of a decision made by the EC Independent Television Publications (ITP) of ITV. The case dealt with the public service broadcasters, the BBC, ITP and RTE (Radio Teletis Eireann) in Ireland and Northern Ireland, which owned exclusive rights to publish their programming schedules, and Magill TV Guide Limited, which wished to publish a programming guide. Magill had started publishing the guide including all programming schedules in 1985 but was prevented from doing so by an Irish court injunction in 1986 (a case brought about by the BBC, ITP and RTE). The decision was overturned by an Irish high court. The case was then taken up by the EC competition authority, which determined in separate rulings that the exclusive licences infringed Article 86 (now Article 82) of the treaty determining dominant market position. An annulment of the Commission decision was sought by the BBC, ITP and RTE at the CFI. The CFI in three separate rulings decided against the BBC, ITP and RTE in support of the EC decisions.[4]

RTE and ITP appealed to the ECJ, which, in a final ruling in 1994, upheld the three CFI *Magill* decisions.[5] These rulings had consequences for all EU Member States. PSBs could no longer enjoy exclusive rights to programming guides.

In the meantime, the EU passed its 1989 TWF Directive, which established a legal framework for the creation of a single audio-visual market.

Following this Directive, there was a dramatic increase in ECJ court cases dealing with media markets (see Appendix 2), which challenged the domain of media policy (as cultural policy) as belonging exclusively to the Member State.

The first of these was the *Commission of the European Communities* v. *Kingdom of the Netherlands* case of 1991.[6] When the first case was brought to the ECJ in 1989, under Dutch cable law, companies were prohibited from 'transmitting programs offered by foreign broadcasting organisations and broadcasters in foreign countries were prohibited from broadcasting programmes with Dutch advertisements to the Dutch audience' (Korthals Altes, 1993: 32). The Court ruled against the Netherlands, claiming that:

> Even if such a restriction forms part of a cultural policy intended to safeguard the freedom of expression of the various social, cultural, religious and philosophical components of society by ensuring the survival of an undertaking which provides them with technical resources, it goes beyond the objective pursued, since pluralism in the audio-visual sector of a Member State cannot be affected in any way by allowing the national bodies operating in that sector to make use of providers of services established in other Member States.

Among other things, the Court's decision meant that domestic companies were no longer obligated to purchase content solely from Dutch providers. The Netherlands subsequently had to make changes to its national Media Act of 18 December 1991, which provoked a greater sector liberalisation than had been envisioned by the Dutch authorities. As Korthals Altes states 'it is European law that opened the Dutch broadcasting system' (1993: 329). The 1991 Dutch Act still represented a relatively strict regulatory regime as all terrestrial frequencies were reserved for the public stations. Private television (national and transnational) was only available through local cable networks. However, the simultaneous enactment of the EC *Television Without Frontiers* in other countries rendered the Dutch Media Act ineffective *vis-à-vis* a large proportion of Dutch broadcasting. As a small country with many bordering countries, the Netherlands had the unique problem of a high level of cross-border transmissions (often in the Dutch language). Circa 40 per cent of audience share in the Netherlands comes from foreign broadcasts (Communications and Information Technology – CIT, 2001). A large proportion of which goes to the Luxembourg-based channels, Radio Télé-Luxembourg (RTL) 4 and 5.

Another case, decided only six days later, further chiselled away at the Member State jurisdiction for broadcasting policy – this time relating to public service broadcasting. The Greek *Elliniki Radiophonia Tilorassi – Anonimi Etairia* v. *Dimotiki Etairia Pliroforissis and Sotirios Kouvelas* case was concerned with the Greek Law No. 1730/1987, which banned commercial broadcasters and, in the ECJ's view, established a 'public television monopoly'. In 1988, the Mayor of Thessaloniki set up a television station and began broadcasting. A Greek court injunction was issued to restrain transmission and ordered seizure of station equipment. The case was taken to a national court, which referred the case to the ECJ. Although this presented a case of sensitive national policy, the ECJ chose to intervene. It decided that the Greek public broadcaster monopolised not only *transmission* but also *exclusive rights*. In this respect, the Court ruled that the establishment of a public broadcasting monopoly 'must be regarded as an ostensibly illegal measure by virtue of the combined provisions of Articles 90 and 86, which cannot be justified by virtue of Article 90(2)'. By this time, perhaps in anticipation of the ECJ ruling, the Greek government had passed a new media Law No 1866/1989, allowing for commercial television stations at the local level. The case is interesting, as the Court did not comment on the fact that the media owner was a prominent politician. The Court of course had no jurisdiction to comment upon this fact, even if it had been requested to do so.

This determination on behalf of the ECJ to intervene in national media policy (often encompassing cultural policy aims) continued in 1992, when the ECJ ruled against the Belgian state in *European Communities* v. *Kingdom of Belgium*. It decided that Belgium had failed to fulfil its obligations under Articles 52, 59, 60 and 221 of the EEC Treaty on four accounts: by prohibiting cable programmes from other Member States, where the programme was not in the language stipulated by Belgian law; by subjecting cable commercial broadcasters from other Member States to prior authorisation, to which conditions might have been attached; by reserving 51 per cent of the capital of the Flemish commercial broadcaster for publishers of Dutch-language daily and weekly newspapers; and by compelling commercial broadcasters to constitute a compulsory part of their programming to cultural interest.

Two years later, another case of TWF non-implementation was brought to Court. The ECJ ruled that the UK had failed to correctly transpose several articles of the TWF Directive into its UK Broadcasting Act 1990 in the 1994 *European Communities* v. *United Kingdom of Great Britain and Northern Ireland* case. This was because the UK treated *domestic* satellite services differently to *non-domestic* satellite services. The implementation of TWF had provided the UK conservative government with a window of opportunity. It was able to legitimise therewith broadcasts from the Murdoch-owned British Sky Broadcasting (BSkyB) channel, which would have been otherwise banned under UK media ownership law. The 1990 UK Broadcasting Act stipulates requirements for satellite licences. Section 43 of the 1990 Broadcasting Act applies a different regulatory regime to non-domestic satellite services than that applicable to domestic satellite services. Companies whose headquarters were in the UK but broadcasting from abroad (i.e. BSkyB)[7] were only required to obtain a non-domestic satellite licence.[8] Non-domestic satellite licences were exempt from both foreign ownership and cross-media ownership rules and a whole host of other domestic rules. This meant that BSkyB did not have to respect UK owner-ship rules even though its parent company, News International, controlled a substantial proportion of the UK press market.

The UK did not even apply TWF provisions to its regulatory regime for non-domestic satellites including rules on alcohol, tobacco products and advertising. Not only was BSkyB exempt from these laws, but so of course was every other company granted a non-domestic satellite licence from the UK. In practice, the 1990 Broadcasting Act allowed the UK to issue licences to any company that wanted to broadcast via satellite to any country any-where in the world.[9] The policy became very controversial for obvious reasons particularly as the UK Independent Television Commission (ITC) has provided non-domestic satellite licences to a number of broadcasters, which were banned domestically.[10] In particular, the lax restrictions on advertising have caused conflict with other Member States. Channels with a UK non-domestic satellite licence were advertising alcohol and tobacco products in France,[11] ignoring advertising rules in Germany and inserting commercials into children's programmes in Norway and Sweden – which went against these Member States' national media laws. But this was of little interest to the ECJ, as public interest regulation did not lie within its jurisdiction. The ECJ was only concerned with the fact that the UK had not applied TWF uniformly.

The ECJ ruled in favour of the Commission and suggested a rewording of the 1990 Broadcasting Act. However, rather than applying *domestic* rules to *non-domestic* satellite licences, the UK chose instead to apply *non-domestic* rules to *domestic* satellite licences. As it now stands, this means that a satellite channel broadcasting directly from a UK satellite to the UK market does not have to take notice of restrictions applied to UK terrestrial broadcasters (such as rules on advertising, content and ownership). The UK subsequently lobbied the Commission to legitimise its domestic policy. The revised 1997 TWF states that a 'broadcaster has its head office in that Member State and the editorial decisions about programme schedules are taken in that Member State' and (if editorial decisions on programme schedules are taken in another Member State) 'a significant part of the work-force involved in the pursuit of the television broadcasting activity operates'.

In its 1996 Act, the UK applied a different regulatory regime to *satellite* broadcasters than to *terrestrial* broadcasters. Moreover, the UK has not yet applied a number of TWF rules to its satellite channels. Williams (2002) observes that over 40 European media companies broadcasting from the UK are actually ignoring TWF provisions on content and advertising. This issue was not resolved under the UK 2003 Communications Act.

The UK's lax regulatory regime for satellite broadcasters has created a situation of regulatory arbitrage in Europe. A significant number of broad-casting companies have relocated to the UK, away from their original loca-tions. Some of these cases arrived in the European court of Justice. One of these was the *VT4 Ltd* v. *Vlaamse Gemeenschap* case. According to Belgian law, the Flemish Executive can license only one commercial television broadcaster at a time. In 1987 this licence was granted to Vlaamse Televisie Maatschappij (VTM) NV to broadcast its station VT4 for a term of 18 years. Under the same provisions, only one broadcaster (radio or television) for the Flemish Community may be licensed to transmit advertising. This licence was also issued to VT4 for a term of 18 years in 1987. In Flanders, VTM therefore holds a legal monopoly in commercial television and television advertising.

With the 18-year licence intact, VTM was bought by Scandinavian Broadcasting SA (registered in Luxembourg) and VT4's company headquarters relocated to London. VT4 secured a non-domestic satellite service licence from the UK permitting it to broadcast to Flanders under UK regulation (pertaining to non-domestic satellite broadcasts). From there it blatantly evaded Flemish media law, particularly that relating to advertising and content. The Flemish Minister of Culture and Brussels Affairs reacted by prohibiting the retransmission of VT4 programming by cable network operators in Flanders from 16 January 1995. This decision, by the Flemish minister, was overturned by the ECJ, which found it to be in conflict with TWF. This rendered Flemish broadcasting law completely redundant, as it was applied to only one market provider – VTM. More generally, the ECJ ruling legitimised the right of media companies to bypass national laws by moving their headquarters abroad. The Court declared in the case that a television broadcaster should be regulated in the state 'where decisions concerning programme policy are taken and the programmes to be broadcast are finally put together'. In the case of VT4, this was the UK.

An analogous case was ruled on the same day against Belgium, again upholding TWF. The UK had this time issued a non-domestic satellite service licence for UK Turner Entertainment Network International Limited (subsidiary of the US American Turner Group) which owns The Cartoon Network Limited and Turner Network Television (TNT) Limited which broadcast via the Astra satellite. On 17 September 1993 Turner International Network Sales Limited concluded an agreement with Coditel, a German cable television company to distribute Turner programming to Brussels. As there was no legislation at that time governing cable television in Brussels, a Royal Decree was issued the day before the agreement (on 16 September 1993) designed to stop the cable company from taking advantage of the regulatory vacuum. Coditel was prohibited from distributing 'TNT' and 'Cartoon Network'. Turner International Network Sales Ltd. took the case to the Tribunal de Commerce in Brussels for an interim order allowing Coditel to carry out its contract. The order was granted by the tribunal on 26 October 1993 and Coditel began broadcasting. In June 1994 the Belgian State brought third-party proceedings against the interim order (of 26 October). In November 1994, the Tribunal de Commerce referred the case to the ECJ and banned Coditel from broadcasting until a decision had been made. This decision was reversed in April 1995 by the Belgian

Cour d'Appel, which withdrew the case from the ECJ. Meanwhile, the Belgian state began separate criminal proceedings against Paul Denuit, the managing director of Coditel, for ignoring the Ministerial Decree of 17 September 1993. The Tribunal de Première Instance referred the case to the ECJ, which ruled in favour of Denuit in 1997 and upheld TWF. Herewith the ECJ again confirmed that companies have the right to circumvent national legislation by broadcasting from abroad – meaning Belgian media law is inapplicable to foreign broadcasts aimed at Belgian audiences.

In the same year, a similar case was ruled against the Swedish broadcasting authorities. In a decision on two joint cases *KO* v. *De Agostini and TVShop*,[12] the Court interpreted European advertising rules. Sweden has strict rules on advertising and prohibits teleshopping and the targeting of advertising to children under the age of 12. The first Agostini case dealt with advertising targeted at children. The Italian group De Agostini, which advertises on the channels TV3 to Denmark, Sweden and Norway and TV4 to Sweden via satellite licensed in the UK with non-domestic satellite licences. On TV4 it advertised its children's magazine *Everything about Dinosaurs* in Sweden. The magazine is printed in Italy and distributed in several languages across Europe. Each issue of the magazine was accompanied with a constituent part of a model dinosaur. The Swedish consumer's ombudsman, the Konsumentombudsmannen (KO), brought the case to the ECJ under the Misleading Advertising Directive (Appendix 1), which allowed Member States to adopt more stringent advertising rules than provided in the Directive. In the *TVShop* case, the company TVShop Europe was broadcasting teleshopping and 'infomercials' for skincare products and detergent on TV3 and the Homeshopping Channel in Sweden. The KO argued that this case went against the new advertising rules laid down in the 1997 TWF on 'advertising, sponsorship and teleshopping'. The Court ruled in both cases that Sweden was permitted to apply more stringent rules on advertising – but it could only apply them to domestic broadcasters, and not to those broadcasting from other Member States. The KO argued that the company should be considered 'Swedish' because 'the announcers all speak Swedish . . . the advertisements are exclusively for the Swedish market given the language in which they are prepared and the products which are marketed'. However, the Court found this position untenable. The ruling concentrated on the importance of *establishment*. As TV3 had been established in the UK, it was therefore considered a British company governed by British media law. In this ruling the ECJ legitimises the right of media companies to bypass national laws by establishing their headquarters abroad – even if the country of establishment (the UK in this case) pays little attention to TWF provisions.[13]

Rather than enforcing TWF provisions, the Court has actually chosen to override them in the Italian Broadcasters Reti Televisive Italiane SpA (RTI) case.[14] A case was referred from the Italian regional court of Lazio, which dealt with the violation of TWF advertising rules by the use of 'telepro-mozione' by Italian broadcasters. The case was brought by the Italian Ministry for the Post and Telecommunications against RTI (C-320/94), Radio Torre, Rete A Srl, Vallau Italiana Promomarket Srl (C-337/94), Radio Italia Solo Musica Srl and Others (C-338/94) and GETE Srl (C-339/94). The Court justified the overruling of TWF provisions by stating:

> the provision by the Community legislature for an increase in the maximum transmission time for direct offers to the public is due to the fact that that type of sales promotion requires more transmission time than spot advertise-ments, and not to the fact that such offers present products which may be directly ordered by telephone, mail or videotext and are intended to be deliv-ered to viewers at home, since the ordering of products by the viewer is a wholly separate operation from the televised presentation with which the directive is concerned. It is therefore normal that other forms of advertising, which also require more time than spot advertisements, should be able to benefit from the increase that is expressly, but not exclusively, provided for in respect of direct offers to the public.

In his analysis of the case, Mastroianni explains, the Court did this by 'equat(ing) *"telepromozione"* with advertising in the form of a direct offer to the public. It held that there is no limitation on the number of times a sponsor may be mentioned during sponsored programmes' (1999: 5). The ruling against TWF was paralleled only by the Court's overturning of the Tobacco Advertising Directive in 1998. Case-376/98 *Federal Republic of Germany* v. *European Parliament and Council of the European Union*, Directive 98/43, which was adopted to prevent the advertising and spon-sorship of tobacco products within the EU, was annulled. Following lob-bying by a number of tobacco companies, the ECJ found that the Directive prohibited trade in goods and services and thus was contrary to provisions in the treaties. A similar case was ruled against a ban on alcohol advertis-ing in 2000. In *Konsumentombudsmannen* (KO) (consumer ombudsman) v. *Gourmet International Products Aktiebolag* (GIP), the ECJ ruled against Swedish law banning alcohol advertising stating that 'a ban which extends to commercial advertisings in periodicals a significant part of whose subject matter is lawfully devoted to alcoholic beverages is in principle unnecessary and ineffective'. This ruling is particularly significant considering the Com-mission's challenge to France's 'Loi Evin' law and the UK's recent propo-sals to ban advertising to children.

The next case of importance was the 1996 Eurovision ruling. It dealt for a second time with PSBs. The case dealt with programming rights acquired by the European Broadcasting Union (EBU) which were for exclusive use of its PSB members.[15] The European Commission had exempted the EBU from EU competition rules under Article 85 (3) (now Article 81 EC) to enable it to share exclusive rights in view of the EBU members' public service role.[16] Although the commercial broadcasters Canal Plus, Télévision

Française Une (TF1) and RTL had been granted membership by the EBU in 1984 and in 1986, three private groups, La Cinq, M6 and Antena 3, were later refused membership. La Cinq, M6, Antena, RTI and Telecinco took the case to the CFI. In two cases (one jointly decided), the CFI ruled against the Commission's decision for the EBU to be opted out of competition rules. In 1994, Métropole Télévision was again denied EBU membership, and asked the Commission to investigate under state aid rules. The Commission refused (Commission decision of 29 June 1999). Métropole Télévision took the case to the ECJ in 1999. The Court decided in March 2001 that the Commission should have investigated the case. This means that the Commission was required to decide on PSB exclusive rights agreements. Accordingly, the European Commission approved the Eurovision System in 2000 exempting the European Broadcasting Union (EBU) from antitrust rules until 2005. This widened the EU's competence in the media policy sphere. However, it marks a clear division between the Commission and the Court in their approaches to PSBs.

The issue of exclusive rights resurfaced in 1997 with the *Tiercé Ladbroke SA* v. *Commission of the European Communities* case. Tiercé Ladbroke SA asked the ECJ for an annulment of an EC Decision of 24 June 1993. In its decision, the EC had rejected a complaint lodged by Tiercé Ladbroke SA against Pari Mutuel Urbain (PMU) and Pari Mutuel International (PMI), the principal French sociétes de courses (horse-racing associations). PMI had granted Deutscher Sportverlag Kurt Stoof GmbH & Co. (DSV) exclusive rights to French horse-racing broadcasts in Germany and Austria. In September 1989, Ladbroke asked DSV to grant it the right to retransmit the broadcasts in Belgium. DSV refused in October 1989 on the grounds that its contract with PMI prevented it from retransmitting the French sound and pictures outside the licensed territory. However, PMI runs a service called 'Courses en direct' that enables horse races in France to be viewed live by satellite. PMI was prepared to licence this service to three Belgian companies: Pari Mutuel Unifié Belge, Tiercé Franco-Belge and Dumoulin – but not to Ladbroke. Ladbroke requested that the EC intervene, but it refused to do so. The ECJ upheld the Commission's decision legitimising cross-border broadcast of a sporting event, even though exclusive rights to the French market had not been granted.

A number of further cases of non-implementation of TWF were ruled in 2000 and 2001. These were brought by the European Commission *Commission* v. *France*, *Commission* v. *Italy*, *Commission* v. *Luxembourg* and *Commission* v. *Spain*. Ruling with the Commission, the ECJ ruled that France had failed to implement Directive 95/47/EC. Italy was found to have failed to implement the 1997 TWF Directive, particularly the provisions relating to advertising. Spain (in trying to block the establishment of a satellite service by the French group Canal Plus)[17] was found to have incorrectly transposed Directive 95/47/EC (standards for the transmission of television signals) by requiring registration of digital television operators as a condition for licensing.[18] Luxembourg was found to have failed to implement the 1997 TWF.

TWF encouraged the evasion of national media rules through cross-border broadcasting. ECJ rulings have been effective in encouraging European firms to engage in regulatory arbitrage. However, at the same time, the Court has not been effective in enforcing minimum standards on content and advertising in broadcasting set out in TWF. The UK's non-domestic satellite policy blatantly disregards minimum provisions set out in TWF. Many other Member States disregard TWF provisions and those set out in related Directives. When faced with a case of non-implementation of TWF, the Court has generally taken an entirely market-oriented approach without regard for considerations of the public interest. The *ARD* v. *ProSieben Media* judgement is a further case in point. As Mastroianni points out:

> the case raises delicate problems regarding the relations between the "economic freedoms" recognised by the Treaty and interests of different nature, namely the promotion of pluralism in the media and the protection of television viewers as "consumers". In deciding to rule in favour of the former, it is submitted in this note that the Court reached an unsatisfactory solution.

The case dealt with the exceeding of national and European advertising limits by the German channel ProSieben (owned by Kirch). The public service broadcaster, ARD, took ProSieben to the higher regional court, the Oberlandesgericht Stuttgart over the issue. The 1997 TWF Directive stipulates in Article 11(3):

> The transmission of audio-visual works such as feature films and films made for television (excluding series, serials, light entertainment programmes and documentaries), provided their scheduled duration is more than 45 minutes, may be interrupted once for each period of 45 minutes. A further interruption shall be allowed if their scheduled duration is at least 20 minutes longer than two or more complete periods of 45 minutes.

This means in principle that a programme which runs for less than 45 minutes should not be interrupted by advertising breaks; a programme of 100 minutes can be interrupted twice, and a programme of 110 minutes can be interrupted three times. According to Art. 11(4) 'a period of at least 20 minutes should elapse between each successive advertising break within the programme'. As it was found to be consistently breaking these TWF rules, the German Court ruled against ProSieben.[19] ProSieben then appealed to the Oberlandesgericht claiming that the ruling went against the *principles* of TWF. The Oberlandesgericht then referred the case to the ECJ for clarification. This presented the ECJ with a clear opportunity to uphold the minimum standards established in TWF on advertising. But the ECJ decided not to uphold TWF. Rather it ruled *in favour* of ProSieben stating that 'the main purpose of Directive 89/552 . . . is to ensure freedom to provide television broadcasting services', therewith completely discounting TWF advertising limits. It stated that 'in order to calculate the 45 minute period for the purpose of determining the number of advertising interruptions allowed in the broadcasting of audiovisual works such as feature films and films made for television, the duration of the advertisements must be included in that period'. As Mastroianni explains well, the decision is not only questionable, but illogical, as it means that advertising should be counted as a part of programming hours *before* a decision can be taken on whether to insert advertising (Mastroianni, 2000: 13). This case clearly illustrates the ECJ's approach to media markets. The Court is intent on the raw interpretation of the Treaties, which are based upon market integration.

Advertising regulation has presented many challenges for the EU. Split screen advertising is practised in the UK and Germany. This form of advertising allows promotions to appear in a corner of the screen without programme interruption. Consumers have the option of clicking on the advertisement in order to connect to the T-commerce site. By storing information, operators then may gain information about viewer preferences, this way allowing them to better target advertisements to programme viewers. However, this form of advertising goes against TWF advertising rules, as time slots need to be separate from programme viewing. As a result, the EC commissioned a study on new advertising techniques (Carat Crystal and Bird & Bird, 2002), and proposals are underway to modify the Directive.[20] Undoubtedly, not only advertising techniques, but also consumer privacy are of issue.

The Court's refusal to uphold TWF provisions has been under much discussion in the legal literature. In a pending case, *RTL Television v. Niedersächsische Landesmedienanstalt für privaten Rundfunk*, the ECJ has again been asked for interpretation of Article 11(3) of TWF, which restricts advertising breaks in the broadcast of feature films for television. This presents an opportunity for the ECJ to clarify its stance on advertising. The case was referred to the ECJ by the Niedersächsisches Oberverwaltungsgericht (Lower Saxony Higher Administrative Court). The ECJ has been asked whether the regulatory authority could restrict advertising breaks, even if a 'serial' has been pre-packed to include them. In its opinion on the case, in May 2003, the Court reasoned that Landesmedienanstalt could indeed impose advertising restrictions. The final ruling will be important for the revision of TWF as it could legitimise or essentially delegitimise TWF advertising rules. As will be shown in Chapter 4, TWF revision is dependent upon interpretations by the Court.

Also awaited by the European Commission is a change in the Court's approach to PSBs. In three recent decisions, the ECJ has been asked to decide if the European Commission should rule on whether the public service television should be prohibited from fund raising through advertising (as an infringement of state aid rules). In a number of decisions in the late 1990s, the Commission ruled that PSB funding is permissable under state aid rules (see Chapter 3). Three cases were brought by private companies in France and Portugal to challenge the EC's approval of state aid to PSBs. The ECJ ruled in each case that the Commission has the authority under the Treaties to judge this issue (*Télévision Française* v. *European Commission* (1999), *SIC* v. *Commission* (2000), *Commission* v. *TF1* (2001)). The EC Directorate for Competition subsequently came out with its 2001 'Communication on the application of state aid rules to public service broadcasting' (CEC, 2001a) in which it recognises PSB importance for maintaining pluralism. The Communication, refers to the 'public service' Protocol of the 1997 Treaty of Amsterdam and quotes the 2000 EC 'Communication on services of general interest in Europe'[21] which states:

> the choice of the financing scheme falls within the competence of the Member State, and there can be no objection in principle to the choice of a dual financing scheme (combining public funds and advertising revenues) rather than a single funding scheme (solely public funds) as long as competition in the relevant markets (e.g. advertising, acquisition and/or sale of programmes) is not affected to an extent which is contrary to the Community interest.

With this as a general rule, future PSB advertising and funding complaints would still have to be decided on a case-by-case basis, and could be brought back again to the ECJ for a final interpretation.

ECJ decisions in press markets

Despite the substantial development of case law in the broadcasting sector, the ECJ has been reluctant to rule cases in the press sector. Perhaps one reason for this is that press markets remain national for linguistic reasons. Another reason is that long-established press markets are more difficult to tackle politically by the European institutions. National press legislation (particularly when dealing with ownership) has often been the result of years of political wrangling and deal making between governments and publishers at national levels. In one of the few early cases concerning the press market in 1981, the ECJ decided to maintain a hands-off approach to national legislation. This case, *Maria Salonia* v. *Giorgio Poidomani and Franca Baglieri, née Giglio*, concerned the 'National Agreement' between the Federazione Italiana Editori Giornali (Italian Federation of Newspaper Publishers) and the Federazione Sindacale Unitaria Giornalai (the United Federation of Trade Unions of Newsagents) made on 23 October 1974. The legality of the exclusive distribution agreement for national newspapers and periodicals was assessed in terms of its compatibility with the articles of the Treaty of Rome.[22] The agreement was looked at only to determine whether it would affect the market for publications from other Member States. The Court ruled that there was no conflict with the Treaty. This hands-off approach was maintained in the *Familiapress* v. *Bauer* case in 1997.

Similar decisions have been made in a number of press cases in recent years.[23] The rulings on press distribution are interesting as they encompass questions of 'essential facilities' (Hancher, 1999). A case in point is the 1997 *Oscar Bronner* v. *Mediaprint Zeitungs, Zeitschriften Verlag and others* dealing with essential facilities. In Austria, the company, Mediaprint has a dominant position on the distribution of national newspapers. It delivers newspapers by post, not by home delivery. It distributes the daily newspapers *Neue Kronen Zeitung* and *Kurier* (both owned by Zeitschriftenverlag GmbH), which hold 46.8 per cent of the Austrian daily newspaper market and 42 per cent of advertising revenues. Mediaprint also distributes the independent daily newspaper, *Wirtschaftsblatt*. However, it refuses to distribute the daily newspaper, *Der Standard*. *Der Standard*'s owner Oscar Bronner brought a complaint against Mediaprint as abusing its dominant position by not including *Der Standard* in the home distribution package. Bronner could not establish a rival home delivery service, as it would be too expensive for a small publisher. The ECJ ruled that Mediaprint, even if it did constitute a dominant position (which needed to be decided by the national competition authority), should not be required to distribute independent newspapers such as *Der Standard*. The case is interesting as it dealt with the essential facilities doctrine, which requires a company with a dominant position on a delivery system to allow competitors to participate in that system (Hancher, 1999). This is analogous to the must-carry rule in cable and satellite broadcasting. As the case dealt specifically with the question of 'essential facilities' it may have significance when applied to other markets, such as broadcasting markets.

Conclusion

This chapter has examined the role of the ECJ in regulating the media markets in the EU. Its role is important, as it, along with the EC competition authority, has represented the only EU institution with the legal resources available to assess national media laws and court decisions, and mandate direct changes to the composition of the media market. The chapter showed how the ECJ has been an important actor in the EU's overall media policy by taking an assertive role in expanding EU legal competence in the area. The Court has been shown to be both an agenda-setter and an assertive political actor, which has required changes to national laws. It was shown that the Court's decisions ruled in favour of market integration to the neglect of public interest regulation. More recently it has made some movements towards the incorporation of public interest considerations in its most recent decisions on state aid to PSBs and advertising. However, a real shift in the Court's approach is not yet apparent.

The Court's role in media regulation is fundamental. Firstly, the development of this body of media case law, and the legal definition of broadcasting as of economic interest in terms of the Treaty of Rome, established the legal competence of the Commission to engage in media policy-making. The 1984 Green Paper 'Television Without Frontiers' (CEC, 1984) makes reference to the *Sacchi* and *Debauve* cases as a legal basis for the Directive. In the most recent (1997) TWF Directive, two more court cases are quoted.[24] The Court's rulings on advertising must be taken into account during TWF's review process. For this reason, the Commission is awaiting the pending RTL case with abated breath.

Secondly, ECJ decisions relating to the media industry have political significance for national broadcasting legislation. This is particularly the case as the ECJ decided that broadcasting should be considered a service. This places broadcasting in the realm of economic policy to be decided at the European level and removes it from cultural policy, which resides with the Member State. The Court has been consistent in upholding this decision in all of its broadcasting decisions. From 1994, the ECJ has upheld all cases of the TWF provision on cross-border transmission brought against Member States by the European Commission. Further, by upholding the TWF clause determining that broadcasting should be governed by the member state of transmission and not the state of reception, it has rendered national law as ineffective *vis-à-vis* foreign broadcasters. In this way, the Court's decisions have *directly* mandated changes to member state broadcasting policy in Belgium, Greece, the Netherlands and the UK.

By opting to reserve discretion for future cases, the Court retains a strong role for itself in future decisions. It has done this in cases on advertising, PSB funding and exclusive rights. For example in the different rulings on exclusive rights between the *Coditel*, *Magill* and *Tiercé Ladbroke SA* cases show that the ECJ is prepared to judge exclusive rights cases separately, rather than set precedence for future rulings. This discretion may not just apply to cases dealing only with the ownership of exclusive media rights, but could be applied to media cases in general. As each case can be determined separately, this leaves the Court a lot of political leeway. In the *Magill* case, it was determined that a dominant producer cannot hold on to exclusive rights if those rights are determined as 'essential facilities'.[25] The *Magill* ruling could possibly be consequential for future media cases determining the status of gateway (access) technologies, sports broadcasting, compulsory bundling or rulings on vertical integration within the media sector. There has not yet been any evidence of such spillover, but these issues are of growing importance at the national level. In particular, the concern over what might constitute essential facilities is building. The Court began to tackle the access issue in a preliminary ruling on the *Canal Satéllite Digital SL/Administracíon General del Estado* case in 2002 – but, rather than supporting open access, the Court ruled *against* the Spanish government which was requiring that all platform decoders must be open.

Thirdly, in the majority of its rulings, the Court has been shown to rarely take into account considerations of the public interest. The *ProSieben, RTI, TVShop* and Agostini cases were most indicative of this. The Court has not made exceptions for national rules prohibiting teleshopping, infomercials or children's advertising. The *ProSieben* case was particularly demonstrative of the Court's liberal stance on media markets wherein the Court ruled against TWF provisions in favour of a market player. In this respect, the ECJ clearly takes a different approach to media market regulation than the European Commission.

A striking example of a divide between the Commission and the Court is their differing stances on PSB. DG Competition has recognised the special role of the PSBs and exempted them from European competition law in its *EBU/Eurovision* decision (Appendix 2). The ECJ has taken a different view. It decided in five rulings that PSBs should not be treated any differently from commercial broadcasters under EU competition law.[26]

The Court hesitated to rule on PSB funding as shown by rulings in the late 1990s. Instead it tossed the ball back into the Commission's court by declaring that the EC did have the legal right to rule on state aid to PSBs. This issue could still be brought back to the Court for a final ruling. The PSB rulings prompted large-scale lobbying to include a protocol on public service providers in the 1997 Amsterdam Treaty. The EBU (representing PSBs) and the European Parliament[27] was successful in lobbying for a public service broadcasting protocol (no. 32) in the Amsterdam Treaty. The protocol states that 'the system of public broadcasting in the Member States is directly related to the democratic, social and cultural needs of each society and to the need to preserve media pluralism'. This protocol and Article 7d (now Article 16) of the Amsterdam Treaty relating to services of general economic interest[28] may provide a basis for a change in the Court's stance on PSBs. As Armstrong and Bulmer observed, the ECJ has been known to provide a progressive interpretation of an Article to further European integration (1997). The PSB Protocol in the Amsterdam Treaty was followed up by the 2001 European Union Charter of Fundamental Rights which recommends that 'the Union shall respect cultural, religious and linguistic diversity'. The Court may take these new pronouncements into consideration on public service broadcasting rulings in the future. In this respect, the Court's actions in the media sector may go full circle as the slow winding process of EU political integration catches up with economic integration. However, it cannot do so without political support from Member States and a definitive change to the Treaties.

Notes

1 In 1957 the founding treaties of the European Community (called the European Union since 1992), separately establishing the European Economic Community (EEC) and the European Atomic Energy Community (Euratom),

were signed in Rome (and are therefore referred to as the 'Treaty of Rome'). The Treaty of Rome has been revised four times: in 1987 (the Single Act), in 1992 (the Treaty of Maastricht), in 1997 (the Treaty of Amsterdam) and in 2001 (the Treaty of Nice).

2   According to Article 21 of the Royal Decree of 24 December 1966 (Moniteur Belge of 24 January 1967).

3   The ECJ also acknowledges in this ruling that Member States could exempt PSBs from this rule. At least the ruling states that under Article 90 (1), 'nothing prevents Member States, for considerations of public interest, of a non-economic nature, from removing radio and television transmissions, including cable transmissions, from the field of competition by conferring on one or more establishments an exclusive right to conduct them'.

4   *Independent Television Publications Ltd* v. *Commission of the European Communities* and *The British Broadcasting Corporation and BBC Enterprises Limited* v. *Commission of the European Communities* (Appendix 2).

5   Joined cases *Radio Telefos Eireann (RTE) and Independent Television Publications Ltd* v. *Commission of the European Communities* (Appendix 2).

6   Two pre-TWF cases dealing with the foreign transmission of advertising also ruled against Dutch cable law: *Bond van Adverteerders* and *Collectieve Antennevoorziening Gouda* (Appendix 2).

7   Sky bought BSB in 1990, which had launched its own satellite Marco Polo with a domestic satellite licence. The new company BSkyB therefore was broadcasting from both Astra and the UK Marco Polo satellites. This contravened UK law, as the company had both a domestic and a non-domestic satellite licence, and went against international satellite law as well. The issue was not resolved until 1998.

8   The 1989 TWF Directive does not stipulate whether or not the location of companies' headquarters are an indication of where they should be licensed. The UK lobbied hard to include this provision in the revised 1997 TWF.

9   For example, under this law one can obtain a UK licence for a channel broadcasting in Arabic to north African states from the Astra satellite.

10   One example of this is the granting of an ITC licence to Wizja TV in Poland, which 'among other things ... has not been obliged to comply with the European quota' (Jakubowicz, 2001: 218).

11   The European Commission actually opened an infringement procedure against France for its law prohibiting advertising of tobacco and alcohol ('Loi Evin'). The law was not seen as justifiable under cultural (or even health) policy, but as potentially discriminating against broadcasts from abroad.

12   Joined cases *Konsumentombudsmannen (KO)* v. *De Agostini (Svenska) Förlag AB* and *TV-Shop i Sverige AB*.

13   Opinion found in Joined Cases E8/94 and E9/94. In a similar case to *De Agostini* the EFTA Court made the same ruling. In *Forbrukerombudet* v. *Mattel Scandinavia and Lego Norge*, Judgment of 16 June 1995, the EFTA Court gave the opinion that the Norwegian prohibition on television advertisements specifically targeting children was incompatible with Television Directive if it applied the rules to a broadcaster established in another EEA State (Appendix 2).

14   Joined cases, *Radio Torre, Rete A Srl, Vallau Italiana Promomarket Srl, Radio Italia Solo Musica Srl and Others*, and *GETE Srl* (Appendix 2).

15 From 1988, the EBU membership was restricted to public service broadcasters following the EBU Marino-Charter (Collins, 1998: 46–9).
16 Commission Decision 93/403/EEC of 11 June 1993 relating to a proceeding pursuant to Article 85 of the EEC Treaty (OJL 179, 1993, p. 23), whereby it granted an exemption under Article 85(3) ('the exemption' decision).
17 The Spanish government tried to prevent the launch of Canal Satélite Digital with two laws: the 1997 Ley 17/97 incorporation of the EC Directive 95/47/CE; and the 1997 Ley 21/97, Reguladora de las Emisiones y Retransmisiones de Competiciones Deportivas.
18 *Canal Satélite Digital SL* v. *Administración General del Estado*, ruling on technical standards and registration rules set by the Spanish government.
19 Judgment of 10 October 1996 of the Stuttgarter Landesgericht.
20 DG Culture ran a public seminar on 'The evolution of advertising techniques/what impact will this have on the review of the TVWF Directive?' in Brussels on 17 January 2002.
21 'Communication on services of general interest in Europe', COM (2000) 580 final, p. 35.
22 In this case, the Agreement was alleged to have produced a dominant position in terms of vertical integration.
23 *Verein zur Förderung des Freien Wettbewerbs im Medienwesen* v. *TV Spielfilm Verlag GmbH* (Appendix 2).
24 *Van Binsbergen* v. *Bestuur van de Bedrijfsvereniging* and *TV 10 SA* v. *Commissariaat voor de Media* (Appendix 2). See Wattel (1995) for discussion.
25 Two later non-media related rulings seem to confirm the ECJ's thinking on rights to 'essential facilities' held by a dominant position: *Hilti* v. *Commission* and *Tetra Pak International SA* v. *Commission* (Appendix 2).
26 *La Cinq* v. *The European Commission; Gestevisión Telecinco SA* v. *Commission of the European Communities; Metropole télévision SA and Reti Televisive Italiane SpA and Gestevisión Telecinco SA and Antena 3 de Televisión* v. *Commission of the European Communities; Elliniki Radiophonia Tilorassi – Anonimi Etairia* v. *Dimotiki Etairia Pliroforissis and Sotirios Kouvelas* (Appendix 2).
27 European Parliament 'Resolution on the role of public service television in a multi-media society', September 1996 presented by MEP Carol Tongue.
28 Article 7d states 'Without prejudice to Articles 77, 90 and 92, and given the place occupied by services of general economic interest in the shared values of the Union as well as their role in promoting social and territorial cohesion, the Community and the Member States, each within their respective powers and within the scope of application of this Treaty, shall take care that such services operate on the basis of principles and conditions which enable them to fulfil their missions.' The Court first interpreted Article 7d in 2003 in the Altmark case (Appendix 2) wherein it decided that state aid could be used for public service obligations (in this case transport). However, it has not yet applied Article 7d to broadcasting.

3

Competition law, beyond the boundaries of the politically possible

Introduction

Under competition policy, the European Commission has direct authority to make decisions which are not subject to approval by the Council of Ministers or the European Parliament but only to review by the ECJ (Brealey, 1994). As such, competition has been recognised as a key policy area of the Commission (McGowan and Wilks, 1995). Within the Commission, the DG for Competition (formerly DG IV) has responsibility for competition decisions and houses the Merger Task Force. Competition law has been utilised in a great number of decisions concerning media markets (Appendix 3). More progressive than the ECJ, DG Competition in its media decisions has taken on board public interest as well as economic considerations.

Following the 1989 Television Without Frontiers Directive and the 1989 Merger Regulation, there was a dramatic increase in the number of cross-national media mergers and joint ventures registered with DG Competition (see Appendix 3). Between 1989 and 1999, the EC made over 50 formal decisions in the media sector. The great majority of decisions were decided positively. However, 8 of the media decisions resulted in negative decisions.[1] This is significant, as in the period 1990–1999, only 11 of a total of 1104 merger decisions (in all sectors) made by the EC were negative.[2] No less than 6 of the 11 negative merger decisions dealt with broadcasting markets. A further 2 negative decisions were taken in the media sector under Article 85 of the Treaty of Rome during the same period.[3] This brings the total of media market prohibitions taken by DG Competition to 8 in a ten-year period. If informal decisions are included, the total number of prohibitions in media markets amounts to much more.[4] This occurred when the EC informally suggested that BSkyB be excluded from British Digital Broadcasting (BDB) when the UK issued digital licences in 1997. Informal negotiations were also attempted to deal with the Premiere/Deutsches Fernsehen (DF1) digital platform until the case was officially registered with the European Commission in December 1997. DG Competition has clearly contributed greatly to the Commission's overall media policy considering this hands-on approach to shaping national markets.

The chapter reviews the instruments of competition policy and the development of DG Competition's policy towards media markets through a chronological examination of decisions taken. It will show how DG Competition has gradually shaped national markets. In particullary, it will show how DG Competition began to take on board aspects of public interest regulation derived from national rationales. The chapter then discusses the decisions in light of the development of EU media policy.

Competition instruments

European competition law is applied through Articles 81, 82 and 86 (these were formerly Articles 85, 86 and 90 under the Treaty of Rome renamed after the Treaty of Amsterdam) (Appendix 4). When discussing specific competition rulings, Articles 85, 86 and 90 will be referred to if a decision was made before 1999 after which the new Articles came into force. Article 81 (ex Article 85) prohibits private sector anti-competitive agreements and Article 82 (ex Article 86) prevents the abuse of dominant position.[5] Articles 81 and 82 are applied to the public sector by Article 86 (ex Article 90).

Article 81 (ex Article 85) states:

§1. The following shall be prohibited as incompatible with the common market: all agreements between undertakings, decisions by associations of undertakings and concerted practices which may affect trade between Member States and which have as their object or effect the prevention, restriction or distortion of competition within the common market, and in particular those which:
(a) directly or indirectly fix purchase or selling prices or any other trading conditions;
(b) limit or control production, markets, technical development, or investment;
(c) share markets or sources of supply;
(d) apply dissimilar conditions to equivalent transactions with other trading parties, thereby placing them at a competitive disadvantage;
(e) make the conclusion of contracts subject to acceptance by the other parties of supplementary obligations which, by their nature or according to commercial usage, have no connection with the subject of such contracts.
§2. Any agreements or decisions prohibited pursuant to this Article shall be automatically void.
§3. The provisions of paragraph 1 may, however, be declared inapplicable in the case of:
– any agreement or category of agreements between undertakings;
– any decision or category of decisions by associations of undertakings;
– any concerted practice or category of concerted practices, which contributes to improving the production or distribution of goods or to promoting tech-

nical or economic progress, while allowing consumers a fair share of the
resulting benefit, and which does not:
(a) impose on the undertakings concerned restrictions which are not indispensable to the attainment of these objectives;
(b) afford such undertakings the possibility of eliminating competition in
respect of a substantial part of the products in question.

Article 82 (was Article 86) states:

> Any abuse by one or more undertakings of a dominant position within the
> common market or in a substantial part of it shall be prohibited as incom-
> patible with the common market insofar as it may affect trade between
> Member States. Such abuse may, in particular, consist in:
> (a) directly or indirectly imposing unfair purchase or selling prices or other
> unfair trading conditions;
> (b) limiting production, markets or technical development to the prejudice of
> consumers;
> (c) applying dissimilar conditions to equivalent transactions with other
> trading parties, thereby placing them at a competitive disadvantage;
> (d) making the conclusion of contracts subject to acceptance by the other
> parties of supplementary obligations which, by their nature or accord-
> ing to commercial usage, have no connection with the subject of such
> contracts.

Prior to 1990, all Commission competition decisions were made under
Articles 85, 86 and 90 of the Treaty of Rome. Under these Articles, DG
Competition could rule against mergers *only after they had already taken
place*. A negative ruling under Articles 85, 86 or 90 requires the divestiture
of a merger or acquisition. For this reason, DG Competition lobbied for a
long time for the enactment of a merger regulation, which would require
companies to pre-notify mergers. The idea for a merger regulation appeared
back in the early 1970s (Cini and McGowan, 1999: 27–29). A proposal for
a 'regulation on the control of concentrations between undertakings' was
first presented to the Council of Ministers in 1973. However, the Council
did not adopt a merger regulation until 1989 following extensive consultation and revision with the Member States. The Merger Regulation came
into effect on 21 September 1990 (Appendix 1).

From 1990 onwards, the bulk of media market decisions were made
under the 1989 Merger Regulation (although some investigations still took
place under Articles 85 and 86, which declare that a dominant position
formed after a concentration had taken place). The 1989 Merger Regulation required proposed mergers with a combined aggregate global turnover
totalling more than ECU 5 billion and an aggregate Community-wide
turnover more than ECU 250 million to notify DG Competition for permission.[6] Notification allowed companies to receive a quick decision from
the Commission (usually within five months during Stages I and II). As 95
per cent of merger cases are decided in Stage I, only 5 per cent reach Stage

III and only a small proportion of these are prohibited (Cini and McGowan, 1999: 123). As noted in the chapter introduction, only 11 MTF cases were decided negatively in a ten-year period, out of which six dealt with broadcasting markets. In April 1997, the Merger Regulation was amended to include joint venture decisions and thresholds were lowered from five to two and a half billion ECU. According to the Merger Regulation markets are defined geographically: 'Whereas the scope of application of this Regulation should therefore be defined according to the geographical area of activity of the undertakings concerned and be limited by quantitative thresholds in order to cover those concentrations which have a Community dimension'.

EC competition law is applicable to European markets when agreements between companies are seen to come into conflict with the creation of a Single Market or there is generally a perceived threat to competition through cartels, monopolies or mergers. At least this is easily understood to be the main rationale behind European competition policy (Cini and McGowan, 1999: 3). However, Cini and McGowan highlight that a key objective of competition policy at national levels is the protection of the consumer, as had been tradition in the US, the UK and many other national competition regimes. This entails 'the defence of the individual against big business, usually for moral or political reasons' (Cini and McGowan, 1999: 4).[7] At the national level, this is where extra constraints on media markets have come into play (as discussed in Chapter 7). For example in the UK the application of competition law has been balanced by the use of the public interest test. Although there is no public interest test as such, the same considerations have entered competition policy at the European level.

These public-interest considerations have manifested themselves in various ways. Most concerns of public interest are dealt with politically, within the *cabinet* of the competition Commissioner where a final decision on all competition cases is taken. Majone (2000) points to the fact that at this stage many Merger Task Force decisions have been made for political reasons rather than based upon technical or economic reasoning. Significantly, the competition Commissioner Van Miert (1993–99) has expressed concern for the concentration of national media markets (Levy, 1999: 82–83). Van Miert presided over nine negative decisions concerning the media industry during his term in office. Interviews revealed that the cabinet of Van Miert often came into conflict with DG Competition over media merger decisions, with the Commissioner taking a stricter line on market concentration than the services. As Cini and McGowan explain 'any competition-orientated analysis that takes place within the MTF can easily be overridden once the decision falls in the hands of the more political College of Commissioners which takes the final decision' (1999: 122). Although the competition portfolio is controlled by one Commissioner only, more controversial decisions are discussed by the College as a whole. As

Cini and McGowan comment further, 'it would certainly be naive to imagine that political/ideological questions do not enter the decision-making' at this stage (1999: 45). Indeed, heated debates have taken place within the College over media merger decisions, many evoking input from national-level politicians.

The recognition of public interest concerns have slowly found their way into official Commission documents. The first clear recognition by the Commission that the media industry is important for preserving media pluralism came in the original 1989 Merger Regulation. Under Article 21 Member States are permitted to enact national media ownership legislation, even though it may contradict European competition law. Under this Article, Member States are allowed to prevent a merger after the Commission has decided in favour, if that Member State believes that the merger can be detrimental to pluralism.[8] Importantly, Article 21 of the Merger Regulation states:

> §2. No Member State shall apply its national legislation on competition to any concentration that has a Community dimension.... §3. Notwithstanding paragraphs 1 and 2, Member States may take appropriate measures to protect legitimate interests other than those taken into consideration by this Regulation and compatible with the general principles and other provisions of Community law. Public security, *plurality of the media* and prudential rules shall be regarded as legitimate interests within the meaning of the first subparagraph. (Emphasis added).

Following the 1989 Merger Regulation, DG Competition began to formulate a more specific policy for the media sector. The EC 1989 TWF Directive was to result in a significant increase in European media mergers (documented in Chapter 6). The anticipation of a corresponding increase in media-related competition decisions and mounting European Parliament pressure for a Directive on media ownership (discussed in Chapter 4) meant that DG Competition needed to delineate its position on media mergers. In 1989, DG Competition commissioned a report, which identified the tendency of the broadcasting markets to concentration vertically and horizontally. This coincided with the Booz-Allen & Hamilton Report commissioned by Directorate General for Industrial and Internal Market Policies (DG III) that predicted a high level of concentration in the broadcasting sector in the decade to come (CEC, 1989).[9] In both Commission studies, the importance of the media industry for ensuring pluralism and diversity was discussed.

In 1990, DG Competition produced its 'Communication to the Council and European Parliament on audio-visual policy' (CEC, 1990). In this Communication, DG Competition clarified its position towards the audio-visual industry. Most significantly, the Communication devotes a paragraph (§2.2.3) to 'Pluralism and Mergers' in which it states that the audio-visual sector is different to other sectors due to a number of 'specific economic and cultural considerations'. It recognises the fact that TWF could allow for a circumvention of national media rules and therefore the Commission should balance this by taking an active role in protecting pluralism. Importantly, the Communication recognises that application of Articles 85, 86 and the Merger Regulation are insufficient for protecting pluralism from the dangers presented by media concentration.

Since its 1990 Communication, DG Competition has continued to build upon its policy, which is unique to the media sector. Significantly, its definitions of media markets have become increasingly narrow. This has been noted both positively and negatively by a number of academic lawyers (Froehlinger, 1993; Kon, 1996; Ungerer, 1996; Lang, 1997a). The idea behind the restriction of media ownership at national levels is to provide for a large enough number of players on the market in order to ensure media pluralism.[10] DG Competition could not openly justify competition rulings on these grounds, as it has no tangible legal basis.[11] Therefore DG Competition's narrowing definition of media markets is interpreted (in this chapter) as a means by which recommendations and decisions, made for pluralist reasons, are justified by economic rationales. This indirect use of competition policy has been noted in the academic literature. Although Cini and McGowan did not specifically refer to the media sector, they comment that 'the Commission uses its merger powers for other policy ends'. This seems to be true of competition decisions on media ownership (Harcourt, 1996; Levy, 1999; Krebber, 2001).

In its 1990 Communication, DG Competition initially delineates three audio-visual markets: (1) production and distribution of cinema and television films, (2) the market for television broadcasts and (3) the market for satellite broadcasting. Over a period of years, Kon (1996) notes that DG Competition has defined six further broadcasting markets: free-access television (advertisments), free-access television (non-advertisments), pay-TV, cable television, satellite broadcasting (general), and satellite broadcasting (wholly dedicated to sport).[12] Similar distinctions for publications markets have since been made. As a DG Competition official explains, publications are separated into 'trade publications, economic and financial magazines, weeklies, women's magazines, television magazines, specialised amateur and professional magazines (motoring, travel, gardening, etc.) and daily newspapers' (Lang, 1997a: 59). There are also distinctions made between 'quality' and 'tabloid' newspapers. Finally, the Commission has segmented the purchasing activity for television into separate markets according to the nature of the content: the acquisition of rights for feature films constitutes a separate market, distinct from made-for-television programmes.[13]

The paradox is that, while DG Competition was developing increasingly narrow definitions of media markets, another DG, for the Information Society, was widening its definition of the communications market. This is of course the convergence initiative that defines communications as 'one market', which *includes* the existing markets of terrestrial broadcasting, pay-TV, cable operators, telephone companies electronic internet, etc. A further dichotomy existed as DG Information Society proposed that dominant position should be assessed when a company reached a market threshold of 30 per cent, whereas DG Competition could begin to assess dominant position when market share exceeds 25 per cent of (Preamble 15 of the Merger Control Regulation). This is particularly interesting as the new Regulatory Framework for Communications (passed in 2002) will most likely rely greatly upon DG Competition for implementation as 'soft' forms of governance are less likely to be effective. Significant Market Power (SMP) is still to be decided under the new regulatory framework at the time of writing. The final division between DG Competition and DG Information Society is in the setting of technological standards. DG Information Society has attempted to set standards in a series of Directives and agreements, whereas DG Competition has enforced market competition in this area. The failure to agree a common approach within the EC on standard setting is perhaps contributing to a detrimental effect upon media markets.

For the purposes of this chapter only decisions of major significance to EU policy are discussed. The chapter makes it clear that DG competition is willing to take on board public interest considerations. This is shown by the strict definitions of media markets and rulings on public service broadcasters in particular.

Chronology of competition decisions 1989–2001

Following TWF, the first negative decision concerning media markets was the 1991 *Screensport/EBU* decision (for all DG Competition cases, see Appendix 3). The European Commission determined that a joint venture between the EBU and News International presented a dominant market position infringing Article 85(1) of the Treaties. In 1988, the satellite sports company, Screensport, had filed two complaints with the European Commission. The first related to its inability to access Eurosport exclusive rights. In its second complaint, Screensport claimed that Satellite Sport Services Ltd, a joint venture between the EBU and News International, presented an undue dominant position in the European market for sports broadcasting. The European Commission decided to split the case in two, firstly tackling the legitimacy of Satellite Sport Services Ltd. In May 1988, 17 Members of the EBU, which is made up of PSBs, had signed an exclusive rights agreement (the Eurosport Consortium Agreement) to share sporting broadcasts. Later that year, in December 1988, the EBU set up the joint venture, Satellite Sport Services Ltd, in collaboration with News International, to provide sports programming. The EBU and News International then signed two exclusive rights agreements with the joint venture company: a Services Agreement and a Facilities Agreement. An additional guarantee was signed between News International and Eurosport. The European Commission ruled in favour of Screensport, and against the EBU/News International, determining an infringement of Article 85(1) as the joint venture excluded third parties access. The complaint against the EBU's exclusive rights agreement was decided later in 1993. In this case, the European Commission exempted PSBs from EU competition rules and permitted the EBU to hold exclusive rights to broadcast sports events (based upon the Eurovision system) (1993 *EBU/Eurovision* case). With this decision DG Competition clearly recognises the PSB role in securing the public interest. The decision was later overturned in the ECJ (as detailed in Chapter 2). In 2000, DG Competition again approved the Eurovision System following the withdrawed of the private group Canal Plus from the exclusive rights aggreement. Eurovision is thus exempted from antitrust rules until 2005. However, DG Competition could face further scrutiny by the court.

The next case of significance was the 1991 *ABC/Generale des Eaux/ Canal+/WH Smith* decision. The proposed joint venture dealt with an agreement between the European Sports Network (known in England as ESPN a subsidiary of Capital Cities/ABC), Générale d'Images (GdI) (a subsidiary of Compagnie Générale des Eaux) and Canal Plus to acquire the television interests of W.H. Smith. Capital Cities/ABC (American Broadcasting Company) was a US communications group, with a particular interest in selling sports programmes (baseball and American football) to European pay-TV channels. Compagnie Générale des Eaux was a large French water company (now renamed Vivendi). Canal Plus was a French pay-TV channel. The three groups acquired WHSTV, which belonged to W.H. Smith. WHSTV owned TESN, ESPN (formerly Screensport), LifeStyle TV, Kindernet, Cable Jukebox and the Molinare Group. (WHSTV also owned Yorkshire TV, but this was not included in the acquisition.) The joint venture between the three companies was eventually permitted to go ahead. However, it is significant that DG Competition used this case to more narrowly define the product market in broadcasting. The Commission determined in its decision that pay-TV and commercial free-access television constituted separate product markets. The case is also interesting because it again dealt with sports broadcasting which was deemed by the Commission to be 'particularly amenable for transnational broadcasting as (it) transcend(s) national, cultural and linguistic barriers'. This was significant for future decisions as sports broadcasting is no longer considered to be restricted to national (geographical) markets, but has been elevated to a 'European' issue.

European Commission investigations of concentrations taking place between the largest German media groups are numerous. In a period of only five years, between 1994 and 1999, DG Competition investigated no less than 14 joint ventures involving German media groups. Nine investigations handled joint ventures taking place solely between German companies within the national German market.[14] Six investigations dealt with German groups seeking joint ventures outside of Germany.[15] In 1994, the European Commission decided the first two of these cases, which dealt with cross-border acquisitions: the *Kirch/Richemont/Telepiù* case and the *Bertelsmann/News International/Vox* case.[16] The latter cases were decided positively, but, in both cases, as in the *ABC/Generale des Eaux/Canal+/WH Smith* case, DG Competition uses a narrower definition of pay-TV and commercial free-access television.

The definition of broadcasting markets was narrowed further still in the 1994 *Kirch/Richemont/Telepiù* case. In this case, Kirch and Richemont[17] acquired joint control of the Italian television group Telepiù S.r.l (divested at the time by Fininvest). The Commission decided to approve the acquisition as the Italian language market presented a new market for the companies involved. On 27 June 1994, Richemont (through its subsidiary, Ichor) acquired CIT (which held 25 per cent of Telepiù) and Kirch (through its subsidiary Beteiligungs-GmbH[18]) increased its stake in Telepiù from 34.72 per cent to 40.73 per cent. The remaining shareholders in Telepiù were the Della Valle Group (23.39 per cent) and Fininvest (10 per cent).[19] The Commission decided in this case that Kirch and Richemont's joint control of Telepiù did not present a problem of co-ordination of competitive behaviour because Richemont and Kirch operated in separate pay-TV markets according to geographic criteria. This opened the Italian market to foreign investment. In its ruling, the Commission reasoned that pay-TV was different to free access television because:

First, pay-TV is primarily financed by subscription fees, whereas free-access television is financed by public authorities and/or by advertising revenue, depending on whether the channel in question is State-owned or a private commercial one. Although a pay-TV channel may take advertising, it is of lesser importance. Secondly, pay-TV offers a more specialised programme-mix in order to meet the requirements of a target audience. This can consist of live coverage of sport events, first television screenings of recent films or well-reputed works, etc. In most countries pay-TV channels acquire the right to broadcast major new films only after they have been on general release on cinemas (the so-called theatrical window) for a period of 6 to 12 months, and after they have been made available on video (video window) for around 6 to 10 months once the theatrical window has expired. The pay-TV channel will broadcast those films (pay-TV window) within a period of 6 to 12 months, after which they will become available for free-access channels. 16. The above factors seem to lead to the conclusion that pay-TV represents a separate market. (Kirch/Richemont/Telepiù No. IV/M.4100)

This division of free-access as opposed to pay-access markets was confirmed in a second decision made by the European Commission in the same year. In the 1994 *Bertelsmann/News International/Vox case*, News International bought a 49.9 per cent stake in Vox, a German free-to-air television channel. Vox was 24.9 per cent owned by Bertelsmann. Because media markets are divided linguistically, DG Competition considered whether the acquisition strengthened either of the companies' dominant positions in the German television market. News International had entered the German language market some years before through a joint venture with Selco (50 per cent owned by Kirch's Pro 7). The Commission decided again that free-access channels and pay channels constituted separated markets. Therefore, because Vox was a free-to-air channel, DG Competition did not consider News International to be increasing its dominance in the German language market as the company was present in two separate markets: free-to-air and pay-TV.[20] The Commission also considered the potential for Bertelsmann and News International to trade film rights. It was concluded that this did not at that point in time present a problem for the German market. However, this again could be an issue, now that Kirch has sold off its film rights to the German market following bankruptcy. This case in point highlights why the EC's reliance on competition policy to govern media markets has been problematic. Media markets are highly volatile. Therefore the market status quo at the time of a decision could alter itself dramatically in a relatively short period of time. It would aid both market investors and public interest regulators if clear rules on media ownership could be agreed at the European level, rather than having to rely on case-by-case analyses.

In 1994, the Commission made the first of what could be labelled four highly controversial negative decisions on joint ventures in the German market.[21] In its 1994 Media Service GmbH (MSG) Media Service decision, the European Commission ruled against a German joint venture for pay-TV called Media Service GmbH (MSG) between Bertelsmann, Kirch and Deutsche Telekom (DT). Proposed was a joint pay-TV service between Bertelsmann AG, Taurus Beteiligungs GmbH (belonging to Kirch) and Deutsche Bundespost Telekom (the public telecommunications group). DG Competition found the joint venture to be incompatible with the common market as it would have created a dominant position in three markets: (1) technical and administrative services for pay-TV (a market in which MSG would have been directly present) (2) cable distribution (DT), and (3) pay-TV (Kirch and Bertelsmann through Premiere). The Commission also considered that MSG was likely to gain a lasting dominant position in the new media markets (of the future), particularly for digital television, where it would exclude market entrance to newcomers. Even though these were economic rationales for preventing the joint venture, it is plain to see that such a joint venture could have presented serious implications for cultural (and political) pluralism in Germany. However, the decision had serious implications for the German market. Two separate digital platforms (Kirch's DF1 and Bertelsmann's Premiere) were launched. However, they chose to use different technologies for set-top boxes. The Commission failed to convince

Bertelsmann to use Kirch's D-box technology. The debate on standards fed the EC initiative for a Directive on Television Standards, which was eventually passed in 1995 (Appendix 1). Standards were only recommended, never imposed at the European level.

The next prohibition was Nordic Satellite Distribution (NSD) in 1995.[22] This related to the capacity of a satellite television transponder. DG Competition found that NSD (a joint venture between Norsk Telecomm, Tele Denmark and Kinnevik) would acquire a dominant position in the market for satellite television transponder services targeted towards Nordic viewers. This would in turn strengthen Tele Denmark's dominant position in the Danish cable television market. The vertical integration of NSD meant that the companies' respective positions in their national markets would reinforce each other. In addition, the Commission reasoned that the NSD would lead to the dominance of Viasat (Kinnevik's subsidiary) in the specific market of pay-TV distribution (to direct-to-home households). In this case, the Commission expressed its wish to ensure that the Scandinavian markets, which were in a stage of liberalisation, were not closed to third parties (*Butterworth's Merger Control Review*, 1995).

Soon afterwards, DG Competition ruled against the 1995 Holland Media Group (HMG) joint venture. The Holland Media Group had proposed a joint venture in commercial television in the Netherlands between RTL4 S.A., Vereniging Veronica Omroeperganisatie and Endemol Entertainment Holding BV (Tucker, 1995b). The Dutch government had requested a ruling on the case under Article 22(3) of the Merger Regulation. Had the Dutch government not referred the case, DG Competition would have had no jurisdiction to judge it as the turnover thresholds were below those required by the Merger Regulation.[23] The Commission ruled that the agreement would lead to the creation of a dominant position in the Dutch advertising market and strengthen Endemol's dominant position for independent Dutch-language television production.[24] Clearly, as this case dealt solely with a purely national case and a venture with a comparatively low turnover, the Commission's concern overstepped those of ensuring a competitive market. When commenting on the ruling Commissioner Van Miert expressed his concern for growing European media concentration: 'today's decision is a further example of the Commission's commitment to protect competitive market structures in media sector. It is also worth mentioning that the strict application of the competition rules can also contribute to maintaining plurality in this sensitive sector' (Lang, 1997a: 42). Later in July 1996, the Commission approved the joint venture following the withdrawal of Endemol from the project. Endemol challenged the Commission over the ruling in the CFI and lost.

The next case to be judged negatively in 1996 concerned the acquisition of Cablevisión by Telefónica de España and Sogecable SA, a subsidiary of Canal Plus España. The Commission found that the acquisition affected the supply of services to both pay and cable television operators. Originally, the companies had notified the acquisition to the Spanish competition authority, but the MTF wrote to Canal Plus España requesting notification to the Commission. Following the negative decision, Sogecable sought an annulment in the CFI. The Court supported the Commission's decision. Just before the Court decision was announced, the operation was withdrawn.

In 1997, five decisions were made on joint ventures within the German media market, which was showing an increasingly high degree of concentration. The two joint ventures between the largest press groups Bertelsmann and Burda, and Bertelsmann, Burda and Springer were examined and approved. In the three broadcasting cases, the MTF reached *negative* decisions. The broadcasting cases dealt with the proposed acquisition and joint control of the German pay-TV operator Premiere and BetaResearch by Bertelsmann and Kirch. Bertelsmann and Kirch owned Premiere and DF1 respectively, which represented the only pay-TV packages in Germany. The plan was to launch a joint-digital platform. Together, the two companies would have controlled the technological standard for digital set-top boxes and extensive programming rights. In the first decision, the Commission pronounced the joint venture as incompatible with the common market as it represented a concentration in the 'European German-speaking market'. The Commission had initially put informal pressure upon the German government and the Bundeskartellamt (the German Cartel Office) to decide the case at the national level. When the German government decided to approve the joint venture (against the wishes of the six Socialdemokratische Partei Deutschlands (SPD) German Länder which refused to license the service), the European Commission warned the three companies that they risked a fine of a maximum of 10 per cent of their combined turnovers if they proceeded with plans to launch the digital service without notifying the European Commission. The MTF opened an investigation even though the Commissioners for Information Society (Bangemann), Education (Cresson) and Culture (Oreja) were initially in favour of approving the joint venture (Levy, 1999: 95). The incumbent Conservative German government lobbied in support of a positive ruling. In particular, Chancellor Helmut Kohl allegedly put informal pressure on the Commission to pass the venture.[25] Despite this political resistance, the Commission was able to prevent the joint venture under EU Merger Regulation. It was only possible for the EC to intervene in the German market because it could argue that the venture effected linguistic markets external to Germany, namely Austria and the German-speaking minorities in the Netherlands and Belgium ('European-German-speaking' market). The success of this ruling, notwithstanding resistance from the powerful Member State, Germany, showed that DG Competition had acquired a considerable degree of legitimacy in arbitrating media markets. This legitimacy was called into question when digital markets across Europe began to collapse (Chapter 6).

The second case (which was filed at the same time as *DF1/Premiere*) was *Deutsche Telekom/Betaresearch*. This second case related to the joint control of the D-Box decoder by Bertelsmann, Kirch and Deutsche Telekom. A negative decision was adopted by the Commission in May, 1998. During the preceedings, the President of the Bundeskartellamt, Dieter Wolf, stated the following at a conference of the International Bar Association: 'the majority of national states lacked both the strength and the courage to do anything about their respective monopolies. A higher political level was called upon to do so, and this is where the European Commission came in' (Dieter, 1997).

This statement indicates that national governments may simply lack the political power to regulate large media mergers. By ruling the case at the supranational level, DG Competition was able to take a decision which went beyond the boundaries of the politically possible at the national level. The Dutch *HMG* and German *Bertelsmann/Kirch/Premiere* cases were further evidence of this phenomenon. The British *BDB* case (below) represents another such case.

The MTF has investigated five cases of dominant position within the British market.[26] In the *British Telecom/MCI* case, DG Competition formally prevented a market concentration. The second case dealt with BSkyB's involvement in BDB. The Department of Trade and Industry (DTI) had approved BSkyB's participation in the creation of British Digital Broadcasting (BDB, renamed ONdigital, which later became ITV Digital). The Commission argued against through a series of informal discussions with UK regulatory bodies. Snoddy (1997) claims that these talks were initiated by the ITC. The Commission argued that the joint venture BDB would strengthen BSkyB's dominant position in the UK pay-TV market and encourage co-operation (rather than competition) between BDB and BSkyB. In particular, the Commission stated that the strengthening of BSkyB's dominant position would be contrary to a principle ruled by the ECJ in *Ahmed Saeed Flugreisen* based on Article 5 of the Treaties (Lang, 1997a: 32). In the end, the UK government requested that BSkyB withdraw from the joint venture.

The Commission's next intervention in a broadcasting market came in Spain. The ruling, in 1996, concerned the joint acquisition of Cablevisión by the telecommunications operator Telefónica, and Sogecable SA (a subsidiary of Canal Plus España). The Commission found that the venture affected the supply of services to cable television operators and prevented new entrants to the markets for pay and cable television. Originally, the companies had notified the acquisition to the Spanish Competition Defence Tribunal (TDC), which vetoed the joint venture, but this was overruled by the Spanish government. Following the government's decision, the Commission wrote to Canal Plus España requesting notification to the Commission. This resulted in a political tug-of-war between the Commission and the Spanish government.[27] The MTF prevented the joint venture. Soge-cable sought an annulment in the CFI and a suspension of the Commis-sion's activities until the Court had determined whether the operation had a Community dimension. The CFI did not suspend the MTF investigation (as it viewed this to be a substitution of the EC's administrative activities), but supported the MTF decision.[28] In any case, just before the CFI decision was announced, the operation was withdrawn due to a change in the Spanish government in 1996 and the opposition of European Commission.

Thus, two satellite platforms, rather than one, were created in Spain, one by Telefónica, the other by Canal Plus. The new Spanish government tried to prevent Canal Satélite Digital from using a different encryption technol-ogy than Telefónica through the enactment of two laws (Llorens-Maluquer, 1998: 578–85).[29] The government mandated the use of one encryption technology (multicrypt rather than simulcrypt) by all market players and mandated the shared use of sports rights. This, it reasoned, would create a level playing field for competition and promote pluralism, and consumer choice. Customers would only have to buy one digital set-top box with access to both services. This should have been legal under the 1995 Tele-vision Standards Directive, which encouraged the use of one technology. However, the Directive did not state that Member States could impose stan-dards on operators. Canal Satélite Digital had chosen simulcrypt, and requested that the Commission intervene in its defence. DG Competition opposed Act 19/97 as anti-competitive and contrary to the free movement of goods and threatened to challenge it in the ECJ. The European Com-mission (through the DG Competition ruling) was effectively going against its own recommendation of the promotion of common standards in the 1995 Directive. As Llorens-Maluquer details well, a long battle between the Commission and the Spanish government ensued resulting in the amend-ment of both laws by Spain (1998).[30] In a parallel development, Canal Satélite Digital (CSD) challenged Act 17/97 in a Spanish court (Tribunal Supremo), which referred the case in turn to the ECJ. Long after the Real Decreto had been revoked, the ECJ ruled with the Spanish court, and against the Spanish government in January 2002.[31] In a recent development, the Spanish government was condemned by the Spanish Tribunal Supremo to pay 26.4 million euros in compensation to Sogecable for commercial damages as a result of the illegal application during six months of Act 17/97. This case in particular illustrates the lack of internal co-operation in the European Commission. The Commission had an opportunity to enable a government to impose a common standard on market operators. It chose not to. The market result was that the two players chose different set-top box technologies, locking customers into one system or another. This decreased competition at the content level. The two platforms eventually merged in 2002. Neither operator was able to generate enough profit to overcome the high costs of technology and sports rights.

In 1997, two further Spanish cases dealt with the cable television company, Cable I Televisio de Catalunya (CTC), in the Spanish region of Catalonia. In the first case, *Cable I Televisio de Catalunya*, joint acquisition of CTC was proposed by the electric company, Endesa, the gas company, Gas Natural (the principle suppliers of electricity and gas in Spain), Stet (the Italian telecommunications operator) and Caixa Catalunya (the leading Catalan bank). In the second case, *Cableuropa/SpainCom/CTC*, the US companies, General Electric (through Cableuropa) and Bank of America (through SpainCom) proposed partial acquisition of CTC. The European companies were dubbed 'the European partners' and the American companies, 'the American partners'. The MTF authorised the acquisitions in both cases, establishing joint control between the American and European partners in CTC. Although the Commission could not justify an intervention, the MTF expressed dissatisfaction with the ruling (*European Bulletin* 1/2, 1998: 25, 1999: 14).

In the 1990s, the Commission faced a number of complaints from private broadcasters against the national financing of PSBs (Levy, 1999: 95–96). Complaints surfaced in France, Spain and Portugal in the early 1990s. In 1997 and 1998, additional complaints came from Germany, the UK and Italy and, later, Portugal. The German association of commercial broadcasters (Verband Privater Rundfunk und Telekommunikation – VPRT) complained about competition from the digital PSB channels Kinderkanal and Phoenix. BSkyB accused the UK government of an illegal application of state aid with the creation of the BBC 'News 24'. In Italy, Fininvest denounced the underwriting of RAI's debts by the Italian government. DG Competition made some attempts to define rules governing PSB funding in a 1998 document. As Hills and Michalis explain it proposed 'to apply the 'net cost' text developed for financing universal service in telecommunications' (2000: 458). This meant that advertising would not be permitted to PSBs receiving a licence fee if 'it exceeded the "net cost" of fulfilling their public service mission' (Hills and Michalis, 2000: 458). DG Competition also proposed that PSBs would be prevented from producing content that went beyond what it considered to be its public service remit, in particular that they would not broadcast major sporting events and entertainment programmes. The proposal naturally came under grave opposition from PSBs and some Members of the European Parliament and was withdrawn.

Under duress, the Commission eventually decided on the three pending PSB cases. In the VPRT complaint, the Commission ruled in 1999 that state funding of digital channels was justified under state aid rules (NN-70/98).[55] In the *News 24* case, the Commission decided in September 1999 that PSB funding from licence fees was admissible under Article 87 of the Treaty (case NN-88/98 and CEC, 1999e).[56] The Commission ruled in this case that the channel was fulfilling a clearly defined public service remit and therefore the aid was proportionate. It stated in the same ruling that PSB funding could also be granted without prior notification and approval (*Competition Policy Newsletter*, 2000).

Private groups challenged the Commission on PSB funding in three cases brought to the ECJ.[32] As detailed in Chapter 2, the ECJ chose not to make a definitive statement on state aid. Instead it called for DG Competition to clarify its position on PSB financing. DG IV therefore published its 2001 Communication on the application of state aid rules to public service broadcasting'[33] in which it recognises PSB importance for maintaining pluralism (Craufurd Smith, 2002; Ward, 2003). The Communication, quotes the 'public service' Protocol of the 1997 Treaty of Amsterdam and the 2000 EC 'Communication on services of general interest in Europe' (CEC, 2001c) as its basis. The Communication states that 'the choice of the financing scheme falls within the competence of the Member State, and there can be no objection in principle to the choice of a dual financing scheme (combining public funds and advertising revenues) rather than a single funding scheme (solely public funds) as long as competition in the relevant markets (e.g. advertising, acquisition and/or sale of programmes) is not affected to an extent which is contrary to the Community interest'. This recognises Member States' right to maintain PSB funding, but means that private sector complaints over PSB advertising and funding need still be decided on a case-by-case basis. The Communication enabled the EC to mandate a number of requirements from Member States relating to their PSBs. It firstly requests that Member States define public service broadcasting activities and to differentiate these from private broadcasters. It also recommends greater transparency of accounts if PSBs are license-fee funded in order to determine whether the fee is being used to cross-subsidise new services. The Communication requests Member States to formally define public service broadcasting (through a formal act of legislation) and to formally establish a regulatory body to oversee it. This is a significant requirement of the Commission. Many Member States (e.g. Spain) had never formally defined public service broadcasting in a legal act. The Commission has prompted a serious assessment of public service broadcasting at national levels. This is leading to greater European co-operation in the definition of public service broadcasting. Following the adoption of the 'European Union Charter of Fundamental Rights' at the 2000 European Council meeting in Nice, an idea for a European Charter for public service broadcasting was floated, but has not yet been realised.

In October 2003, the Commission ruled on public service television financing in Italy and Portugal. It found that provisions to fund PSBs, adopted during the 1990s in Italy and Portugal, were in line with EU state aid requirements. However, in 2004, DG Competition opened an investigation into Dutch public broadcasting spending. It is investigating whether the Dutch government has spent 110 million euros too much on public broadcasting since 1992. In particular, the Commission is concerned that the Dutch broadcaster utilises public funding for commercial activities. This would not be permissible under state aid rules, which stipulate that public funding only be used for non-commercial purposes.

With the amendment of the Merger Regulation in April 1997, paragraphs 1 and 3 of Article 85 were extended to joint ventures to determine whether or not a dominant position is created or maintained.[34] The Commission had planned to lower turnover thresholds from five to two and one half billion ECU under the new rules. However, Member States could not reach an agreement on this, so the thresholds were maintained, and the lower thresholds were adopted only for those mergers which had to be notified in several EC countries. Only a small number of cases are expected to utilise the lowered thresholds due to the organisational requirements involved (Fine, 1997). The new rules became effective on 1 March 1998. The *Telia/Telenor/Schibsted* case, which related to the provision of internet and audio-visual interactive services in Scandinavia, represented the first media case to which the new rules applied in 1998. In January 2004, the European Union passed a new merger regulation which will come into force in May 2004 at the same time as the European Union's enlargement. It strengthens the Commission's role and enforcement, but thresholds remain unchanged.[35]

The number of media mergers and joint ventures is on the rise, but since 1999 when Van Miert left office, DG Competition has made no prohibitions in the media sector. This is most likely to a number of factors: the reluctance to intervene in broadcast markets following the collapse of digital markets in Europe, the enactment of the new regulatory framework for communications which widens definitions of communications markets and perhaps the approach of the new Commissioner who inherited the competition portfolio in 1999, Mario Monti.

Conclusion

This chapter showed that the EC's Competition Authority has had substantial influence on the development of media markets in Europe, particularly in the case of digital television. It discussed how the MTF narrowed the definition of media markets over the years. This approach has permitted DG Competition greater scope in media market decision-making and irrevocably expanded the EU's scope for media regulation.

Unlike the Court, DG Competition has taken into consideration the public interest. Indeed, DG Competition has singled out the media sector as unique from other sectors due to regard for pluralism. This was shown most clearly in its PSB financing cases, but also in cases concerning national media concentration. In a maturation of its thinking on this, DG Competition stated in 1999:

2.2.3. Media plurality While the competition rules are of general application, they must take account of each sector's special characteristics. In the case of television, there are many such characteristics which will be discussed in the annex on market definition. However, one quite specific point should be stressed here, namely the *dangers inherent in the creation or strengthening of dominant positions for media plurality. The goal of media plurality must, therefore, always be kept in mind.* (emphasis added) (*Competition Policy Newsletter*, Number 1, February 1999, p. 7.)

With this, the Commission recognised that it must consider public interest as well as economic responsibility in decision-making. This was also demonstrated in Van Miert's public declaration in the *Endemol* case that 'that the strict application of the competition rules can also contribute to maintaining plurality in this sensitive sector'.

Despite the extensive use of competition policy in regulating European media markets, there have been concerns that it is the wrong instrument for ensuring public interest goals. The key problem is that the MTF needs to justify rulings through market definition. DG Competition's reliance on instruments designed to guarantee the economic functioning of the Single Market cannot easily encompass issues of pluralism. Even with the 1997 changes to the Merger Regulation, without specific rules for the media industry, DG Competition is experiencing difficulties in justifying media decisions and a significant number face appeal. Indeed, when concentrations are prevented 'the MTF is frequently accused of taking an overtly political approach to decision-taking' (Cini and McGowan, 1999: 126).

DG Competition faces a clear dichotomy in its approach. The ECJ has categorised the broadcasting market as a single European market in order to justify jurisdiction. However, DG Competition has respected the public interest as demonstrated in its policy documents and by Van Miert's case comments. The consideration of the public interest is of course comprehensible because (as Chapter 6 shows) if European national policy shares nothing else, it shares a historical tradition of public service broadcasting and media markets regulated in view of cultural goals. However, DG Competition risks the overturning of its decisions in the ECJ. The Commission is hampered not only by the fact that EU law excludes jurisdiction in cultural areas, but also by the ECJ's unwillingness to make progressive rulings in this area.

Indeed, DG Competition needs to find a better foundation for decision-making rather than simply the narrowing of market definitions. Not only is it an economic argument that is easily fallible in Court, but the method will have to end with the implementation of new regulatory framework for communications which conceives of all communication markets to be part of 'one' combined market. Increasing integration and internationalisation of media markets has already made the regulation of media markets in terms of economic policy problematic for DG Competition. But the passing of the new regulatory framework in 2002 will complicate decision-making further. This was recognised by a DG Competition official at a conference in 2002 who wrote: 'as a main result from the convergence debate: regulation should no*t separate sectors and technologies in a rigid manner* but will have to depend more and more on a *dynamic assessment of actual audience and market power*' (original emphasis) (Ungerer, 2002). This pronouncement is of further interest as DG Competition herewith ponders the potential use of the 'audience share' instrument as was proposed by DG Internal Market in its Draft Directive on media ownership. Audience share is innovative, but, as will be shown in the next chapter, lacks a legitimate legal basis. Neither can DG Competition feasibly define the 'the public interest' without Treaty basis.

With media companies expanding into adjacent markets, the definition of media markets is becoming increasingly difficult, making judgements politically controversial. When asked if he were in favour of harmonising Member State media ownership laws, Van Miert stated:

> My personal opinion is that I am convinced of a need for European legislation on media concentration. From a democratic point of view, it is necessary. When we said no to the Nordic satellite case, the ruling was considered to be difficult. We cannot use competition rules to govern democratic issues.[36]

In effect, the former Commissioner took the position that European competition policy instruments are inadequate for judging cases that effect goals of democracy and pluralism. The next chapter will discuss EU efforts to regulate media markets through instruments other than competition law. The focus will be the initiatives on *ownership* and *convergence*.

Notes

1   These are specifically the 1994 *MSG Media Service Nordic Satellite Distribution*; *RTL/Veronica/Endemol*; *Telefónica/Canal Plus/Cablevisión*; *Deutsche Telekom/Betaresearch*; and *DF1/Premiere*.
2   Between 1990 and 1999, 1,168 mergers were pre-notified to the Merger Task Force under the Merger Regulation in all sectors. 1,104 of these cases resulted in an official decision by DG Competition. See EC 'Competition statistics on European merger control', *http://europa.eu.int/comm/competition/mergers/cases/stats.html*. Under line 8.3 (Prohibition) a total of 11 negative decisions were recorded under the Merger Regulation 1990–1999. Cini and McGowen also note the high occurrence of negative decisions in the media sector, amounting to 4 out of 7 by 1996 (1999: 130). Other authors have also commented upon this phenomenon (Kon, 1996). Since this time (1999–2002) a further 865 decisions were taken – meaning a total of 1,969 have been made by the MTF between 1995 and 2002, 18 of which were prohibitions.
3   *Screensport/EBU* and *Tiercé Ladbroke*.
4   Many of these are decided in letters, although there is a problem with this as letters have no legal validity. For discussion see Tucker (1997b).

5   Articles 81 (ex 85), 82 (ex 86) and 86 (ex 90) are to be found in the Consoli-
     dated Version of the Treaty Establishing the European Community under Title
     VI (ex Title V) of the 'Common rules on competition, taxation and approxi-
     mation of laws', Chapter 1 (Rules on competition), Section 1 (Rules applying
     to undertakings).
6   An exception to this is when each of the companies has more than two-thirds
     of its Community-wide turnover in one Member State only, in which case
     national law would apply.
7   Cini and McGowan state that when DG IV was set up, 'an identifiable con-
     sumer culture provided evidence of a public interest dimension within the
     policy' (1999: 24). At the time, consumer policy was also situated within DG
     IV.
8   The European Court of Justice would have to decide in this case whether the
     Member State decision was acting within Community law.
9   Booz-Allen and Hamilton (1992) 'study on pluralism and concentration in
     media – economic evaluation', Brussels, 6 February, Report to the Commission
     of the European Communities, DG III.
10   Gibbons (2003) has argued that there is general European agreement that this
     should be 3–4 players.
11   This is because the EU has no jurisdiction in cultural policy (which continues to
     be protected by the principle of subsidiarity), and there is yet no Directive for
     media ownership. Further, as the ECJ has identified the broadcasting as a service,
     legally it should be equal to other industrial sectors under competition law.
12   This tendency to narrowly define markets has been recognised by a number
     of lawyers. See in particular discussion by Kon (1996: 33–7) and Lang (1997:
     20–3).
13   This was determined in the 2000 *Vivendi/Canal Plus/Seagram* case.
14   *MSG Media Service, N-TV Bertelsmann/Burda/Springer Hos MM, Bertels-
     mann/Burda Hos Lifeline, Deutsche Telekom/Betaresearch, DF1/Premiere,
     Bertelsmann/Burda/Futurekids* and *Havas/Bertelsmann/Doyma*.
15   *Kirch/Richemont/Telepiù Decision, Bertelsmann/News International/Vox
     Decision, Vox (II), Kirch/Richemont/Multichoice /Telepiù, Bertelsmann/CLT
     (Ufa), Betaresearch/Bertelsmann/Kirch* (1998).
16   *Kirch/Richemont/Telepiù, Bertelsmann/News International/Vox*.
17   Compagnie Financière Richemont AG.
18   Ptb Pay TV Beteiligungs GmbH.
19   Through its subsidiary, Reti Televisive Italiane SpA.
20   DG Competition measured the market through advertising and audience share.
     It compared the advertising market shares of Vox (2.5 per cent) with RLT (35
     per cent), SAT1 (27 per cent), ARD (9 per cent) and ZDF (7 per cent) and the
     audience shares of VOX (2 per cent) with ZDF (17.8 per cent), RTL (21.8 per
     cent), ARD (16.8 per cent) and SAT1 (14.7 per cent).
21   The 1994 *MSG Media Service*, 1998 *Deutsche Telekom/Betaresearch*, 1998
     DF1/Premiere and 1998 *Betaresearch/Bertelsmann/Kirch*.
22   For further discussion Tucker and Carnegy, 1995a.
23   If a case is referred to the European Commission under Article 22(3) of the
     Merger Regulation, the companies are permitted to go ahead with their pro-
     posed concentration while the case is being examined.

24   Endemol is the largest independent producer of Dutch-language television programmes.
25   'Freund Kohl in geheimer Mission', Süddeutche Zeitung, 17 December 1997.
26   BBC/BskyB/Football Association, British Telecom/MCI, British Telecom/MCI (II), BDB, Microsoft/Liberty Media/Telewest.
     Case No. IV/M.856 [14.05.97]; 1997 *BskyB/British Digital Broadcasting* Case IV/M. 300.
27   Politically (Llorens-Maluquer suggests), this choice may have been a battle between the defence (on the behalf of the Commission) of a 'European champion' (Canal Plus) against a 'national' champion (Telefónica).
28   1996 *Sogecable SA* v. *Commission of the European Communities*.
29   1997 Ley 1/97 incorporation of the EC Directive 95/47/CE; and 1997 Ley 21/97 Reguladora de las Emisiones y Retransmisiones de Competiciones Deportivas.
30   Real Decreto Ley 16/97 amends Ley 17/97 with the changes mandated by the Commission.
31   2002 *Canal Satélite Digital* v. *Spain*.
32   *Télévision Française* v. *European Commission* (1999), *SIC* v. *Commission* (2000), *Commission* v. *TF1* (2001).
33   Communication from the Commission on the application of State aid rules to public service broadcasting – and Commission clarifies application of State aid rules to Public Service Broadcasting Press Release – IP/01/1429 – 17 October 2001.
34   The amended version of the Merger Regulation is to be found in *Official Journal of the European Communities* (OJ) L 257, 21 September 1990, p. 13. As amended by Regulation No. 1310/97, OJ L 180, 9 July 1997. A correction of the Act is found in OJ L 40 of 13 February 1998.
35   The 2004 Merger Regulation includes: a test based on a 'Significant Impediment to effective competition'; more flexibility in the timetable for merger review; a reinforced 'one-stop-shop'; and higher fines for non-compliance.
36   In response to a question by the author at the *Future of Merger Control in Europe* conference.

4

The Commission, the Parliament and media market regulation

⌐ it will soon be impossible to separate telecoms from computer-based communications and broadcasting: the future regulatory framework for communications and media in Europe therefore needs to be open, flexible and
adaptable. . . . Convergence between telecommunications, computer, audiovisual, and publishing technologies, services, and industries will constitute the
greatest challenge to policy-makers in the years to come. (Martin Bangemann,
Geneva, 1997)
 The (DG XIII) Report (on convergence) takes a one-sided, ideological
approach that does not take account of the reality of the diversity of opinion
in European society as a whole or in the European Institutions. It calls into
question the whole European regulatory framework on audiovisual policy,
and with it all the efforts of the Parliament and the Commission so far in this
field. (Carol Tongue, Brussels, 1996b)

The academic literature on the EU indicates that the European Commission
is the most important actor in policy formation. Often overlooked is the
important role of the European Parliament, particularly as an agenda setter.
This chapter will explore the roles of both the Commission and Parliament. It focuses on the parallel initiatives of *media ownership* and *convergence*, two initiatives that pushed at the boundaries of the regulatory state.
Impediments to policy-making are explained by the lack of a Treaty basis,
increasing politicisation of the policy processes due to the democratic goals
of media regulation at national levels and the Commission's (consequent)
over-reliance on economic policy instruments. The chapter will access how
these obstacles presented limitations to the EU's expansion as a regulatory
state.

Initiation by the European Parliament

Following the 1980 Debauve ruling of the European Court of Justice, the
European Parliament launched a debate on the regulation of media markets.
Two party groupings, the Party of European Socialists (PSE) and the

European People's Party (EPP) led this debate in two separate reports (European Parliament, 1980a and b). As Collins (1994) and Krebber (2001) detail **NB** the reports represent two contrasting views of media market liberalisation. The 1980 PSE Report argued for legislation which would protect public service broadcasters and prevent media concentration. The 1980 EPP Report assessed the potential of the European market for economic growth and jobs. The latter recommended the establishment of a pan-European broadcaster modelled on Luxembourg's RTL which would report on European affairs. This was followed by an official report (the Hahn Report)[1] from the Committee of Youth, Culture, Education, Information and Sports. The report largely reiterated the goals set out by the PSE. It encompassed the EPP recommendation for a pan-European broadcaster which, the Hahn Report envisioned, would report directly on the activities of the European institutions. This, it was believed, would better integrate citizens into European-level decision-making. The proposal was that the European institutions would fund such a channel.

The Commission was opportunistic in its response. It took advantage of the Hahn Resolution to initiate its Green Paper on 'Television Without Frontiers'. In a 1983 Communication, the Commission expressed support for the EP proposal for a pan-European channel (to be established in partnership with the EBU) in the report 'Realities and tendencies in European television: perspectives and options' (CEC, 1983). However, it reasoned that it was infeasible due to the costs involved.[2] Importantly, the Commission used the 1983 Communication to outline its own developing approach to media market regulation. This included a general regulatory framework for new technologies (cable and satellite), the proposed harmonisation of technical standards (at that time PAL and SECAM were under discussion) and support measures for European content production. Following consultation with relevant interest groups, the Commission published its 1984 Green Paper Television Without Frontiers (TWF) (CEC, 1984). The Green Paper looked remarkably different to the initiative of the European Parliament. As Humphreys details well the Green Paper received substantial input from large media groups and the advertising industry (Humphreys, 1996: 268–72). The Commission had relied heavily on cognitive resources external to its civil service, with extensive use of a report prepared by the European Association of Advertising Agencies (EAAA) entitled 'New communication developments' (Humphreys, 1996: 268–72).

The key focus of the Green Paper was the liberalisation of cross-national broadcasting. The EP responded to the Paper by expressing concern over the EU's limited competence for controlling media concentration. Certain Members of the European Parliament (MEPs) from the UK and Italy led the debate fearing a repeat at the EU level of national scenarios, wherein liberalisation of media markets coupled with insufficient legislation had led to concentration in press or television markets. The EP produced four resolutions[3] between 1984 and 1989 requesting that the Commission include measures within the TWF Directive for protecting media pluralism. The 1987 resolution in particular requested the Commission protect cultural diversity from the dangers of media concentration. The EP did not view media concentration as a problem of market inefficiency rather as a threat to democracy, the freedom of speech and pluralist representation. This reflected national rationales on media market regulation which was at the same time coming into being at the Member State level. However, whereas national regulation was ultimately dependent on democratic approval by national parliaments, the EU suffered from a democratic deficit. National ministers in the Council (for the internal market) would ultimately pass any Directive proposed by the EC, with no guarantee of input from the EP.

The TWF initiative became a member of a package of Directives initiated in the 1987 Single European Act (SEA) (Appendix 4).[4] The 1985 White Paper 'Completing the internal market' leading up to the SEA stated that the media industry represented one of only three future growth sectors in Europe (Appendix 2). Accordingly, the Commission planned to liberalise the media sector in the interest of Single Market objectives. DG III (for Industrial and Internal Market Policies) was given the responsibility of drafting TWF. The timing and the context of the debate therefore set the stage for the initial framing of the issue by the Commission as one concerning industrial and internal market policy, whereas the EP had chosen to frame the issue within the context of pluralism. Broadcasting, like any other service or good, required free access to the internal market.

After five years of negotiation,[5] the TWF Directive was adopted in 1989 (Appendix 2). The 1989 TWF Directive typifies a Single Market regulatory policy (Fraser, 1996). The Directive established a legal framework for the cross-border transmission of television programmes, thereby seeking to create a single audio-visual market. The Directive stipulates a harmonisation of national legislation relating to the free movement of television services. Under the 1989 Directive, a media company could only be regulated in the country of transmission, not reception.[6] Herewith the Commission aimed to strengthen the competitiveness of national media industries by buffering the European market against wider forces in the international market (Humphreys, 1996).

Unlike at the national level where the liberalisation of the broadcasting industry was accompanied by rules protecting the public interest,[7] the Commission Directive contained few such measures despite substantial calls from the EP and interest groups to do so. As Humphreys (1996), Collins (1994) and Krebber (2001) analyse, public pressure to include provisions based upon democratic goals was reasonably high. Significantly, the French president Mitterand insisted that the EC formally create a Council of Ministers of Culture during this time (established in 1989).[8] Despite this pressure, it was not the Culture Ministers who decided on TWF.[9] According to the Treaty Articles upon which it was based, the Directive was to be ratified by national ministers holding the 'internal market' portfolio. This was because the Directive was framed as a single market initiative. Only as such could it be ratified in the Council. As a single market initiative it only required qualified majority voting rather than unanimity.[10] Thus, the Commission was unable to balance market regulation with public interest regulation due to limitations of the EC Treaties. As a result, EU media regulation was grounded in an economic framework. In a last minute political move the French Presidency transferred the TWF dossier from the Internal Market Council to the General Affairs Council (dealing with trade policy) in an (unsuccessful) attempt to strengthen European content quotas (Krebber, 2001: 117). TWF was ultimately ratified by national ministers for trade.

The EC was marginally successful in that it was able to add some provisions to TWF issues that went beyond market regulation. TWF required that: a majority proportion of transmission time is reserved for European works; 10 per cent of transmission time or 10 per cent of programming budget for European works is created by independent producers; interruption of films by advertising is limited to once every 45 minutes; advertising during news, current affairs programmes, documentaries, religious programmes and children's programmes is excluded; advertising cigarettes, prescription medicines and medical treatment is prohibited; advertising time is limited to 20 per cent of the daily transmission time and 20 per cent within a given clock hour; minors are to be protected; and incitement to hatred on grounds of race, sex, religion or nationality is prohibited. However, Member States managed to annex 21 protocols to the Directive, which opted them out of specific rules. For example, Italy exempted the Fininvest channels from European quota requirements (Hirsch and Petersen, 1992: 49). This was quite remarkable as Italy was one of the Member States that lobbied heavily for inclusion of the provision in the first place. In addition, many Member States failed to implement many provisions of the Directive. France and Germany continued to advertise prescription medicines and medical treatment, the UK permitted single advertising spots and Italy continued advertising breaks in religious broadcasts. As detailed in Chapter 2, the ECJ was not interested in the implementation of these public interest goals, most probably because they lay outside its jurisdiction. The only provision it found relevant was that on cross-border broadcasting.

TWF's consequence for European markets was the encouragement of cross-border broadcasting and increasing co-operation between the largest European media groups (Lang, 1997a). TWF's depoliticisation during the policy process was hard won by the Commission. However, immediately following TWF ratification the European Parliament again took issue with the Commission over media concentration. This time requesting a separate initiative from the Commission, the EP published three resolutions and five reports on media concentration between 1990 and 1992.[11] The 1990 EP 'Resolution on media take-overs and mergers' states 'restrictions are essential in the media sector, not only for economic reasons but also and above all, as a means of guaranteeing a variety of sources of information and freedom of the press'. It requests that the Commission:

> put forward proposals for establishing a special legislative framework on media mergers and take-overs together with anti-trust laws to ensure that: (a) minimum professional standards are guaranteed; (b) journalistic ethics are protected; (c) the risk of subordination of small companies is eliminated; and (d) freedom of expression for all those working in the media is safeguarded.

Importantly, the Resolution also calls upon the Commission to require those Member States that do not have media ownership rules to adopt them. (Immediately following this Resolution, DG IV produced its 1990 'Communication to the Council and Parliament on audio-visual policy' which is discussed in Chapter 3). The 1992 EP 'Resolution on media concentration and diversity of opinion' restates the request to the Commission to 'submit a proposal for effective measures to combat or restrict concentration in the media, if necessary in the form of an anti-concentration Directive, with a view to: (a) harmonise national provisions on the concentration of media ownership, and (b) guarantee diversity of opinion and pluralism where the proposed concentration is on a European scale'. This Parliament pressure accompanied by some pressure from national levels and an increasing EP alliance with DG X led the Commission to embark upon an initiative for media ownership.[12]

The media ownership initiative

At that time, the Directorate Generals involved in media policy were DG I (External Relations), DG III (Industry), DG IV (Competition), DG X (Culture), DG XIII (Information Society) and DG XV (Internal Market). The Commissioners of the DGs who are responsible for co-ordinating media policy are outlined in Table 4.1.[13]

The European Commission began to consider media ownership legislation in 1991. When the Commission embarked upon the initiative, the portfolio was given to DG III author of TWF then responsible for both internal market and industrial policies. DG X had requested the portfolio at the time, but DG III had convincingly argued that the Commission only had the competence to legislate for media pluralism if it defined the issue as a problem of the internal market. This was also important, as such, a Directive would only require the QMV procedure in the Council. In 1991, DG III announced the idea for a Green Paper and interest groups were mobilised to submit opinions (see Chapter 5 for discussion of consultation).

Table 4.1 Directorate Generals and Commissioners holding media portfolios' 1989–2004

Group composition:	1989–92	1993–94	1995–99	1999–2004
President	Delors	Delors	Santer	Prodi
DG I (External relations)	Andriessen	van den Broek	Brittan	Lamy
DG III	Bangemann	*Bangemann*	Bangemann	
DG III	*Bangemann*			
DG IV (DG Competition)	Brittan	van Miert	van Miert	Monti
DG X (DG Culture)	Dondelinger	Deus de Pinheiro	Oreja	*Reding*
DG XIII (DG Information Society)	Pandolfi	Bangemann	Bangemann	Liikanen
DG XV	Scrivener	Scrivener		
DG XV (DG Internal Market)		d'Archirafi	*Monti*	Bolkestein
DG XIX		Schmidhuber	Schmidhuber	Liikanen

Note: Commissioners responsible for the media ownership portfolio are indicated in italic.

Soon after the initiation of the policy process, a conflict began to surface within the Commission as to the organisational domain relating to the responsibility for policy-making. In 1992 the DG III portfolio for industry and internal market was separated into DGs III and XV respectively. Responsibility for internal market initiatives was moved to DG XV. However, due to political reasons, the portfolio and unit dealing with media ownership did not come under the (French) Commissioner Scrivener's cabinet (DG XV) but remained with Bangemann (DG III) under temporary status. Bangemann did not wish to relinquish a portfolio dealing with the media industry to a French Commissioner. Even though the unit was linked to Bangemann's industry portfolio, the question as to whether media ownership constituted industrial or internal market policy remained and the utilisation of both arguments in the 1992 Green Paper is more than apparent.

In both of the Commission Green Papers on media ownership (1992 and 1994) the chief concern is the effect of national media legislation upon the EU's internal market. After consultation, DG III released the Commission's first Green Paper entitled 'Pluralism and media concentration in the internal market' in December 1992 (CEC, 1992a), which argues that Europe's media industry was hindered by different ownership rules in each Member State where media companies were attempting to pursue their activities and investments. The main argument throughout the paper is for the harmon-

isation of Member States' media ownership rules, as the Commission perceived that a 'disparity' of national anti-concentration laws could be seen
to 'brake structural adjustment' in the internal market. |

The Green Paper is divided into 4 parts. Intriguingly, Part I concentrates
on definitions of pluralism. Three options are discussed in this respect.
Whether pluralism be assessed (a) by content, (b) by the number of channels or titles or (c) by the number of media owners/controllers. The Paper
concludes that the latter option was preferred because 'concentration of
media access in the hands of a few is by definition a threat to the diversity
of information'. Part II of the Paper, based upon a 1992 Booz-Allen &
Hamilton Report, presents a picture of the EU audience reached by 'controllers'. It does not differentiate between public and private broadcasting
channels. Conclusions reached are that there has been an increase in the
diversity of controllers in television and radio, but 'public controllers
account for the majority in most EU states'. Private broadcasters meanwhile
were seen to be 'forced' to expand (particularly abroad) to produce
synergies. This statement was based upon the Booz-Allen & Hamilton
Report, which claimed that limiting ownership nationally tends to encourage partnerships between large media companies which would otherwise
be competing with each other (Booz-Allen & Hamilton, 1990: 37). It is
argued that Axel Springer Verlag (in Germany), Comcosa (in Spain) and
News International (the UK) are seen to be forced into forming national
alliances in this respect. This argument is ponderous as these companies would most likely have sought alliances transnationally, whether or
not national rules require the dilution of share ownership in subsidiary
companies.

Part III of the Green Paper entitled 'National measures to ensure pluralism' contains a country-by-country breakdown of measures/restrictions
(including charts). This part is engrossed with concerns of over-regulation
of the media industry by Member States. It notes that there is an increase
in national legislation after the mid-1980s, which is when national markets
were liberalised. This is picked up later in the paper (p. 56) and explains
the increase in national legislation as directly linked to the TWF Directive.
Restrictions created by national measures are outlined in detail, with particular attention paid to the disparity between national laws. This part also
notes that Belgium, Germany and Portugal continue to restrict foreign ownership of media companies *contrary to European competition law*. This is
stated in the 1991 Green Paper even though the Commission had already
exempted national media ownership laws from competition policy in DG
IV, 'Communication to the Council and European Parliament on audio-
visual policy' (1990) and Article 21 of the 1989 Merger Regulation (as discussed in Chapter 3).

Part IV of the 1992 Green Paper discusses the legal competence of the
European Commission in proposing a harmonisation Directive. At the start,

it is stated that pluralism is not stipulated in the Treaty of Rome. Here the Commission is itself communicating that its power to legislate in this area is limited. The remainder of Part IV, attempts to justify Commission legislation by attributing harmonisation of media ownership rules as beneficial to achieving Single Market objectives – an area in which the Commission does have jurisdiction. National ownership laws are seen to 'interfere with the Single Market' as they place 'restrictions on free movement of services' (pp. 94–5). Part IV, section II, which spells out this argument, constitutes the majority of the Green Paper (pp. 62–100). Legislating for media pluralism under the EC's 'Audiovisual policy' portfolio is ruled out in Part IV section IIC of the Paper. Article F(2) of the Treaty of Maastricht (with respect to fundamental rights which incorporates ECJ Case 11/1970 1125) is stated as a possible source for future Directives, but hailed as an unlikely basis for legislation. Section IIIE goes on to recognise that competition law is inadequate for regulating media ownership. The objectives of pluralism and competition policy are judged to be 'fundamentally different'. The limits to applying competition law to multimedia mergers are further identified by DG III as problematic due to difficulties in market definition and the high thresholds defined in Article 1(2) of the 1989 Merger Regulation. The Green Paper states that the Canal/ESPN and Sunrise, and Sky/British Satellite Broadcasting (BSB) are examples of mega-media mergers, which fell below the Merger Regulation limits. The Conclusion of Paragraph A (section 1 in the paper, p. 85) is that EU competition law is 'inadequate' for ensuring pluralism. This brief reference to the pluralist argument is quite contradictory to the lengthy arguments made in Section II, Part VI that media ownership laws are preventing obstacles to the growth of the Single Market.

Clearly, DG III which was at the time both anxious to kick-start its information society and eager to create conditions favourable to the growth of European champions was particularly concerned with the growth in media regulation at the Member State level. Accordingly, the Green Paper noticeably focused upon fortifying strong European media firms, which would be able to compete globally. It was plainly intent on the removal of ownership rules, but not for motivations of pluralism or the public interest. In this respect, further concentration of European media markets was perceived positively by DG III as fulfilling an industrial policy designed to make Europe's media industry more competitive.[14] DG III argued that concentration of major European multimedia companies could fend off competition from non-European multi-media firms. This explained to some extent why when it later handed over the media ownership portfolio to DG XV, DG III withdrew support of the initiative. It considered that any subsequent draft might weaken European firms.

With the Green Paper intact, the Commission had framed media ownership as a problem of the Single Market. However, it very quickly realised that *political* acceptance of the issue on these terms was not easy to attain because *national* media ownership policy had been formulated to ensure goals of pluralism and democracy. For this reason, DG III systematically sought support for the initiative from the other EU institution and interest groups (Beltrame, 1996). Official opinions were sought and given by the EP[15] and the Economic and Social Committee.[16] Following the Green Paper the Commission sent two studies and a Questionnaire to interest groups requesting them to consider three possible courses of action. These were quite simply: (1) no action, (2) transparency action, and (3) harmonisation action. This was followed by a public hearing and a second Questionnaire. In this way, by seeking legitimacy, DG III began to open up the policy process to a wide number of groups, which were not usually considered during technocratic policy-making. (This is discussed in Chapter 5.)

Advocacy of audiovisual policy by the European Parliament and DG X

Due to its political sensitivity and the fact that the EP had increased its powers following the 1992 Maastricht Treaty, it was particularly important for DG III to gain the support of the EP in order to promote its initiative (Beltrame, 1996). This proved an impossible task as DG III had framed the problem of media ownership as one concerning industrial policy and the internal market, whereas the EP had initiated the issue over concerns of pluralism. The EP wanted an initiative from the Commission but disagreed with the internal market argument.

Following the 1992 Green Paper on media ownership, the EP opposed the liberalising proposals of DG III in its 1994 'Resolution on the Commission Green Paper "Pluralism and media concentration in the internal Market"'. The EP criticised the 1992 Green Paper and urgently called for tough restrictions on European media ownership. The Resolution requested legislation to prevent European media companies from controlling too many media outlets and for measures to ensure pluralism and diversity as 'national media legislation alone was no longer sufficient to safeguard diversity of opinion and pluralism in Europe'. These requests were strongly supported in official opinions by the Economic and Social Committee and the Committee of the Regions.[17]

Three EP committees in particular were involved. These were the Committee on Economic and Monetary Affairs and Industrial Policy, the Committee on Legal Affairs and Citizens' Rights and the Committee on Culture, Youth, Education and the Media. The Economic committee was in favour of the initiative but cautious as to the Commission's competence to propose it. Interestingly, interviews suggest that the Economic committee, which has been long responsible for reviewing EC competition law (Bowler and Farrell, 1995), was thought to have influenced DG IV in some key decisions concerning media concentration during the 1990s.

The Legal Affairs committee also focused upon the issue of community competence. There was hesitation on the part of this committee particularly because the Rapporteur, a German, considered media ownership policy to fall under the state competence of the German Länder.[18] It was the Legal committee however that had been most adamant about the problem of media concentration during the mid 1980s. It stated its Barzanti Report 'the Community must put up a determined struggle against the pathological tendencies to destroy fair competition and real variety. If the market is to be dominated by a few media companies, we risk losing freedom of choice'. The Italian national interest was of course a large factor as it was during this time that Berlusconi was coming to the fore in the Italian national market

For the Culture committee competence was not an issue, but pluralism was exceedingly important. It rejected DG III's Single Market approach. (The Culture committee was to become the most outspoken on media concentration in the late 1990s.) Due to this focus, DG III pursued its initiative without the direct support of the EP at this stage of the policy process due to its differing opinions on the issue.

A principal debate surrounding media ownership concerns the way in which it should be legislated. DG X opposed DG III's proposal to base the Directive on Articles 100a Treaty (now Article 95 (4–9)) on harmonisation which defined media as a product of Article 52 (now Article 43) on freedom of establishment which defined media as a service. It argued that such a Directive would harmonise media ownership laws with the objective of promoting the Single Market, whereas the national laws it sought to harmonise had been initiated to protect pluralism. DG X preferred the Directive to be judged in the Council of Ministers, not by Ministers for the Internal Market, but by the Ministers for Culture. Along this line, DG X supported an initiative based on Article 151 (ex 128) (introduced at Maastricht) which refers to cultural concerns and could possibly provide a potential legal basis for legislating for pluralism. Article 151 (ex 128) provides that the Community *'shall contribute to the flowering of the cultures of the Member States'* and *'take cultural aspects into account in its action under other provisions of the Treaty'*. However, it should be noted that this option would have been politically infeasible because of restraints presented in the Treaties. Whereas Articles 100a or 52 required the co-decision procedure (under Article 189b), which requires review by the EP and qualified majority voting in the Council, Article 151 (128) requires co-decision in the EP and unanimity in the Council. When the TWF Directive was adopted under qualified majority voting (by economics ministers), two countries, Denmark and Belgium, voted against. The feasibility of a Directive being passed in the Council under unanimous decision-making on such a politically sensitive issue is next to impossible. The only possibility would be if revision EU Treaties (i.e. the European Constitution) was to extend qualified majority voting to Article 128, which does not look likely.

It should be noted here that many authors have singled out DG X as embodying EU cultural policy and representing a lone stand *vis-à-vis* the overwhelmingly liberal policy framework advocated by the remaining DGs (Collins, 1994b; Schlesinger, 1995; Venturelli, 1998). Some of these authors see DG X as presenting the only rightful home for EU media policy. However, DG X (now DG Culture) thus far is not in a position to *regulate* the media industry (as are DGs IV, XV and XIII) due to a lack of a Treaty basis. Although many authors point to Article 151 (ex 128) as providing the correct basis for cultural policy, the weakness of the Article cannot be overlooked. There is the possibility however that Article 151 may provide a basis for a future European Court ruling. The same could be said of other articles on state aid as providing a basis for the recognition of the PSB importance for pluralism. A court ruling could be a legitimate basis for legislation, meaning that a revision to the EU Treaties would not be necessary. However, the ECJ has not yet moved in this direction and it does not look, based on the evidence presented in Chapter 2, as if it is likely to without an explicit Treaty statement from EU Member States.

Collins has labelled DG X's approach towards media regulation as interventionist, or similar to the French 'dirigiste' style of regulation. This is based on the view that DG X units were influenced by successive French Ministries for Culture (1994b: 30). However, the administrative culture of the DG X cannot easily be seen to reflect the French 'dirigiste' regulatory style which would imply central economic planning and the support of national or European champions (see Hayward, 1995 for discussion of *dirigisme*). As stated, DG X does not possess such regulatory role within the European Commission. Rather, DG X's approach can perhaps be seen to reflect the views of equivalent regulatory bodies at national levels (UK Department of Culture, Media and Sport (DCMS), French Ministry for Culture, the German Landesmediananstalten, etc.) *vis-à-vis* economic ministries (UK Office of Telecommunications (OFTEL), the German Federal Cartel office, etc.). 'Dirigiste' may better describe the EC approach as a whole, which has been more intent on the support of European champions to the sacrifice of establishing efficient market regulation. In this respect, DG XIII – particularly in its choice of the high definition television (HDTV) standard – may be considered to have been particularly 'dirigiste'.

In 1993, the unit responsible for the media ownership portfolio was split into two separate units (*data protection* and *media and information society*). The media ownership portfolio came under the *media and information society* unit (E5) and was moved to DG XV, which became its permanent home. The portfolio came under the Commissioner d'Archirafi (who took office in 1993). As an Italian, Commissioner d'Archirafi came under intense lobbying for and against the ownership initiative from the national level, where Berlusconi had attained a dominant position in broadcasting markets.

After Bangemann relinquished the media ownership portfolio, attempts emerged to restore it to him under the umbrella of the information society. In June 1994, the Council of Ministers Higher Level Group (Bangemann I – see Table 4.2), produced a paper entitled 'Europe and the global information society' (referred to as the 'Bangemann Report') (CEC, 1994e).[19] The report, which is preoccupied with Europe's competitiveness in the global information market, includes a section entitled 'media ownership', which calls for immediate European legislation to ensure 'the global competitiveness of Europe's media industry' (CEC, 1994e: 13). It also reiterates internal market concerns stated in the first DG III Green Paper by referring to national media ownership rules as 'a patchwork of inconsistency which tends to distort and fragment the market' (CEC, 1994e: 14).

The inclusion of media ownership in the Bangemann Report was taken as a sign of support by Commissioner d'Archirafi for the DG XV initiation who, shortly afterwards, submitted a Draft Directive on media ownership to the College of Commissioners on 21 September 1994 (Tucker, 1994; Tech Europe, 1994; Fuller, 1995). The Bangemann cabinet rejected the draft. This came as a surprise to DG XV. After all, the Draft Directive had been drafted whilst within Bangemann's portfolio and the 1994 Bangemann Report had contained a whole section devoted to the importance of EU legislation of media ownership. Other objections (including a strong objection from the competition Commissioner Van Miert) secured the draft's withdrawal from the College. Following this political setback, D'Archirafi began to lose interest (Tucker, 1994). The DG XV civil service staff continued to work on the initiative over the next two years, without the support of their Commissioner. During this time, DG XV increasingly sought alliance over the portfolio with DG XIII and the media ownership initiative began to incorporate aspects of information society policy objectives.

One month following the rejection of the September draft, DG XV produced a second Green Paper in October 1994 entitled 'Follow up to the consultation process relating to the Green Paper on "Pluralism and media concentration in the internal market – an assessment of the need for community action"' (CEC, 1994a). This paper differed from the first in two significant ways: Firstly, although it still focused on the competitiveness of European firms, it did not stress the liberalisation but rather the harmonisation of Member States media ownership laws. Secondly, it sought additional support by linking itself to the information society debate, which increasingly through Bangemann Group I was gaining political prominence within the European Commission.

The alliance sought with DG XIII is evident throughout the second Green Paper which, in its opening pages, declared itself to be both a follow up to the 1992 Commission Green Paper and an initial response to the Bangemann Report. The paper noticeably focuses upon the *information society*. In particular it is argued that national restrictions on media

Table 4.2 Members of the High-Level Group on the Information Society (Bangemann Group I)

Martin Bangemann	European Commission	Germany
Peter Bonfield	Chairman and CEO of ICL	UK
Enrico Cabral da Fonseca	Campanhia Comunicaçaoes nacionais	Portugal
Etienne Davignon	President Société Générale de Belgique and member of the European Round Table of Industrialists (ERT)	Belgium
Jean-Marie Descarpentries	Bull	
Peter Davis	Chairman, Reed Elsevier	Netherlands
Carlo de Benedetti	President Olivetti and ERT member	Italy
Brian Ennis	Managing Director, IMS, company founded in 1986 which provides software to the NHS	UK
Pehr Gyllenhammar	Former executive chairman Volvo and ERT member, and later appointed Reuters Trustee (in 1997)	Sweden
Hans-Olaf Henkel	CEO of IBM Europe and later appointed head of the Bundesverbandes der Deutschen Industrie (BDI), the national association for German industry in 1998	Germany
Lothar Hunsel	Chairman, T-Mobil and D1[a]	Germany
Anders Knutsen	Administrative Director, Bang & Olufsen	Denmark

Pierre Lescure	Canal+	France
Constantin Makropoulous	Former Managing Director, Hellenic Information Systems	Greece
Pascual Maragall	Mayor of Barcelona, Vice President of POLIS	Spain
Romano Prodi	Director General, IRI, a 'state owned industrial holding company'[b]	Italy
Andre Rousselet	Former President Director General, Canal Plus	France
Pierre Suart	Président, Alcatel	France
Gaston Thorn	Président du Conseil d'administration du Luxembourgeoise de Telediffusion / CLT	Luxembourg
Jan Timmer	COE, Philips Electronics and ERT member	Netherlands
Cándido Velázquez-Gastelu	Telefónica / ERT	Spain
Heinrich von Pierer	CEO, Siemens / ERT	Germany

Source: Bomberg, and Peterson, 1999: 225.

Notes: [a]T-Mobil, Motorola and Nokia introduced the new digital Trans European Trunked Radio (TETRA) into Germany. A 1997 trial acted as a platform for the introduction of TETRA into mainland Europe. TETRA was standardised by the European Telecommunications Standards Institute (ETSI). DF1 is Germany's leading mobile phone company.

[b]After working at IRI, Prodi became Italian Prime Minister from 1996 to 1998 of a centre-left coalition, after which he was appointed President of the European Commission in 1999. Like Berlusconi, Prodi has been investigated for corruption (although never charged). He came under two court investigations for alleged corruption while he was head of IRI. In the first case, he had an alleged conflict of interest, firstly in connection with contracts awarded to his own economic research company. In the second case, he was accused of corruption over the sale of a state-owned food conglomerate to the multinational Unilever, for which he had for a time been a paid consultant. For detail see BBC News 'World: Europe Profile: Romano Prodi', 10 May 1999.

companies constrict the growth of the information society within the Single
Market. As well as indicating the differing national regulatory systems for
media ownership, it referred to shortcomings in national law for *new technologies*, which it claimed are also leading to fragmentation of the internal
market. This focus on the information society can be found in two academic publications by DG XV officials (Crabit and Bergevin, 1995; and
Crabit, 1995).

The 1994 paper provides detailed discussion of policy instruments.[20] The
Commission also detects a shift in opinion between responses to the first
and second Questionnaires in favour of utilising audience share as the crucial
criterion for measuring and controlling concentration. The choice of audience share rather than traditional instruments[21] is significant because it dif-
ferentiates media ownership legislation from competition law. The paper
concludes by suggesting the initiation of new consultations, that audience
share be used in measuring media ownership, and that the Commission
initiate a further study of controllers based on national experience and law.
Finally, in the 1994 Green Paper, the Commission argues that the
responses to the first Paper and subsequent Questionnaires support future
legislation on media ownership by the European Commission.[22] In line with
the internal market frame, DG XV wished to harmonise national laws, but
in such a way that they did not interfere with the internal market. Clearly,
DG XV did not want disparate national rules on media ownership to
impede realisation of the Single Market in broadcasting foreseen by TWF.
This illustrates the differentiation between DG XV, which views media ownership as a 'traditional internal market problem' that requires 'the harmonisation of national rules concerning media ownership', whereas DGs
III and XIII view the media market as a prime target for liberalisation to
harvest capital investment and jobs.

After the induction of the new Commission in 1995 Commissioner
d'Archirafi was replaced by the Italian Commissioner Monti. DG XV bureau-
crats, responsible for the media ownership portfolio, found an ally in Monti
who gave priority to their initiative. Immediately after Monti took up office,
DG XV launched a third consultation with interest groups in January 1995.
A third Questionnaire was sent out to the interest groups which had
responded to the 1992 paper. Along with the Questionnaire, two technical
studies on possible policy instruments were sent for comment; one on
audience share measure, from a UK *ad hoc* consultancy group Goodhall,
Alexander, & O'Hare (GAH) and the other on the definition of the controller
from the European Institute for the Media (EIM) (discussed in Chapter 5).

The convergence initiative

From 1995 onwards, DG XIII began work on its convergence initiative,
which drew upon a much wider definition of the media market than the

ownership initiative. DG XIII (now DG Information Society) holds the portfolio for communications and technology markets under the umbrella of the information society.[23] This is a particularly successful DG having produced a large number of Directives dealing with telecommunications (leading up to full EU liberalisation in 1998) and satellite communications during the preceding decade. It is clear that Bangemann considered the media market to be a part of the 'communications market' and there was much pressure on him to aid the realisation of the Global Information Society to which he promised his commitment at the 1995 G7 meeting in Brussels.[24] During the G7 meeting, the issue of convergence between the media and telecommunications industries (driven by technology) had been a key theme. Significantly, Union of Industrial and Employers Confederation of Europe (UNICE), the federation representing European industry, declared at the meeting that 'distinctions between broadcasting and information services will become irrelevant'.

Accordingly, DG XIII set up an internal *ad hoc* working committee dealing with the issue of convergence (CEC, 1996e). From mid 1995 onwards, DG XIII began to publish studies and policy papers on convergence between telecommunications and audio-visual sectors. In an academic paper by two DG XIII officials, it is stipulated that convergence lies at the 'heart' of the information society (Schoof and Brown, 1995). They argue that the information society requires a policy framework, which encompasses all communication technologies and seeks to eradicate inconsistencies between policies in different media sectors. A similar paper, 'Regulating the convergence of telecommunications and broadcasting', was presented at the same time by the Commission official Marcel Haag at the International Conference 'The social shaping of information highways' a DG XIII sponsored workshop in Bremen, in October 1995.

This was followed in September 1996 with DG XIII, 'Public policy issues arising from telecommunications and audiovisual convergence', by the consultancy group, KPMG. The report makes no distinction between telecommunications and distinct media markets, and public service enterprises were deemed monopolistic or unnecessary. The KPMG Report produced a fair amount of political backlash in the national press and from the European Parliament.[25]

The KPMG Report in particular spells out some key differences between approaches to media market definitions formulated by the different DGs. Firstly, DG XIII did not differentiate between telecommunications, media or public and private enterprises (for discussion of the convergence initiative see Hills and Michalis, 2000; Murdock, 2000; McKenna, 2002; Ward, 2002), whereas DG XV distinguished between telecommunications and media; defined print, radio and television broadcasting and new service markets separately; and distinguished between public and private companies. For this reason, the more liberalising convergence initiative found support from large commercial media companies, such as News Corporation and Springer, which favoured greater market liberalisation[26] and met with opposition from smaller market players and from public broadcasters such as the BBC, ARD and RAI (discussed in Chapter 5). This discrepancy between media market definitions is not atypical of course to the European Commission, but reflects different approaches taken to media market regulation by national regulatory authorities (e.g. the ITC and OFTEL at the UK level).[27] In 1997, the debate was launched politically with the Bangemann Group II (the 'High-Level Group of Experts' – see Table 4.3) report on convergence, which was largely based upon the KPMG study (CEC 1997e).[28]

The trade factor

Convergence at that time was high on the international agenda. Indeed, international arguments for liberalisation of European communications markets had for a long time come from the USA and OECD (Brenner, 1993; OECD, 1992a; 1992b; 1993; OECD/DGXIII, 1997). Pressure for market liberalisation from large European companies was particularly felt after the enactment of the 1996 US Telecommunications Act. European companies argued that they might be left behind US firms if they were not also permitted to compete in adjacent markets. The OECD promoted market liberalisation under its convergence proposals (Fenoulhet, 1997; OECD, 1998). At a 1997 EUI workshop an OECD representative stated that with technological convergence 'there will be no need to have separate broadcasting and telecommunications regulators' (Ypsilanlï, 1997). Similar views were expressed by a World Trade Organisation (WTO) representative at the same workshop.[29]

The Directorate General for External Relations met with strong opposition by US broadcasters, networks and producers to the European programming provision included in the 1989 TWF Directive and the US government took the issue to GATT (Garrett, 1994). When the Uruguay Round eventually ended in 1994, the EU managed to obtain an opt-out for audio-visual products. However the US is continuing to protest against the opt-out in official contexts.[30] In parallel, industry lobbying is fierce. The US studios, represented globally by the Motion Picture Association of America (MPAA),[31] is lobbying against the European content quota in the revision of TWF. At the same time, in the USA, the MPAA is opposed to opening the US market to non-US satellite systems. In particular, it is 'unalterably opposed to granting entry to satellites licensed outside the United States if that country's marketplace is closed to, or severely restricts US satellite systems that distribute video programming. In determining whether markets are closed or restricted, the Federal Communication Commission (FCC) should consider foreign restrictions on US content, such as content quotas

Table 4.3 High-Level Group of Experts (Bangemann Group II)

Martin Bangemann	European Commission	Germany
Hans Blankert	Chairman of the Dutch Employer Organisation VNO/NCW and Chairman of NOC-NSF (the Dutch sports platform) and Chairman of the Dutch Olympic Committee	Netherlands
Gerhard Bosch	Head of Labour Market Department, Institut Arbeit und Technik, Gelsenkirchen	Germany
Manuel Castells	Research Professor, Consejo Superior de Investigaciones Científicas, Barcelona	Spain
Liam Connellan	former Director General of the Confederation of Irish Industry, Dublin	Ireland
Birgitta Carlson	Senior Advisor, Telia AB, Farsa, Sweden	Sweden
Ursula Engelen-Kefer	Deputy President, Deutscher Gewerkschaftsbund (DGB), Düsseldorf	Germany
Chris Freeman	Emeritus Professor, Science Policy Research Unit, University of Sussex	UK
Lisbeth Knudsen	Chief Editor, Det Fri Aktuelt, Copenhagen	Denmark
Yves Lasfargue	Director, Centre d'Etude et de Formation pour l'Accompagnement des Changements (CREFAC)	France
Isabelle Pailliart	Professor, Institut de la Communication et des Médias, Université Stendhal, Grenoble	France
Armando Rocha Trindade	President, Universidade Aberta, Lisbon	Portugal
Jorma Rantanen	Director, Finnish Institute of Occupational Health, Helsinki	Finland
Luc Soete	Professor, Director, Maastricht Economic Research Unit on Innovation and Technology (MERIT), University of Maastricht	Netherlands
Pier Verderio	Director, International Relations and Training, Federazione Informazione e Spettacolo – Confederazione Italiana Sindacati Lavoratori (FIS-CISL)	Italy

Source: Building the European Information Society for us all. Final policy report of the High Level Expert Group (CEC, 1997c).

or advertising restrictions'.[32] The latter reference is clearly referring to the TWF provisions.

DG External Relations is therefore wary of restrictions on communications markets due to possible US retaliation in the form of trade sanctions.[33] The issue is highly politically sensitive. In return for the Uruguay Round opt-out for audio-visual products, the US was granted permission to apply 'anti-dumping' duties against European film imports due to European film subsidisation policies. It has not yet done so because European film imports are so low (Zampetti, 2003). The US has also not raised much official objection to the European support systems for film production and distribution, mostly because US film presently enjoys a large share of the European market. For its part, the European Commission has yet not queried US monopolisation of film distribution in Europe under EC competition rules or the off-loading of US content on to the (secondary) European market under WTO 'dumping' rules (Herold, 2003). Revisions to the WTO opt-out are expected particularly, following the EU's liberalisation of telecommunications markets. Although the Doha talks failed, the GATS discussion on the liberalisation of services continues. At the time of writing however, the present (French) European Commissioner for Trade, Pascal Lamy, has been successful in keeping the audio-visual trade issue off the GATS agenda due to its political sensitivity.[34]

The policy processes for ownership and convergence: inside the College of Commissioners

In 1995, DG XV's new Italian Commissioner Monti embraced the media ownership initiative and sought political alliance. The first task was to seek the support of DG X and the European Parliament, particularly the EP's Committee on Culture, Youth, Education and the Media, the most vocal of the pluralist argument. Monti firstly tried to muster support from the committee informally, reasoning that, considering the limited competencies of the EU, the internal market logic offered the only way in which a Directive could be proposed (Beltrame, 1996: 4). However, in return for its support of the internal market argument, the Parliament wanted *public* commitment from the Commissioner for pluralist concerns.[35] Accordingly, in a September speech before the Cultural Committee, Monti declared himself to be personally in favour of an initiative which would 'safeguard pluralism'. He also promised to the European Parliament that the Commission would embark on a Directive for media ownership: 'En conclusion, je demanderai a mes services de preparer une proposition de Directive en matiere d'acces a la propriete dans les medias, proposition que j'entends soumettre a la Comission dans les premiers mois de l'annee prochaine.'[36] The Commission repeated this view in a Communication to the EP in October 1995. The Cultural Committee responded with the 1995 'A resolution on pluralism and media concentration' (CEC, 1995a) which re-stressed the pluralist issue. From this time onwards, the Draft Directive began to incorporate arguments of the pluralist frame and became much stricter as a consequence (*Agence Europe*, 1996a). By 1996, the draft included a special opt-out for public service broadcasters, lowered ceilings for audience share and new rules on cross-media ownership (as discussed below). None of these new provisions were considered before 1995.

After six years of consultation, a proposal for a Directive on Media Ownership was submitted to the College of Commissioners by Commissioner Monti on 24 July 1996 (*Agence Europe*, 1996b, 1996c). The draft was agreed upon in principle, with objections mainly to policy instruments. Stronger objections came from Commissioners Brittan and Bangemann who found the draft too strict (*Agence Europe*, 1996d; Jones, 1996). The draft suggested a tiered system of audience share to be set at 25 per cent at the regional level, 14–15 per cent at the national level and 10 per cent at the European level. This system would apply to cross-media ownership as well as mono-media ownership. Van Miert and Oreja supported the initiative. The draft was reconsidered by the Chefs du Cabinet and resubmitted on 4 September 1996 (*Agence Europe*, 1996d). Initially, a major objection was raised during the September 4 meeting, which was not expected by the Monti cabinet (Jones, 1996). This came from Commissioner Oreja and it was on grounds of pluralism. The failure to anticipate Oreja' objection was a political oversight by the Monti cabinet.

The reasons why the pluralism argument reappeared were political. The submission of the media ownership draft was badly timed as it coincided with the renewal of the 1989 TWF Directive. The 1996 ratification of the TWF Directive became so politically mired, as it went through the new Maastricht-established co-decision procedure, that it took one year of negotiation between the Council and the EP before an agreement was reached. The EP made 44 amendments to the Directive in February 1996. All of the EP amendments were rejected by the Council of Ministers in its 1996 summer sitting (*Agence Europe*, 1996e).

Significantly, the proposed amendments were linked to protection of the public interest: content of programming, protection of minors against harmful programmes, the strengthening of advertising rules and extending the scope of the Directive to new services (European Report, 1996c). In direct contrast to the EP amendments, the final Directive actually lifted existing limits on advertising. The daily and hourly time allowed for advertising and teleshopping were almost doubled (Mastroianni, 1999). In the new version of Arts 18 and 18A of the Directive, the 'teleshopping windows' were excluded from the total ceiling of advertising time and any form of advertising 'other than advertising spots and teleshopping spots' were excluded from the hourly ceiling of 20 per cent. 'Telepromotions' was also excluded from the hourly ceiling of advertising – based upon the Decision reached by the Court in the RTI case as discussed in Chapter 2. Flexibility was introduced to the European quota provision (see Krebber for detail, 2001: 152).

The outcome of TWF seriously drew into doubt the ability of the Commission to commit itself, as promised to pluralist objectives. Commissioner Oreja, who held the TWF portfolio, had largely been in agreement with the Culture Committee over revision to the TWF Directive. Accordingly, Commissioner Oreja objected to Monti's September 1996 draft because the Directive would not be based on principles of pluralism, but on the internal market. Soon after the September submission of the media ownership Draft Directive to the College of Commissioners, the European Parliament published the Tongue Report on 'Pluralism and media ownership' (1996a) which seriously criticised the draft directive on media ownership. In particular its suggestion of audience share was denigrated as 'fail[ing] to take into account of pluralism content controls'.

The summer rejection of the TWF amendments led to a second reading in November 1996 by the European Parliament at which 314 votes were needed to modify the Council decision. Only 291 votes were attained and TWF was eventually ratified but excluding the amendments suggested by the European Parliament, which were aimed at protection of the public interest. The decision went to conciliation stage and eventuated in the 1997 TWF Directive. Through the TWF revision, the Commission was drawn into a wider debate of EU democratic concern. The loss of the vote drew attention to the problem of a lack of democratic legitimacy in the EU. The EP, as an elected body, even with a large majority, was unable to influence the decision of the Council. Particularly, because the amendments to the TWF had involved issues of democratic relevance, the reality of the near miss dismayed MEPs on the Culture Committee. For this reason, support by the EP for a media ownership initiative, based solely upon internal market principles, became less likely.

Shortly afterwards, on 18 December 1996, Monti resubmitted the media ownership draft to the College of Commissioners (European Report, 1996d, 1996e, 1996f). The same objections were again made by Commissioners Bangemann, Brittan and Oreja (European Report, 1996f). As the initiative was not going to go through as it stood, and only two more votes were needed to pass the draft by simple majority, a coalition contract was sought. In order to accomplish this, Commissioner Monti organised a special forum in January between himself, Bangemann and Oreja to discuss the issue. At this forum, Monti succeeded in consolidating support for his initiative, which was publicly declared by the two Commissioners (Jones, 1997). Bangemann's support in particular came as a surprise to a number of interest groups and to the German government. The details of the January meeting can only be surmised. It seems that the Commission's bureaucratic competence in the area of media policy was delineated.[37]

In February 1997, a new version of the Draft Directive was circulated internally to the European Commission. The February draft introduced some changes, which reflected compromises between the different actors. Firstly, there was a title change from 'Concentrations and pluralism in the internal market' to 'Media ownership in the internal market'. Herewith the Commission attempted to move the focus of attention away from the issue of pluralism. Secondly, a 'flexibility clause' was inserted into the draft. The clause allows Member States to raise the upper limit of audience share to 30 per cent at the national level (this would accommodate German law),[38] and to opt designated companies out of this 30 per cent limit (for up to 10 years) provided that the media company did not exceed this limit in more than one Member State. The limits of 25 per cent at the regional level and 10 per cent at the European level were dropped and replaced by a national audience share measure of 10 per cent for multimedia and 30 per cent for monomedia (Doyle, 2002). Notably, the proposed rules continued to apply to cross-media ownership (rather than solely monomedia). Thirdly, the draft included suggestions for measures to be taken against a media company found to be breaching audience share limits. Suggestions of these 'appropriate measures' stated in the draft were the requirement of 'windows for independent programme suppliers' or the establishment of a 'representative programming committee'. Fourthly, in light of the Carol Tongue Report on public service (1996b) and the public service protocol in the Amsterdam Treaty, the revised draft included a special opt-out for public service broadcasters. A 1998 European Commission study summarised the draft as follows:

> 30% for 'monomedia' concentrations for television and radio, respectively; under this standard, a single undertaking could not control another (new or existing) undertaking if the total audience share of the services offered by the combined undertaking equalled or exceeded 30% in the relevant geographic area concerned; and 10% for 'multimedia' concentrations for a combination of different media; accordingly, an undertaking already active in one media could not control an undertaking in a different media (new or existing) if the total audience share of its combined media equalled 10% or more in the relevant geographic area concerned. Public service broadcasters were said to be exempt from these proposals. Opposition from the broadcasting industry and the press resulted in the Commission giving consideration to the adoption of a 'flexibility' clause which would allow Member States to authorise domestic media companies to exceed the proposed thresholds where considered appropriate. Such flexibility was claimed to be necessary because the proposed thresholds are already exceeded in a number of Member States and because regional broadcasters would be adversely affected by the proposal, even though their relevant geographic areas of operation constitute only a small fraction of the overall national territory. For example, under current estimated market shares based on audience coverage, *France*'s TF1 has approximately 39% *Belgium*'s VTM has 43%, Italy's three networks run by the Berlusconi

Fininvest group have over 40%, while the *United Kingdom*'s ITV Association
would hold in excess of 30% in small regions' European Commission (CEC,
1998c: 107).

The media ownership draft was resubmitted to the College on 12 March
1997 (*Agence Europe*, 1997a). This time Bangemann and Oreja supported
the draft and for the first time a simple majority of 11 out of 20 Commissioner votes was achieved – enough to pass the initiative in the College.
Brittan had raised the usual objections, and Papoutsis, even though pos-
sessing an unrelated portfolio, expressed his domestic concern over the liberalisation of the Greek print market. A key objection was raised however
by Santer. This came about due to intense lobbying against the initiative,
in particular by News International, Springer, ITV and Compagnie
Luxembourgeoise de Télédiffusion (CLT), which had targeted the Commission President. As a Luxembourg Commissioner, Jacques Santer was
particularly sensitive to the arguments of large media companies that
brought a lot of income to his government. The objection by the president
was too significant. Even though Monti had enough support in the College
for the initiative, he was convinced he had to withdraw the draft until lobbying efforts had subsided. As the Luxembourg presidency of the Commission commenced shortly afterwards on 1 July 1997, there was no point
in resubmitting the draft until the following year (*European Voice*, 1997;
Agence Europe, 1997b; Tucker, 1997; *Wall Street Journal*, 1997). During
1998, it was decided due to intense lobbying that the draft could not be
resubmitted until after the intake of the new Commission (which was meant
to take place at the end of 1999). In March 1999, the whole of the
European Commission resigned *early* due to a public scandal over corruption and mismanagement of the annual EU budget.[39] The make-up of the
new Commission and the restructuring of the DGs meant that the initiative
was shelved in 1999.

The ownership portfolio was inherited in 2000 by the (renamed) DG
Education and Culture (DG EAC) overseen by the Luxembourg Commissioner Viviane Reding. Reding has given no support for the initiative most
likely due to the importance of the media industry at the national level
in Luxembourg. Reding has stated often that the European Commission
should only step in when media market fails (Reding's press releases
2001–3).[40] Therefore, the civil servants would need to await the new intake of the Commission in 2004 for any submission of the draft to be
considered.

In the meantime, the DG Information Society initiative on convergence
gained steam after the intake of the 1999 Commission. Up until 1999, the
convergence initiative had stagnated. Following the KPMG report, a 1997
Green Paper entitled 'Convergence of the telecommunications, media and
information technology sectors, and the implications for regulation' was

published. The paper was much more cautious in its approach than the KPMG report and showed evidence of wide internal consultation (Ward, 2002). Its fundamental recommendation remained the convergence of national telecommunications and media policies, which it ambitiously suggested be regulated by one European regulatory authority. The paper foresaw competition between the sectors, predicting what it termed a 'struggle between computer, telecommunications and broadcasting industries for the control of future markets' (CEC, 1997a: 10). It called for the liberalisation of national markets to allow media operators to enter the telecommunications market and vice-versa. Ownership is not much mentioned, the issue 'already being dealt with in Community initiatives'. This phrase in particular showed that competence for the ownership and convergence portfolios had been delineated. The paper only indirectly refers to ownership in one paragraph:

> Current restrictions in some Member States (and not others) regarding what types of services can be carried on different infrastructures could make it difficult for operators to formulate unified strategies addressing pan-European markets. It may also prevent economies of scale being realised. The resulting higher unit costs, and hence tariffs, could hold back the delivery of innovative services'. (CEC, 1997a: 27)

The Commission seemed at this stage (in 1997) to plan to liberalise national media markets with its harmonisation proposals on media ownership (to create a level playing field). Then to follow with the convergence initiative once incumbent telecommunications companies had lost market power due to pronounced competition and new services had been allowed to grow without regulatory constraint. However, as stated, the draft directive on ownership was never resubmitted to the College of Commissioners and was, indeed, dropped due to political obstacles. But the convergence initiative went ahead.

During 1998 and 1999, the convergence proposal underwent substantial public consultation the results of which were published in 1999 (CEC, 1999). Consultation unveiled fierce resistance to the application of the regulatory framework to content regulation. As a result, content regulation was opted out of the final regulation package (Ward, 2003). Content regulation can continue to be sector specific ('vertical') according to Member States' social, cultural and political preferences. This came in Part A of the Annex of the Authorisation Directive which states that Member States *may* be permitted 'to attach conditions' to some communications operators, and 'additional conditions relating to content' found in national broadcasting law and TWF.

In 1999, DG Information Society published its Communication, 'Towards a new framework for electronic communications infrastructure and associated services – the 1999 communications review' (1999a), which proposed a detailed regulatory framework for communications. The European Commission then adopted a package of legislative proposals in July 2000, which led to Council approval of the 2002 regulatory framework for electronic communications and services. As described in Chapter 1, the Commission approved six Directives under the Framework: a 'framework' Directive and five accompanying Directives (Authorisation Directive, Access Directive, Universal Service Directive, Data Protection Directive and the Liberalisation Directive). Also included in the package was a Commission 'Decision on radio spectrum' (the 'Spectrum Decision'), a 'Market recommendation and guidelines for significant market power' (SMP).

In 1999, DG Information Society was successful in breaking up ownership in cable markets. The 1999 Cable Ownership Directive[41] mandated that telecommunications operators separate their cable interests into structurally separate companies. The Commission was then able to require divestment by incumbent operators at national levels (the examples of Deutsche Telecom and Royal PTT Netherlands are given in Chapter 6). Interestingly, during consultation for the Directive, the European Parliament and Economic and Social Committee called for limited implementation of the cable Directive (EP, 1998; ESC, 1998).

Lobbying over the ownership initiative continued, firstly in 2000 with the Economic and Social Committee report, 'Pluralism and concentration in the media in the age of globalisation and digital convergence' (CEC, 2000). In the same year, 2000, a European Union 'charter of fundamental rights' was adopted by the Presidents of the European Parliament, the Council and the Commission at the European Council meeting in Nice on 7 December 2000 (European Union, 2000). Article 11.2 of the Charter contains the statement 'the freedom and pluralism of the media shall be respected'.

The European Parliament was less active in pursuing the media ownership issue following the election of Berlusconi. During the Italian Prodi government, the European Parliament's CULT committee was balanced in favour of introducing concentration measures.[42] After the election of Berlusconi, the CULT committee was split over the issue due to disagreements among Italian committee appointees, which has meant that there has been little EP agreement on proposed resolutions on media ownership since 2000. However, in a 2001 Resolution, the EP stated 'whereas the importance and impact of the audiovisual sector on the European cultural landscape is strongly affected by the ownership of media and its concentration within a few large corporations'(EP, 2001).

The ownership initiative gained momentum in 2002 when a report was published by the UK conservative MEP Roy Perry calling on the Commission to draft an updated Green Paper on media ownership and to monitor levels of media concentration in Europe (EP, 2003b). The Culture Committee eventually adopted the report. Then on 20 November the European Parliament adopted a Resolution calling for an updated Green Paper on media pluralism by the end of 2003 in both Member States and applicant countries (EP, 2002). The Resolution called for measures to ensure that the media in all Member States is free and diversified, and called for a European media market to be established. This Resolution came immediately after a high-profile conference, entitled 'Media, power and democracy,' sponsored by the Green-EFA party group .of the European Parliament in Brussels on 13 November 2002.[43]

In 2003, the European Commission responded to this in its Green Paper on services of general interest (2003d) which states:

> Whilst the protection of media pluralism is primarily a task for the Member States, it is for the Community to take due account of this objective within the framework of its policies. Currently, secondary Community legislation does not contain any provisions directly aiming to safeguard the pluralism of the media. However, Community law allows the application of national safeguards with regard to media pluralism. This is highlighted, for example, in Art. 21(3) of the Merger Regulation, which explicitly provides for the possibility of applying national measures protecting the plurality of the media alongside Community merger rules or in Article 8 of the Framework Directive on electronic communications which provides that national regulatory authorities may contribute to media pluralism. . . . Ten years later, given the progressing concentration of the media sector and the proliferation of electronic media, the protection of media pluralism remains an issue, including within the context of the Amsterdam Protocol on public broadcasting. Views are sought as to whether the Commission should re-examine the need for Community action in this field in more detail.

Then, in September 2003, the Committee on Citizens' Freedoms and Rights, Justice and Home Affairs issued a report calling for a 'Comprehensive EU policy against corruption' containing a paragraph calling

> on the Commission to prepare proposals for the introduction of rules and codes of conduct aimed at preventing and avoiding conflict of interest for public authorities whose activities are susceptible to private-sector interests (in such areas as media ownership, award of public concessions, etc) . . . along the lines of those set out by the OECD in its recommendation of June 2003 on guidelines for managing conflict of interest in the public service. (EP, 2003)

In October 2003 the European Parliament's political groups (the Conference of Presidents) authorised the Civil Liberties Committee to produce an own-initiative report on the state of media freedom in the European Union and Italy in particular. It is expected to single out Article 7 of the Nice Treaty, which states that the Council could suspend a country's voting rights if it persistently violates fundamental rights as applicable to the Italian situation.

In April 2004, the European Parliament (Committee on Citizens' Freedom and Rights, Justice and Home Affairs) published a Resolution on the 'risks of violation, in the EU and especially in Italy, of freedom of expression and information' (2003/2237/INI). It is a highly detailed report criticising the state of media pluralism in Member States and requests the Commission to take action particularly in the area of media ownership.

In March 2004, the Commission published a report on the public consultation on the Green Paper on Services of General Interest. Section 4.6.2. of the paper is entitled 'little support for a Community initiative on media pluralism at this stage'. This was followed in May 2004 by a White Paper on Services of General Interest. It restates that the issue of pluralism 'should be left to Member States at this point in time'. It recommends increased media monitoring and 'the need for closer co-operation between the Commission and national regulatory authorities'.

At the same time, in 2003–4 the European Commission was reviewing its TWF Directive under the Reding cabinet. TWF revision was targeted by Berlusconi under the Italian presidency of the EU, which initiated an 'informal' Council meetings in 2003.[44] The Italian government in particular was lobbying for a loosening of advertising rules to take into account new technology, particularly 'virtual and interactive advertising' and recommending increased self-regulation. Also recommended was an increase in European subsidies for production, digital set top boxes and for operators that invest in digital broadcasting.

In 2003 the Commission carried out a TWF consultation based on six themes: access to events of major significance for society, the promotion of cultural diversity and competitiveness in the European programming industry, the protection of general interest of television advertising, sponsorship, teleshopping and promotion, protection of minors and public order, and the right to reply (for discussion, see Crauford Smith, 2003). A likely outcome is that existing rules on teleshopping and telepromotions will be loosened, particularly following ECJ rulings. The TWF provision requiring that a majority of programming be of European origin is also being questioned due to implementation problems, the trade factor and the lessened French pressure.[45] The revised Directive is also expected to propose systems for self-regulation and co-regulation for implementation. The regulation of ownership was also discussed, but it is unlikely that any such provision will be included in a final draft.

Following the consultation, the Commission decided that there was a broad consensus in favour of retaining the quotas, protection of minors and events of major importance. Hence these Articles are unexpected to change. Three 'focus groups' are to be set up to reflect on the regulation of audiovisual content, advertising and the right to short reports and access to information respectively. Meanwhile, a Communication covering new forms of advertising and other revision issues is to be issued along with a Recommendation on the protection of minors and human dignity. At the time of writing, the first proposals for TWF revision are to be made public in 2005 at the earliest, with a Directive not expected before 2008.

Conclusion

This chapter has illustrated the main reasons for the failure of the media ownership initiative compared with the relative success of the convergence initiative. Chiefly, the Commission lacked a legal basis upon which to base its ownership directive. At the same time, national governments and NRAs have resisted attempts to move the policy arena to the European level. The EP's role is hampered by the EU's democratic deficit. Consultation on the directive brought about a more restrictive draft based upon a national rationale for media market regulation – media pluralism. However, this deemed the Directive political infeasible. The EU has proven incapable of encompassing public interest goals in its policy-making. It was shown to be ever reliant on economic instruments for regulating media markets. This approach is not expected to change with the revision of TWF. As argued in Chapters 2 and 3 only a change to the EU Treaties could make a difference in the media policy field. The impetus for change exists. Chapter 8 shall discuss the possibilities for policy change. Firstly, the next chapters (5–7) look at the input of interest groups into the policy process and the effect of policy outcomes on the development of markets and national policies.

Notes

1 The Report was adopted as the 1982 Hahn Resolution. The MCP Wilhelm Hahn was former Minister for Culture for Baden-Württemberg.

2 This was not to be realised until 2003 when the European institutions began to fund ITN's Euronews service. The funding was granted upon the condition that ITN increase its reporting of EU affairs in particular.

3 1985 'Resolution on the economic aspects of the common market for broadcasting', 1986 'Resolution on the Fifteenth Report of the CEC on competition policy', 1987 'Resolution on the Sixteenth Report of the CEC on competition policy' and two amendments to the Draft Directive TWF in the Barzanti Report.

4 Single European Act *Official Journal of the European Communities* L 169, 29.06. 1987.

5 For detailed analyses of the policy process leading to TWF see Collins (1994b: 53–84) and Krebber (2001: 79–135).

6 The Directive was changed in 1997 to state that the a company should be regulated in the country of *establishment*, based on ECJ rulings, but this still does not necessarily mean the country of *reception*.

7 The French 1986 Press and Freedom of Communication laws; the German 1987 Inter-State Agreement on the Regulation of Broadcasting, the Italian 1987 Publishing Law, the Luxembourg 1989 Law on Electronic Media, the Dutch

1987 Media Act, the Spanish 1988 Law on Commercial television and the UK 1990 Broadcasting Act. See Chapter 7 for details.

8   The Ministers for Culture first met in 1985 organised by French Minister of Culture, Jacques Lang upon request from the French President Mitterand (Krebber, 2001: 91). These meetings were formalised by the Council in 1989.

9   The Council of Ministers is composed of one representative at ministerial level from each Member State, who is empowered to commit a Member State to legislation. Which Ministers attend each Council meeting varies according to the subject discussed. National Ministers for Culture never decided upon EU media regulation. Instead, Member States designated their national Ministers for Economic Affairs.

10 Qualified majority was set at 62 votes out of 87 (71 per cent). Member States' votes are weighted on the basis of their population and corrected in favour of less-populated countries as follows: France, Germany, Italy and United Kingdom, ten votes each; Spain, eight votes; Belgium, Greece, the Netherlands and Portugal, five votes each; Austria and Sweden, four votes each; Denmark, Ireland and Finland, three votes each; Luxembourg, two votes. The Nice Treaty amended qualified majority which is reached when two conditions are fulfilled: the decision receives a set number of votes (which will change as new countries join) and is agreed by a majority of Member States; a Member State may request that it be verified that the qualified majority represents at least 62 per cent of the total population of the Union. If this is not the case, the decision is not adopted.

11 1990 'Resolution on media takeovers and mergers', 1992 'Resolution on media concentration and diversity of opinions', 1992 'Resolution on media concentration and pluralism of information', 1990 'Albor motion for resolution on concentration of information', 1990 'Ferri motion for resolution on anti-trust legislation for the media', 1990 'Ortega motion for resolution on local television in Europe', 1991 'Titley and others motion for resolution on importance of diversity in the media', 1991 'Titley and others motion for resolution on tendency towards the concentration of ownership in the media industry'.

12 This alliance between DG X and the European Parliament over media issues has been noted by Collins (1994b: 30) and Humphreys (1996: 279). See also *Le Monde* newspaper (10 July 1991) wherein DG X Commissioner Dondelinger expresses his support for requests for media concentration legislation.

13 Up until 1993, Commissioners were appointed for four years. In 1995 there was a break in term due to enlargement and changes in DG portfolios. From 1995, Commissioners were appointed for five-year terms.

14 On EU industrial policy see Hayward (1995).

15 The 1993 Resolution on the Commission Green Paper, 'Pluralism and media concentration', was in favour of harmonisation.

16 The Economic and Social Committee 1993 'Opinion on Commission Green Paper', was also in favour of harmonisation (Davis, 1997).

17 German members of the Committee of the Regions opposed the initiative as it would weaken Länder jurisdiction for media policy *vis-à-vis* the Federal government. The German members argued for the exclusive competence of

Member States. However, the majority of representatives to the Committee of the Regions rejected the German position in favour of a positive vote.

18 According at that time to state broadcasting laws in the 1987 Rundfunkstaatsvertrag (an interstate broadcasting treaty).

19 The Bangemann Report (1994d) was a report of the (Bangemann chaired) Council of Ministers Higher Level Group, entitled 'Europe and the global information society' as the submitted to the European Council for its meeting in Corfu on 24–25 June 1994.

20 For an excellent overview of measurements of media markets considered by the European Commission, see Isofides, 1997. See also Congdon, Graham, Green, and Robinson, 1995.

21 At national levels, media markets have been limited by multiple licences, shareholding limits, cross-media restrictions, advertising revenue and/or subscription revenue.

22 In total, three Commission Questionnaires were sent to interested parties. Written responses to the second 1993 Questionnaire are compiled in a five volume Commission document XV/9555/94. Responses to the remaining Questionnaires were compiled by Beltrame (1997). These are discussed in Chapter 5.

23 As outlined in the 1994 Bangemann Report, which has provided a general policy framework for a significant number of Commission policy initiatives.

24 Bangemann like Delors before him, was clearly providing political leadership to the College of Commissioners and his 1994 White Paper on Europe and the global information society, like Delors' White Paper on Growth, competitiveness and employment', was clearly providing a general framework for a significant number of policy initiatives. As Bangemann held both the DG III and DG XIII portfolios and was a senior member of the Commission, his opinion on the regulation of media markets carried considerable weight.

25 In particular, EP concern about the report was expressed in an open letter to all EU Commissioners sent by Carol Tongue (1996b). The attack on public broadcasters fuelled the EBU lobbying effort to insert a protocol (no. 32) into the Amsterdam Treaty. The protocol states that 'the system of public broadcasting in the Member States is directly related to the democratic, social and cultural needs of each society and to the need to preserve media pluralism'.

26 Some companies, which supported the DG XV initiative up until 1995, withdrew their support in favour of the more liberalising DG XIII initiative.

27 A later study produced by DG X challenges the DG XV market definition approach: 'Economic implications of new communication technologies on audio-visual markets'. This was prepared for the draft Green Paper on new audio-visual services, March 1997. The study was carried out by Norcontel (Ireland) Ltd in conjunction with National Economic Research Associates (NERA), *Screen Digest* and Stanbrook and Hooper. The same authors at NERA had previously been commissioned by the DNH to carry out a similar study at the UK level. The study was published again in 2000 by DG Culture and is available on-line.

28 European Commission, High Level Group of Experts (1997), 'Building the European information society for us all', Final version, April 1997.

29   Dimitri Ypsilanti speaking at the workshop on 'The aftermath of liberalisation: multi-level governance in the regulation of telecommunications', organised by the EUI Working Group on Telecommunications and the Information Society, European University Institute, Florence, 14 November 1997.

30   The TWF provision for European content has been consistently opposed by US representatives to the WTO table and Brussels as a barrier to trade. When appointed to the position of US Representative to the EU, Vernon Weaver, stated 'I will not be shy about defending key US industries, such as the audio-visual industry, against new protectionist measures, however packaged' (in an interview with *European Voice*, 25–31. July 1996). Indeed, he proved a keen advocate of European media market liberalisation whilst in office. Weaver was replaced by the Bush appointed Rockwell Anthony Schnabel in 2001 who has also been a devoted proponent of market liberalisation.

31   Formerly the Motion Picture Export Association of America, it changed its name to the Motion Picture Association in 1994. Members include the Walt Disney Company, Sony Pictures Entertainment, Inc., Metro-Goldwyn-Mayer Inc., Paramount Pictures Corporation, Twentieth Century Fox Film Corp., Universal Studios, Inc. and Warner Bros.

32   www.mpaa.org.

33   Another concern DG External Relations has about the EU media regulation is its commitment to the European Commission/United States Government Competition Agreement, which was signed by DG I on 23 September 1991 and enacted into EC law in 1995. This calls for notifications and regular exchanges of information on antitrust enforcement activities and for the co-ordination of enforcement agencies. Any initiative on ownership could be questioned under this agreement as it involves competition policy.

34   Commissioner Lamy, acting on behalf of the Member States, has made it clear that three policy areas will not be liberalised by EU Member States: health, education and culture.

35   Stated in interviews with Members of the Cultural Committee.

36   'In conclusion, I will ask my services to prepare a draft Directive on Media ownership. I plan to submit this draft to the commission in the first month of next year.' 'Pluralism and Media Concentration' speech to the Committee on Culture, Youth, Education and the Media, 26 September 1995 by Commissioner Monti. Quoted in Beltrame (1997).

37   As one DG X official explained there was recognition that any legislation on media ownership must come from a politically stronger DG in order for EU policy to be maintained in the area. Shortly after the meeting, DG X began drafting its paper on new audio-visual services and DG XV started to show support for the convergence initiative.

38   More specifically, the 30 per cent rule applied to any area in which a station could be received. In most cases, this would mean nationally. However, these limits could have determined a dominant position for certain ITV companies regionally. For this reason, many ITV companies withdrew support for the draft (see Chapter 6).

39   This was following a report by Commission official Paul van Buitenen who claimed that 5 per cent of the EU budget could not be accounted for. There were some accusations of fraud which were subsequently widely publicised in

the press, but most was down to mismanagement of the Commission budget. The figure may have been lower than that not accounted for in national budgets, but the Commission complacency over the issue led to national calls for increased EU transparency. At the time of writing, the Commission is facing another highly publicised case of fraud allegations in the allocation of European Statistical Office (Eurostat) funds and calls for resignation. The president of the European Commission, Romano Prodi, gave a speech at the Conference of the Presidents of the European Parliament Strasbourg, on 25 September 2003, to clarify the Commission position.

40 http://europa.eu.int/comm/commissioners/reding/press_en.htm.

41 Commission Directive 1999/64/EC amending Directive 90/388/EEC in order to ensure that telecommunications networks and cable TV networks owned by a single operator are separate legal entities.

42 Of course, there were Italian CULT members during that time who were decidedly against such rules, such as the Northern League Member, Umberto Bossi.

43 www.greens-efa.org/pdf/TMT_policy/events/Panels/intro.htm.

44 Informal Council of Audiovisual Ministries, Siracuse, Italy, 12–14 September 2003 and European eGovernment Conference organised by the European Commission and the Italian Presidency, Villa Erba, Como, 7–8 July 2003.

45 This is due to French difficulties with content requirements on domestic media companies.

5

Interest group participation in the policy process

Introduction: gaining consensus, the consultation process

When the first Green Paper 'Pluralism and media concentration in the internal market' (CEC, 1992a) was published in December 1992, the majority of European media companies were not aware that the Commission had been considering media ownership legislation. This does not mean that there had been no interest from industry in the initiative prior to the Green Paper. On the contrary, industry input to the formulation of policy options took place at an early stage of the policy process – before the drafting of the first 1992 Green Paper. But only a handful of interest groups were involved at this point. This is when the ideas for using audience share and definition of the controller were introduced. At the time, DG III had taken advantage of the implementation of the 1989 TWF Directive to stir national debates over the deregulation of media ownership rules. As a result, a number of British and Italian companies considered the possibility of European-level action to achieve deregulatory results that were not forthcoming at the national level.

After the publication of the Green Paper, DG III began a selective consultation process. It advocated its initiative to a small number of large media groups. This technocratic approach was to fail. Technocratic regulatory policies are defined as those processed in relative isolation from public debate (Rhodes, 1988; Jordan and Richardson, 1979). Although consultation began selectively, the Commission very quickly lost control over the number of groups involved. The change in portfolios in 1993 had resulted in a withdrawal of interest in the initiative from the College of Commissioners. As a consequence, the Commission services increased the consultation of interest groups. This was used as a tool to create a debate at the European level and to enforce an agenda that was inherently fragile within the Commission itself.

By seeking legitimacy, the Commission introduced a wide number of groups to the policy process, which were not usually considered during technocratic policy-making. The consultation process took on a momentum of its own as it experienced increasing politicisation. The services of the Commission found themselves turning increasingly to smaller interest groups and the Parliament for advocacy of its initiative. This input brought about a decisive change to the policy process away from the originally liberalising plans of DG III and towards the more restrictive Draft Directive produced by DG XV (the 1997 Draft Directive). Policy formation became more democratic. Thus, the policy process was moving away from the traditional technocratic style that characterised the European Commission policy-making (Majone, 1996) towards a more transparent and consensual style.

This significant change deemed the initiative politically infeasible at the European level. Although the initiative failed, a number of consequences arose from what resulted in a five-year consultation process. Namely, the Commission was firstly successful in raising the issue of media ownership to the European level. As discussed in Chapter 4, the possibility of including media ownership rules in the TWF Directive had been suggested by the European Parliament as early as 1984, so the issue had been placed on the European agenda long before publication of the 1992 Green Paper. However it was the Commission that gave the debate a public profile. Secondly, it indirectly filtered European policy suggestions through consultation to the national level. Thirdly, DG XV brought wider interests into the policy process, which resulted in a more democratic input than originally envisioned by the DG III. This in turn had a knock-on effect on subsequent Commission initiatives in related areas (e.g. convergence initiative, electronic commerce, data protection and parental control). It became increasingly difficult, if not impossible, for the Commission to continue to make policy in areas of democratic significance without consulting a large range of interest groups (for subsequent initiatives, interest group statements were often submitted and published on line).[1] Even Bangemann's convergence initiative, which began behind closed doors (Ward, 2002: 114) in what could be considered the Commission's technocratic style, underwent extensive public consultation.

Industry lobbying prior to the 1992 Green Paper

Informal consultation with large media groups was undertaken before publication of the 1992 Green Paper. Although media ownership rules were not included in the 1989 TWF Directive, the Directive's implementation meant that it was necessary for Member States to revise their national media laws. Any revision of national legislation inevitably meets with calls for further deregulation. Revision gave rise to a reconsideration of existing media ownership rules at the national level. This gave the Commission the opportunity to court media companies that were involved in lobbying their national administrations over ownership revision: particularly, those in Italy and the

UK. In informal discussion with the Commission, British and Italian companies warmed to the idea that the EU take a role in regulating media ownership – albeit for differing reasons. Some companies called upon the
Commission for a liberalisation of ownership laws, others raised concerns
at the weakness of national restrictions. Companies presented their own
policy recommendations at this point in time.

In 1989, News International was one of the companies in favour of a
Commission initiative. News International was frustrated at the time with
media ownership restrictions in the UK. In 1989 it commissioned a study
from the Washington-based consultancy group, the American Enterprise
Institute, which was sent to the European Commission just before the completion of the 1989 TWF Directive. The study, entitled 'Measures of media
concentration', was authored by William Shew (who also acted in the
capacity of media consultant to the FCC). In the report, *audience share*, as
opposed to traditional instruments,[2] is recommended as the best instrument
with which to regulate media ownership. The Commission was strongly
influenced by the arguments of the Shew study. In the December 1992 Green
Paper, 'Pluralism and media concentration in the internal market', DG III
devotes five pages (pp. 106–10) to the advantages of utilising audience share
as a legislative instrument at the European level. This policy instrument was
later utilised in Commission Draft Directives and eventually found its way
into national legislations (see Chapter 7 for discussion). One year after the
release of the 1992 Green Paper, the Commission published a similar study
to the Shew study entitled 'Audience measurement in the EC' (GAH, 1993).
A second Commission study on audience share was published in 1994
(GAH, 1994). Hence, the original idea for audience share (which has subsequently been adopted in the UK, Germany, Ireland and Romania) came
from the media company News International plc.

Before the release of the 1992 Green Paper, the British group ITCA (Independent Television Companies Association) expressed a different opinion
to the European Commission. Its concern was the increased market share
of the Murdoch-owned media in the UK following the launch of Sky in
1989 from the Luxembourg Astra satellite. The TWF Directive had allowed
Murdoch to circumvent UK media ownership legislation. ITCA's concerns
deepened when Sky took over the rival British Satellite Broadcasting (BSB)
company (to form BSkyB) in 1990. On 20 December 1991 ITCA sent a
letter to competition Commissioner Leon Brittan, pointing out 'disparities
arising between different Member States of the Community as a result of
different national restrictions on media ownership . . . This creates distor-
tions of competition in terms of access to ownership of EC media companies, and in terms of operating in the European marketplace' (quoted in
Beltrame, 1997).

Around the same time, the European Commission was receiving letters
from Italian groups. Similar concerns about the influence of controllers were

raised. Many Italian publishers (in particular groups owned by the industrialists and publishers Agnelli and De Benedetti) and politicians (national
and MEPs) expressed concern about the rising influence of Berlusconi who
had bought the Rete Quattro channel (from Rizzoli) and Italia 1 (from
Mandadori) at the end of the 1980s.

The first Questionnaire and the 1993 hearing

By embarking upon the ownership initiative, the Commission clearly saw
an opportunity to expand its legislative powers. The European Parliament
had already placed the issue on the agenda. After the publication of its first
Green Paper in 1992, the Commission actively sought support for its initiative. The Commission embarked upon a consultation process, which was
to result in a five-year long intense debate over ownership policy. As the
years wore on the Commission lost support from large industrial groups,
and turned increasingly to interest groups advocating the pluralist argument. Although the policy process was in the end much more transparent,
it proved impossible for the Commission to move the resulting draft
forward due to political restraints.

The first step was to acquire support from other EU institutions. After
the 1992 Green Paper was published, it was submitted to the European Parliament and Economic and Social Committee (ECOSOC) for opinions (as
discussed in Chapter 4). Shortly afterwards, in February 1993, DG III
launched what it called a 'parallel consultation' by approaching relevant
European federations and a handful of media companies with a short
Questionnaire. Questionnaire I (Table 5.1) was sent out to 16 European
federations, 15 media companies and two consultancy groups.

The Commission directly consulted national media groups in line with
the Commission's new transparency policy, which had been announced at
the 1992 Edinburgh Summit. Prior to 1992, the Commission had only (officially) invited European federations to place their views on internal policy
documents. Since 1992, the Commission was permitted to openly consult
national groups and individual companies. However, Questionnaire I was
mainly sent out to large groups and, in particular, those interest groups
which had already expressed an informal interest in the initiative prior to
the Green Paper.

Upon closer examination, the 15 companies consulted turned out to be
representing only six main interests. Only British, German and Italian media
companies were consulted. Significantly, no French companies were
approached (not even through the European federations). Questionnaire I
was sent out to six British, five Italian and two German companies (Table
5.2). Of the six British companies, two (BSkyB and News International plc)
belonged to Murdoch's News Corporation group (which at the time supported the initiative). Three were a part of the British ITCA network

Table 5.1 Respondents to Questionnaire I

European Federations/Associations	Media companies	Consultancies
European Association of Advertising Agencies (EAAA)	BSkyB	The European Institute for the Media (Düsselfdorf)
European Advertising Tripartite (EAT)	News International plc	Institute for Information Law (IIL) (Amsterdam)
World Federation of Advertisers (WFA)	Pearson plc	
Association des Television Commerciales Européennes (ACT)	ITCA (Independent Televisionq Companies Association)	
	Channel 4 Television	
European Broadcasting Union/Union Federation Européenne des Radios Libres (FERL)	Zweites Deutsches Fernsehen (ZDF)	
Association Européenne des Radios (AER)	Rundfunkanstalten der Bundesrepublik Deutschland (ARD)	
European Publishers Council (EPC)	Bundesverband Deutscher Zeitungsverlager e.V.	
European Newspaper Publishers' Association (ENPA)		
European Group of the International Federation of Journalists (IFJ)		
Europaische Grafische Föderation (EGF)	Editoriale l'Espresso	
Comite des Industries Cinematographiques et Audiovisuelles des Communautes Européennes et de l'Europe extracommunautaire (CICCE)	Fininvest Comunicazioni	
	Federazione Radio Televisioni (FRT)	
	RCS Editori 'Rizzoli Corriere delle Sera'	
Broadcasting Entertainment Cinematograph & Theatre Union (BECTU)	Federazione Italiana Editori Giornali	
European Committee of Trade Unions in Arts, Mass Media and Entertainment (EGAKU)	Reuters	

(Pearson, the Independent Television Commission and ITCA). Of the five Italian companies, two (Federazione Italiana Editori Giornali, and Rizzoli Corriere delle Sera) were controlled by the industrialist Agnelli (who supported the initiative), one (Editoriale l'Espresso) was owned by De Benedetti (who supported the initiative), and the other (Fininvest Comunicazioni) was owned by Berlusconi. The only German companies to be consulted were the two public broadcasters ARD and Zweites Deutsches Fernschen (ZDF). German private broadcasters were not involved at this point in time. In effect, DG III only consulted six private interests: Murdoch, Agnelli, De Benedetti, Berlusconi, ITV and Reuters. Most were precisely those groups with which DG III had had contact before the Green Paper was released. Most apart from Berlusconi (who had not yet been consulted) were in favour of DG III's proposals. These groups supported the initiative for different reasons from one another and from very different reasons to the media unions. This industry support was to turn to opposition at a later stage.

A number of European federations were consulted. There were three advertising associations, EAAA, the World Federation of Advertisers (WFA) and the European Advertising Tripartile (EAT) and two publishing associations, ENPA and the European Publishers Council (EPC). In addition, the Association of Commercial Television (ACT) was consulted and the International Federation of Journalists (IFJ). No consumer groups, such as the European Consumers' Association (BEUC) responded at this point in time. This was most unusual given BEUC's role in TWF formation. In comparison, BEUC had played a decisive role in the formation of the TWF Directive, having lobbied for a ban on alcohol and tobacco advertising (Krebber, 2001: 89). Interviews revealed that European federations were unable to respond to the Questionnaire, as the deadline was too short to gather a representative response from their members. This shows how the role of European umbrella associations had initially diminished after the Edinburgh Summit.

Four unions were also consulted on the first Questionnaire: the Europaische Grafische Föderation (EGF), Comite des Industries Cinematographiques et Audiovisuelles des Communautes, Européennes et de l'Europe extra-communautaire (CICCE), the Broadcasting Entertainment Cinematograph and Theatre Union (BECTU) and the European Committee of Trade Unions in Arts, Mass Media and Entertainment (EGAKU) (see Appendix 5 and Table 5.1). The unions were in favour of a European initiative supporting pluralism and it was precisely these unions which had lobbied the European Parliament to that effect during the policy process leading up to the TWF Directive.

Responses to Questionnaire I were mixed. Some groups, which had originally supported the initiative before the Green Paper (notably News International), withdrew their support. Most groups raised questions over the exact nature of the policy instruments to be employed in a proposed Directive. The Commission had not considered traditional criteria, reasoning that technology would abrogate the need for these. Instead, questions were centred around two policy instruments: audience share and definition of the controller. There was a mixed response to Question 4 of the Questionnaire, which related to the proposed use of audience share. The advertising groups the EAAA the EAT, and WFA refused to get involved in the debate and expressed a neutral opinion. The groups EPC, ENPA, AER, Federation Européenne des Radios Libres (FERL), News International and Fininvest opposed an initiative in any form, stating that national law was adequate.

The ITCA, Channel 4 and Pearson and Editoriale L'Espresso supported an initiative, but only if it meant liberalisation for their particular groups while at the same time curbing the expansion of Murdoch and Berlusconi. Arguments from these groups focused on the creation of a level-playing field. The EBU and the four unions (CICCE, EGAKU, the EGF and British BECTU) were in favour of legislation, but only if it meant strict regulation of media ownership at the European level to preserve cultural and linguistic identities. The EGF in particular was concerned about the dangers of media concentration and the increasing transnational links between the largest European media companies. The IFJ took a different view. It agreed in principle with European legislation. However, it heavily criticised the Single Market approach of the Commission, which it viewed as industry-rather than citizen-oriented. It stressed that any European regulation must guarantee that Member States could continue to regulate for pluralism at the national level.

In order to stimulate the dialogue at the European level and clarify ideas set out in the Green Paper the Commission organised a hearing on 26–27 April 1993. The Commission was optimistic about the hearing. However, it turned out to be a significant step along the road to untenable politicisation of the policy process. The Commission limited invitation to the hearing to those groups who responded to Questionnaire I (Appendix 5). The gathering of such diversely opposed groups under one roof was reportedly chaotic (Beltrame, 1999). The discussion was unfocused and no agreement could be reached, even on the general principles of the Green Paper. Large industry fundamentally expressed opposition to a European-level initiative. Most participants wished to know more detail of the proposed rules.

The structure of the Commission itself during this time was undergoing change. Between the release of Questionnaire I (February 1993) and the hearing (April 1993), the media ownership portfolio had changed hands from DG III to DG XV. A change over from Bangemann to d'Archirafi was underway.

The second Questionnaire 1993

Commission officials classified the 1993 hearing as wholly unsuccessful. The consensus from industry that had been carefully constructed before the release of the Green Paper had come undone. However, the hearing brought together many national interests at the European level for the first time. The Commission was not successful in fostering agreement, but it was successful in bringing the debate closer to the European level and bringing national groups closer to their foreign counterparts. It was simple to glean from the hearing that there was a clear misunderstanding of policy instruments outlined in the Green Paper. The Commission sent out a second Questionnaire to interest groups to clarify questions on the specification of policy instruments. Questionnaire II (entitled the 'complementary Questionnaire') was sent to European federations on 26 July 1993. The same Questionnaire was sent out to media companies and other interests on 28 July. It requested that interest groups consider three possible courses of action: (I) no action, (II) transparency action or (III) harmonisation action.

Questionnaire II (Appendix 5) posed questions on the use of real audience and of the definition of the controller as regulatory instruments. The Questionnaire was only one page in length and not particularly in-depth so easier to comprehend. The Commission took the opportunity therewith to find out from national interest groups what the Member States were planning in the area of media ownership legislation. Questions were asked about the 'potential development of national legislations' and the influence of new technologies on national licensing. Indeed, Questionnaire II could be seen as a fact-finding mission to discover the proposal of national governments and perhaps even to discover which interest groups had direct access to national administrations. Question B3 in particular asks what might prompt a revision of national ownership rules: 'new broadcaster authorisations, case law developments, political debates, ineffectiveness of national rules, over-stringent rules, etc.?' Question B4 asks how long it took to draw up the last ownership rules.

The questions on audience share were not clear. The Commission had not yet commissioned or published any studies on audience share. The measure had never been discussed at national levels and indeed was absent from the 1990 UK, German and Italian Broadcasting Acts. The only information on the potential of audience share had been provided in the five pages of the 1992 Green Paper. Many interest groups informally stated to the Commission that they did not comprehend the significance of the proposed instrument. In an attempt to clarify definitions, DG XV commissioned a study entitled 'Audience measurement in the EC' from the GAH consultancy group (1993). Questionnaire II had been sent out in July 1993. The GAH study was published in September 1993. Copies were sent out to the groups, which expressed difficulties in understanding Questionnaire II.

Table 5.2   Respondents to Questionnaire II

Comments from European associations and federations	Comments from interested parties other than European federations or associations
European Group of Television Advertising (EGTA) Association des Television Commerciales Européennes (ACT) European Broadcasting Union (EBU) Association Européenne des Radios (AER) European Publishers Council (EPC) Federations des Editeurs europeens/ Federation of European Publishers (FEE/FEP) Federation of Associations of Periodical Publishers in the EC (FAEP) Association Européenne des Editeurs de Journaux (ENPA-CAEJ) International Federation of Journalists (IFJ) Groupement europeen des Societes dAuteurs et Compsiteurs (GESAC) Europaische Grafische Föderation (EGF)	News International ITC (Independent Television Commission) ITV Network Pearson plc Channel 4 Television Bertelsmann A.G FUNK (Fragen Unabhängiger Neutraler Kommunikation) RTL Plus Deutschland Fernsehen VDZ Verband Deutscher Zeitschriftenverleger e.V.Zweites Deutsches Fernsehen (ZDF) Fininvest Comunicazioni Global Media Italia SRL L'Espresso RCS Editori Federazione Italiana Editori Giornali OLON Organisatie van Lokale Omroepen (Dutch)

A deadline of 18 October 1993 was given for responses to the Question-naire (Table 5.2).

There were over 70 responses to the consultation process. This fact was stated in the Commission's second Green Paper entitled 'Follow up to the consultation process relating to the Green Paper on "Pluralism and media concentration in the internal market – an assessment of the need for com-munity action"' in October 1994 (CEC, 1994a). The statement is not quite accurate. There were in fact 28 responses to Questionnaire II (12 federa-tions and 16 companies). In their calculation of 70, the Commission counted responses to both Questionnaires I and II and the companies and organisations which were represented by European federations. The main consultation was of key industrial groups: chiefly those owned by Murdoch, Berlusconi and Agnelli, with the addition this time of the German group

Table 5.3 Company response to Questionnaires I and II

Company responses to Questionnaire I			Company responses to Questionnaire II		
(Murdoch)	BSkyB	UK	*(Murdoch)*	News International	UK
(Murdoch)	News International	UK	*(ITV)*	ITV Network	UK
(ITV)	Pearson plc	UK	*(ITV)*	ITC	UK
(ITV)	ITCA	UK		Channel 4	UK
	Channel 4	UK		ZDF	DE
	ZDF	DE			
	ARD	DE			
(De Benedetti)	l'Espresso	IT	*(Bertelsmann)*	RTL Plus	DE
(Berlusconi)	Fininvest	IT	*(Bertelsmann)*	Bertelsmann A.G	DE
	FRT	IT	*(De Benedetti)*	L'Espresso	IT
(Agnelli)	Rizzoli	IT	*(Berlusconi)*	Fininvest	IT
(Agnelli)	Federazione Italiana		*(Berlusconi)*	Global Media Italia	IT
	Editori Giornali	IT	*(Agnelli)*	Rizzoli	IT
	Reuters	NE	*(Agnelli)*	Federazione Italiana	
				Editori Giornali	IT

Bertelsmann (Table 5.3). Again, only British, German and Italian groups were consulted. French groups remained absent from the consultation process.

At first glance, it appears that a different group of federations responded to Questionnaire II than did to Questionnaire I. However, many of the same groups had responded under a different name. For example, the three advertising agencies (EAAA, EAT and WFA) responded jointly this time as the European Group of Television Advertising (EGTA). The European Newspaper Publishers' Association (ENPA) responded under its French name, the Association Européenne des Editeurs de Journaux (CAEJ). Two new groups appeared, representing similar interests to ENPA: the Federation of Associations of Periodical Publishers in the EC (FAEP) and the Federations des Editeurs Europeens/Federation of European Publishers (FEE/FEP). This meant key industrial interests were represented more than once. Responses from unions and consumer groups were noticeably absent from Questionnaire II. Three of the unions, which had responded in Questionnaire I, CICCE, BECTU and EGAKU, did not respond to the second questionnaire. The EGF and another union, the Groupement Europeen des Societes d'Auteurs et Compositeurs (GESAC), responded.

Responses to Questionnaire II were again mixed and there were few changes in opinion. Some companies were warming to the idea, but were reluctant to commit themselves to an initiative if they did not know the precise implications of the policy instruments proposed. Most interest groups interpreted the absence of a clear position on behalf of the Commission with suspicion. The majority of submissions were dissatisfied with the status quo and favourable to a change in the legal framework. However, each case of dissatisfaction was naturally related to the participant's specific case.

As prompted by the Questionnaire, the majority of respondents concentrated on the impact of new technologies on sector developments. In particular, large industrial groups argued that the new media (satellites and digital compression) would make the national legislation obsolete (and by the same token any community initiative). Many of these expressed concern that by legislating the Commission would run the risk of posing regulatory obstacles to technological and economic growth.

The European Group of Television Advertising (EGTA representing the EAAA, the EAT and WFA) expressed no opinion. The written response of EGTA shows perhaps the difference between formal and informal consultation. In interviews, the EAAA, representing 80 per cent of advertisers in Europe, strongly advocated DGX III's convergence initiative and expressed opposition to the ownership initiative.

Fininvest was opposed to the use of audience share in response to Questionnaire II and sent its own study relating to audience share (prepared by the consultancy, Global Media Italia SRL). The study concentrated on the futility of legislation by any means due to the advent of new technologies, in particular digital compression. It argued that any measure should take into account the whole of the communications market, a measure which had been introduced in the Italian 1990 Broadcasting Act. This is particularly interesting as it is a measure which was subsequently taken up in the convergence initiative. In the 1996 KPMG report, commissioned by DG Information Society, it was proposed that dominant position should be assessed when a company reached a threshold of 30 per cent of the whole of the communications market. News International was also heavily opposed to an initiative. Shortly after its submission, it too sent a second study on audience share. This study was also authored by William Shew but this time on behalf of Arthur Andersen Economic Consulting (Shew, 1994). It also expressed the need for a wider market definition.

The EPC slightly changed its view from the first Questionnaire stating that it may not be opposed to a European initiative and the use of audience share if it was deregulatory in nature. At the time, the internal membership of the EPC had changed slightly to include more Italian publishers (Agnelli and De Benedetti), meaning that News International had a less dominant view. The ACT had also had a change in membership. Up until this time, ACT was dominated mainly by the large commercial broadcasters, CLT, Sky, and Fininvest (Humphreys, 1996: 128). As Humphreys notes, Silvio Berlusconi was the ACT's first chairman (1996: 128). By 1994, the ITV companies had joined ACT and their opinion split with Fininvest (ITV in favour, Fininvest against). For this reason there was no response submitted to the second Questionnaire by the ACT.

ITCA, Channel 4 and Pearson and Editoriale L'Espresso supported Option III (harmonisation), but only if it meant expansion of their own enterprises and the reining in of Murdoch and Berlusconi. Support for a European initiative (Option III) also came from the IFJ and the two unions (GESAC and EGF). The IFJ repeated its criticism of the Single Market argument. It stressed that European legislation was urgently needed, however that it must guarantee that the regulation of pluralism could be left up to the Member States. The EBU took a stronger line in its response to the second Questionnaire that European legislation was absolutely vital. It pointed to increased vertical integration in the private sector and heightened competition for programming rights for public service broadcasters. The EBU and ZDF, expressed their concern that national legislation could be overridden with the increased use of satellites. They rejected Option III that harmonisation of national rules would solve this problem as private companies would merely broadcast from outside the European Community. Rather they stressed the need for transparency (Option II). Both organisations called for a public service opt out for any European legislation, particularly if it concerned the use of audience share. This suggestion was eventually adopted in the 1997 version of the Draft Directive.

Written responses to Questionnaires I and II were compiled in a five volume Commission document (XV/9555/94). On 21 September 1994, d'Archirafi was convinced by the services that a Draft Directive be submitted to the College of Commissioners based upon the 1992 Green Paper. This Draft Directive was rejected (as discussed in Chapter 4), not only by the majority of Commissioners in the College, but also by Commissioner Bangemann. The loss of support from Bangemann (who had strong ties to industry) was a major setback.

The Commission's second Green Paper entitled 'Follow up to the consultation process relating to the Green Paper on "Pluralism and media concentration in the internal market – an assessment of the need for community action"' was published in October 1994 only one month following the rejection of the September draft (CEC, 1994a). As discussed in Chapter 5, the Commission focused on new technologies in this second Green Paper. There was a definite move away from core industrial arguments for liberalisation and a move towards harmonisation of national ownership laws. DG XV attempted to recoup Bangemann's support by linking the Green Paper to the information society. This strategy was not to succeed.

The publication of the second Green Paper in 1994 had a number of consequences. It fuelled lobbying activity at the European level. The Commission kept up on-going informal consultations with interest groups but only gained small successes. The majority of groups remained against a European-level initiative. However, the Commission was successful in other ways. Frequent contact with national interest groups enabled DG XV to keep up with national regulatory developments and to influence debates at national levels. Meetings also enabled interest groups to build up trans-national networks. In this way, Commission offices became a platform for the exchange of ideas.

Commission officials attributed the lack of support in responses to Questionnaire II to confusion on behalf of the interest groups over the technical policy instruments of audience share and definition of the controller (Beltrame, 1997). Up until this time, no study on audience share had been publicly released by the Commission. Therefore the DG XV commissioned two studies on technical instruments. These were on the policy instruments of audience share and definition of the controller: one the 'Feasibility of using audience measures to assess pluralism' prepared by British Goodhall, Alexander, and O'Hare (GAH) Group and the other 'La Transparence dans le contrôle des médias' prepared by the German European Institute for the Media (EIM, 1994).[3] Both studies were published in November 1994. The studies were distributed to interest groups along with a third Questionnaire in January 1995. In the same month, DG XV gained a new Commissioner, Mario Monti.

The third and final 1995 Questionnaire

Questionnaire III was sent out to the European Parliament, ECOSOC, European federations, companies and national administrations. Deadlines for responses were 15 April for the European institutions and companies and 15 May for Member States. Questionnaire III was four pages in length and concentrated on the content of an eventual initiative (Appendix 5). Its questions did not differ much from Questionnaires I and II, but greater focus was given to the type of policy instruments to be used. Summarised, the questions covered (A) the need for Community action, (B) scope of a possible initiative, (C) principles underpinning the internal market, (D) conditions governing access to media ownership to be included in a possible initiative, (E) criteria for defining the media controller, (F) criterion of actual audience, (G) disqualified persons, (H) transparency and exchange of information, (I) European committee and (J) type of Community instrument.

In answer to the Questionnaire, there were 36 written responses (Table 5.4): 18 from companies, 13 from federations and 5 from Member States. Included in the submissions from Member States were submissions from separate authorities: OFTEL, the Department of National Heritage (DNH) and the ITC in the UK, four Länder in Germany and the Swedish competition authority, the Swedish Ministry of Culture and the Swedish Parliamentary Media Committee in Sweden. There was little participation from consumer associations, unions or academic institutions (the GESAC and the EGF did not submit this time around). Many of the same groups responded to Questionnaire III as did to I and II. However there was some new input from groups from Denmark, Spain and Portugal and the new Member States, Sweden, Austria and Finland.

Table 5.4 Respondents to Questionnaire III

Comments from European Associations and Federations	Comments from companies	Comments from National Authorities
ACT (Association des Television Commerciales Européennes)	ARD ZDF	Bavaria Nordrheinwestfalen
ENPA (Association Européenne des Editeurs de Journaux)	Bertelsmann RTL (Bertelsmann) Politiken Newspapers	Berlin Schleswig-Holstein
EBU (European Broadcasting Union)		
AER (Association Européenne des Radios)	PRO7	UK Department for National Heritage
FAEP (Federation of Associations of Periodical Publishers in the EC)		UK Office for Telecommunications UK Independent Television
EPC (European Publishers Council)	BBC	Commission
Eurocinema	(ITV) Pearson	
	(ITV) Carlton	
IFJ (International Federation of Journalists)	(ITV) Meridian	Swedish competition authority
German Association of Journalists	Channel 4	Swedish Ministry of Culture
National Union of Journalists	British Telecommunications (BT)	Swedish Parliamentary Media
Fundación Comunicación Social		Committee the Swedish Television Authority
BECTU	Fininvest	
European Group of Television Advertising (EGTA)	RCS (Rizzoli) Federazione Italiana Editori	Luxembourg Denmark
Instituto do Consumidor Journalistförbund (Finnish)	Giornali L' Espresso	Japan
	RTVE Grupo Prisa	
	Mediaraad Sveriges Television Time Warner MTV (Finish company)	

Of the companies, the British groups BBC, Pearson, Meridian, Channel 4; the Italian groups Rizzoli, De Benedetti and Fininvest; the German groups RTL, and PRO7, the Spanish Grupo Prisa and the Finnish company MTV[4] were in favour of an initiative (Beltrame, 1997). As were the federations AER, IFJ, BECTU, and the Fundación Comunicación Social. The ACT, EBU, ITC, Sveriges Television and Bertelsmann were undecided. Those against were: the ENPA (of which Springer was a member), FAEP (of which News International was a member), the German public broadcasters ARD and ZDF, Carlton, Politiken Newspapers, the Spanish RTVE, Time Warner and the Dutch Mediaraad. Of the Member State submissions, Germany and the UK were against any initiative; Luxembourg and Denmark were neutral; Sweden could not agree internally on an official position. The Japanese government was also consulted this time around. It did not express an opinion either way but raised questions as to the feasibility of audience share and gave information about regulation of the media in Japan. It is interesting to note that no US groups or US representatives (officially) submitted to any of the Commission questionnaires.

More or less the same European federations submitted to the third Questionnaire as did to the first and second. There were some slight shifts in opinion between the second and third Questionnaires. Fininvest by this time had lost its influence within the ACT (the Fininvest associated director retired). The irony was that Fininvest now supported the European initiative and there was increasing dissent amongst the ITV companies whose view became prominent within the ACT, due to the sheer number of them. Fininvest's switch to support of a European initiative in 1995 could be explained for two reasons. First, shortly after the release of the second Green Paper (in October 1994), DG XV Commissioner D'Archirafi made some assurances to Fininvest in a speech to the European Parliament on 24 November 1994 in which he stated:

> As regards the Fininvest group, the competitive situation of this group is not due to a recent concentration with a community dimension, which would fall under the Merger Regulation. The channels of the group were bought at the time when they were much smaller, with no evident Community dimension, and when no appropriate regulations on media ownership or on concentrations existed in Italy. The channels then expanded through internal growth up to their present size. Outside the framework of a concentration, a dominant position as such, if it was proved to exist, is not forbidden by any Community competition rule: article 86 or the Treaty only deals with abuses of dominant position. (quoted in Beltrame, 1997)

Secondly, the Italian constitutional court in the same year declared that Italian national ownership limits be set to 20 per cent of national channels by the end of August 1996 (Lane, 1997). Fininvest was ordered to divest its interests. Fininvest stated in its submission to Questionnaire III dissatisfaction with national media ownership laws that the 'existing channels method is not appropriate'. However, the company was unsurprisingly opposed to any kind of European rules governing vertical integration.

The ACT declared that it was not against an initiative as long as harmonisation of national laws represented a liberalising policy. The AER professed that it was in favour of community action as long as the public service broadcasters did not receive a special opt out ('pas de privileges pour le service public'). It particularly feared the concentration of satellite services. The EPC, which was the most vocally opposed to the initiative in its response to Questionnaire I, actually submitted a favourable response to Questionnaire III. The reason for this is that the Italian publishers, Rizzoli and De Benedetti had been instrumental in out-voting News International within the EPC (Beltrame, 1997).

The Portuguese communications federation, the Fundación Comunicación Social, expressed favour as long as such an initiative only dealt with the concentration of broadcasting markets and not press markets. This most likely reflected the view of Portuguese publishers, whose broadcasting interests were coming under increasing competition from foreign groups. The Spanish publishing company, Grupo Prisa, submitted a similar response to that of the Portuguese Fundación's. It favoured an initiative, but only if it solely dealt with broadcasting markets. This group answered 'no' to question B.4: 'Should a possible Community initiative cover concentration between press enterprises?' Pearson declared a similar view. It was in favour of a regulation on media ownership at the European level but only if it dealt with broadcasting. In the same vein, Bertelsmann stated that it was open to the idea of European legislation, but only if cross-media ownership was not restricted. Bertelsmann's answer to question B4 was a firm 'no' adding that any initiative 'should certainly not add to national, regional and European rules resulting in increased restrictions'.

The ENPA response (representing Springer) was unchanged in its opposition and maintained that European competition law was adequate for controlling the concentration of markets. The ENPA was particularly opposed to any European legislation which would cover concentration between press enterprises. It was less opposed to the regulation of broadcasting. The ENPA was internally divided over the issue of whether public service broadcasters should be included. It did state however that 'there is no doubt that international investment in the media can be hindered by the disparity of regulation in the Member States'. The FAEP (of which News International was a key member) was adamantly against any initiative arguing that 'cross border traffic remains small'. In response to question E relating to definitions of the controller, the FAEP stated that 'the clearest objective measure is 51 per cent majority share'. The small Danish group, Politiken Newspapers, was also against an initiative, stating that 'existing Danish Press and Media Responsibility laws . . . are sufficient'.

Those most concerned with the protection of pluralism at the European level were the IFJ, BBC and BECTU. The IFJ favoured harmonisation at the highest possible level. In particular, it considered lack of transparency and concentration in the advertising market to be of most salience. The IFJ suggested that 'within national boundaries no single operator should be allowed to control more than 30 per cent of the advertising market in which they operate'. Separate submissions by the British NUJ and the German Association of Journalists supported the IFJ response. The group Eurocinema was also strongly in favour as was BECTU, but BECTU stressed the need for a 'more sophisticated measure of concentration' than audience share. The Portuguese consumer association, the Instituto do Consumidor, also expressed favour for the initiative.

The EBU had doubts about the initiative, but was not against. This reflected internal division. It stressed the need for a public service opt out and argued that definitions of the controller should be made on a case-by-case basis. Significantly, the BBC was in favour of a European initiative, but stated that 'any regulation must provide Member States with an incentive to regulate in the majority of cases, recognising that there will always be situations where Member States do not have any incentive to regulation (in which case the Commission should intervene)'. The BBC however was reluctant about audience share, favouring instead 'a weighted points system which combined several measurements criteria may represent the most reasonable approach'.

The German public service broadcasters, ARD and ZDF, were staunchly against any European initiative this time around. This was not because they were supporting the view of the German Länder (which had been consulted for the first time around), but because they believed that any European initiative would represent a liberalising proposal and allow for expansion of large groups in Europe. It was evident by this time that the German operator, Kirch, was in favour of an initiative (represented through PRO7 and the VPRT). The German ARD and ZDF were also strongly opposed to the possibility that public service broadcasters might be regulated along with private broadcasters. The Spanish public service provider RTVE shared this opinion. Other groups were opposed to the initiative for a different reason. FAEP, Carlton, Mediaraad, Time Warner groups favoured total sector liberalisation and the sole utilisation of competition law to regulate media markets.

The ITV company, Meridian, was in favour of a European initiative, but felt that including new services would be premature. Channel 4 also expressed favour. The German company, RTL, was in favour of an initiative (although Bertelsmann stressed neutrality) as long as 'public channels were subject to the same rules as private channels'. Rizzoli Corriere della Sera (owned by Agnelli) was strongly in favour of an initiative as was L'Espresso and the Federazione Italiana Editori Giornali. The Federazione

Italiana Editori Giornali was opposed to audience share, instead proposing a combined criteria for measuring concentration: an economic measurement (such as market share) plus the number of channels. Remaining groups expressed no opinion.

No French groups submitted any formal responses to any of the three Commission Questionnaires. This perhaps says more about the lobbying style of French groups (informal) than their actual opinions. Representing some of the largest media groups in Europe, it is hard to conceive that French groups were completely silent on the issue.

In their responses, a number of groups agreed that a level playing field should be created in the internal market (BBC, Pearson, British Telecom, Bertelsmann, RTL, Fininvest, Rizzoli, L'Espresso, Grupo Prisa, ACT, EPC). Many private companies expressed the need for increased investment and Commission support for European competitiveness in a global market (ENPA, EPC, BBC, Bertelsmann, Pearson, RTL). Some interest groups thought that the initiative should be linked to the Information Society (ACT, EPC, Bertelsmann, Fininvest, Grupo Prisa, RTL). Two Italian companies (Fininvest and l'Espresso) pointed to the risk of increased disparity between national ownership rules, particularly in the light of the current revisions in national laws taking place in the Member States. A number of publishing groups were worried that European proposals for audience share would limit multimedia activities (e.g. cross-media ownership) (Fininvest, Meridian, Pearson, Politiken Newspapers). Other groups believed that the Commission should propose both monomedia and multimedia ownership limits (OFTEL, Espresso, Rizzoli, Sverige TV). Bertelsmann suggested that monomedia limits should be set at 33 per cent of audience share. Meridian suggested that audience share be tiered at 25 per cent at the regional level, 14–15 per cent at the national level and 10 per cent at the European level. This latter suggestion was adopted in the July 1996 Draft Directive on media ownership (which did not succeed). The larger ITV groups (notably Carlton, Pearson and Granada) were strongly opposed to the Draft at this point. In particular, they objected to the use of regional criteria.

In 1994, the European Institute for the Media study was sent out to interest groups. Four criteria to identify a controller were identified: (1) contractual links (upstream and downstream), (2) financial links, (3) personal links and (4) property links (via share-ownership). In response to the Question E.3 on definitions of the controller, L'Espresso and RTVE stressed the importance of contractual links, whereas Fininvest and MTV were against. Bertelsmann, the ITC and RTL doubted the possibility of identifying controllers. Others groups, notably the IFJ, the German Association of Journalists, Eurocinema, Fundación Comunicación Social, Rizzoli, and RTL were in favour. Question E.7 asking 'should family links be taken into account in identifying the media controller?' turned out to be a contentious issue. Fininvest and the Finnish group, MTV, were strongly against the idea.

Other groups, such as the EBU, BBC, IFJ, the German Association of Journalists, Eurocinema, Fundación Comunicación Social, Rizzoli, L'Espresso (Rizzoli) and RTL were in favour of identifying family links.

Questions G, relating to disqualified persons, received little attention. It was reported that most national media ownership legislations list categories of people who are not permitted to control a television station. Questions G asked who should be included in such a list. The few replies listed political parties, public authorities, public networks and advertising companies. Surprisingly, the disqualifying of individual politicians from media ownership was not of issue. Question I asked whether or not a European watchdog should be established. The idea for a watchdog was proposed in the European Parliament Resolution. The majority of interest groups were opposed to this idea. Therefore the Commission decided not to propose an authority in its Draft Directive.

Of the Member States, Germany, Denmark, Italy, Greece, Sweden and the UK were all revising their national media laws in 1995. Italy and Greece did not respond to the Questionnaire. Denmark, Germany and the UK expressed opposition to a European proposal. Although opposed, the UK and Germany both adopted the Commission's proposal of audience share in their 1996 Acts. The Commission has since argued for an initiative based upon the 'German model'.

The Commission received responses from three regulatory authorities in the UK: the DNH, the ITC and OFTEL. The DNH sent the official response, which opposed any Community initiative. In order to respond to the Commission's Questionnaire, the DNH had surveyed UK interest groups and submitted a summary of the survey along with an official response to the Commission through the UK permanent representative to the EU on 18 October 1995. The UK regulatory authority, the DNH maintained that the Commission approach was overly Single Market focused and that pluralism was of secondary concern. The DNH further pointed out that News Corporation only came in third place in an estimation of UK newspaper circulation according to the proposed EU measurement (audience share). The DNH argued to the Commission that an EU Directive would be more restrictive than UK legislation for the ITV companies (1996c). Granada would have more than 30 per cent of audience share in the Northwest of the UK according to the proposed regional measurement. The DNH also pointed out that a Commission Directive would hasten the decline of daily regional newspapers in the UK. The DNH objected to what the Commission was proposing as essentially 'cultural legislation', which went against the principle of subsidiarity. For its part, the Independent Television Commission (ITC) took a neutral position, but both BT and OFTEL expressed support for a Commission initiative (Beltrame, 1997).

The Commission followed a similar strategy in its consultation of Germany. The state of Bavaria submitted the official response to the Commission on behalf of all the German Länder, which stated opposition to any European initiative (Bayerische Staatskanzlei, 1996). Support for the initiative came however from three German Länder: Berlin, Nordrheinwestfalen and Schleswig-Holstein (New Media Markets, 1994, 1995). The director of the Landesmedienanstalt in Berlin was a strong supporter of the German Duales System and wished to preserve the rights of the public service broadcasters. He subsequently organised expert hearings at the national level to which Commission officials were invited. Nordrheinwestfalen also came out publicly in support of a European initiative (depending upon the form it took) after it was dissatisfied with the outcome of the 1995 revision of the German 1991 Rundfunkstaatsvertrag. Nordrheinwestfalen firstly stated its position publicly in a meeting with supporters of public service broadcasters. Then its support was given in October 1996 in a speech given by the NRW head of chancellery (Frohn, 1996). A third speech was given in Straßbourg to the European Parliament by the German Minister for Federal and European Affairs (Dammeyer, 1996). The Land, Schleswig-Holstein, also expressed support for the initiative.

The Commission consulted different regulatory authorities in Sweden as well. This fuelled the national debate. Sweden attempted to introduce media ownership rules nationally during 1995 (which were never passed). The Commission received four responses to Questionnaire III from different Swedish regulatory bodies: the Swedish competition authority, the Swedish television authority, the Swedish Ministry of Culture and the Swedish Parliamentary Media Committee. The Swedish Ministry of Culture and the Swedish Parliamentary Media Committee were in favour of a Commission initiative, whereas the Swedish competition authority and the Swedish television authority were against.

DG XV put together the results of the Questionnaire in July 1995.[5] With these responses, it was able to demonstrate to the Cabinet that interest groups were in favour of an initiative (Beltrame, 1997). Shortly afterwards, Monti made his September 1995 speech to the European Parliament, declaring that he would authorise the drafting of a Directive on media ownership. From this time onwards, a number of internal drafts were presented to the Cabinet. One year passed before the chef du cabinet decided that the proposal was politically viable and a Draft Directive was first presented to the College of Commissioners in July 1996 (as discussed in Chapter 4). Meanwhile, a plethora of informal meetings between DG XV and interest groups took place during 1995 and 1996. This had a definitive effect on the shaping of the eventual Draft Directive. Following Monti's October speech to the EP, wherein he committed himself to pluralist concerns, the remaining large companies began to withdraw their support for the initiative as they grew increasingly sceptical of the Commission's intentions and began to proffer opposition to any Directive (*Agence Europe*, 1997f). ITV turned against the initiative when it realised that it had won its battle on home territory – in the revision of the 1996 Broadcasting Act. Pearson reportedly turned against in 1996 directly following its purchase of *Les Echos* in France (Beltrame, 1997).

Following the second submission of the Draft Directive to the College of Commissioners in December 1996, lobbying efforts against the initiative stepped up. Of the large European media groups, News International, Springer, ITV and CLT were most strongly opposed. The European Publishers Council (representing News International) publicly reported its opposition in a *Financial Times* article, stating that a pan-European media ownership initiative was unnecessary and would only hinder the development of European media companies (Tucker, 1997). In February 1997, the EPC sent a letter to Commissioner Santer stating its opposition to the Directive. According to interviews, the letter was drafted solely by News International and sent to Santer without consultation with other EPC members. In particular, the Italian publishers were never consulted on the position. In response, representatives of Rizzoli and L'Espresso circulated a letter internally to the EPC denouncing the letter sent to Santer. This letter also found its way to the Commission. Other groups (allegedly, Springer and CLT) directly lobbied the Commission president, Jacques Santer, against an initiative.

Up against such hefty opposition, the Commission increasingly sought the support of small and medium-size companies, public service broadcasters and journalist and consumer organisations. Assurances were made to these groups that a Community initiative would curb the expansion of large industry.

As the policy process proceeded, the 1996 proposal became more and more restrictive in nature, reflecting the views of smaller groups. The draft included a special opt-out for public service broadcasters and lowered ceilings for audience share (according to the suggestions by Meridian). Audience share was set at 25 per cent at the regional level, 14–15 per cent at the national level and 10 per cent at the European level, and introduced new rules on multimedia enterprises (e.g. cross-media ownership). None of these provisions had been planned until the final stages of the policy process.

Internal consultation of the Draft Directive began in the summer of July 1996. As documented in Chapter 5, the Draft in this restrictive form was unacceptable to the more liberal members of the College of Commissioners. However, the Draft had reached a stage of political bargaining. As discussed in the last chapter, political compromise led to a final loosening of the Draft rules. When the final draft was submitted on 12 March 1997, it contained a number of changes. In particular, the restrictive measures for audience share were abandoned and replaced by a national audience share measure of 10 per cent for multimedia and 30 per cent for monomedia (Doyle, 2002). The 'flexibility clause' was inserted into the draft. However, the opt-out for public service broadcasters remained.

In March 1997, a simple majority of the College voted in favour of the initiative and the only reason why the Directive did not go through was due to political dissent of Commissioner Santer. It is remarkable indeed that political consensus on a draft was achieved despite heavy handed opposition and negative feedback from the largest European media companies.

Conclusion

As shown in this chapter, consultation of interest groups in this case was used by the Commission to build internal support for its initiative, to retrieve information from national levels and to disseminate ideas. Only large groups were consulted before the release of the 1992 Green Paper. News International introduced the idea for audience share at this point in time as tool for introducing sector liberalisation. Since the initiative had originally been proposed by the European Parliament, DG III also invited those groups which had advocated a Directive on media ownership to MEPs: the unions of media professionals. Lack of political support in the College led to wide consultation following the 1992 Green Paper.

This move away from the technocratic policy-making style of the Commission was significant. A technocratic policy process is best administered by a closely knit policy community (Rhodes, 1988; Jordan and Richardson, 1979), and is hampered by the active involvement of MEPs, the media, national political parties, regions or Länder and ultimately citizens. The invitation for democratic enquiry meant the death of the policy initiative. It led to increased politicisation and the loss of support of large industry as a result.

Even though the 1997 Draft Directive failed, the consultation process itself produced a number of results. Firstly, the issue of media ownership was considered for the first time at the European level. Secondly, policy instruments suggested by the European institutions were filtered down to national levels through national interest group consultation. The use of the audience share instrument for measuring was adopted in Germany, the UK, Ireland and Romania (as discussed in the next chapter). Thirdly, wide consultation and the input of smaller voices meant increased democratic input into the policy process. It represented a clear change in the Commission's opaque technocratic style towards a more transparent style of consultation – an experiment which proved unsuccessful in this case. Fourthly, the move away from technocratic policy-making meant that subsequent initiatives which had cultural significance required a similar wide consultation of interest groups (e.g. convergence, electronic commerce, data protection and parental control). The political obstacles that the Commission encounters in such cases may be forcing ever-more reliance on self-regulatory instruments which forego this process. Lastly, the on-going debate over media ownership at the European level had a significant effect on overall

European policy. The European debate on ownership had an effect on the direction of DG competition law as rulings in the field took into consideration issues of media pluralism.

However, the chapter showed that, due to the make-up of the EU polity, the Commission essentially needs the support of large industry or strong political backing in order to push an initiative in the media field. The more balanced proposal resulting from a wide and transparent consultation process was doomed to failure. Democratic policy-making is not feasible within the EU as a regulatory state. The successful initiative was therefore *convergence*, as explained in Chapter 4. The convergence initiative underwent an even wider consultation process than the *ownership* initiative.[6] In contrast, however, it received overwhelming support from large industry and dissent from smaller media groups, consumer groups, unions and PSBs.[7] Although, the academic literature comments extensively upon the fact that the latter groups managed to exclude national content regulation from the scope of the new regulatory framework (Levy, 1999: 140; Hills and Michalis, 2000; Ward, 2002), the fact remains that the EU can only push the policy agenda forward on one front, market liberalisation, and not in policy areas which aim to protect the public interest.

Notes

1 The 1996 Commission Green Paper 'Commercial communications' (CEC, 1996f) received 400 responses from interest groups, many of them very small. Comments on the 2003–4 consultation on the revision of TWF are also available on-line.

2 Traditionally, media markets have been limited by multiple licences, shareholding limits, cross-media restrictions, advertising revenue and/or subscription revenue.

3 In the European Institute for the Media study, four criteria to identify a controller were identified: (1) contractual links (upstream and downstream); (2) financial links; (3) personal links; and (4) property links (via share-ownership).

4 Support from the Finnish group is curious as MTV was the only private operator in Finland and held 40 per cent of the Finnish television audience market.

5 The results of the third questionnaire were never made publicly available but were commented upon at length in a PhD thesis at the University of Milan by Beltrame (1997) who was the stagiaire responsible for compiling questionnaire responses within DG XV at the time.

6 For discussion of interest group consultation during the convergence initiative, see Hills and Michalis (2000), Murdock (2000), McKenna (2002), and Ward (2002). For discussion of interest group consultation during TWF see Collins (1994b), Humphreys (1996) and for TWF revision see Krebber (2001).

7 For the consultation process on the convergence initiative see Levy (1999), Hills and Michalis (2000: 452–5), Ward (2002).

6

Whither a European media market?

Last week I attended a media conference in New York. Most of the media barons were there. They boasted (probably with accuracy) how their companies would be one of the six or seven media groups that would dominate the next decade. They listed the members of the priestly tribe — News Corp, Viacom, Time Warner, Disney and so on. I heard no mention of Bertelsmann, Kirch, Canal +, Polygram, the BBC, Prisa, Carlton or any European group. (Michael Kuhn, President of Polygram Filmed Entertainment, Birmingham, 1998)

The previous chapters showed how EU media regulation came into being and the goals and rationales upon which it is based. This chapter shows the impact of European media policy on market development.[1] It assesses how far the stated goals of European policy have been met. The main goals were identified as job creation, market growth, the defense of European champions and the protection of European and independent content production. Additional goals of course are found in individual provisions of the TWF and other Directives, such as the protection of minors and limitation of advertising, etc.

The first finding is that the inconsistency in EU policy is contributing not to market growth but to failure at national levels. As shown in Chapter 3, national attempts to create single national platforms for pay-TV and impose technological standards were vetoed by DG Competition. The Commission's insistence on increased market competition has led to overdue strain on media markets, contributing to the collapse of pay-TV platforms and huge losses for Europe's parent groups.

The second finding is that EU policy has encouraged cross-border investment and cross-border alliances between the largest European groups. At the same time, vertical concentration has been discouraged at the national level. This marks a key difference between the goals of the EU and Member States. Traditionally, national competition policy and media ownership laws targeted horizontal concentration. Vertical agreements were viewed as beneficial, as they allowed firms to internalise externalities (Gibbons, 2003).

This has changed over the last 15 years largely under the direction of the EU institutions. Thus, more focus has been given to limiting vertical integration and encouraging horizontal cooperation. The result is an increasingly high level of co-operation at the European level between the major European media groups. Media groups have been encouraged (through TWF) to outsource to independent production companies rather than produce in-house. However, the increased expense has led European groups to rely on cheaper production than is provided by European independent production companies.

A third finding is that media companies have evolved into corporations listed on stock exchanges. This has led to increased transparency and divorce from political and state ties. However, the drive for profitability to please shareholders means that companies are investing less in content and perhaps suffer a loss of editorial independence as well. The search for greater supply and ever-cheaper sources of content has made European companies increasingly reliant upon production imports.

Growth of European media companies

Of the press and broadcasting companies operating in Europe, the majority of large players have been dominant at the national level since markets began operation. Most European media groups are subsidiaries of large industrial conglomerates, which draw the bulk of their income from activities other than the media. The media market has generally not proven itself to be a profitable sector. Rather it tends to be a high-risk market, in both press and broadcasting, with many companies dipping into the red for years at a time. Established players are compelled to compete with new markets, which diminish their existing market share. Newspaper markets faced near collapse from rising advertising competition from television in the late 1970s to mid-1980s. The fast pace of technological advance in the broadcasting sector requires heavy capital investment for new technologies. In the 1990s, investment in digital markets toppled many companies, apart from those that cross-subsidised their media holdings from other business areas. The market was too lightly regulated at national levels, due to EU intervention. At the same time, the EU failed to replace the regulatory vacuum through European-level initiatives (e.g. on ownership and standard-setting). The liberal regulatory environment was lethal for European firms. Once companies, which had risked investing in new markets, fell into difficulty they could no longer rely on government bail-outs (due to restrictions on state aid), which might have been forthcoming in the past.

Notably prominent in European media markets have been single media owners (e.g. Black, Burda, Dassault, Hersant, Lagardère, Maxwell, Murdoch, O'Reilly) or family firms (e.g. Agnelli, Aller, Berlusconi, Bonnier, De Benedetti, Fellner, Hersant, Holtzbrinck, Kirch, Mohn, Mondadori,

Springer), which oftentimes practiced political partisanism. It has been argued that many industrialists deliberately invested in the media to gain direct political influence or to fend off government intervention in other markets (Blumler, 1992; Mancini, 1999; Herman and Chomsky, 2002). An example of this is Lagardére in France who allegedly invested in the media to fend off nationalisation of a family-owned industry. Another view is that media groups were dependent on successive governments' decision-making to continue to be viable in media markets. However, as time progresses, shareholder-owned, rather than family-owned, companies are becoming more common place. This seems to lessen partisanism to one political party.

A small number of press groups have consolidated at national levels, due to processes of concentration over long periods of time (CEC, 1977, 1978). Before the 1980s, only Italy and the UK had some private sector competition in broadcasting markets. The majority of Member States granted the exclusive right to broadcast to one company or public entity. Most EU Member States had a state-owned public service broadcaster. This was initially permitted at that time under the EEC Treaty of Rome, as broadcasting was seen to be of non-economic public interest. As detailed in Chapter 2, the ECJ overturned the right to maintain a national public service monopoly in the 1970s in rulings in Italy and Greece. As markets were liberalised from the 1980s onwards, spectrum scarcity restricted competition to a small number of private broadcasters. In the 1990s, the digital broadcasting allowed for a greater number of channels, but access to these channels remained controlled by a handful of national gateway operators.

In most Member States, investment in private broadcasting in the 1980s came either from large press conglomerates, industrial 'national champions' or privatised utilities companies, most of which have been around for 100 years or longer and many of which have since grown into multinationals. For example, in Greece, Ireland and Italy, investment came from established industrial families. In France, investment came from privatised utilities companies, mostly water and public works companies. Investment in European cable and satellite markets largely came from established US corporations, such as AOL/Time Warner, Liberty, News Corporation, NTL, UPC and Viacom. Member States deliberately attracted US groups in order to encourage investment in new technology. There seemed to be some expectation that the US groups would come in, lay the lines, then leave. However, US groups, once established in markets rarely exit them, even in the face of considerable debt. They remain until eventually companies become profitable.

There has been a higher level of integration and co-operation between the largest European media groups since the 1985 SEA and 1989 TWF Directives, with a number of cross-national mergers and acquisitions, take-overs and joint ventures in both print and broadcasting markets

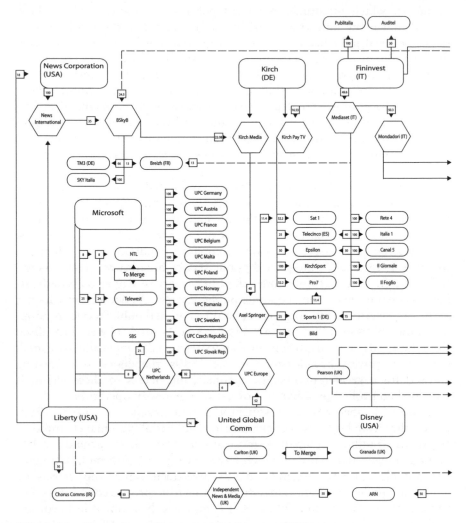

Figure 6.1   European media ownership, January 2003

(Figure 6.1). This co-operation has been strongly encouraged by the European institutions. Of the 50 largest European media companies (by turnover), 93 per cent are located in just seven Member States: France, Germany, Italy, Luxembourg, the Netherlands, Spain and the UK (Figure 6.2). This chapter will concentrate on these Member States. The chapter overviews national media markets in Europe, then examines pan-European co-operation. The conclusion provides observations about the outcomes of EU policy.

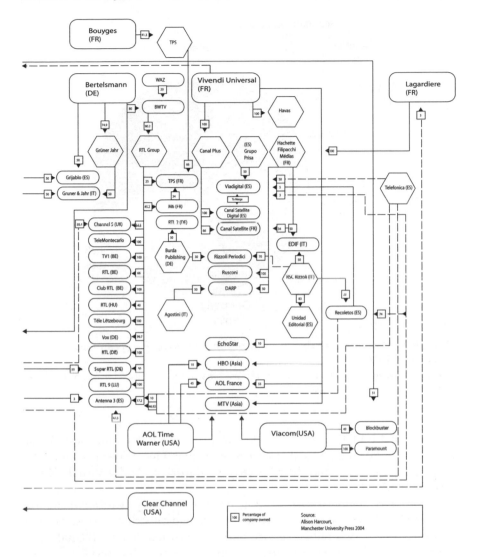

National media markets in Europe

France
France is home to a number of large European players with Lagardère and Havas in publishing and Bouygues and Vivendi in broadcasting. All of these firms have substantial international activities. It was estimated that by as early as 1988 Hachette (of the Lagardère group) derived 50 per cent of its turnover from international income (Bundgaard, 1990: 29). Havas[2] (of the Vivendi group) ranks amongst the top ten global communications groups (the only other European group in the top ten is Bertelsmann) with a

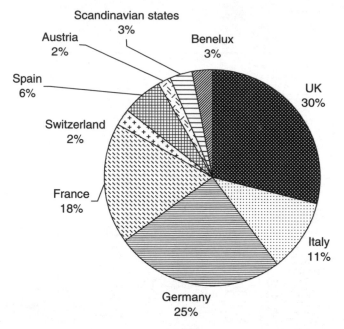

Figure 6.2   Breakdown of the turnover of the 50 leading European media companies, 2001

Source: European Audio-visual Observatory *Economy of the audiovisual industry* Yearbook (2002: 32).

turnover of 14.9 billion Euro in 2001 and is active in 91 countries. Of the world's top 50 audio-visual companies, Canal Plus (Vivendi) and TF1 (Bouygues) ranked 5 and 30 respectively (European Audio-Visual Observatory, 2002: 32).

France has demonstrated striking growth in the privatised television market since 1985. Up until this time, France had only three terrestrial television channels, two public service and one private channel (Canal Plus) (Kuhn, 1995). Following liberalisation in 1986, the public service channel TF1 was privatised (in 1987) and the issuing of licenses began for further private channels. Most investment came from privatised water and public works companies, particularly Bouygues, Générale des Eaux (renamed Vivendi in 1998) and Lyonnaise des Eaux (now Suez-Lyonnaise),[3] which increased their shares in media holdings overtime. For these companies, the greatest income is derived from French public sector contracts.[4] Further investment came from France's largest publishing group, Havas, which invested in Canal Plus, and TF1 before being merged into Vivendi.

In 2003, in France, there were four PSB stations, France 2, France 3, La 5éme and Arte; 3 commercial channels consisting of TF1 (Télévision

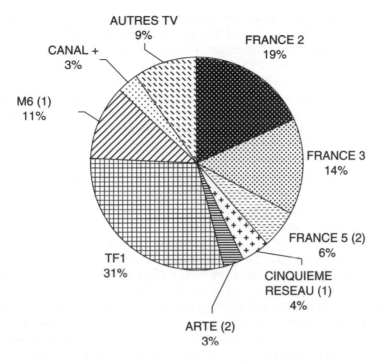

Figure 6.3 France's TV audience share by channel, 2002
Source: Médiamétrie 2002 www.mediametrie.fr.

Française 1), M6 and Canal Plus; 40 cable operators and three digital satellite services. The two commercial companies with the largest audience share
are TF1 and M6 (Figure 6.3). The former public service, TF1, is controlled
by the group Bouygues[5] which owned 41.3 per cent of the company in
December 2002 (TF1 Annual Report, 2002). M6 is controlled by Bertelsmann which held 45.2 per cent in 2003 (Bertelsmann Annual Report).[6] The
terrestrial channel La Cinq ran from 1986–1990 as a joint venture between
Berlusconi and the French publisher, Hersant (now Socpresse), but closed
due to financial losses. The pay-channel Canal Plus occupied La Cinq's terrestrial frequency in 1990 following the station's collapse (but continues to
run as a subscription channel). All television stations holding licences within
France are required to finance the French film industry by the national regulatory authority, the CSA. This is known as the as 'l'exception culturelle'.
The pay service Canal Plus was created under the Mitterand socialist government with the agreement that it would counterbalance the influence of
US content in France by financing the French film industry. Canal Plus
is required to spend 20 per cent of its French turnover on French film
production.

Canal Plus launched the first subscription satellite service in France in 1992 with CanalSatellite. Canal Plus later launched a digital satellite service in 1996, Canalsatellite Numérique. France's second digital satellite service Télévision par Satellite (TPS) was launched in December 1996. TPS was jointly owned by TF1 (66 per cent) and M6 (34 per cent) in December 2003 (TPS Annual Report). The French government did not impose a common technology standard for set top boxes. The European Commission was unsuccessful in convincing TPS to choose the same technology as Canal Plus for its set top boxes (Levy, 1999: 65–7). A smaller third digital satellite service (AB Sat) was started by AB Productions in March 1997. Canal Plus and AB Productions use the same set-top box technology and under the 'simulcrypt' agreement are able to offer each other's programme packages to their subscribers. This has rendered TPS less competitive and the group sunk into considerable debt as a result.

Due to diversification and Europeanisation, Canal Plus for a time became Europe's most successful private television operator. After its merger with the Dutch/South-African company NetHold in September 1996 it became, according to some, the 'largest television group in the world' (Dempsey, 1996). In 1998, it launched digital platforms in Belgium, Italy, the Netherlands, Poland, Spain and Scandinavia. In 2000, Canal Plus was fully acquired by Vivendi. In its search for content, Vivendi merged with the Canadian distillery group Seagram[7] in 2000, thereby acquiring the film production companies Universal and Polygram. Canal Plus also owned 24.5 per cent of BSkyB in the UK between 1999 and 2002.[8] Since this time, however, Vivendi/Universal has been downsizing its media assets due to huge losses.[9] Its March 2003 Annual Report showed a corporate debt of EUR 23.3 billion (the net debt was EUR 12.3 billion) and announced that it would divest 7 billion worth of assets in 2003. In an effort to compensate for its debt, Vivendi would sell off Havas Advertising and some other non-American assets to Lagardère SCA, for EUR 1.28 billion in 2003. The European Commission opened an investigation in July 2003. In September 2003, Vivendi's entertainment assets were acquired for USD 14 billion by the US media group NBC, which belongs to the US utilities group General Electric. The new group will be called NBC Universal.

All the large French multimedia groups have extensive international holdings. The largest global player is the industrial conglomerate Lagardère, which is active in the car, weapon, aerospace and telecommunications industries. In publishing, the group is active in most EU countries, including ownership of the Hachette publishing group (France), Rusconi Editore (Italy) and Filipacchi Presse (Spain). In broadcasting, Lagardère has a 34 per cent stake in CanalSatellite and holdings in the production company Multithématiques. In France, Hachette (founded as a publishing firm in 1826) and Matra were slowly acquired by Jean-Luc Lagardère (deceased in 2003), who was CEO of the telecommunications firm, Matra. In 1996

Hachette and Matra were fully absorbed by Lagardère, which has since been floated on the stock market — according to CIT, no one shareholder owns more than 5 per cent (2001).

The second largest group is Vivendi. Vivendi is no longer 'French' as such, as the majority of its stockholders are US citizens since it was listed on the New York exchange in 2000. Vivendi is a global leader in water, waste management, energy, and construction. In publishing, it is Europe's largest trade magazine publisher and educational publisher (Williams, 2002: 14). In broadcasting it owns Canal Plus and 10 per cent of EchoStar in the US. It continues to own the digital platforms Canalsatellite Numérique (France), Canal+ (the Netherlands) and holds shares in Canal Satélite Digital (Spain).[10] But sold off many stakes in other European platforms in an attempt to reduce media debt. These were Scandinavia (Canal+ Nordic and Canal Digital), Italy (Telep+), Poland (Canal+Polska), Belgium (Canal+ Vlaanderen and Canal+ Belgique) and Germany (Vox). The group hung on to its assets in content production: Universal Studios, Polygram Film International and Abbey Home Entertainment. The national regulatory body, the CSA, has taken exception to the fact that Vivendi is US-owned and vertically integrated with US content providers delivering US content to French viewers. It is concerned that Canal Plus may bypass the 'l'exception culturelle'. However, CanalSatellite is broadcast from the Luxembourg satellite Astra. Under TWF it could easily relocate its headquarters and broadcast to France, bypassing CSA requirements even if its licence is revoked nationally. When the CSA issued digital terrestrial television (DTT) licences in 2003, it granted a licence to Canal+ along with TF1 and M6.[11]

The groups Amaury and Socpresse had the largest share of the daily newspaper share in 2001 (CIT). However, the leading dailies (see Table 6.1), were *Ouest France* (a regional newspaper) and *Le Parisien*, which are owned by the Association pour la Défense des principes de la démocratie humaniste directed by François Régis Hutin. The second leading newspaper, *Le Monde*, is majority owned by the Society of the Editors of *Le Monde*, an association of employees. These newspapers tend to lie to the left of the political spectrum (Kuhn, 1995), whereas, newspapers owned by Socpresse and Lagardère[12] tend to lie to the right. The conservative national newspaper *Le Figaro* was owned by Robert Hersant from 1975 until his death in 1996.[13] The US Carlyle Group owned a minority share in *Le Figaro* Group from 1999 to 2002, when 100 per cent ownership passed to Socpresse. The Dassault family through Dassault Aviation SA bought a 30 per cent stake in Socpresse in 2001 (Earnest and Young, 2002). Dassault took a further 50 per cent from Hersant heirs in 2004, bringing the Dassault taking stake in Socpresse to 82 per cent. Remaining shareholders are the heir Aude Hersant (13 per cent) and the head of Socpresse Yues Chaisemartin (5 per cent).

Table 6.1 French newspaper market, 2001

Title	Daily circulation	Ownership
National dailies		
Le Parisien	481,000	Groupe Amaury
Le Monde	399,000	Society of the Editors
L'Equipe	393,000	Groupe Amaury
Le Figaro	363,000	Hersant Press Group
Libération	173,000	Pathe
France Soir	163,000	Hersant Press Group
Regional dailies		
Ouest France	783,000	Francoise Hutin
Sud Ouest	345,000	Hersant Press Group
La Voix du Nord	331,000	Hersant Press Group (through Rossel)
Nice Matin	276,000	Lagardère

Source: CIT publications (2001).

Germany

Germany represents the largest media market in Europe. Similar to France, the market is highly concentrated with a high degree of cross-media ownership and co-operation between the major groups. Germany is home to three of Europe's largest publishing companies: Bertelsmann, Bauer and Springer. The three hold dominant positions in the national market for daily newspapers (Springer) and magazines (Bertelsmann and Bauer) (Röper, 2002) (see Table 6.2). Axel Springer Group holds 23.7 per cent of the daily newspaper market, the Westdeutsche Allgemeine Zeitung (WAZ) Group 5.9 per cent, Verlagsgruppe Stuttgarter Zeitung 5 per cent, and Gruner + Jahr,[14] 3.4 per cent (Kleinsteuber and Thomaß, 2002). Kleinsteuber and Thomaß indicate a fair degree of political partisanism in Germany with 'most of the large media conglomerates (Kirch, Springer, Bauer, Burda) tend(ing) towards the CDU, the Bertelsmann company acts in close association with the SPD'. This can be inferred to some extent. Bertelsmann is headquartered in North Rhine-Westphalia where the SPD has been in power for 40 years. Kirch headquarters are located in Munich and Kirch is close to the conservative Bavarian government from which it has received financial support in the form of loans through the state bank. However, the German press have not engaged in political partisanism to the same degree as press groups in other EU Member States (notably the UK).

All major German media groups have invested in broadcasting and have substantial interests abroad. The publishing groups Bertelsmann, Axel Springer, Bauer, Holtzbrink and WAZ have television and radio interests both nationally and internationally (particularly in the emerging markets of Central and Eastern Europe). The smaller publisher Burda also holds

Table 6.2   German newspaper market, 1999

Title	Daily circulation	Ownership
National dailies		
Bild	4,484,000	Springer
Die Zeit	445,000	Holtzbrink
Süddeutsche Zeitung	430,000	Süddeutscher Verlag
Frankfurter Allgemeine	405,000	Frankfurter Allgemeine
Die Welt	257,000	Springer
Handelsblatt	161,000	Handelsblatt
Regional dailies		
CAN, Düsseldorf	1,432,000	Rheinische Post
ZTG-G-WAZ	1,085,000	Zeitungsgruppe WAZ
Hannoversche Allgemeine	623,000	Madsack Daily
Wirako, Hamburg	576,000	Lübeck Nachrichten
Stuttgarter Zeitung	526,000	Stuttgarter Zeitung

Source: CIT publications (2002).

shares in RTL-Plus (Bertelsmann), Springer and Antenne Bayern radio station. Bertelsmann is by far the largest company with a turnover of EUR 18.9 billion in 2002 (Bertelsmann Annual Report). The company is represented in the world's top ten multi-media firms (Zenith, 2002).

In television, Germany has six public service channels, and six private terrestrial channels. Satellite subscription is low in Germany due to high cable penetration. Germany is Europe's largest cable market. Krebber points out that this was due to 'an ambitious cable television infrastructure project' supported by the Kohl government, which led Germany to the highest number of cable connections in Europe (2001: 17). Hence, state action has been more effective in realising cable reach than market solutions (as in the UK). The project was executed by the state-owned company Deutsche Telekom, which dominated ownership in the cable market until the European Commission pressured for the sale of its cable networks. The 1999 Cable Ownership Directive required that cable networks be declared separate legal entities. The US Liberty Group proposed to buy Deutsche Telekom's remaining six (debt-ridden) regional networks in 2001 but this was blocked by the German Federal Cartel Office.[15]

According to audience share, the three leading commercial terrestrial channels are RTL, SAT1 and PRO7 (Figure 6.4). Controlling interests in the majority of commercial channels have until the present day been held either by the Kirch Group or by Bertelsmann (for detail see Humphreys, 1997; Röper, 2002). According to German law, only publicly traded companies need to disclose their accounts. Transparency has therefore been low in the family-owned Kirch group. But this changed with Kirch liquidation.

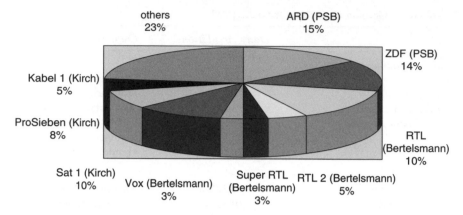

others
23%

ARD (PSB)
15%

ZDF (PSB)
14%

Kabel 1 (Kirch)
5%

ProSieben (Kirch)
8%

RTL
(Bertelsmann)
10%

Sat 1 (Kirch)
10%

Vox (Bertelsmann)
3%

Super RTL
(Bertelsmann)
3%

RTL 2 (Bertelsmann)
5%

Figure 6.4   Germany's television audience share by channel, 2000
Source: CIT 2001.

The public service channels ARD-1 and ZDF became the first German channels to broadcast in digital in December 1995. They began transmission via satellite in May 1997. RTL, Sat-1, Pro 7, Vox and most commercial channels are now digitally broadcast. In July 1996, the Kirch Group launched the DF1 digital satellite service. At the end of 1996, despite much higher estimates, subscribers to the service only numbered 30,000 and the Group was predicted to suffer huge losses until at least the year 2004 (Lang, 1997b). In February 1997, the pay-channel Premiere (which was owned at the time by Bertelsmann, Canal Plus and Kirch) started to use digital decoders and launched a new service, Premiere Digital with four pay-per-view services. This formed the basis for a joint venture between Premiere and DF1 with the collaboration of Deutsche Telecom for a digital service. As detailed in Chapter 3, the joint venture was blocked by the European Commission despite support from the German CDU government. Kirch subsequently acquired Premiere in 1999 to form 'Premiere World'.[16]

The Kirch Group was family owned. Until 1999, it was 100 per cent owned by Leo Kirch and his son Thomas after which other partners (Berlusconi, Murdoch and Prince Al Waleed) took shares. The Group was reorganised into KirchMedia and KirchPayTV in 1999. KirchMedia owned the national channels Kabel 1, Deutsches SportFernsehen (DSF) and N24. It also held 52.52 per cent of ProSiebenSat1 (which owns the channels Sat1 and ProSieben) (CIT, 2001). ProSiebenSat1 was floated on the stock market in 2000.[17] The Kirch PayTV branch housed the digital satellite service, Premiere World. As predicted, Premiere World consistently lost money until KirchPayTV filed for insolvency in August 2002. Kirch owed EUR 1.4 billion to its bank creditors and EUR 500 million to its US content providers, Paramount, Warner Bros and Disney. BSkyB was seeking the conditional return of its 22.03 per cent equity interest in KirchPayTV in 2003. Kirch's chief creditor was the state bank of the Bavaria, Bayern LB, which is headed by Edmund Stoiber, who is Bavaria's Minister and Chairman of the Christian Social Union (CSU) party. It is estimated that the State of Bavaria risked a loss of EUR 2.3 billion due to the financial collapse of the Kirch Group (Hooper, Cassy and Milner, 2002). In August 2003, ProSiebenSat1, Germany's biggest broadcaster, was sold to the US media owner Haim Saban for GBP 915m.

By contrast, Germany's largest group Bertelsmann is thriving. Its core business was once book publishing, but now television (in particular CLT/Ufa) has become more important in terms of turnover and profits in recent years. It was founded in 1835 as a printing company of religious books and has been active in the US book market since 1901. In 1977, Johannes Mohn, who had inherited the company in 1887, established the Bertelsmann Foundation. In 2003, Bertelsmann AG was owned 57 per cent by the Bertelsmann Foundation, 17.3 per cent by the Mohn family and 25.1 per cent by the Groupe Bruxelles Lambert S.A. (GBL) (Bertelsmann, 2003 Annual Report). GBL acquired its shares in 2001 in exchange for Bertelsmann's acquisition of GBL's shares in the RTL Group. In May 2001 the European Union approved the acquisition. From this time onwards, Bertelsmann was listed on the stock exchange.

In broadcasting, Bertelsmann owned 67 per cent of the RTL Group in 2002. RTL comprises of the Luxembourg television group Compagnie Luxembourgeoise de Télédiffusion (CLT) and the television arm of the UK group Pearson. CLT owns 24 television channels and 18 radio stations in ten European countries and is the largest global content distribution company outside the US. It is active in 35 countries. Through RTL, Bertelsmann controls the German broadcasting channels, RTL, RTL-2 (34.5 per cent), SUPER RTL (50 per cent with Disney), VOX and RTL Radio. In publishing, Bertelsmann owned the Gruner Jahr Verlag. Through Gruner Jahr, Bertelsmann owns a number of daily newspapers in Germany and Central Europe, but the company policy is presently to retreat from newspaper markets and concentrate on magazines. Bertelsmann also owned 86.5 per cent of the Springer Verlag (a publishing group unrelated to the Axel Springer group) until selling it off in 2003.

Italy
Compared with other Member States, Italy does not have a highly concentrated press market, but the private company, Mediaset, and the public broadcaster, RAI, dominate the broadcasting market.

Italian newspaper readership has been one of the lowest in Europe (Satori, 1996). For this reason, publishing in Italy was unprofitable and receiving state aid until 1989. A financial crisis in the newspaper publishing market in the 1970s, led to market entry by large family-owned industrial groups (Satori 1996: 137). Prominent industrialist families entering the publishing sector during this time included: Agnelli (Fiat), Berlusconi (construction), De Benedetti (Olivetti computers), Caltagirone (construction), De Agostini, Feruzzi (chemicals, sugar, agricultural products), and Monti (oil). In 2003, the newspapers with the largest national circulation were owned by the family groups: Agnelli,[18] De Benedetti,[19] Berlusconi,[20] Monti-Riffeser,[21] and Rusconi.[22] The newspapers holding the largest market share are owned by Agnelli and Rusconi (Tables 6.3 and 6.4). As stated, com-

Table 6.3   Market share of the five major Italian press companies, 1998

Press company	Market share (million Lira)	Number and types of newspapers and periodicals	Major shareholders of the press company
R.C.S. Editori S.p.A	2,554	2 dailies, 23 periodicals	Gemina (100%) (Agnelli)
A. Mondadori Ed. S.p.A.	2,152	more than 40 periodicals	S. Berlusconi Holding Ed. S.p.A (47%)
L'Espresso Group	1,119	14 dailies and periodicals	CIR S.p.A. (60%) (De Benedetti)
Sole 24 Ore	476	1 daily	Confindustria (100%)
Rusconi Ed.	293	more than 20 periodicals	Rusconi family (100%)

Source: Council of Europe, Committee of Experts on Media Concentrations and Pluralism (1998).

Table 6.4   Italian newspaper market, 2001

Title	Daily circulation (000s)	Ownership
National dailies		
Il Corriere della Sera	620,000	Rizzoli
La Repubblica	562,000	L'Espresso Group
Il Sole 24 Ore	388,000	Confedindustria
La Gazzetta dello Sport	380,000	Rizzoli
La Stampa	355,000	Rizzoli
Il Messaggero	286,000	L'Espresso Group
Corriere Sport+Stadio	264,000	Rizzoli
Il Giornale	220,000	Berlusconi
Il Resto del Carlino	185,000	Monrif Group
La Nazione	151,000	Monrif Group

Source: CIT publications (2001).

pared with other European States the Italian newspaper market is not highly concentrated. However, there is significant co-operation between some of the family groups. For example, Carlo de Benedetti acted as chief executive of Agnelli's car company FIAT in 1976 and chief executive of Olivetti in 1978. The newspaper *La Republicca* was founded in 1976 as joint venture between Benedetti and Mondadori. An OECD study shows that corporate culture within these companies is hierarchical with a vertical chain of control from the principle owner[23] (Goldstein and Nicoletti, 1995).

Cross-media ownership is not common in Italy with different groups operating in press and broadcasting markets, but there are some exceptions. The industrialist Francesco Gaetano Caltagirone has southern broadcasting as well as publishing interests. Paolo Berlusconi (the brother of Prime Minister Silvio Berlusconi) owns the Milanese newspaper *Il Giornale*, but other publishers have not retained their presence in broadcasting. Rusconi sold Italia 1 to Fininvest in 1982. In the same year, the Mondadori publishing group sold Rete 4 to Fininvest.

Of the adult Italian population 82 per cent depend only on television for news, which represents the highest percentage in Europe (Norris, 2000). Italian television is dominated by the company Mediaset, which is controlled by the Berlusconi family. As in Germany, privately owned groups are not required to publicise accounts in Italy, so transparency of the Berlusconi family-owned Fininvest holding company is low. It is estimated that the Berlusconi family owns around 96 per cent of Fininvest.[24] In 2002, Fininvest owned 48.6 per cent of Mediaset, 30 per cent of Auditel,[25] 100 per cent of the advertising group, Publitalia,[26] 19 per cent of the telecommunications group Albacom, 100 per cent of the production company Mediadigit, 100 per cent of the film company Medusa, 100 per cent the football club A.C. Milan, 51 per cent of home video chain Blockbuster (with Viacom) and 50.3 per cent of Italy's largest publishing company, Mondadori, which is managed by Berlusconi's daughter, Marina Berlusconi (Williams, 2002). Fininvest's broadcasting division ran up heavy debts (circa USD 2 billion) in the 1990s but is now profitable. Silvio Berlusconi was elected Prime Minister in 2001. His clear conflict of interest, as head of the state with a major share in national television operators and control of PSB board appointments, has been criticised at national and international levels. Notably, the President of the Italian Republic, Carlo Azeglio Ciampi,[27] has publicly criticised the situation as damaging for media pluralism and democracy. The legitimacy of Fininvest's financial history has also been called into question.[28]

In 1992, 'Mani Pulite' (Operation Clean Hands) led by a group of magistrates in Milan began to expose the extent of corruption by bringing over 2,000 business and political leaders to trial. The magistrates claimed that Italy's political parties were being illegally financed by industry. This was dubbed 'Tangentopoli', or 'Bribesville', by the Italian press. The trials broke the ruling power of the Christian Democratic Party and weakened its rival, the Socialist party, creating a window of opportunity for a third political party, Berlusconi's Forza Italia which proclaimed itself as a fresh political face which supported the clean-up operation. However, in 1994, magistrates began to investigate Berlusconi's links with the former Prime Minister Bettino Craxi. Pension reform led to the collapse of the Berlusconi government in 1994.[29] When Berlusconi was re-elected in 2001 one of the cases was still pending.[30] A mounting number of cases have since been accumulating against Berlusconi in Milan. In June 2003, the Italian parliament voted to pass an immunity law, protecting Berlusconi from prosecution during his term in political office. In January 2004, Italy's Constitutional Court overruled Prime Minister Silvio Berlusconi's immunity from prosecution. The trial is to begin on 16 April 2004.

The Italian television market saw substantial concentration in the 1980s when Fininvest bought the failing Rete Quattro channel from the publishing group Rizzoli and acquired Italia 1 from Mondadori. Fininvest at that time already owned the channels Canale 5, Telepiù 1, Telepiù 2 and Telepiù 3. By December 1994, Fininvest's channels had reached an audience share of over 40 per cent prompting the Italian Constitutional Court to declare that the ownership limit be set to 20 per cent of national channels by the end of August 1996. Berlusconi's government (lasting eight months in 1994–95) instead suggested the privatisation of RAI to provide private competition to Fininvest and thereby diluting the ownership requirements (this initiative did not succeed). Fininvest eventually sold Telepiù in 1996[31] and Fininvest floated its remaining broadcasting interests by establishing Mediaset (initially 20 per cent of stock was sold).[32] In this way, Fininvest adhered to Italian media ownership rules introduced in 1990 (25 per cent of national channels), but not those mandated by the national Court (20 per cent), which were never introduced in Italy (as detailed in Chapter 7). The Prodi government was unable to come to an agreement on the Court's decree (Lane, 1997). Prodi was also unable to gain parliament consensus on a 'conflict of interest' law while in government which would have prevented media owners from holding political office. In 2002, the Italian Constitutional Court ruled that Rete 4 cease analogue broadcasting by December 2003. However, in January 2004, the Italian government pushed through a decree to prevent Rete 4 from being moved to satellite. President Carlo Azeglio Ciampi ordered the decree to be reconsidered by parliament. What is clear is that Mediaset is not selling off any of its channels.

In 2002, Italy had three public television channels (RAIuno, RAIdue and RAItre), 11 terrestrial commercial channels (Retequattro, Canale 5, Italia 1, Europa 7, Telemarket, Rete Mia, Italia 9, Cinquestelle, TV Italia, TMC1 and TMC2) and three satellite channels (Telepiù Nero, Bianco, Grigio and Calcio). Mediaset (controlled by the Berlusconi family) owns Retequattro,

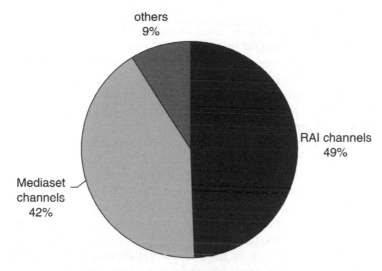

Figure 6.5 Italy's television audience share by company, 2000
Source: Auditel (2000). Statistics can be downloaded from www.auditel.it or received through the Communications Regulatory Authority (Agcom).

Canale 5 and Italia 1. Telepiù was bought by Rupert Murdoch's News Corporation in 2003. Telemontecarlo (which ran the channels TMC1 and Videomusic)[33] is now owned by SEAT (controlled by Telecom Italia). Cecchi Gori Communications sold off Telemontecarlo to gain a terrestrial licence from the Authority of Communications (to meet requirements of the 1997 Maccanico Law). SEAT used the frequencies to establish two new national channels: La7 and MTV Italia. Of the commercial companies, Mediaset channels have by far the largest audience share at 42 per cent of national viewing in 2000 (Figure 6.5). Mediaset and the public service channels together accounted for 91 per cent of audience share. This is surely having an effect on content as broadcasters compete for the widest possible audiences during prime time hours with little reserve on content. Higher-quality programming is pushed to later hours or reserved for radio broadcast.

The first Italian digital satellite service was offered by Orbit Satellite Television and Radio Network in 1996.[34] Telepiù began satellite broadcasting in March 1996 and broadcast digital from 1999. A third service, Stream, which has been providing a video-on-line service since 1995, went digital in 2000. Stream was slowly acquired by News Corporation with the European Commission approving both acquisitions in 2000 and 2003.[35] News Corporation merged Telepiù and Stream in 2003 to form Sky Italia, which is 80.1 per cent owned by News Corporation and 19.9 per cent owned by Telecom Italia.

Luxembourg

Compagnie Luxembourgoise de Telediffusion (CLT) and Européen des Satellites (SES) are the two largest media players seated in Luxembourg. CLT is
a large multi-national company, which has been controlled by Bertelsmann
since it was merged with the Bertelsmann subsidiary, Ufa, 1997.[36] It also
owns a number of production companies in Germany, the UK and the USA.
In 1997, CLT was merged with the Bertelsmann subsidiary, Ufa to create
Europe's second largest television company after the Canal Plus/NetHold
merger (*Frankfurter Allgemeine Zeitung*, 10 November 1996; *Financial
Times*, 6 November 1996; Lindermann, 1996). Its film distribution
company, CLT-UFA International, is a global competitor. In publishing, CLT
has holdings in France and Spain (where it owns 100 per cent of Telestar).

Although small, Luxembourg was allocated the same number of satellite frequencies as the rest of Europe. Whereas other Member States granted
frequencies to their PSBs, the Luxembourg government granted its allocation of satellite frequencies to the Astra satellite company in 1983 with
which SES, Europe's first partly privately owned satellite television system,
was created (the government still owned 16.7 per cent in 2003).[37] As the
1989 TWF Directive stipulates a broadcaster can only be regulated by the
country of origin and not by the country of reception, many companies
were able to circumvent national media regulations by transmitting from
the Astra satellite. A number of companies established themselves in
Luxembourg to broadcast to other Member States (some to avoid national
legislations, some simply due to domestic spectrum scarcity).

Indeed, *Astra* has proved the most popular satellite for European broadcasters, hosting both analogue and digital channels, which broadcast to
markets in almost all EU Member States, and an increasing number of
non-EU states. Chalaby notes that Astra hosts over 1,000 television and
radio channels to 87 million European households (2002: 7). Significantly,
the large national players in France (Canalsatellite), Germany (DF1), the
Netherlands (NetHold), Spain (Sogecable) and the UK (BSkyB) chose to
launch satellite platforms from Luxembourg. Astra hosted digital platforms
for Canal Plus in the French, Polish, Spanish and Dutch markets and provided further capacity for Kirch, ARD, ZDF and ORF-SRG. NetHold
(which is based in Amsterdam) transmits PayCo and FilmNet channels to
much of northern Europe (e.g. FilmNet broadcasts to Belgium, the Netherlands, Denmark, Norway, Sweden and Finland). In addition, a number of
single stations are now hosted on *Astra*, which broadcasts to most of
Europe. Including much broadcast content which would be otherwise
strictly regulated at national levels (e.g. chat-show channels, music channels, religious stations, fashion channels, regional channels and 'adult film'
channels). Hence, the broadcasting sector became very important for the
Luxembourg economy and the biggest tax contributor from 1997
onwards.[38] For this reason, Luxembourg has taken great interest in

European media policy. It was the Luxembourg Commissioner Jacques Santer, acting in his capacity as EC president, who blocked the media ownership Directive in 1997. Luxembourg attained the post of EC Commissioner for DG Education and Culture in 1999, which houses the media policy portfolio, of which Luxembourg Commissioner Vivien Reding is now in charge.

The Netherlands

The Dutch national market has provided the European market with a number of large media companies with NetHold (Network Holdings), Polygram, Reed Elsevier, PCM Uitgevers, Philips,[39] Wolters Kluwer and VNU (Grisold, 1996). Most of these companies have extensive international interests. NetHold was acquired by Canal Plus (Vivendi) in September 1996.[40] The film production and music company, Polygram, which ranked ninth amongst the world's leading audio-visual companies in 1996 (European Audio-Visual Observatory, 1997: 55) is also owned by Vivendi.[41]

The Dutch newspaper market is highly concentrated with PCM Uitgevers dominating ownership in national dailies and Wegener dominating the regional press market.[42] The reason why the leading Dutch publishers, Reed Elsevier, Wolters Kluwer, VNU and HMG, abandoned the domestic market for overseas markets was that the Dutch market represented only a fraction of their operations. Reed Elsevier[43] sold off the dailies 'NRC-Handelsblad' and 'Algemeen Dagblad', to PCM Uitgevers in 1997. VNU, which formerly owned stakes in both press and broadcasting markets, sold off its broadcasters VTM (Netherlands) and HMG (Belgium) in 1998, its Dutch regional newspapers[44] (to Wegener) in 1999 and the remaining newspapers in 2000 (see Table 6.5).

The Netherlands has eight public television stations, three national (Ned-1, TV 2, Ned-3) and five regional (represented by NOS). The main commercial channels are RTL 4, RTL 5, Veronica, SBS 6, Net 5, Fox 8 and the Music Factory. The Bertelsmann-owned RTL channels had the highest share of audience at 21 per cent in 1999 (Figure 6.6). The greatest radio share goes to the PSB station (c. 40 per cent) and News Corporation's Sky Radio (15 per cent).

As in Germany, cable reach is high in the Netherlands. This is because the incumbent telecommunications company (Royal PTT Netherlands) laid most of the lines. It has since sold off its main cable networks to comply with the 1999 Cable Ownership Directive. Most were bought mainly by foreign companies. Of the 50 cable operators in 2002 the US group Liberty (through UPC) owned by far the largest number. Canal+ Netherlands presently represents the only digital satellite platform in the Netherlands, which is to be sold, as it is suffering from heavy debt. A new digital terrestrial service Digitenne was launched in 2003, backed by KPN, Nozema, NOB, SBS and Canal+. This consortia approach of all the Member States'

Table 6.5   Dutch newspaper market, 2002

Title	Daily circulation (000s)	Ownership
National dailies		
De Telegraaf	796,000	De Telegraaf
Algemeen Dagblad	358,000	PCM Uitgevers
De Volkskrant	346,000	PCM Uitgevers
NRC Handelsblad	274,000	PCM Uitgevers
Trouw	125,000	PCM Uitgevers
Het Financieele Dagblad	64,000	Het Financieele Dagblad
Regional dailies		
Hazewinkel Pers	185,000	Hazewinkel Pers
Dagblad De Limbruger	174,000	De Telegraaf
De Gedlderlander	164,000	Wegener
Brabants Dagblad	159,000	Wegener
Nordhollands Dagblad	156,000	Wegener
BN/e Stern	146,000	Wegener
De Twentsche Courant Tubantia	138,000	Wegener
Eindhovens Dagblad	125,000	Wegener
Haagsche Courant	117,000	Wegener
Rotterdams Dagblad	102,000	Rotterdams Dagblad

Source: CIT publications (2001).

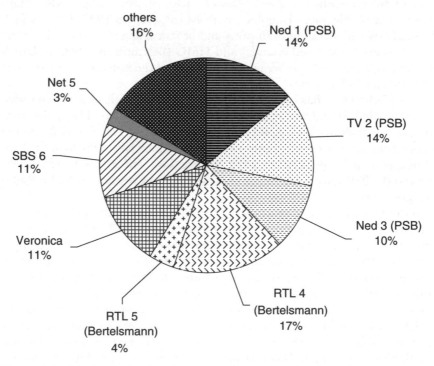

Figure 6.6   The Netherland's television audience share by channel, 1999
Source: CIP Publications 2001.

main players has been recently been lauded by the European Council within the eEurope initiative. As a smaller Member State, the Netherlands in particular has argued for the importance of maintaining pluralism through public service broadcasting. Smaller markets are at risk of higher concentration (Austria, Slovenia, Belgium have also stressed this importance) and the neglect of minority interests in the media.

Spain

There are not many large European operators originating in Spain, but the market is interesting for its quick embrace of digital technology and the rapid development of the Spanish digital satellite market. Ownership within media groups is comparatively diverse, due to stringent ownership laws. However, cross-media ownership is high with investment in broadcasting coming from established publishing groups and the incumbent telecommunications operator, Telefónica. The Spanish national market has also seen a high level of infiltration by well-established European groups, namely: Bauer, Havas, Hachette, Canal Plus, CLT, Fininvest, News Corporation, Pearson, Kirch, Bertelsmann and Springer and VNU. Sanchez-Tabernero claims this is due to the commercial weakness of Spanish media groups (1993: 97). Vilches (1996) attributes this rather to the dual requirement upon the Spanish media to rapidly adapt to both the new Spanish democracy and the impact of the single European market.

The largest Spanish group is Grupo Prisa, which has both publishing and broadcasting interests. It is also the only Spanish media group with substantial foreign holdings. Prisa publishes a number of daily newspapers, including the leading dailies, *El Pais* and *Cinco Dias* (in Barcelona), and magazines. It runs 395 radio stations (through its 80 per cent stake in Radiofónicos Union Radio) comprising of 80 per cent of the market (Williams, 2002). In 2002, it held shares in Sogecable together with Vivendi, and in Vía Digital together with Telefónica and Recoletos.

The second largest publishing group is Grupo Recoletos owned by the British group Pearson and the Italian group RSC (MUDIA, 2002). Recoletos publishes the second leading daily Marca (a sport newspaper) in addition to *El Mundo*, *Expansión* (in Madrid) and *Diario Médico* (through its subsidiary in Unidad Editorial SA (known as Unedisa)). In broadcasting, Recoletos has shares in Antena 3 (together with Telefónica) and the digital pay-TV platform Vía Digital (together with Telefónica and Prisa) and in radio, Radio Marca Digital and Radio Marca Madrid. The third largest publishing group is Grupo Correo, which owns a stake in Telecinco (together with Berlusconi and Kirch) and a number of local channels.[45] Telecinco in turn owns the production companies Atlas and Estudios Picasso and the advertising companies Advanced Media and Publimedia Gestión (see Table 6.6).

Radio audience is high in Spain compared with other EU Member States. Five national networks exist: three private, one public and one owned by

Table 6.6   Spanish newspaper market, 2001

Title	Daily circulation	Ownership
National dailies		
El Pais	435,000	Prisa
Marca	397,000	Recoletos
ABC	293,000	Prensa Espa ola
El Mundo del Siglo XXI	285,000	Recoletos
Regional dailies		
La Vanguardia	205,000	La Vanguardia
El Periodico de Catalu a	195,000	Grupo Zeta
El Correo Espa ol	132,000	Grupo Correo
La Voz de Galicia	109,000	Grupo Voz
Sport	113,000	Grupo Zeta

Source: CIT publications (2001).

the church. The public service is provided by the company RTVE. Two private networks, SER, Antena 3, are both controlled by PRISA. The third private station Onda Cero was actually considered a private company but was owned by the government company, Organización de Ciegos de España (ONCE) until recently bought by the privatised telecommunications group, Telefónica. Apart from Onda Cero, ONCE had interests in the commercial channel Telecinco and several newspapers. ONCE has been criticised for its private activities (Vilches, 1996: 191). The fourth national radio network is Candena de Ondas Populares de Espana (COPE). COPE is owned and operated by the Catholic Church. To balance concentration of ownership in national Spanish radio networks, local and regional radio flourishes in Spain. Many stations are unlicensed. The publishing groups Grupo Timon and the television group Antena 3 have regional radio holdings.

   Private television did not exist in Spain until January 1990, although the public service was provided by the private company RTVE (private radio was established in 1924) (de Mateo, 1997).[46] Up until 1983, RTVE was funded publicly, now over 95 per cent of its funding is derived from advertising. There are now two national public television channels in Spain TVE-1 and TVE 2 and eight regional. Private stations consist of three terrestrial stations, Antena 3,[47] Telecinco,[48] and Canal+ Espana (owned by Canal Plus). There are 15 regional stations, 650 local stations, 42 cable franchises (delivered through two cable operators) and three satellite platforms. The commercial stations with the greatest share of audience are Antena 3 and Telecinco (Figure 6.7). Antena 3 was purchased by the telecommunications group Telefónica until an enquiry by the European Commission prompted divestment.

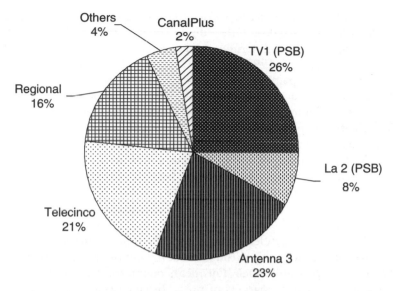

Figure 6.7 Spain's television audience share by channel, 1999
Source: CIT, 2001.

Canal Plus España (whose main investors were Canal+ France and Prisa) was the first to offer terrestrial pay-TV in Spain in 1990. In 1996, Telefónica de España and Canal + España, announced a new joint venture, Cablevisión, to create a platform of digital pay-TV via cable systems. As Chapter 3 detailed, the Commission blocked the acquisition,[49] ensuring that two platforms were established at the national level. Sogecable, through its subsidiary Canal Satélite Digital was the first to go digital in January 1997. Vía Digital launched its satellite service in September 1997. The government wanted to force both players to use the same set top box technology. However, the EU blocked this compelling market players to compete with different technologies.

The two platforms merged into Digital+ in 2003. This means that, since September 2003, there is only one digital satellite platform in Spain. Both Canal Satélite Digital (CSD) and Vía Digital encountered heavy losses. Telefónica and Sogecable announced the merger of the two pay-TV services (Vía Digital and Canal Satélite Digital respectively) in mid 2002 into Sogecable.[50] The conditions of the merger are that Telefónica pay the debt of Vía Digital and purchase 20 per cent of Sogecable's shares. The management of Sogecable is controlled by PRISA group (20 per cent of the Sogecable shares). Groupe Canal + (France) has 16 per cent of Sogecable and 30 per cent are floating on the stock market. Warner Bros has taken 10 per cent share.

A third digital pay service, Quiero, established by a terrestrial network in 1998, collapsed in 2002. Other digital players include the main cable providers, Spaincom and Grupo Auna. Spaincom owns ONO, which started cable services in 1995 (then as Cableuropa). Telefónica owns cable licences in each of Spain's 42 regions (each region issues two licences). In addition, there are dozens of local cable companies in Spain, many yet unregistered. Télefonica, rather than continuing its development of the cable networks, is presently developing the ADSL network and it is planning to offer broadcasting services via the ADSL network rather than via cable. The fact that the incumbent telecommunications operator is laying the lines most likely means that Spain will become one of the more advanced countries in Europe in terms of broadband reach.

The United Kingdom
The UK for a long time differed from continental media markets as it maintained diversity in ownership through strict regulation, particularly in cross-media ownership. Unlike their European counterparts, UK groups have operated in the separate markets of press, broadcasting and telecommunications. Media tends to be the core activity of UK groups, rather than investment coming from industrial champions, as in other Member States. These factors have meant that home-grown companies are smaller in size than European companies in both press and broadcasting. However, few restrictions on foreign ownership meant entrance to the UK market by a number of large US groups in publishing and cable and satellite markets (NTL, TeleWest and News Corporation). Rapid concentration within national press and broadcasting markets (both terrestrial and cable) has occurred since the 1996 Broadcasting Act.

As in Germany, daily newspaper readership is high in the UK at around 60 per cent of the population, largely due to the presence of tabloids, price competition and freesheets (Gustafsson and Weibull, 1997). There are ten national newspapers, which practice a high degree of political partisanism. The largest four companies account for 83 per cent of sales (News International, the Trinity Mirror Group, Northern and Shell, and Daily Mail and General Trust) (Figure 6.8). Individual and family owners have long dominated the British press market (Koss, 1984; Curran and Seaton, 1997). Share ownership is more common today, but further individual owners entered the national market during its slump in the 1980s (Sparks, 1995). These were the (mostly foreign) businessmen Murdoch (Australian) buying *The Times* and *Sunday Times* in 1981, Robert Maxwell (Australian) buying the Mirror Group in 1984, Conrad Black (Canadian) buying the *Daily Telegraph* in 1994 (through Hollinger International, which also owns the *Chicago Sun-Times* and the *Jerusalem Post*).[51]

The company with the largest national newspaper circulation has for a number of years been News International, controlled by Rupert Murdoch's

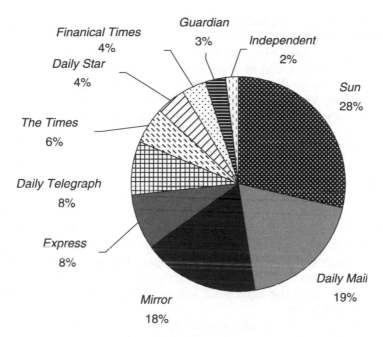

Figure 6.8 Percentage of UK newspaper circulation, 2000
Source: Audit Bureau of Circulations (year ending December 2000). Statistics from the Audit Bureau of Circulations Statisties can be downloaded at www.abc.org.uk.

News Corporation, which publishes *The Times, The Sunday Times, Sun* and *News of the World*. The company's national share of newspaper circulation has been relatively stable at around 35 per cent (36.8 per cent in 1995 and 34 per cent in 2000 according to CIT) with the *Sun* holding the highest circulation with around 4 million copies sold daily. News International also owns the magazine with the greatest national circulation *Sky Customer Magazine* (Bromley, 2001).

The company with the third greatest share of the national newspaper market is the Trinity Mirror Group. Nationally, it publishes the *Mirror* newspaper, but its greatest market share is in the regional market where it owned 278 newspapers in 2002 (Annual Report).[52] Following the death of Maxwell in 1991 and the disentanglement of assets from offshore holdings, the Mirror group was floated on the stock exchange. In 1996, United News and Media merged with MAI, forming United MAI. The chairman of United was Lord Stevens and the managing director of MAI was Lord Hollick. United MAI increased its market share by acquiring Midland Independent Newspapers in 1997 and merging with Trinity in 1999. As a condition of merger, United News & Media was required to divest its Express Group of newspapers. In 2000, Richard Desmond's publishing company, Northern & Shell, bought the Express newspapers from United News &

Media, acquiring therewith the newspapers the *Daily Express, Sunday Express* and *Daily Star.*[53]

In 2002, the Daily Mail and General Trust group printed the national daily the *Daily Mail*, the *Mail on Sunday* and the *London Evening Standard*, plus 17 regional papers and 27 regional free newspapers. The group was owned by Vere Harmsworth (third Viscount Rothermere since 1978) until his death in 1998. His heir, Jonathon Harmsworth (fourth Viscount Rothermere) now has a controlling share in DMGT. The *Daily Mail* supported Prime Minister Thatcher during the 1980s, and continued to support the Conservative Party in the 1990s. Following the 1997 UK elections, political allegiance has been less pronounced. DMGT's greatest newspaper acquisition occurred in 1994, when it bought T. Bailey Forman's regional and local newspapers (e.g. *Nottingham Evening Post*). DMGT acquired Pathe's film archive in 2003, which is operating together with ITN. According to the *Daily Mail*, the acquisition has created 'the world's biggest commercial source of news and history footage, containing half a million hours of historical material dating back to 1896' (www.dmgt.co.uk). The agreement will last for five years selling through ITN's global network.

In 2002, the BBC public service broadcast two national television stations, BBC 1, BBC 2 (which offer regional programming), and two cable/satellite channels, BBC Choice and BBC News24. These stations are wholly publicly funded and carry no advertising. The BBC also broadcasts two worldwide services, BBC World and BBC Prime, which are funded by advertising revenue. The BBC has commercial interests both nationally and globally. At the national level it has a stake in UKTV, which broadcasts four cable/satellite channels: UK Gold, UK Horizons, UK Style and UK Arena. The BBC launched a further eight digital television stations in 1998 (and broadcasts digital radio stations (DAB)).

The UK has three national commercial networks: ITV, Channel 4 and Channel 5. Each has specific content requirements stipulated by the present licensing authority, the ITC. The network with the largest audience share is ITV (Figure 6.9). In 2003, ITV was licensed through 15 regionally based franchises.[54] The shareholder-owned companies Carlton[55] and Granada[56] owned 12 of the 15 licences. The two companies, which have seen substantial losses in recent years through their investment in digital television, had their proposal to merge approved by the Secretary of State for Trade and Industry in October 2003. In 2003, the UK Communications Act will remove ownership restrictions and open the UK television market to non-EU owners. Press predictions are that Viacom[57] will buy the ITV companies.

Channel 4 uniquely is a public service 'programme publisher' broadcaster financed entirely commercially, but it is not privately owned. It has a statutory duty to provide for minority audiences. Bromley points out that the channel's low production output has encouraged independent produc-

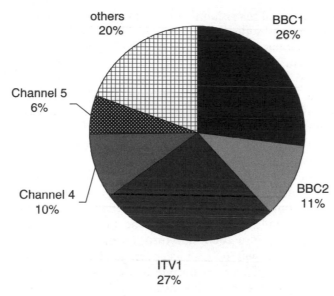

Figure 6.9   UK's television audience share, 2002

Source: ITC (2002). The Independent Television Commission posted statistics on-line. At www.itc.org.uk. However, the ITC was disolved in 2003 and statistics are available through the new regulatory authority OFCOM www.ofcom.org.uk.

tion in the UK (with purchase from circa 1,500 companies). Channel 4 started the subscription channels FilmFour in 1998 and E4 in 2001, both of which have seen huge losses totalling GBP 60 million in 2001.

Channel 5 is presently 65 per cent owned by Bertelsmann. Press rumours indicate that there is a political deal[58] to sell Channel 5 to Murdoch's News Corporation following implementation of the Communications Act, although Murdoch has denied any interest. Any take-over will be subject to approval from the Competition Commission as News Corporation holds 35 per cent of BSkyB, and circa 35 per cent of the newspaper market through News International.

The first UK private satellite operator started in 1980 with Satellite Television Ltd, which became Sky in 1984 (it was bought in 1982 by Murdoch). Sky started broadcasting its package service in 1989 from the Astra satellite. British Satellite Broadcasting started a rival service later in the same year, but was acquired by Sky with which British Sky Broadcasting (BSkyB) was formed in November 1990. BSkyB is currently the only satellite service operative in the UK. It is controlled by News Corporation through Sky Global Networks, Inc[59] (which holds 35.4 per cent of BSkyB), the remaining major shares were floated on the market between 2000 and 2003 after the withdrawal of previous partners Vivendi, Kirch, Pearson and Granada (due to their financial difficulties).

A digital terrestrial television (DTT) licence for a second digital satellite service was granted by the British government authority, the ITC, in June 1997 to BDB, a joint venture between BSkyB (33 per cent), Carlton (33 per cent) and Granada (33 per cent). Under pressure from the European Commission (DG IV) the UK government asked BSkyB to withdraw.[60] The resulting joint venture, ONdigital (renamed ITV Digital), was established by Carlton (50 per cent) and Granada (50 per cent). The two companies sank into considerable debt (GBP 402 million) and ITV Digital was terminated in April 2002. The greatest debt is owed to the content providers Sky TV (GBP 210 million) and the Football League (GBP 179 million). ITV withdrew from ITN in 2003. ITN's Euronews channel is now run by a consortium of European public service broadcasters. In an interesting move, the European Commission and European Parliament announced in May 2003 that they would fund Euronews. The European Parliament firstly pledged EUR 3 million in 2003. In return, Euronews service is opening an office in Brussels and will increase its coverage of EU affairs.

The UK is seeking to attract outside investment to establish a satellite service to rival BSkyB. For the time being, the ITC issued the existing ITV digital licences to the BBC and Crown Castle. The BBC's digital terrestrial television service is called 'Freeview'. It includes the eight digital television channels, BBC 1, BBC 2, BBC Choice, BBC 4, CBeebies, CBBC, BBC News 24 and BBC Parliament, In addition it has one interactive channel, BBCi, seven BBC radio networks (BBC Radio Five Live, Five Live Sports Extra, 1Xtra, 6 Music, BBC World Service, BBC Asian Network and BBC 7). Viewers can access 'Freeview' through buying a set-top box. Many set-top boxes were available gratis before Ondigital collapsed.

The cable companies NTL and Telewest dominate the UK cable business. Between them they have 60 per cent share of the broadband market. Concentration in the cable sector occurred in 1996 when Cable and Wireless's Mercury telecommunications business merged with the UK cable operators Nynex CableComms, Bell Cablemedia and Videotron to form C&WC (now NTL). The US Liberty Group bought an 8 per cent holding in NTL in 2002. It already had 24 per cent of Telewest by that time. The US company Microsoft bought a 23.6 per cent share of NTL in 2000, but sold it at a loss in 2003. In 1999, the European Commission decided not to put any conditions on the purchase after its brief concern that Microsoft (which had also invested in Telewest and UPC) could overly influence the technological choices made by the European cable company. In 2000 Microsoft and Liberty announced that they would take joint control of Telewest, but the European Commission expressed reservations over TeleWest's (inevitable) choice in set-top box technology, which would effect the UK market as a whole. Hence, the proposal was withdrawn. Microsoft has since divested its European cable companies. Telewest and NTL have since announced plans to merge in 2004.

Building bulk: horizontal and vertical concentration

Following liberalisation of the European market by the Single European
Act, the late 1980s witnessed an increase in co-operation between the
largest of media companies across Europe. The 1989 TWF Directive accelerated this growth resulting in a number of cross-national joint ventures,
and mergers and acquisitions in the broadcasting sector. Indeed, it seems
now possible to identify camps of alliance between the large European
firms, particularly in pay-TV television.

The first pan-European joint venture in analogue pay-TV was Premiere,
which started Germany's first and only pay-TV channel in 1989. This
involved joint ownership by the German firms Bertelsmann and Kirch and
the French company Canal Plus. Bertelsmann was next linked to Murdoch's
News International, which bought a stake in Bertelsmann's ailing private
channel, Vox in 1994 (now sold). Since this time, there has been a sharp
rise in pan-European activity. Leading this was the group Canal Plus.[61]
Before its acquisition by Vivendi, Canal Plus had established joint venture
satellite platforms with other key European groups[62] in Belgium, Italy, the
Netherlands, Poland, Spain and Scandinavia. Other broadcasters followed
suit, forming alliances with partners across Europe. Berlusconi attempted
to expand in Europe by buying into Kirch in Germany and the (now collapsed) La5 in France (with Hersant), but was more successful in the
Spanish market, with Telecinco (with Kirch), and investment in the publishing groups Unidad Editorial and Grijalbo. Kirch in turn bought into
BSkyB, Telepiù and Mediaset (since divested).

The large-scale pan-European mergers began during the race for the
European digital television market from 1996 (Lang, 1997b). The biggest
group was formed by the merger between French Canal Plus and Dutch
Nethold in 1997. The second largest had occurred a few months earlier,
with the merger of Luxembourg's CLT into the German Bertelsmann subsidiary Ufa. In publishing, the largest merger came in November 1997 when
the UK Reed international merged with the Dutch publisher Wolters
Kluwer. The second largest publishing merger was formed in 1997–99 with
Lagardère's merger of Hachette and Filipacchi Presse and purchase of
Rusconi Editore. The market has evolved into the situation today wherein
all major European groups have sought cross-border co-operation
(as shown in Figure 6.1). This has been encouraged by the European
institutions.

With the sharp increase in channel availability in Europe, media companies find themselves scrambling for programming supply. Consequently,
there has been a parallel increase in vertical integration. Media companies
are increasingly acquiring production companies or establishing exclusive
rights contracts with programme producers. There are many examples of
the acquisition of production companies. Vivendi has taken the lead in

acquisitions to the cost of its near collapse.[63] Bertelsmann followed suit. The groups Kirch and Fininvest already owned production companies and went into broadcasting as an outlet for their content libraries.[64] The Kirch Group was the owner of Europe's largest film library with 18,000 titles until it was sold to the US owner Haim Saban in 2003.

More frequent than acquisitions are the purchase of exclusive broadcasting rights (particularly for film). European broadcasters rely mostly on US imports, particularly for film and children's programming. This is not because there is a high consumer demand for US content. Rather US imports are inexpensive compared with European production. This is because US producers have already made a profit in their home markets and can therefore afford to sell their productions more cheaply in Europe. Sales are cumulative as US producers are also selling rights 15 times over in Europe, as exclusive rights are granted geographically. The European Commission has yet not queried this activity under WTO 'dumping' rules, reasons for which were discussed in Chapter 4. It must also be considered that many European channels are viable due to the availability of cheap US content. As European markets are often small, many broadcasters might not survive without the provision of cheap content.

In 2002, European pay-TV services spent around USD 1.5 billion on US production which represented 20 per cent of US studio income (Kagan, 2003). The largest content producers in the US are Viacom,[65] AOL-Time-Warner,[66] Disney,[67] Vivendi,[68] MGM/UA,[69] 20th Century Fox[70] and Columbia Pictures.[71] All of the major studios have strong distribution networks in Europe. European producers by contrast suffer from weak distribution structures. Equally important as to the building up of film libraries has been the acquisition of sports rights such as football matches (e.g. national teams, the Premiership, the UEFA Champions League, the World Cup), golf (e.g. Open golf championship, European golf tour), tennis (e.g. Wimbledon), and Formula Racing. Competition for sports rights has driven purchasing costs sky-high with no regulatory intervention. This led the European Parliament to draw up its amendment to the TWF Directive in 1997 requiring Member States to draw up lists of 'events of major importance for society', which should be made widely accessible to the public.

Conclusion

The chapter showed how the actions of the EU institutions have impacted the structure of national media markets. The clearest example is in pay-TV, where Member States initially preferred one platform of their key national players. The Commission enforced, through competition law, the establishment of at least two platforms. The second most prominent example is in the choice of technological standards. The EC competition authority wanted to let the market decide. National attempts, as in the example of

Spain, to impose a single encryption technology (e.g. multicrypt) at the national level were vetoed by the European Commission which ensured that there be a market choice. This decision-making had consequences for the whole of the European media market. The EC did not mandate a standard but did not permit Member States to do so either.

The creation of multiple pay-TV platforms with competing technologies increased pressure on a market already saturated from existing competition in terrestrial and cable broadcasting. At the same time, vertical integration and in-house production was discouraged. The scramble for content led to rising costs leaving the market unsustainable. The situation rapidly dissolved into the status quo as pay-TV platforms experienced heavy losses and even bankruptcy across Member States (e.g. Canal Plus, ITV Digital, Kirch, Quiero, Vía Digital) New market entrants placed strain on established markets, with terrestrial and cable operators making losses as well. Industrial conglomerates began to off-load their media interests on to the market. The remaining players, chiefly BSkyB and Fininvest, barely survived substantial losses, but only due to investment by their parent companies and cross-advertising of their media products.

Thus, the EC produced with its framework of light-touch regulation intense market competition, which weakened rather than strengthened European media companies (ultimately terrestrial television operators and publishing groups). Few of the major European players remain in sound financial shape. The dilemma that the European institutions now face is that many European terrestrial and digital players are vulnerable to foreign (e.g. non-European) take-overs. Europe already finds itself in a situation wherein initial investment in the new media markets of the early 1990s (cable and satellite) largely came from established US corporations such as AOL/Time Warner, Liberty, News Corporation, NTL, UPC, and Viacom.

A weakened market has meant a high cost for companies, jobs and regulatory cost to governments across Europe. The EC policy goals for competitive markets set out in the mid 1990s were not met. In each Member State only one digital gateway remains often owned by a single company. National regulatory authorities (NRAs) are faced with potential monopoly power from owners that not only control encryption technology (CA, Multiplex, etc.), EPGs and APIs but also exert control over upstream or downstream markets. Further potential negative externalities exist in terms of the public interest (e.g. media pluralism).

The chapter starkly points out the difficulties caused by a lack of policy co-ordination within the European Commission. As detailed in the last chapter, the discrepancies between the DGs grew out of differences in the delineation of markets. DG Information Society defined communications markets (widely) differently than DG Competition (narrowly). Whereas DG Information Society recommended light touch regulation and greater market concentration in emerging markets, DG Competition enforce through individual decisions that there was national competition in each specific market (cable, satellite, digital television, etc.). Whereas DG Information Society recommended the use of one digital standard (in the 1995 TV standards Directive), DG Competition insisted on competition in the choice of gateway technologies. DG Market opted for a middle ground approach that recommended that a certain number of media owners be maintained at the national level, at least 3–4 in each market. It came into difficulties when delineating those markets, and produced an ownership Directive based upon public interest goals, which was politically infeasible

If governments had been permitted by the European Commission to mandate the use of a single encryption technology this may have resulted in a more even playing field for competition and the survival of more than one digital service at national levels. The European Commission did not have to stipulate a European-wide standard but could have discussed a preferred standard during decision-making. Some Member States have reacted to market failure by attempting to push forward their original agenda within the European Council. This has been integrated into the aforementioned (in Chapter 1) eEurope initiative (CEC, 2002b), which calls for greater public–private co-operation in the establishment of nascent markets, particularly the establishment of digital platforms.

It can be contended that developments in media markets have managed to fissure traditional ties between political parties and media groups. Generally, diversification of ownership within media companies has diluted tendencies towards political partisanism. In many EU Member States, family/individual-owned media companies have now been floated on the stock market (e.g. groups owned by Bertelsmann, Berlusconi, Kirch, Lagardère, Maxwell, Murdoch, Mediaset, Rusconi), although Berlusconi and Murdoch retain substantial interest through controlling shares. Shareholder-owned groups are less likely to have close ties to political parties than individual owners. Particularly in newspapers, political partisanism, which was pronounced in the 1980s, has lessened to a considerable degree. Whether this is 'good' or 'bad' for democracy is debatable. Although shareholder-owned companies have less political allegiance and increased transparency, there is the concern that they invest less in content and may sacrifice editorial independence in favour of profitability.

Stock market floatation has increased financial transparency in media holdings, but transparency in private companies still remains a problem as Austria, Belgium, Germany, Luxembourg and Switzerland (where many Italian groups bank) still have banking secrecy laws.

A notable finding in the chapter is that EU policy has been promoting the growth of large European groups with media interests in many Member States (such as Canal Plus, and CLT) rather than permitting the further concentration of national champions (hence the negative EC decisions on the expansion of Bertelsmann, Kirch, News International, Telefónica, etc. in

national markets). Consequently, there has been a high degree of co-operation between the largest players at the European level. The question can be raised as to whether the market can be truly competitive if so many media groups are co-operating with each other at the European level. On this phenomenon, the European Commission competition directorate has stated the following:

> the Commission will take a positive attitude under the competition rules to the creation of cross-border alliances between companies active in different geographic markets. These are unlikely to result in the creation of dominant positions. Moreover, they contribute to the creation of companies in the European audio-visual sector which can benefit from economies of scale and scope. There is only one caveat, namely that if a network of strategic alliances between all major European players were to be created, the impact of individual operations would have to be assessed against such a background. There might be a risk of partitioning of national markets and a consequential creation or strengthening of dominant positions in those markets, in particular if two companies with strong market positions were to ally. However, such an effect would have to be proved (and has not yet materialised). (*Competition Policy Newsletter*, No. 1, 8 February 1999)

Clearly, from this statement, the trade factor remains of ultimate importance in media market regulation – the creation of large groups to defend Europe against 'foreign' (American) players. The defence of European industry appears to be an ingrained policy discourse unaffected by the realities of the market.

Hence, the Commission is showing very little concern about the pan-European network of strategic alliances taking place amongst Europe's large media groups. The only interest in this respect is over the bidding for exclusive rights in programming on which a Commission study is taking place in 2003. In the same year, DG Competition opened investigations into the joint selling of media rights to the English Premier League by the UK Football Association Premier League (FAPL).[72] The European Parliament for a long time lobbied for an end to exclusive rights to sports broadcasting. This culminated in a change to the *Television without Frontiers Directive* in 1997 wherein Art. 3a (2)[73] mandates Member States take measures to ring-fence a list of 'events of major importance for society', which cannot be granted exclusive rights contracts. This has not amounted to much in the way of national policy. Only six Member States have thus far produced guidelines and implementation is patchy.[74] The UK Office of Fair Trading (OFT) considered putting an end to the UK sports deals by ruling that sports' unions and leagues were acting in the capacity of cartels in agreeing exclusive contracts. However, OFT decided in 1999 not to block the Premiere League's exclusive sports rights agreement with BSkyB as it was found to be in the 'wider public interest'.

With its concentration on programming acquisition, Europe may be overlooking the salient issues of media concentration, content production and distribution. It has been theorised that content producers may in future choose to acquire their own stations and broadcast directly to viewers in Europe without the need to sell to European broadcasters (Dellarte, 1996). Ironically, this move could be justified precisely by the dissatisfaction of producers, from the (highly concentrated) US groups in particular, with increasing concentration of the European broadcasting industry. Complaints about European media concentration have been made to the EC competition directorate by many of the big US studios, including Disney, Universal, and Warner Brothers. Upon expiry of exclusive rights contracts, these producers may one day not renew programming deals. Considering the high percentage of US content in European broadcasting could have a further detrimental effect on the market, as the purchase of European content is more costly, and European broadcasters may be forced to find content from ever cheaper sources. Distribution networks for European content remain fragmented due to national and linguistic factors (Lange and Newman-Baudais, 2003).

Notes

1   The chapter can only provide a snapshot of European media markets at the time of writing. Information has been gathered from company reports, market analysis reports (e.g. CIT, 2001 and Earnst and Young, 2002) and newspaper reports (chiefly, *The Financial Times*).
2   Havas was nominated as a state news agency in 1835. It has since grown into a large multinational company active in publishing, telecommunications, travel, energy and construction industries. The French government sold off its last stake in Havas in 1987. Vivendi bought 100 per cent of Havas in 1997 and 1998 but begun selling off group assets from 2000 onwards.
3   La 'Lyonnaise des Eaux' merged in 1996 with the Financial company Suez; the joint venture is the group Suez-Lyonnaise.
4   In France, Générale des Eaux (now Vivendi) and Lyonnaise des Eaux senior executives were convicted of corruption to win public sector contracts in 1994 and 1996 respectively (Davies and Hall, 1999). Générale des Eaux, Lyonnaise des Eaux and Bouyges have also been under corruption investigation for construction contracts (Davies and Hall, 1999). The three companies Vivendi (formerly Générale des Eaux), Suez-Lyonnaise des Eaux and Bouygues dominate the French water market and allegedly hold 70 per cent of the global water market (Hall, 1998). Lyonnaise des Eaux (through its subsidiary Sita) and Vivendi (through its subsidiary Onyx) also represent the top five waste management multinationals. Hall has criticised the companies for co-operation on a global scale (1998: 121–2).
5   Bouyges is a family-owned firm active in public works, telecommunications, utilities and construction markets (roads and property).

6 According to CIT Publications 2001, M6 was owned by Bertelsmann (41.9 per cent through the RTL Group) and Lyonnaise Communications (a subsidiary of Lyonnaise des Eaux and France Télécom) (37 per cent), Compagnie de Suez (3.3 per cent) and UAP (3.3 per cent).

7 In 2002, Seagram owned the Universal Television Group, Polygram, the Brillstein-Grey Entertainment (50 per cent), Multimedia Entertainment (which produces the talk show, Jerry Springer), USA Networks Inc. (45 per cent formerly the Home Shopping Network Inc.) and the distribution company Universal Pay Television. Seagram also has shares in HBO Asia, Telecine (Brazil), Cinecanal (Latin America), Showtime (Australia) and Star Channel (Japan).

8 In 1999, Canal Plus acquired a 24.5 per cent stake in BSkyB, but was obliged by a Decision of the European Commission to sell its holding. Instead it used its share in BSkyB to secure a bank loan from Deutsche Bank to offset debt. Deutsche Bank floated the shares in 2002.

9 See http://finance.vivendiuniversal.com for details of Vivendi's financial status.

10 The group still has television interests in Africa through NetHold and Asia, Australia and Latin America through Seagram.

11 Other licencees were Direct 8, i-MCM, M6 Music, NRJ TV, NT1, TMC and eight public broadcasters.

12 Lagardère owns the newspapers *La Provence, Nice-Matin, Var-Matin, Corse Matin, Corse, Votre Hebdo, Le Parisien, 'Equipe and L'Alsace.*

13 Before his death in 1996, Hersant owned the national papers: *Le Figaro, France-Soir* and regional papers, *Le Progrès, de Lyon, Le Dauphiné, Libéré, Le Progrès, Dimanche, La Dauphiné, Paris-Normandie, Les Dernières, Nouvelles, d'Alsace, Nord-Matin, Nord-Eclair, Le Havre-Libre, Le Havre-Presse, Midi-Libre, Journal, Rhone-Alpes, L'Espoir, L'Independent, L'Union, La Tribune, Le Courier, de Soame-en-Loire, Les Depeches, Liberte, du Morbihan, Loire Matin, Lyon, Figaro, Matin, Midi, Libre, Nord, Eclair, Nord, Matin, Presse, Ocean, Vaucluse,* and *Matim*. The assets of the Hersant Press Group (now SocPresse) have disbursed.

14 Gruner + Jahr was owned by Bertelsmann AG (74.9 per cent) and the Jahr family (25.1 per cent) in 2003 (Bertelsmann Annual Report).

15 These were eventually sold to a consortium of Apax, Goldman Sachs Capital Partners and Providence Equity in March 2003.

16 Kirch owned 25 per cent of Premiere until 1998 when it purchased Canal Plus' share in Premiere in return for Kirch's 34.72 per cent stake in Telepiù. It bought remaining shares in 1999 leaving Bertelsmann with around 5 per cent, which Bertelsmann sold to Kirch in 2001.

17 The publishing group Axel Springer owns 11.4 per cent of ProSiebenSat1. In turn, 40 per cent of Axel Springer is owned by the Kirch Group (40 per cent of which was taken over by Deutsche Bank AG in 2003 as a part of the Kirch liquidation).

18 The Agnelli family controls the national papers *Corriere della Sera, La Stampa* and *La Gazzetta dello Sport* through its controlling stakes in the publishing groups Rizzoli and FABBRI. Rizzoli is owned by the Holding di Partecipazioni Industriali (Hdp) in which the Agnelli family have a controlling stake. The Agnelli family is active in aerospace, car and energy markets.

19 De Benedetti retained control of the Espresso Group which is a subsidiary of

the Berlusconi controlled Mondadori Group. The Espresso Group owns the national newspaper, *La Repubblica* and the regional newspapers, *Il Tirreno*, *La Nuova Sardegna*, *Messaggero Veneto*, *Il Piccolo*, *Alto Adige*, *Corriere delle Alpi*, *Bolzano*, *Gazzetta di Mantova*, *Il Mattino di Padova*, *La Provincia Pavese*, *Il Centro*, *La Tribuna di Treviso*, *Gazzetta di Reggio*, *La Sentinella del Canavese*, *La Nuova Ferrara*, *Nuova Gazzetta di Modena*, *La Nuova Venezia* and *La Città*. Carlo de Benedetti was convicted of fraud in 1992 in connection with the 1982 collapse of Banco Ambrosiano.

20 Fininvest owns 50 per cent of the Mondadori publishing group. The share was awarded to Fininvest in a Roman court decision following a battle for a controlling stake between De Benedetti and Berlusconi. Berlusconi was charged in 1991 for bribing Roman judges in the case but he was acquitted under Italy's statute of limitations in 2000. In another case Berlusconi was charged over bribing judges for the takeover of SME supermarket. Berlusconi is still being charged for this but the Italian Parliament passed an immunity law in 2003 to postpone the trial until after Berlusconi's term in office. The Italian parliamentary vote reflected a bi-partisan effort to avoid the embarrassment of a potential ruling during Italy's six-month presidency of the EU. Antonio Maccanico (of the center-left Margherita party), who drafted the 1997 Italian Media Act under the Prodi government, was a sponsor of the immunity law.

21 The Monrif Group owns the newspapers *Il Resto del Carlino*, *La Nazione* and *Il Giorno* which are prominent in Bologna, Florence and Milan respectively.

22 Rusconi has since been bought by the French group Lagardère.

23 The same study shows the high occurrence of equity linkages between the largest industrial groups in Italy (Goldstein and Nicoletti, 1995).

24 A detailed study of media ownership in the Italian market is provided by the Istituto Economia dei Media in a publication entitled 'L'industria della comunicazione in Italia'. www.fondazionerosselli.it/.

25 Auditel is responsible for official figures on television audience share and newspaper circulation.

26 Publitalia holds 60 per cent of the Italian advertising market (Williams, 2002: 22).

27 The President's wife, Franca Ciampi, has been outspoken about the poor depiction of women on Italian television.

28 In 2001, the Italian newspaper, *La Repubblica*, claimed in a series of articles that there exists a KPMG report on Fininvest commissioned by a Milanese public prosecutor, Franceso Greco, who has filed charges for tax evasion and fraud against Berlusconi and Fininvest officials ('KPMG, la procura chiede che Berlusconi sia processato' by Pier Francesco Fedrizzi, *La Repubblica* 29 June 2001). The newspaper claims that KPMG found that Fininvest organised its corporate structure into two groups. In the early 1990s, Fininvest allegedly used 'Group B' companies to take significant stakes in Spain's Telecinco and Italy's Telepiu, acquisitons that would otherwise not have been permitted under national ownership laws. La Repubblica alleges that KPMG claims that Group B companies assisted Fininvest in retaining shareholdings in companies without having to comply with national obligations to deliver information to regulatory authorities. Fininvest has denied the charges claiming that the named companies of Group B were not a part of Fininvest. According to the Republica

newspaper, a Fininvest lawyer allegedly informed KPMG of Fininvest's Group B activities. The lawyer, David Mills, is the husband of British Minister for Culture, Tessa Jowells (Leonard, 2003).

29 Pension reform remains Berlusconi's toughest political challenge. In October 2003, 1.5 million state employees went on strike against pension reform. Newspaper journalists have joined the union strike. The Berlusconi government wants to raise the qualification requirement for a full state pension from 35 to 40 years. This has been highly contested particularly as the state remains an employer for a significant proportion of the Italian working population.

30 In 1991 and 2003, Berlusconi was on trial for two cases of bribing judges in the 1980s ('Berlusconi faces court on bribery charges', *Guardian*, Tuesday 17 June 2003). Berlusconi's lawyer, Cesare Previti, was sentenced in May 2003 for 11 years on the charge of bribing judges in Rome to facilitate the Fininvest takeover of the Mondadori publishing house. In June 2003, Previti was sentenced a second time for five years on charge of bribery in the SME case. The Roman judge Renato Squillante who took the bribe annulled the sale of the state-owned SME to Berlusconi's rival, De Benedetti, allowing Berlusconi to buy SME. Squillante was sentenced to eight years. Berlusconi claims that he is a victim of political plot against him.

31 In 1996, 23.4 per cent was sold off to Berlusconi's close associate Renato Della Valle (until bought by Kirch in July 1996), 32.5 per cent to Nethold and 10 per cent retained by Fininvest. Today Telepiù is owned by Rupert Murdoch's News Corporation.

32 Kirch bought 7.6 per cent, Nethold 7.3 per cent, Prince al-Waleed bin Talal bin Abdul (Saudia Arabia) 2.6 per cent, British Telecommunications 2.4 per cent and Banca Nazionale del Lavoro 2.4 per cent. Smaller stakes are now held by ABN Amro (Dutch banking group), BZW (investment banking arm of Barclays of the UK), Morgan Stanley, and the Abu Dhabi Investment Authority.

33 Videomusic was owned by Beta Television, SpA Rete A by Rete A Srl and Cecchi Gori Communications. SEAT now uses the channel to transmit the American music channel MTV Italy, which replaced the home-grown channel Videomusic.

34 Orbit Satellite is owned by the Mawarid Group of Companies based in the Saudi Arabia, whose chairman is the Saudi prince, Khalid bin Abd al-Rahman, who is a cousin of King Fahd. The company is active in construction, electronics, computers, food and banking and investment sectors.

35 Stream was originally owned by Telecom Italia but was floated in 1999. News Corporation gained a 35 per cent stake, Cecchi Gori Communications 18 per cent and four Italian football teams (Fiorentina, owned at that time by Cecchi Gori, Lazio, Parma and Roma) owned 12 per cent. News Corporation bought out the football teams in 2000.

36 In 2003, CLT was active in television markets in Belgium (RTL TVI 66 per cent, Club RTL 66 per cent), France (M6 43.8 per cent, RTL9 35 per cent, TMC 23.8 per cent), Germany (RTL 100 per cent, RTL 2 35.9 per cent, Vox 99 per cent, Super RTL 50 per cent, RTL 50 per cent with Disney, RTL Shop, 100 per cent), Hungary (RTL KLUB 49 per cent), Luxembourg (RTL Tele Letzebuerg 100 per cent), the Netherlands (RTL4 100 per cent, Yorin 100 per

cent, RTL5 100 per cent), Poland (RTL7 100 per cent), Spain (Antena 3 17 per cent) and the United Kingdom (Channel 5 65 per cent). In radio, it is active in Belgium (Bel RTL 43 per cent, Radio Contact 35 per cent), France (RTL 100 per cent, RTL2 100 per cent, Fun radio 100 per cent), Germany (104.6 RTL 100 per cent, Antenne Bayern 16 per cent, Radio Hamburg 29 per cent, Radio NRW 16 per cent, Berliner Rundfunk 30 per cent, RTL RADIO Die grossten Oldies 100 per cent), Luxembourg (RTL Radio Letzebuerg 100 per cent), the Netherlands (Yorin FM 100 per cent), Spain (Telstar 100 per cent), Sweden (WOW 1055 100 per cent, RTL 104.7 49 per cent) and Romania (Radio Contact 35 per cent).

37   SES (Société Européene des Satellites) is owned by a number of shareholders. The Luxembourg State, the Luxembourg bank, Banque et Caisse d'Epargne de l'Etat (BCEE) and Société Nationale de Crédit et d'Investissement (SNCI) hold key voting interests.

38   SES, which owns the Astra satellites, became Luxembourg's biggest tax contributor in 1997 with a input of LFr2.06bn in taxes. ('Survey-Luxembourg: Space age role for chateau', *Financial Times*, 5 May 1997).

39   Philips developed the HDTV standard.

40   Up until 1996, NetHold was 50 per cent owned by Richemont and 50 per cent owned by Multichoice. Both Richemont and Multichoice are South African companies. Richemont is a based in Switzerland and controls the tobacco companies Rothmans International plc and Luxco SA. MultiChoice has pay television interests in South Africa. MultiChoice was established in October 1993 out of the subscriber service (SMS) and Comtech divisions of the larger South African group, Electronic Media Network Limited (M-Net).

41   Polygram was bought from Royal Philips Electronics by Seagram in 1998, which was acquired by Vivendi in 2000.

42   PCM Uitgevers was up for sale at the end of 2003. The British equity group Candouer is bidding for purchase.

43   Elsevier merged with UK Reed International in 1993, but both companies remain separated on the London and Amsterdam stock exchanges for tax reasons.

44   NB/DE Stem, Brabants Dagblad, Eindhovens Dagblad, De Gelderlander and Uitgeversmaatschappij De Limburger.

45   In publishing, Grupo Correo owns the regional newspapers, *El Correo* (Bilbao), *La Voz de Galicia*, *Diario Vasco* (San Sebastián), *El Diario Montañés* (Santander), *La Rioja* (Logroño), *El Norte de Castilla* (Valladolid), *La Verdad* (Múrcia), *Ideal* (Andalucía), *Hoy* (Badajoz), *Sur* (Málaga), *Andalucía Costa del Golf* and *El Comercio* (published in Lima). The Group also publishes magazines.

46   RTVE also runs stations in Latin America and Asia.

47   In 2002, Telefónica owned 46.92 per cent and the Recoletos Editorial group 10 per cent.

48   In 2002 Telecinco was owned by Correo (25 per cent), Mediaset (40 per cent) and Kirch (25 per cent). In the mid-1980s, Berlusconi bought 80 per cent of Telecinco in defiance of Spanish media ownership laws. The Spanish government forced divestment. When the Bank of Luxembourg began to sell off its 15 per cent share in 1997, Kirch and Fininvest were prevented from increas-

ing their share ownerships as the companies had already reached their percentage limit according to Spanish ownership law (*El Pais*, 11 October 1997). The 4 per cent was eventually bought by Grupo Correo, which has since upped its stake to 25 per cent.

49 1996 Case No. IV/M.0709 [OJC 228/05, 7 August 1996].

50 The merger was approved in November 2002 subject to conditions (particularly in respect to football rights).

51 Conrad Black, who was investigated by the US Securities and Exchange Commission in 2003, has resigned from chairman of Hollinger International. Black is selling off his controlling stake in the *Daily Telegraph*. The group was bought by the brothers David and Frederick Barclay in 2004.

52 Another UK newspaper publisher, Newsquest plc, holds the largest number of UK regional newspapers with more than 300 titles in 2003. Newsquest is a wholly owned Gannett subsidiary (acquired 1999).

53 Richard Desmond also owns a number of 'adult' television channels and magazine, which include *Big Ones* and *Horny Housewives*. It is interesting to note that Desmond made around £17 m in 2003 from a single television station (the 'Fantasy' channel). In the same year he only made £28 million from the whole of the Northern & Shell group.

54 Anglia, Border, Granada, LWT, Meridian, Tyne Tees, Yorkshire, Carlton, Central, HTV, Westcountry, Grampian, Scottish, Ulster, Channel.

55 Carlton, Central, HTV, Westcountry.

56 Anglia, Border, Granada, LWT, Meridian, Tyne Tees, Yorkshire.

57 Viacom was predicted to buy ITV following Tony Blair's meeting with Viacom Chairman Sumner Redstone on 12 November 2002. Viacom already owns MTV, CBS, Paramount film studios, Blockbuster Video, the UCI cinema chain, the Paramount Comedy Channel and all the advertising spaces on London Underground.

58 The political deal is allegedly to gain press support over UK entry into the Euro.

59 BSkyB is 35.4 per cent owned by Sky Global Networks, Inc., which is majority owned by Sky Global Holdings, Inc., which is majority owned by News International Plc, which is majority owned by Newscorp Investments Limited, which is 100 per cent owned by News Corporation Limited.

60 The only other contender for the licence, Digital Television Network (DTN) (a joint bid between cable operator NTL and United News & Media) had filed a formal complaint with the European Commission about the award of the DTT licence to Carlton and Granada.

61 On the growth of Canal Plus, see Guillou (1991) and Johnson and McCormick (1996).

62 1996 Canal Plus Belgique negotiated a joint venture with 20 local cable distribution companies for a Belgian digital launch (Canal Plus Belgique 33 per cent). It co-operated with German groups in Canal Plus Deutschland (50 per cent) and invested in Premiere. It bought Telepiù in Italy bringing competition to Berlusconi and acquired Nethold in the Netherlands. It co-operated with Telenor in Norway (Canal Digital) and with Telefónica and Recoletos in Spain (Canal Plus España), and invested in the UK (with 10 per cent of TVS). In 1997 Canal Plus made a deal with Telecom Italia, Rai, Mediaset and Cecchi Gori to develop digital television in Italy with Stream.

63 Vivendi bought up the US and European production companies: Universal Studio, Universal Pictures, October Films, Universal Studios Home Video, Interscope, Propaganda, Cinea, PolyGram, Pan Europeenee Production, Noe, Propaganda Television, TedPoly, Meteor Films and Sogepaq.

64 Kirch owned TaurusProduktion, CBM, Janus Glücksrad, Filmproduktion Janus, Janus Pearson Television, KirchMedia Entertainment, Prima Idee, ndF and Roxy. Bertelsmann owns UFA Film & TV Production, Trebitsch Production, Delux Productions, Cinevideo, Holland Media House and First Choice. Mediaset owns the largest Italian production house, Medusa Films.

65 Viacom owns Paramount Pictures, Spelling Films, Paramount Television, Spelling Entertainment, MTV, M2, Nickelodeon, Nick at Nite, Nick at Nite's TV Land, VH1, Showtime, The Movie Channel, Flix and Paramount Stations Group.

66 AOL–Time-Warner (created through a merger in 1999) owns Warner Brothers (WB), WB television Network, WB TV Animation, Hanna-Barbera Cartoons, Telepictures Productions, Witt-Thomas, Warner Bros. International TV, Castle Rock, HBO, Cinemax, HBO Pictures/HBO Showcase, HBO Independent Productions, HBO Downtown Productions, HBO Animation, HBO Home Video, HBO Sports, Time Warner Sports, CNN, Turner Entertainment Group, TNT, TBS Superstation, Cartoon Network, Turner Classic Movies, New Line Cinema, Fine Line, Turner Sports, Turner Home Satellite, Turner Original Productions and America Online (AOL).

67 Disney owns Disney, Touchstone, Caravan, Hollywood Pictures, Miramax, Buena Vista International, Buena Vista Home Video, Walt Disney TV, Walt Disney TV Animation, Disney Channel, Buena Vista TV, Disney TV International, ABC TV Network, ESPN, A&E Networks, Lifetime TV, and Disney/ABC International.

68 Vivendi (through Seagram) owns Universal Pictures, Brillstein-Grey Entertainment, Universal TV Enterprises, Universal Family Entertainment, and Universal Cartoon Studios, Inc.

69 MGM/UA owns the production companies MGM Pictures, United Artists Pictures, Samuel Goldwyn Pictures, and Orion Pictures.

70 20th Century Fox (owned by Rupert Murdoch) owns Twentieth Century Fox, Fox 2000, Fox Searchlight, Fox Family Films, Fox Animation Studios, Fox Broadcasting Company (television), Fox Entertainment, Fox Children's Network and Fox Sports.

71 Columbia Pictures (Sony) owns Columbia Pictures, TriStar Pictures, Sony Pictures Classics and Columbia TriStar TV.

72 Commission Press release COMP/38.453 – statement of objections into the selling of rights to BSkyB by Arsenal Football, Aston Villa Plc, Blackburn Rovers, Bolton Wanderers, Charlton Athletic, Chelsea Football, Everton Football, FA Premier League, Fulham Football, Ipswich Town Footbal, Leeds United Plc, Leicester City Football, Liverpool Football, Manchester United, Middlesbrough, Newcastle United, Southampton, the Derby County, the Sunderland Asso, Tottenham Hotspur and West Ham United. Commission Press release COMP/38.173 – statement of objections into the selling of rights by the Football Association Premier League Limited to the English Premier League. 20 December 2002.

73   Published in the Official Journal of the European Union C 100 of 26 April 2003.
74   The six Member States which have produced lists are: Denmark (OJ. C 14 of 19 January 1999, then revoked in OJ. C 45 of 19 February 2002); Italy (OJ. C 277 of 30 September 1999); Germany (OJ. C 277 of 29 September 2000); the UK (OJ. C 328 of 18 November 2000); Austria (OJ. C 16 of 19 January 2002); and Ireland.

7

Engineering Europeanisation at the national level

> there are signs that in some important respects the key role of national uniqueness is ending. (Moran and Prosser, 1994: 148)

Introduction

Chapters 2 to 6 detailed the actions of the EU institutions in regulating media markets. This chapter investigates ways in which the EU institutions have affected the development of national regulation.[1] As Moran and Prosser comment, 'It is now a truism to remark that legal and policy-making processes are strongly shaped by the institutions of the European Community, and we would make the further claim that, even in Great Britain, the constitutional elements we found lacking in relation to British privatisation are to be found in Community law' (1994: 148). This chapter investigates the extent to which the institutions of the European Union (the Commission, Court of Justice and European Parliament) have between them promoted a process of convergence in national regulation.

European models of media regulation

All European Union (EU) Member States have developed specific regulatory regimes to govern their media industries, each differing substantially in approach. Although there is wide variance in regulatory structures between EU states, most share a common model of a dual system of public and private broadcasting (Humphreys, 1996; Picard, 2002). Each Member State provides for a public service broadcaster (PSB). PSBs have traditionally dominated the broadcasting sector, and continue to do so (although their audience share has declined since the 1980s). PSBs are meant to contribute to the quality of public discourse, promote societal integration and emphasise news and education, as opposed to entertainment. A further PSB role is the representation of minority interests, as well as the promotion of national culture.

In practice, the intended functioning of the PSB varies widely from state to state (Humphreys, 1996). Blumler (1992) points to the PSB 'place in politics', which may entail the tendency towards the politicisation of editorial boards, intervention by political parties and, in the worst scenario, the transformation of the public service broadcasting into the 'voice of the state'. In France and Italy PSBs are thought to be particularly prone to political actors, such as supervisory boards being appointed by the ruling parties. In Greece, Ireland, Portugal and Spain, ruling parties are seen to interfere directly in political reporting 'by giving direct instructions or banning . . . news items' (Voltmer, 2000: 36). The German and British PSBs are viewed as relatively independent. The German model includes the participation of societal groups on PSB supervisory boards (*Rundfunkrat*).

Member State regulation of commercial broadcasting focuses on ownership limits, caps on advertising and rules on media content. Laws provide percentage requirements for news and documentary programming, the promotion of European and national content and time devoted to minority audience programming or representation of identifiable societal groups.

The press has traditionally been recognised as a bulwark of democracy and therefore has not been heavily regulated (Humphreys, 1996). Policy instruments regulating the press have concentrated on ownership structures: the limitation of shares, multiple ownership and cross-media ownership. Right of reply rules exist in most Member States. Content laws have not been applied to the press, as in broadcasting, but state subsidisation of newspapers, particularly political party newspapers, still exist in Europe (although less so nowadays) (Murschetz, 1998).

Transparency measures differ from state to state. Financial transparency is high in the UK, the Netherlands and the Scandinavian states. But transparency as stated in the last chapter in private companies still remains a problem in Austria, Belgium, Germany, Luxembourg and Switzerland, which have banking secrecy laws. In most states, media companies are made to report to broadcasting councils, courts or national ministries, but these accounts are not necessarily made available publicly.

Convergence in Member State media policies

The beginnings of convergence in national media policies took place in the mid-1980s and accelerated after 1990 when EU Member States implemented the TWF Directive. The degree to which the Directive was implemented in the Member States was initially dependent upon how well the Directive 'fitted in' with the widely varying national regulatory structures. However, dissatisfaction of the EU institutions with the mode of implementation led to pressure for revisions to national media laws. The pressure exerted by the ECJ and MTF was effective. As shown in Chapters 2 and 3, in some cases, the dual actions of these EU institutions ran roughshod over the preferences of the Member States despite objection from national ministries and political leaders.

To complement actions of the ECJ and the MTF, the European Commission (EC) simultaneously practised an indirect approach to influencing national legislation through the suggestion of best practices, models and solutions. This was done specifically through the promotion of regulatory instruments in Commission reports, green papers and draft directives. Consultation with national administrations and interest groups as detailed in Chapter 6 enabled the dissemination of suggested policy instruments to national levels. In order to observe the phenomena of convergence, the chapter examines the media policies of France, Germany, Italy, Luxembourg, the Netherlands, Spain and the UK. As outlined in Chapter 6, the choice of these countries is because this is where most media revenue in Europe is generated (Figure 6.1).

Convergence in national policy

From the mid-1980s, a gradual pattern of market liberalisation, regulation and deregulation began to emerge in the countries under observation. Three key regulatory overhauls of national media policies can be distinctly marked as occurring just after the EU's 1986 Single European Act (SEA), the 1989 TWF Directive and during the mid-1990s.

The SEA may not have been a direct catalyst of media market liberalisation; however its liberal market philosophy was extremely significant. Following the 1986 SEA, many European countries liberalised their media markets. Regulation that accompanied liberalisaton was found in: the French 1986 Press and Freedom of Communication laws,[2] the German 1987 Inter-State Agreement on the Regulation of Broadcasting,[3] the Italian 1987 Publishing Law,[4] and the Spanish 1988 Law on Commercial television.[5] These laws resulted in the appearance of commercial broadcasters, which began to stress the need for further deregulation to attract investment for new technologies. The new laws' manifold implications presented the Commission with a window of opportunity to introduce the TWF Directive.

In 1989, the TWF Directive required formal revisions to national broadcasting regulation. National media acts implementing the 1989 directive included: the French 1994 Broadcasting Law,[6] the German 1991 Interstate Broadcasting Agreement,[7] the Italian 1990 Broadcasting Act,[8] the Spanish 1994 Televisión Sin Frontera Law[9] and the British 1990 Broadcasting Act. At this point in time, national administrative cultures still played a large role in implementation at national levels. This was to change as the EU institutions expressed dissatisfaction with TWF implementation.

Deregulation occurred again at the end of the 1990s with: the French 1996 Information Superhighway Law,[10] the German 1996 Interstate Agreement on the regulation of broadcasting, the Italian 1997 New Media Act,[11] the Spanish 1998 Law on digital television and the British 1996 Broadcasting Act. The content of these laws was shaped both formally by decisions of the ECJ and the EC and informally by EC policy proposals.

The simultaneous appearance of new media acts in France, Germany and the UK in 1996 has not gone unnoticed. Levy, discusses this phenomenon (Levy, 1997). He argues however that the coincidental timing of the acts is not actual evidence that policy convergence has occurred. Instead, he argues, media policy represents a limitation to policy convergence. This argument is based upon the classic literature on policy style, which considers national cultural considerations (beliefs, values, historical experience, etc.) to diffuse the influence of European policy. This observation is important as media policy has traditionally been influenced by cultural variables. However, as Moran and Prosser (1994) point out arguments of national style, particularly in the regulatory field, are diminishing in importance. This is significant when examining media market regulation at national levels. Levy focuses in his article on regulation of digital television. However, a closer examination of these three national media laws shows that a great proportion of them dealt with the dismantling of previous instruments, than the promotion of digital television as such. To clarify, it does not appear that these 1996 laws were created specifically for the regulation of digital television, but rather the advance of the 'digital age' was used as an argument for deregulation (Humphreys, 1997). It is argued in

Table 7.1 Media laws of selected EU members states, 1986–98

	1986–89	1990–94	1995–98
France	1986 Press Law No. 86-1210; 1986 Freedom of Communication Law No. 86-1067	1994 Broadcasting Law No. 94-88	1996 Information Superhighway Law No. 96-299
Germany	1987 Inter State Agreement on the Regulation of Broadcasting	1991 Interstate Agreement on the regulation of broadcasting	1996 Interstate Agreement on the regulation of broadcasting
Italy	1987 Publishing Law No. 67	1990 Broadcasting Act No. 223	1997 New Media Act No. 249
Spain	1988 Law on Commercial television	1994 Television Without Frontiers	1997 Law on digital television
UK		1990 Broadcasting Act	1996 Broadcasting Act

this chapter that there has been rather a high occurrence of policy convergence between these countries, and not only these countries, but between a majority of the Member States of the European Union. The policies of the European Union have had a substantial effect upon this convergence.

A full understanding of how this has occurred and in particular how formal decisions of the ECJ and MTF have mandated revisions to national laws requires an analysis of each national case. The following sections provide such an analysis.

Germany

European intervention in German media policy has been strongly opposed by German Länder which have considered media policy to be exclusively the domain of the state (Chrocziel and Dieselhorst, 1996; Humphreys, 1997). In response, the EU institutions have taken an increasingly active role in regulating German media markets through competition law and decisions of the ECJ. Indirect influence came through national adoption of the audience share model.

German regulation of broadcasting markets

The 16 German Länder are responsible for regulation of broadcasting (Humphreys, 1994, 1996a: 220).[12] Regulation at the state level is balanced by the media decisions of the German Constitutional Court[13] and jurisprudence. Many Constitutional Court cases have dealt with ensuring plurality of opinion, editorial independence and protection of the media from government influence. But they have also dealt with questions of media ownership and programming rights. In particular, an early Court decision[14] ruled that media concentration could affect pluralism and therefore should be regulated against by the Länder (this resulted in rules in the interstate broadcasting treaties) (Robillard, 1995; Chrocziel and Dieselhorst, 1996). The actual model for legislation is left up to the state legislators, but the Court gave some general guidelines.[15]

Before implementing TWF, the Länder challenged the European Directive in the German Constitutional Court in 1989. Initially the state of Bavaria (seat of the company Kirch) brought the case (Robillard, 1995). Bavaria was joined by all the German Länder, except for Baden-Württemberg. The Federal government had signed the Directive on 3 October 1989. The Länder claimed that the Federal government had committed an illegal act in adopting the Directive as Chapter III of the Directive concerning quota regulations lay within the jurisdiction of the Länder. In 1995, the German Constitutional Court ruled against the Länder.[16] Since the case was brought, the European Commission has been trying to gain the support of the Länder for its media policy on a case-by-case basis. This led to some amendments of Articles in the 1997 TWF Directive (Krebber, 2001: 123).

Notwithstanding this development, the EU institutions have had a significant say in the regulation of the German media market and the development of media policy at the Länder level. MTF decisions on mergers and joint ventures involving German media groups are numerous. As documented in Chapter 3, the MTF dealt with no less than 14 cases involving German groups in the period 1994–99. Four cases were decided negatively.[17] During the last case (the proposed acquisition and joint control of the German pay-TV operator Premiere and BetaResearch by Bertelsmann and Kirch), the Commission firstly put informal pressure upon the German government and the Cartel Office to block the agreement at the national level. Only when the German government decided to approve the joint venture, did the MTF open an investigation. Under Kohl's leadership, the German government at the time responded angrily to this decision. Despite this political resistance, the Commission prevented the joint venture under the EU Merger Regulation. In a later case, *Kirch/BSkyB/Kirch Pay-TV*, Kirch and BSkyB proposed to take joint control over Kirch Pay-TV. The Commission expressed concern that Kirch would strengthen its already dominant position in pay televison markets with access to BSkyB's financial resources, marketing and distribution capabilities. As a compromise the companies offered to other operators increased access to Kirch's platform. In particular, interactive television companies could access the platform and utilise their own technologies. The Commission therefore did not oppose the merger.

To complement decisions of the MTF, the EC was able to indirectly influence policy formation at the Länder level. This was in the choice of the policy instrument used to regulate media ownership: audience share. Until 1996, a limit of 49 per cent ownership of media company shares was imposed on companies holding a licence for nationwide broadcasting or news channels, and there was a limit of two television stations and two radio stations (this was very similar to the French limit of 49 per cent and a licence for two television stations, nationally and regionally). As Humphreys and Lang explain, the regulation of media ownership at the state (Länder) level has only resulted into a regulatory race to the bottom as Länder attempted to attract sector investment (Humphreys, 1998; Humphreys and Lang, 1998). Under the 1996 Interstate Treaty on Broadcasting' a shareholder is allowed to control 100 per cent of the capital of a broadcasting company. (The limit of 50 per cent for national radio stations still applies.) There is no longer a limit to the number of television stations one can own. In place of the old rules, a new policy instrument was introduced in the 1996 treaty: that is, that companies are limited to 30 per cent of national audience share of the combined television stations they own (Poll, 1996; Ridder, 1996). The idea for this policy instrument was suggested in the GAH study which was sent out by the EC to national authorities in 1993 (GAH, 1993). The one hundred page, cross-country study strongly recommends the use of audience share as an effective instrument for guaranteeing media pluralism. Interviews reveal that diffusion of the idea was aided by the organisation of meetings in Germany by an EC head of unit, wherein national media experts discussed possible policy instruments for the new interstate treaty. German policy-makers were convinced of the utility of the instrument, and audience share was adopted as a key regulatory instrument in the 1996 interstate treaty.

It should be pointed out that the implementation of Commission Directives also accelerated market liberalisation in Germany. Before 1987, the German Länder agreed national treaties separately for terrestrial, cable, satellite and radio broadcasting; the financing of public service broadcasters; and the subsidisation of film and independent production (Holtz-Bacha, 1991; Herkströter, 1994; Humphreys, 1994). In 1987, the first Interstate Treaty on the Restructuring of Broadcasting was enacted. Implementation of TWF mandated a revision of the 1987 treaty. The resulting 1991 Interstate Treaty on Broadcasting which implemented the EU 1989 TWF Directive incorporated all previous separate Länder treaties. Presently, all the German Länder regulate their broadcasting with the 2003 Interstate Treaty on Broadcasting (Rundfunkstaatsvertrag). Although media markets are still regulated at the state-level in Germany, it undoubtedly represents a uniform policy nationally. As a result of regulatory competition between the Länder (Humphreys, 1998; Humphreys and Lang, 1998), the German treaty represents the most liberal regulatory framework for media markets in Europe.

The EU institutions have had a direct hand in shaping the German media market, in particular the development of digital television. Through its decisions, the European Commission and Court of Justice have halted further concentration in the (already highly concentrated) German market. Through its suggestion of policy instruments, the European Commission has presented its own solutions to the regulation of broadcasting markets at the state level. However, due to its federal structure, Germany is a long way from the introduction of a single regulator for the converged sectors as recommended by the European Commission. Germany has produced its own distinctive approach to regulating new media services with continued Länder regulation of those services relevant to broadcasting, and federal regulation of delivery systems (Levy, 1999).

German regulation of press markets
In contrast to Community direction in broadcasting, the EU institutions have been less interventionist in German press markets despite a high level of market concentration. According to the 1949 Grundgesetz (Articles 30, 70 and 75), the German states (Länder) are responsible for cultural policies, which include press policies (Humphreys, 1994). There is therefore no federal press law. The press is regulated by 16 different state press laws

(Landespressegesetze). This state level regulation has been balanced by the German Constitutional court (Bundeserfassungsgericht) which has made a number of decisions relating to the press industry (Humphreys, 1994; Robillard, 1995). Many of these decisions have related to pluralist representation, freedom of expression and assurance of unbiased news reporting. The federal Court has recommended regulation of press ownership, but the Länder have not yet considered such regulation as imperative. Significantly Germany has no conflict of interest law. In 2004 Schroeder's Social Democratic Party bought a stake in the regional newspaper *Frankfurter Rundschau*.

The 16 Länder press laws are all fairly similar in content.[18] All guarantee freedom of establishment for publishers, meaning that there is no licensing. There are no limits on press circulation as in France, nor are there distinctions between different press markets. The laws do include provisions for freedom of expression, dissemination and accuracy of information. Somewhat contradictorily, however, the state laws also protect the right of the publisher to specify the political line of the publication (Tendenzschutz). This gives owners of publishing companies considerable editorial control (Lange and Van Loon, 1990).

The federal government can of course apply general market laws to press markets. According to the Grundgesetz, the federal government is responsible for economic law according to Articles 73, 74, 75 and 79. Therefore competition law is applicable at the federal level, in addition to Länder media law (Humphreys, 1994; Ladeur, 1995).

However, concentrations have ofentimes been allowed above the threshold limits (Kleinsteuber, 1997: 81). Two recent decisions in the press sector have however been decided negatively by the Cartel Office utilising these thresholds.[19] No ownership provisions for the press sector are stipulated by the Länder beyond the turnover thresholds laid down in the federal 1973 Law on Restrictive Practices. Over the years, a number of national press commissions have been set up and carried out studies on the influence of the press. They have recommended ownership legislation as press concentration is viewed as a threat to freedom of information. The Länder however have never come to agreement on such measures. They do not wish ownership law to be imposed from the Federal level as it would mean a loss of political power. This applies also to Länder objection to European legislation.

Transparency of media holdings is required by a number of different federal laws (these apply to all companies, so to both press and broadcasting groups). The 1987 Commercial Law (Handelsgesetz updating the Commercial Law of 1897) requires that limited companies provide the names of all members of the board of management and name the seat of the parent company. Consolidated company accounts must be made public. The 1965 federal Corporation Law (Aktiengesetz) further requires companies to make an immediate public announcement as soon as shareholdings

of 25 per cent or 50 per cent are reached. The 1965 Accounting Law
(Buchführungsgesetz) imposes further requirements on the publication of
company accounts. The extent of publication depends on the legal form a
company takes. As mentioned in Chapter 6, there are no provisions in
Germany which require the disclosure of financial sources on privately
owned companies (including advertising companies). This presents serious
limitations to transparency of ownership (Humphreys, 1994). Some further
transparency measures are applied at the state level. State (Länder) laws
require publishers to print a listing in their newspapers about their staff
(including the name of the editor and publisher), operation and circulation.
But generally the Länder have produced weak regulation for transparency.
In 1997, the Kommission zur Ermittlung der Konzentration in Medien-
bereich (KEK) was set up to monitor ownership and regulatory compliance.
However, it is dependent upon information provided by the Länder which
is not always forthcoming.

The Netherlands

Due to its small market size and historical reasons, the Netherlands has
strongly resisted the move towards liberalisation of its broadcasting market.
For this reason, the Netherlands has come under much scrutiny from the
EU institutions. In particular, two European Court of Justice rulings has-
tened the Netherlands towards liberalisation of its broadcasting markets.

Dutch regulation of broadcasting markets
In 1987, the first Dutch Media Act regulated the provision of public service
broadcasting and licensed private radio stations. Private television companies were not permitted to broadcast independently, but were contracted to
provide public service programming. The Act set strict content provisions
for public service programming: 25 per cent of which needed to be news,
25 per cent entertainment, 20 per cent culture and 5 per cent education.
Each private company granted public service broadcasting time must set up
an internal programme charter which states the rights of journalists. The
1988 Act introduced a new regulatory body, the Commissariaat voor de
Media. The Commissariaat voor de Media, is an independent regulatory
body which regulates both private and public broadcasting. In 1991, the
Dutch introduced a new Media Act.[20] This Act encated the TWF Directive
and the ECJ case, *Commission of the European Communities* v. *Kingdom
of the Netherlands*. Under Dutch media law, foreign companies which
obtained air time on the national broadcasting network were obliged to
provide a certain number of radio programmes and to purchase their programming material from Dutch companies. The ECJ ruling in the *Commission of the European Communities* v. *Kingdom of the Netherlands* case,

meant that domestic companies were no longer obligated to purchase content material solely from Dutch providers.

The second Dutch case, the *TV10 SA* v. *Commissariaat voor de Media*, was brought to challenge the Dutch broadcasting law in 1991 (eventually decided in 1994). TV10, a company based in Luxembourg, was commercially broadcasting to the Netherlands. According to the 1987 Dutch Media Act, commercial broadcasters were not permitted.[21] The Commissariaat voor de Media, the Dutch regulatory body for broadcasting, challenged TV10 in a Dutch national court. The Dutch court referred the case to the European Court of Justice (Voorhoof, 1995; Wattel, 1995). The ECJ found that the Commissariaat voor de Media had legitimately prevented TV10 from broadcasting through cable from Luxembourg to the Netherlands (CMLR, 1995: 1257–1276). In the Court ruling, the ECJ stated:

> The Treaty provisions on freedom to provide services cannot therefore be interpreted as precluding a Member State from treating as a domestic broadcaster a broadcasting body constituted under the law of another Member State and established in that State but whose activities are wholly or principally directed towards the territory of the first Member State, if that broadcasting body was established there in order to avoid the rules adopted by the first Member State as part of a cultural policy intended to establish a pluralist and non-commercial radio and television broadcasting system.

The ECJ had accepted that TV10 had deliberately relocated abroad in order to avoid Dutch national law. However, the TV10 ruling was to prove exceptional. In most rulings, as detailed in Chapter 2, the Court recognised the right of broadcasters to relocate abroad. In any case, the Dutch government had to legitimise foreign broadcasts according to this TWF provision, which it did in Article 77) of the 1991 Act.

The Dutch 1991 Media Act was drafted to liberalise the domestic private market and promote Dutch production. However, once it reached the stage of enactment, it restricted private broadcasting to cable transmission. All terrestrial frequencies were reserved for the public stations. A system arose wherein cable licenses were issued by the Ministry for Culture and required separately from each local authority (of which there were over 700 in the Netherlands). Broadcasting solely at local and regional levels was restricted to public service providers. The 1990 Act contained some provisions on cross-media ownership in that any broadcaster with over 60 per cent audience reach, could not own a newspaper with beyond 25 per cent national reach. There were no limits on internal ownership of private companies (100 per cent ownership is possible).

Regarding transparency, the 1991 Act required that broadcasters permitted inspection of their accounts to the Commissariaat voor de Media upon request. Transparency of media holdings is high in the Netherlands. According to general company law, all companies (also non-media) must

publish annual accounts. There is an additional obligation for all companies to report significant stock changes publicly (in a newspaper). Significant stock changes are considered to be when a share holder reaches 5, 10,
25, 50 and 66 per cent share of a company. All shares must be registered
nominally.

The 1994 Media Act revised the 1991 Act. The revision was prompted
by a McKinsey consultancy report on the viability of public service television. The 1994 Act loosened programming rules for public service broadcasters, allowing them to better compete with commercial broadcasters. The
Act did not introduce any further private sector liberalisation. In 1995, DG
IV ruled against the 1995 Holland Media Group merger (Tucker, 1995).
When the only three Dutch domestic broadcasters (RTL, Veronica and
Endemol) proposed a joint venture in commercial television, the Dutch government requested a ruling from DG IV. Had the Dutch government not
referred the case under Article 21 of the Merger Regulation, DG IV would
not have been permitted to judge it. DG IV ruled that a dominant position
would be created and the concentration was blocked.

The Netherlands was one of the first European countries to privatise its
national telecommunications operator, PTT Telecom, in 1989. In 1995
licenses were issued for further private operators. The rapid development
of telecommunications systems (including wide cable reach) prompted the
Dutch government to amend its 1990 Media Act through its new 1998
Telecommunications Law[22] and 2001 Media Act.[23] Rules amending the
Media act included the licensing of local and regional level private broadcasters and the provision of new services by public broadcasters. In 2000
the PSB licence fee was dropped and funding was allocated by top-slicing
income tax. In 2004 the European Commission initialed an investigation
of overspending by the Dutch PSB. This most likely arose from national
criticism of overspending, as the levy on income tax makes PSB spending
much more visible to citizens.

Dutch regulation of press markets
The Netherlands has no specific regulation relating to the press and there
are no special provisions for press concentration under competition law.
However, Dutch publishing companies practice a form of self-regulation.
In 1993, Dutch publishing companies agreed to limit their publications to
one-third of the national newspaper market (newspaper markets tend to be
national in the Netherlands and not regional). This was agreed through the
platform of the national publishing trade association (Lange and Van Loon,
1990).

From 1956 all Dutch companies were regulated by competition law: the
1956 Economic Competition Act (No. 401), updated by the 1989 Economic
Competition Act (No. 57) and the 1997 Competition Act (No. 242). The
1997 Competition Act was based upon European competition law and

became effective on 1 January 1998. Under the new law, an autonomous Dutch Competition Authority was established to monitor and prevent instances of dominant position. Before 1998, decisions of this kind were taken solely by the Dutch Minister for Economic Affairs. Now they are taken independently by the director general of the Competition Authority.

United Kingdom

As in Germany, the institutions of the European Union have become involved directly in the regulation of the British media market. In 1994, the ECJ demanded a rewording of the 1990 Broadcasting Act (detailed in Chapter 2). The MTF has investigated many cases of dominant position within the British domestic market.[24] In two cases, British Telecom/MCI (1993) and BSkyB/British Digital Broadcasting (BDB) (1997), the Commission prevented market concentrations. It was the ITC that had asked the MTF to intervene to exclude BSkyB from British Digital Broadcasting (BDB) in 1997 (Snoddy, 1997). In a third case, *Microsoft/Liberty Media/Telewest* (2000)[25] the MTF expressed concern that the proposed joint control of the UK cable group would effect the choice of set-top box technology. The proposal was withdrawn before a decision was taken.

British regulation of broadcasting markets

In contrast to its light-touch regulation of press markets, the UK has regulated broadcasting markets to a comparatively greater extent than other EU Member States with a clear separation of markets (Humphreys, 1996: 221).[26] The UK has been slow to liberalise commercial terrestrial television. ITV, Channel 3 (the first commercial channel) was first licensed in 1955. However, it was held to strict content requirements to protect pluralism, as was the BBC. Channel 4 was licensed in 1982 as a 'minority' channel. It was not privately owned and further restricted in terms of content and a portion of its advertising revenue was allocated to ITV.

The 1990 Act introduced some liberalisation under the Thatcher government (Glencross, 1991). ITV licence holders were permitted to own up to 20 per cent in a company owning another ITV licence. The Act stipulated that the ITV companies would in future have to bid for their licences through a 'licence auction' (following the Act, 3 of the 15 ITV companies lost their licences). This resulted in a concentration in the market with Granada, Carlton and UNM strengthening their market positions through acquisitions. Permission was granted for a fifth terrestrial television station (Channel 5, which eventually aired in 1997). The 1990 Act established competency for broadcasting under the Radio Authority and the (pre-existing) Department of National Heritage. The Independent Television Commission (ITC) was also set up (replacing both the Independent Broadcasting Authority (IBA) and the Cable Authority).[27] As explained in Chapter 3, the TWF

Directive enabled the UK to establish its non-domestic satellite policy with which it has generated a high amount of capital investment.

As detailed in Chapter 3, the European Commission was unsatisfied with TWF implementation, as the UK had established a separate regulatory regime for terrestrial and satellite broadcasting. After a series of formal letters sent between the Commission and the UK,[28] the Commission took the UK to the European Court of Justice in 1994. The ECJ ruled in favour of the Commission and suggested a rewording of the 1990 Broadcasting Act. However, the UK continued to apply different rules to domestic than to non-domestic broadcasters, and, significantly, still did not apply TWF provisions to non-domestic satellite licences. At the same time, the UK claimed jurisdiction over foreign broadcasts aimed at the UK market (i.e. BSkyB). The UK objected in particular to the TWF rule that broadcasters should be regulated in the country of transmission, because it would mean (if applied) that it could not authorise control over BSkyB broadcasts from Luxembourg. This led the UK government to lobby for a revision in the 1997 TWF Directive. Article 2, Paragraph 3 of the 1997 TWF Directive was revised to state that a Member State has jurisdiction over a broadcaster if:

(a) the broadcaster has its head office in that Member State and the editorial decisions about programme schedules are taken in that Member State;

(b) if a broadcaster has its head office in one Member State but editorial decisions on programme schedules are taken in another Member State, it shall be deemed to be established in the Member State where a significant part of the workforce involved in the pursuit of the television broadcasting activity operates; if a significant part of the workforce involved in the pursuit of the television broadcasting activity operates in each of those Member States, the broadcaster shall be deemed to be established in the Member State where it has its head office; if a significant part of the workforce involved in the pursuit of the television broadcasting activity operates in neither of those Member States, the broadcaster shall be deemed to be established in the Member State where it first began broadcasting in accordance with the system of law of that Member State, provided that it maintains a stable and effective link with the economy of that Member State;

(c) if a broadcaster has its head office in a Member State but decisions on programme schedules are taken in a third country, or vice-versa, it shall be deemed to be established in the Member State concerned, provided that a significant part of the workforce involved in the pursuit of the television broadcasting activity operates in that Member State.

This revision permitted the British government to continue to regulate BSkyB without disruption to its satellite licence policy. These TWF provisions were incorporated into British law in the 1997 Satellite Television regulations and the 1998 Television regulations, since which time there have no larger been 'non-domestic satellite licences', merely 'satellite licences.' The UK still has not applied TWF provisions to satellite licences.

Although the UK has been keen to encourage cross-border broadcasting to continental Europe, it has been less keen to receive signals from abroad. Rather than ban this directly, the UK indirectly banned transmission through the illegalisation of smartcards. Under Section 177 of the Broadcasting Act 1990 (still in force) the ITC could recommend to the Secretary of State for Culture that a foreign channel be made the subject of a proscription order if it is satisfied the channel repeatedly 'offends against good taste and decency'. A proscription order makes it a criminal offence in the UK to sell smartcards and decoders or subscriptions, to publish programme information or to advertise designated services. The UK banned the selling of smartcards for a number of channels broadcasting hardcore pornography (Red Hot Television, Red Hot Dutch, Eros TV, TV Erotica (also known as xxxTV), Channel Bizzare, Rendezvous Channel, Satisfaction Channel, Satisfaction Club, Television Eurotica, Rendez Vous and Adult X).

The European Commission, as in Germany, was successful in influencing the choice of a key policy instrument used in the UK 1996 Broadcasting Act – that of audience share. The new market measurement limits audience share of broadcasters to 15 per cent (for both television and radio stations). As with Germany, this idea was adopted from proposals in the two Commission studies (GAH, 1993 and 1994) and the 1994 Green Paper on media ownership. The NERA and BMIG studies (assessing audience share) came after the Commission studies (NERA, 1995; BMIG, 1995). When asked in an interview, the DNH official who drafted the 1996 UK Broadcasting Act stated:

> The team was informed about audience share measure by the European Commission Green Papers. The Commission was looking at this. Initially 'revenue' was preferred by the DNH as a more desirable measurement. However, audience share distinguishes this legislation from competition law. Revenue and audience share was also long considered as well as traditional methods (such as licensing). At a late stage in the policy process, there was an amendment to the Act.

With the new instrument, limits to license ownership were removed, that is, as long as the combination of company ownership and their corresponding license holding did not exceed 15 per cent. The measurement is based upon a media owner's audience share accumulated over a number of channels (as in Germany). The Act remained restrictive compared with other Member State laws. No legal entity could control more than one ITV channel for the same area. Control of both an ITV licence and Channel 5 was not allowed. There was a restriction of ownership of one FM and one AM station licence in a local area. Three licences could be granted subject to a public interest test. No one could own more than one national radio station (DNH, 1996a, 1996b). All of this is of course about to change with the enactment of the UK Communications Act in 2003.

Under the 1996 act, national newspapers with less than 20 per cent market share were permitted to own one private broadcaster (radio, television or satellite) and have full control of a non-domestic satellite broadcaster. A publisher could also own up to three local radio licences if it has less than 20 per cent of local circulation (subject to a public interest test). If a local newspaper has between 20 per cent and 50 per cent of local circulation it could only own one local FM radio station and one AM station. If a local newspaper has over 50 per cent of local circulation it could only own one local radio station (subject to a public interest test). Terrestrial broadcasters could own up to a 20 per cent stake in national newspapers and non-domestic satellite licences. Regional publishers were allowed to own one regional broadcaster, as long as there was no major overlap between the licensed area and the paper's circulation area. In the same year, the Royal Charter was renewed; the BBC's licence fee was upheld and it was given permission to expand commercially; and the Department of National Heritage (DNH) became the Department of Culture, Media and Sport (DCMS).

Since its privatisation, British Telecomm (BT) has been under regulatory supervision of the Office of Telecommunications (OFTEL). BT's expansion was allowed only on a case-by-case basis. BT has not been permitted cable interests (until some limited recently) and other cable companies were encouraged to invest in telephony to break up the monopoly of the privatised BT. The UK deliberately attracted US companies to invest in cable and telephony rather than have the incumbent operator lay the lines (as in Germany and the Netherlands).

OFTEL and the DCMS were enthusiastic about the DG Information Society's convergence initiation. The British legislative initiative for communications ran parallel to the EC's convergence initiative. There was a high degree of dialogue between DG Information Society and the UK regulatory authorities. A joint team was set up to work on a British convergence initiative in 1998. The UK published a Communications White Paper, 'A new future for communications' (Cm 5010), in December 2000. The Communications Bill was introduced in the House of Commons in November 2002 and the House of Lords in March 2003 and, following much discussion, was eventually passed in July 2003.

The UK was thus the first to implement the EC new regulatory framework for communications. The 2003 Communications Act implements the Authorisation, Access, Universal Service and Framework Directives.[29] All eyes are presently on the UK as to the success of its new regulatory framework. The prior licensing system is being replaced with a new framework for the regulation of electronic communications networks and services. The first step was the establishment of a joint regulatory authority for broadcasting and telecommunications, the Office of Communications (OFCOM) which was a key recommendation of the European Commission. OFCOM is replacing existing regulatory bodies (these are the Broadcasting Standards Commission, the Director General of Telecommunications, the Independent Television Commission, and the Radiocommunications Authority). Similar to Italy's *Autorita per le garanzie nelle comunicazioni,* essentially OFCOM will take on board all existing tasks of the UK's previous regulatory authorities. Schedule 1 of the Act transfers all powers previously assigned to other regulatory authorities to OFCOM. These include the licensing of broadcasting services (television, radio, cable, satellite, digital), regulation of Channel 4 Corporation, minority channels, reservation of digital capacity to the BBC, listed events, fairness and privacy in broadcasting and standards for transmission services.

The key change in the Communications Act, as in most broadcasting act revisions, is in ownership regulation, which has produced the most political debate. Press owners are no longer prevented from acquiring 100 per cent of broadcastering companies. With the exception of a the prevention of a press owner with more than 20 per cent of the press market from purchasing ITV (i.e. the Murdoch-controlled News International). The 20 per cent limit on shareholdings in ITN has also been lifted. Significantly, the Act will open the whole of the UK media market to foreign owners in 2003 (including non-EU owners). Press predictions are that Murdoch will buy Channel 5, Viacom will buy the ITV companies, and Clear Channel (another large US company) will buy Capital Radio.[30] The Act will allow increased competition between broadcasters and telecommunications operators. Although ownership restrictions have been relaxed, the same standard requirements should cover all broadcasters (those standards relating to pluralism, advertising, content, protection of minors, etc.). Additional specific requirements will apply to the BBC (e.g. content requirements and programming quotas). In addition, there are mechanisms for self-regulation. This reflects the principles set out in the EC's 1999 Communication on 'Principles and guidelines for the Community's audiovisual policy in the digital age' (CEC, 1999c). Although OFCOM was designed as a 'super regulator' independent of government control, any media merger will have to be eventually approved by the Secretary of State who can issue an 'intervention notice' which considers the effect on viewer choice and quality. This actually brings media market decision-making under closer political scrutiny than before the Act was in place.

A number of requirements for pluralism were introduced in the Act. It requires television channels to use separate news providers. It has strengthened children's programming requirements. It has produced guidelines on 'localness' meaning that programmes cannot be pre-packaged from one studio (be it located in London or abroad). 'Localness' requires that a certain number of programmes are to be relevant to people in a given area and created in that area, relating to news, local information, speech and music. The Act also establishes a Consumer Panel and Advisory committees for different parts of the United Kingdom and for elderly and disabled persons.

British regulation of press markets

The present structure of the UK market differs from other Member State in that there has been relatively diverse ownership in the broadcasting market and a highly concentrated and polarised press market (Curran and Seaton, 1997). This has come about because the UK has no specific ownership regulation relating to the press. The Minister for Trade and Industry can block a transfer of a newspaper taking into consideration a 'public interest test'. Weymouth and Lamizet attribute the lack of UK press regulation to the dominance of tabloids on the market (1996). They view a large part of the British press as 'unruly and unregulated' (1996: 210).

Otherwise, general competition law applies to market concentrations. Up until recently, competition law was determined by a number of different acts, chiefly the 1980 Competition Act. Under the law, dominant position was determined if a company had over 25 per cent of a relevant market. A concentration could be blocked if it totalled over £30 million. As in many countries, political considerations often rode roughshod over media merger decisions. For example, a press market concentration was exempted from competition law during 1981 when News International was permitted to buy *The Times* and *Sunday Times* from Thomson Ltd. This development was thought to be politically motivated as *News International* at the time supported the political line of the Conservative government. The same happened in 1994, when DMGT acquired T. Bailey Forman's regional and local newspapers. The Monopolies and Mergers Commission (MMC) opposed the acquisition, but was overridden by the then Minister for Industry, Tim Eggar. Eggar at the time imposed a number of conditions subjecting DMGT to impartiality but these were repealed in 2001.

The UK has since implemented European competition law with the 1998 Competition Act. The 1998 Competition Act introduces the prohibition of anti-competitive behaviour (based on Article 81, formerly Article 85 of the EC Treaty) and a prohibition of abuse of dominant position (based on Article 82, formerly Article 86 of the EC Treaty). The 1998 Competition Act replaces the 1973 Fair Trading Act, the Restrictive Trade Practices Act 1976, the Resale Prices Act 1976, the 1980 Competition Act and related provisions found in other legislation concerning competition. After an interim period, the Act was fully effective from March 2000. An independent competition authority should have introduced greater impartiality in press market decisions. However, the 2003 Communications Act reintroduces potential political scrutiny into concentration of media markets.

Luxembourg

Rather than creating a public sector broadcaster for such a small population, Luxembourg licensed Europe's first private radio broadcaster, Radio Luxembourg and Télé Luxembourg in 1930. CLR was restructured into Compagnie Luxembourgeoise de Télédiffusion (CLT) in 1954. As detailed in Chapter 6, CLT has since grown into a large multi-national company presently active in French, Belgian, Dutch, German, UK and Spanish television and radio markets.

The policies of the EU institutions have undoubtedly had a direct effect upon the shaping of the Luxembourg media market and on its domestic media policy. The most obvious direct effect is that of the 1989 TWF Directive upon the growth of Luxembourg's tax revenue. Luxembourg's liberal policy framework has proved extremely attractive to outside investors wishing to broadcast programming from the *Astra* satellite to other Member States (as discussed in Chapter 6). TWF turned the media sector into a very important sector of the Luxembourg economy. Unsurprisingly, Luxembourg's politicians have been keen to keep this liberal framework in place to guarantee media sector growth. The European institutions for their part have taken advantage of Luxembourg's liberal policy *vis-à-vis* foreign broadcasters to open up media markets in other Member States. The European Court of Justice, in two cases dealing with Luxembourg, decided in favour of cross-border broadcasting. As detailed in Chapter 2, in both cases (*TV10 SA* v. *Commissariaat voor de Media* and *VT4 Ltd* v. *Vlaamse Gemeenschap*) Luxembourg-based companies were allowed to continue to broadcast even though their broadcasts contravened Dutch and Belgian media laws.

The TWF Directive at the same time required that a media law be introduced in Luxembourg for the first time. Up until 1991, Luxembourg had no media law to speak of. The most significant change was the introduction of advertising rules which had been absent from Luxembourg up until this point. When it introduced its Electronic media Law of 27 July 1991, it introduced media ownership restrictions for the first time. In order not to discourage foreign investment, these rules applied only to domestic radio broadcasting and not to television or broadcasts to other Member States (i.e. from the *Astra* satellite). Ownership in domestic radio stations is limited to one company only and no more than 25 per cent of the shares or voting rights in such a company (including indirect holdings). Transparency rules were also introduced in the 1991 Act. Companies applying for broadcasting licences transmitted 'via low-power transmitters' must detail a complete list of their owners, directors and managers. Any foreseen funding and advertising income of a company had to be indicated and a copy of the accounts had to be delivered to the government every year.

Spain

Spanish media regulation did not come about until the establishment of an independent media following the death of Franco in 1976. The Spanish press market has grown quite rapidly since this time, as has the broadcasting market since its liberalisation in 1988. Up until 1998, Spain had strict media ownership rules for radio and television compared with most EU countries, but not for the press or cross-media ownership (as in the UK). The European institutions have shown a keen interest the development of Spanish broadcasting regulation in recent years.

Spanish regulation of broadcasting markets

Spain has no national regulatory authority for broadcasting (unlike federal Germany) even though Spain is a unitary state. However (like Germany) it is monitored by a constitutional court. This has meant that, in practice, some of the regions have relative autonomy in certain policy areas, including broadcasting (Blanco and Vandenbulck, 1995).[31] But only Catalonia has its own regional authority for the media.[32]

Following the collapse of the dictatorship in 1976, Radio Nacional de España, and TVE were abolished in 1977. A 1980 broadcasting law established Radio Televisón Española (RTVE) as the Spanish public service broadcasting company, for both radio and television (from 1983, this also included regional television). Television remained a public monopoly until the 1988 Law on Private Television.[33] The 1987 Telecommunications Law[34] which was passed in 1987 prohibited publishers from having broadcasting interests.

The Spanish 1980 and 1988 broadcasting laws set out comparably strict media ownership rules for radio and television relative to other Member States. Under the rules, companies were permitted to own only one television station each and shares therein are capped at 25 per cent of capital. Foreigners were not permitted to own Spanish broadcasting companies, but could own up to 25 per cent of capital. This occurred with ownership of Antena 3, Telecinco and the French-controlled group, Canal Plus España. However, the rules never worked in practice. Not only because the rules were not adhered to regionally (there were circa 600 illegal local radio stations in Spain (de Mateo, 1997), but even the government decided to ignore them. In 1994 Spain's largest media group, PRISA, bought Spain's second largest media group, SER. An acquisition which the Spanish government at the time approved regardless of Spanish media ownership rules. Divestment by PRISA in SER was never required and PRISA went on to invest in numerous radio stations, including the national network, Antena 3. Fininvest also overstepped ownership limits in Telecinco but afterwards divested to meet to the legal 25 per cent limit.

Under a 1992 amendment to the 1987 Telecommunications Act,[35] companies holding a licence for a satellite television service were subject to the same ownership rules as terrestrial companies. The 1987 Act set the same limits for private radio stations. Radio licences were restricted to one licence per owner for a medium wave station. Regarding transparency, there are rules (still valid) requiring television companies to register the membership of their management boards with the Ministry of Transport and Communications. All shares in broadcasting must be nominative. Any changes in capital need to be reported to the register. Private broadcasting companies are subjected annually to an external audit, the results of which are registered with the Ministry of Transport and Communications.

In 1994, Spain passed a law entitled, Televisión Sin Fronteras (Television Without Frontiers)[36] which implemented the European TWF Directive.[37] This introduced foreign competition to the Spanish market. Accompanying the law was the Law on Cable Television (eventually passed in 1995), which requires cable companies to adhere to the same rules (De Mendivil, 1995; Suarez Lozano, 1996). From this time, the EC's Merger Task Force and the European Court of Justice were active in shaping the development of Spanish media markets, particularly the digital television market.

In 1996, the MTF prevented the Telefónica/Canal Plus/Cablevisión joint venture. As mentioned in Chapter 3, the Commission had to put up a considerable fight to wrench the decision away from the Spanish government. The Prisa group then proposed to Canal Plus France and other investors the creation of a new firm called Sogecable to launch a new Spanish digital platform by satellite, Canal Satélite Digital, and the management of the analogue terrestrial pay-TV channel Canal +. The conservative Spanish government, the Partido Popular, tried to prevent the use of the simulcrypt standard by Canal Satélite Digital in two laws (Llorens-Maluquer, 1998: 578–85).[38] As detailed in Chapter 2, the Commission forced Spain to amend both laws in 1997.[39] Act 17/1997 had mandated in Article 136 that all platform decoders must be open and all conditional access services must be registered. This requirement was struck down by the Court of Justice in a preliminary ruling as DG Competition found it to be unjustified.[40] Consequently, in 2003, the Spanish government was committed by the Spanish Tribunal Supremo to pay 26.4 million Euro in compensation to Sogecable for commercial damages as a result of the illegal application over six months of the 17/97 Act.

Hence, Spain had initially preferred one digital platform of its key national players, Canal Plus España and Télefonica, rather than requiring the two players to establish separate platforms. The Commission forced, through competition law, the establishment of two market players. Spain then attempted to impose a single encryption technology (multicrypt) at the national level. Simulticrypt is less expensive for the viewer, but multicrypt has the advantage of being able to build many different encrypted services into the set-top box (Scheuer and Knopp, 2003: 12). Again, the European Commission ruled against the Spanish government, ensuring that there should be a market choice. The two national players, naturally, chose different systems. Although, as Llorens-Maluquer (1998) points out, there may have been political favouritism at work at the national level, one has to question the wisdom of EC decision-making in this case. Not only did enforcing national competition go against the EC's own recommendation, under the 1995 TV standards Directive, to encourage the use of one digital standard, but the market outcome was far from ideal. As detailed in Chapter 6, the choice of different digital set-top boxes meant increased financial difficulties for market players leading to the eventual merger of the platforms Canal Satélite Digital and Vía Digital and the bankruptcy of a third (DTT) market entrant, Quiero, in 2002. If the government had been permitted by the EC to enforce a single technology (e.g. multicrypt) then had been simply required to guarantee licensing of different operators, this may have resulted in a more stable market environment.

In 1997, the Spanish government embraced the Commission's convergence initiative and drew up plans for the 'Liberalisation and reorganisation of the convergent industries of telecommunications, cable and television' (de Mateo, 1997: 2). This required revision of existing broadcasting and telecommunications laws (Hopewell, 1996). At the end of 1997 the Spanish government drew up a package of measures designed to ensure a total transition to digital transmission by the year 2001 (linking the measures to a renewal of the broadcasting licences of the country's commercial terrestrial channels, which expired at the end of 1999). The resulting 1998 Law on Commercial Television encompassed recommendations in the European convergence initiative. The 1987 and 1988 laws were abrogated by 1998 rules. Significantly, ownership limits in a single stakeholder were raised to 49 per cent of a commercial television station. This allowed Telecinco and Antena 3 to concentrate their shareholding structures. Local radio was completely liberalised. National radio ownership limits remained with a company limited to ownership of not more than one digital AM licence or more than two FM licences in one region. In October 2002 Spain amended the 1998 Law of Commercial Television to allow a single stakeholder to own 100 per cent of a commercial television station.

Spanish regulation of press markets
During the Franco dictatorship (1939–76), the media was strictly controlled by the Ministry of Information. A state press company, called Prensa del Movimiento, was established by the Franco regime (which continued to exist as a private company after government collapse in 1976). A similar state radio company, Radio Nacional de España, was set up to broadcast nationally, as was the Cadena de Ondas Populares Españolas (COPE), which was jointly run by the Vatican and the Franco government. A law on press censorship was passed in 1940 and the National Press and Information Office was set up to censor the press. A similar body, the Informa-

tion Service, controlled the radio. Some private press and radio groups were tolerated by the Franco regime. Of the private press groups tolerated (numerous resistance papers existed illegally), Barcelona's *La Vanguardia* and Madrid's *ABC* and *YA* were most popular. By 1970, private press groups had 74 per cent of the market (Nieto, 1973, quoted in Vilches, 1996: 175). The private radio Sociedád Española de Radiodiffusión (SER) (established before Franco) continued under Franco. The state television, TVE 1, was set up in 1956. Vilches reports that 'programming policy meandered on in contexts dominated either by indirect political control, or the grossest manipulation of information content' (1996: 184). It remained so until Franco's death in 1975.

There are presently no restrictions on newspaper ownership in Spain. The 1978 constitution contains provisions on freedom of expression and freedom of the press. In 1986, Spain joined the European Union and foreign ownership of the press was allowed for the first time 'to adapt Spanish legislation to the regulation of the European (Community)' (de Mateo, 1997: 197). Until 1984, some newspapers were still owned by the state. There remain some restrictions on cross-media ownership.

Italy

Italy has often looked to Europe to solve difficult domestic disputes. The specific Italian problem of media concentration represents such a dispute. Italy has been fairly successful in regulating media ownership of the press, but has failed conspicuously to control increasing concentration in broadcasting. However, the EU has not intervened in media markets in Italy as it did in Germany. The private company, Mediaset, and the public broadcaster, RAI, dominate the terrestrial broadcasting market. There is little competition from satellite and cable.

Italy's failure to regulate concentration in the broadcasting market has led domestic Italian politicians and Italian members of the European Parliament to lobby the Commission to introduce European rules on media ownership. The first 1987 EP report on ownership was written by the Italian MEP, Roberto Barzanti. This was followed by a deluge of European Parliament reports on media diversity as discussed in Chapter 4. Most of these resulted from the Committee on Culture, Youth, Education and the Media (CULT) which during Prodi's government had no less than 17 Italian Members. Italian MEPs were generally united in their support of European quotas in TWF. But the most intense discussions were over media ownership and these reflected political divisions at home.[41] In particular, CULT's rapporteur, the Italian MEP Luciana Castellina, of the Italian Rifondazione Comunista party, spoke out against European trends in media concentration. This in-depth treatment of the issue that led the European Commission to embark on a policy initiative for media ownership.

At the same time, Italy provided ample opportunity for the EU to expand its competence for media policy due to the willingness of Italian courts to refer media cases to the ECJ. Three of Italy's regional courts, Biella, Lazio and Ragusa, referred cases. The first was the *Sacchi* case that was referred to the European Court by the Biella Court. As discussed, in the *Sacchi* case, the ECJ ruled that television signals could be classed as services ruling which formed the basis for the TWF Directive.

In the second case, *Maria Salonia* v. *Giorgio Poidomani and Franca Baglieri, née Giglio,* an Italian regional court again looked to the Luxembourg court to solve a case which was in fact of high political salience. This case, brought by the regional court of Ragusa in Sicily (*Tribunale civile di Ragusa, Sezione civile, Ordinanzadel*), was the third media case to be brought before the ECJ (after *Sacchi* and *Debauve*). The Court queried the exclusive rights agreement between the Italian Federation of Newspaper Publishers and the United Federation of Trade Unions of Newsagents. Under the 'national agreement' signed in 1974 between publishing groups and the unions, publishers could only supply newspapers to shops with licences granted by 'inter-regional joint committees'. In the town of Ragusa, Maria Salonia wished to sell newspapers but was not granted a licence by the Sicilian committee. Specifically, the court questioned whether the agreement constituted a dominant market position (via vertical integration) according to definitions under Article 85 of the Treaty of Rome. Italian magistrates expected the ECJ to make a similar ruling as it did in the Netherlands in a 1978 case in which it broke up a similar agreement between the producers and retailers of Dutch bicycles. However, the ECJ proved itself unwilling to become involved in the Sicilian dispute. It ruled that there was no conflict with the Treaty, as the agreement did not affect any Member State other than Italy. Even though it had been argued that the agreement affected the distribution of foreign as well as domestic newspapers.

The third Italian case dealt with reference for a preliminary ruling by the regional court of Lazio (Tribunale amministrativo regionale del Lazio) on the interpretation of the TWF Directive 89/552/EEC relating to advertising.[42] As detailed in Chapter 2, the Lazio court requested an interpretation of Article 17(1)(b) of TWF. The case, which eventually ended in 1996, gave the Court an opportunity to override TWF's rules on advertising. This had significance for the 1997 amendment of the 1989 TWF Directive. This case in particular presented an instance where the ECJ could have ruled in favour of protecting public interest goals as stipulated by the European Parliament – but it did not.

The MTF has not been much involved in the regulation of Italian media markets. Much of the concentration of the Italian broadcasting market occurred before the 1989 Merger Regulation. The only two MTF cases dealt with foreign investment in the Italian company Telepiù.[43] The MTF was able to set some conditions in the second case. Telepiù had originally belonged to Berlusconi, but its sale was forced by an Italian Constitutional Court ruling. After a series of share swapping at the European level, Telepiù is presently 100 per cent owned by News Corporation, acquisition of which was approved by the MTF in 2003. As Gibbons comments, even though 'the merger would create a near-monopoly in the Italian pay-TV market' and 'Stream and Telepiù would together hold exclusive rights to premium films and major Italian football coverage, their potential rivals would be foreclosed from obtaining so-called "driver" content for pay-TV ... it seemed clear that Stream would otherwise be closed down by Newcorp' (2003: 11). As a condition of approval, the MTF insisted that parties offered third-party access to the platform and premium content until 2011. Responsibility for implementation was given to the Italian competition authority.

Italian regulation of broadcasting markets

The 1975 Broadcasting Law[44] officially affirmed the public service station, RAI, as the sole national broadcaster in Italy. It also permitted cable broadcasting at local levels. Private interests challenged the law in court. This led to a Constitutional Court ruling of 1976,[45] which opened the national market to cable broadcasters. However, both legal and technical restrictions meant that cable never really flourished in Italy. Terrestrial broadcasting remained restricted to the regional level. There was a proliferation in radio stations (Satori reports 4,000 by the mid-1980s, 1996: 150). Private terrestrial television began operation from this time onwards. Although broadcasting was only permitted at the regional level, regional broadcasters networked nationally. These commercial stations were in effect illegal until a further 1988 constitutional court ruling legitimised national broadcasting by private operators.[46] By 1990, unrestrained concentration had led to a duopoly with the public service, RAI, and the private broadcaster, Fininvest, each roughly sharing 50 per cent each of the market.

The necessity to implement the 1989 TWF Directive forced the Italian parliament to come to an agreement on its first law regulating private broadcasting. This was the Broadcasting Act of 6 August 1990.[47] The law was largely based upon the French Law on Freedom of Communication. It implemented into statutory law the Constitutional Court ruling allowing private broadcasters to apply for national broadcasting licences. The 1990 Act lays down rules relating to media ownership and transparency.[48] It further defines the principles of pluralism, diversity in opinion, and the objectivity and impartiality of news coverage.[49] Importantly, it introduced advertising rules, which had not been present in Italy up until that point. Interestingly, even though Italy had been, along with France, instrumental in inserting the

'European quota' rule into TWF, Italy itself was successful in 'exempting from the quota clauses "local television broadcasts not forming part of a national network" – known as the "the Berlusconi article"' (Hirsch and Petersen, 1992: 49). For that reason the regionally broadcast (but nationally networked) Fininvest channels were exempt from the quota rule. The Act established a new regulatory authority, the Press and Broadcasting Authority (Garante per la radiodiffusione e l'editoria) which replaced the Press Council (Garante dell'editoria). (This authority was replaced in 1997 by the Authority for Communications.)

Similar to the 1985 French Law on Freedom of Communication, the 1990 Italian Broadcasting Act lays down different ownership rules for national and regional television. A company was limited to owning no more than three national broadcasting channels. It could only own two channels if its existing channels consisted of 25 per cent of the number of all national broadcasting channels. A company was also restricted to 25 per cent of the total income of the national communications market, a rule which never worked in practice as the total income of the national communications market could, of course, never be properly defined. However, this instrument was later proposed to the European Commission in a Fininvest study (as related in Chapter 5). DG XIII contemplated the measurement in its convergence initiative.

In 1990, local television licences were limited to three regional stations, provided that they covered different broadcasting regions. If owners held three local television licences with bordering regions, they could not exceed a combined population of 10 million viewers. Local radio licences are restricted to seven licences nationally or an audience reach of 10 million, and to one licence regionally. Foreign ownership by legal entities situated within the EU (or within countries with similar trade agreements) was not restricted. However, foreign (non-EU) companies were not allowed to own a majority shareholding in a broadcasting company. The Act's provisions regarding ownership were criticised as it merely confirmed the market status quo (Mazzoleni, 1999). Mazzoleni commented that 'the 1990 Broadcasting Act (the so-called Mammì Law) only gave political ratification to (a) de facto situation' of market concentration (1999: 12).

However, the 1990 Act should be seen as quite an accomplishment considering the hurdles presented to the Italian parliament in producing statutory legislation (most policy is issued by decrees in Italy which only last five years (Della Sala, Vince and Amie Kreppel, 1998)). It managed to place a regulatory framework on a market which had already developed in a regulatory vacuum. This was no easy task, as demonstrated by other countries which attempted to do the same (e.g. Spain and Hungary).

One accomplishment of the Act was that it halted media concentration. In particular it addressed (and perhaps prevented) cross-media concentration. The Act restricted cross-media ownership, preventing publishers with a circulation of over 16 per cent from owning television stations, or with a circulation of 8 per cent from owning more than one station. A publisher with less than 8 per cent combined national circulation was limited to two television stations. The holder of a national television licence was prohibited from owning a licence for a local television or radio station (and vice versa). The holder of a local television licence could own a licence for a local radio station, as long as there was no scarcity in the allocation of local frequencies. It forbid an owner of three television stations from the purchase of a newspaper. It prevented Fininvest from expanding its number of channels further than the status quo.

Regarding transparency, companies holding a broadcasting licence had to enter the names of their shareholders (over 2 per cent), the number of their respective shares and the value of those shares in the *National Register for Radio and Television Companies* (now the *Register for Communications Operators*). The regulatory authority had to be informed of any transfer of shares amounting to over 10 per cent of capital. Companies quoted on the stock exchange had to notify any transfer of shares amounting to over 2 per cent of capital. Broadcasting companies had to provide an annual financial report of their accounts to the regulatory authority. Information on company revenue (subscriptions, advertising, sponsorship) had to be appended to this annual report.[50] This injected transparency into what had been up until that point a fairly murky business environment.

According to TWF, the 1990 Act stipulated that 51 per cent of programming needs to be of European origin. It further required that half of this quota should be Italian.[51] The advertising rules contained in TWF are incorporated into the Act. Television and radio advertising cannot surpass 15 per cent of daily broadcasting time or 18 per cent of hourly broadcasting time. Private companies holding national broadcasting licences are required to broadcast a daily news programme. Such requirements did not exist in Italy before 1990. There were no requirements on advertising up until the implementation of the TWF Directive. However, as detailed in Chapter 2, many of the TWF advertising requirements were overturned by the European Court in Italian cases.

As stated, under the 1990 Act, Berlusconi's channels exceeded the ownership limits. In order to present a solution to the problem, the Italian government adopted a law in 1993 (Gagliardi, 1994)[52] which stipulated that Fininvest had a period of four years to meet regulatory requirements. In order to force Berlusconi's hand, the law specified that that Telepiù's three channels (Telepiù 1, Telepiù 2 and Telepiù 3) could only continue to use terrestrial frequencies for four more years after which time they had to find an alternative means of transmission. Accordingly, Telepiù began satellite broadcasting in 1994. Eventually, in order to adhere to the ownership provisions in the 1990 Act, Fininvest divested Telepiù in 1996. Fininvest's three remaining channels (Retequattro, Canale 5 and Italia 1) were within the legal limits set down by the 1990 Act because the company owned no more than three national broadcasting channels, which consisted of exactly 25 per cent of the national total.[53]

Silvio Berlusconi was elected Prime Minister by the Italian parliament in 1994. By December that year, Fininvest's three terrestrial channels had reached an audience share of 40 per cent which led the Italian constitutional court to declare that the law's ownership limit be set to 20 per cent of national channels by the end of August 1996 (Lane, 1997). The Italian Constitutional Court ruled that ruled that Article 15, paragraph 4 of the 1990 Broadcasting Law was unconstitutional as it ignored Article 21 of the Italian Constitution (dealing with monopolies). Paragraph 4 limited ownership of national television stations to 25 per cent of the total number of channels. The Court found these limits to be insufficient.[54] A reform of the 1990 Broadcasting Act within three years time (i.e. by 1997) was mandated. After the Berlusconi government fell in December 1994, Prime Minister Lamberto Dini attempted to overcome parliamentary stalemate on a conflict of interest law with three referenda in 1995. They were to: 1) prohibit ownership of more than one television channel by a single entity; 2) to ban advertising breaks during films; and 3) to partially privatise RAI. The majority of voters voted against all three proposals.

Meanwhile, Fininvest was floated as Mediaset in July 1996 as a compromise (20 per cent of stock was sold), but the company did not sell any of its channels. In July 1996, the Prodi government drew up proposals for a new Media Act which would allow telecommunications companies to compete with broadcasters. Significantly, the drafting of the new law was substantially influenced by the 'convergence' initiative promoted by the European Commission. The Italian government essentially decided that the only way to deal the Berlusconi problem was to expose him to market competition. However, in practice, there was no competition.

In 1997, at the end of the three year period, the new law was agreed upon (labelled the 'Maccanico Law' after the Minister of PTT, Antonio Maccanico, at that time).[55] The Act established an Authority for Communications (Autorita per le garanzie nelle comunicazioni). The authority was set up in 1998 replacing the Press and Broadcasting Authority. It is situated within the new Ministry for Communications located in Naples. Similar to the previous authority, the new Authority issues broadcasting licences. It established a *Register for Communications Operators*. As suggested in the Commission's 1996 Green Paper, the Italian authority will register not just companies with television and radio interests but all companies offering communications services. The new Authority monitors media mergers and acquisitions (across all media, including telecommunications and new services) and draws the attention of the competition authority to any undesired market concentration. The old rules on ownership remain in place under the new Act. The only innovative measure is that no company can own more than one pay-TV service. This prevented Berlusconi from moving into satellite and cable markets. With the Act, Italy adopted the European Commission 'convergence' recommendation that no one could control 30 per cent of the financial resources of the *entire* communications market. The definition is so wide and vague that it cannot possibly decide on market concentrations below what competition law could account for. Nevertheless, change was expected in the widening of existing market definitions on media markets. In 1999, the Channel Europa 7 won a government to broadcast on frequencies occupied by Mediaset's Retequattro.

In 2002, a further Constitutional Court ruling mandated that Mediaset's Rete 4 be moved to satellite by the end of 2003. In January 2004, the Berlusconi government passed its decree actually overturning the Constitutional Court's decision. President Carlo Azeglio Ciampi has ordered the degree to be reconsidered by Parliament.

In 2003, the Berlusconi government proposed its 'Gasparri Law' (after the Minister of Communications, Maurizio Gasparri). It aimed to lower ownership requirements to meet with the 30 per cent rule (on communications markets), as introduced under the Prodi government. However, an amendment to the bill passed in April 2003, kept cross-media ownership restrictions in place. The Gasparri Law would restrict a single legal entity from owning licences that allow broadcasting of more than 20 per cent of television programs or more than 20 per cent of radio programs that can be transmitted on terrestrial frequencies over the national area. This is basically very similar to the previous rules which set limits to 20 per cent of national channels. There is an additional limit of 20 per cent for revenues as a percentage of total resources of the entire communications market ('Integrated Communications System') which is reduced to 10 per cent for a legal entity who has more than 40 per cent of revenues in telecommunications services (i.e. Telecom Italia). The law also restricts a legal entity owning more than one television network from own shares in publishers of daily newspapers until December 2008 (i.e. Berlusconi). The bill was ratified in December 2003 but President Ciampi sent it back to Parliament for reconsideration.

Italian regulation of press markets
The first Italian law to regulate the publishing industry was the Press Law No. 47 of 1948.[56] The law dealt with the registration of publications, fundamental rights of journalists and requirements of editors (right of reply, libel and moral and civil responsibilities). It contained no provisions on ownership or transparency.

Following a financial crisis in publishing during the 1970s, Italy introduced a new Press Law No. 416 in 1981.[57] This law, which largely outlined allocation rules for subsidies to industry, introduced Italy's first rules on market share, ownership and transparency. It also established a Council for the Press (Garante dell'editoria) (which was later replaced by the Press and Broadcasting Authority in 1990 and the Authority for Communications in 1997).[58] The 1981 rules on market share restricted publishers to 20 per cent of circulation at the national level and 50 per cent at the regional level (including sports newspapers).[59] As in France, the government fixed newspaper prices until price fixing was abolished in 1988. However, price fixing still continues in Italy by way of informal agreement. The law forbade publishers (or majority shareholders) of a newspaper, magazine or a press agency (which employs more than five journalists) to register holdings abroad. The 1981 Press Law introduced Italy's first rules on transparency of press ownership. Title one of the law required publishers to register their newspapers and magazines with the National Press Register (which was replaced in 1997 with the Register for Communications Operators). Publishers (with over five full-time journalists) have to provide the relevant regulatory body (presently the Authority for Communications) with an annual financial statement according to requirements laid out in the law. These financial reports also had to be printed in the companies' publications. Any transfer of shares had to be reported immediately to the Authority for Communications. The Publishing Law of 1987[60] made some amendments to the 1981 Press Law. It states that company shares can be annulled by Parliament if a dominant position is achieved (a company has 6–12 months to rectify the situation).[61] As Satori notes, however, rules on cross-media ownership, where there was a 'distinct need for regulation' (Satori, 1996: 141), were absent.

In 1995, Italy's press ownership rules were put to the test. Agnelli's holding company, Gemina, (which owns Corriere della Sera, La Stampa and La Gazzetta dello Sport) succeeded the ownership/circulation limits imposed by the 1981 Press Law. The Press and Broadcasting Authority launched a lengthy investigation into the case, however no action was taken. The Prodi government drew up proposals to reform the 1981 Press Act. The draft proposal aimed at liberalising broadcasting ownership limits, to allow the press sector greater concentration and cross-media ownership. Transparency measures were to be tightened, but the draft never went to Parliament.

Italian competition law
Italy's embrace of European policy solutions is most demonstrated by its Competition Law which was passed in 1990.[62] Italian law did not provide for concentration control until then. Prior to this time, the Italian Civil Code of 1942 provided some definitions of dominant position. In particular, Article 2359 of the Italian Civil Code defined dominance (control) as occurring when a legal entity has 50 per cent or more shares of a company's voting rights.

The 1990 Italian Competition Law[63] is almost a word-for-word translation of European competition law (as stipulated in Treaty of Rome articles) and the 1989 EU Merger Regulation. Article 2 of the Italian competition law directly translates Article 85 of the 1957 Treaty of Rome, Article 3 translates Article 86 and Article 4 translates the third paragraph of Article 85 (relating to the exemption of cartels). The law established Italy's first Antitrust Authority, which was autonomous.[64] According to competition law, a company is defined as holding a dominant position when it reaches 50 per cent of revenue of a certain market. The law does not prohibit dominant position, but, if a company achieves dominant position in a market, the Antitrust Authority can impose certain restrictions on that company's operations (restricting further expansion, annulling contracts, etc.). Italy introduced a further law in 1995, including a paragraph on regulating competition in utilities markets.[65] The law established an Authority for the Regulation of Public Utilities, which also has powers to ensure competition in utilities markets.[66]

France

Having observed the other national cases (particularly Germany and the UK), the influence of the European institutions in steering French media markets would be expected to be high. However, a detailed examination of the French case shows European intervention to be negligible. Despite a high degree of market concentration between the largest French media groups, the ECJ and the MTF have taken no interest in curtailing their expansion. This is quite remarkable, considering the high degree of cross-media ownership.

The ECJ has handled no cases concerning French media companies apart from complaints by private operators against the French PSB. The MTF has made some decisions concerning French groups but only to approve expansion. In 1991, DG IV investigated the joint venture between the French companies, Generale des Eaux and Canal Plus with ABC and WH Smith. It was approved in the first consultation round without revision. In the second French case, the Commission did actually prevent Canal Plus from forming an alliance with the Spanish telecommunications company, Telefónica. However, Telefónica's exclusion from the deal allowed Canal Plus to singularly launch Spain's first digital satellite television in January 1997 (under its subsidiary, Canal Satéllite Digital) defying the political pressure of the incumbent Spanish government (Llorens-Maluquer, 1998: 582). Without the support of the European Commission, this would not have been possible. In the third (French) case, the European Commission investigated the digital satellite television venture between the French television company TF1 and the utility company Lyonnaise des Eaux. The joint venture between the two large French companies was approved without constraint on 10 March 1999.

In contrast to this lack of formal intervention by the EU institutions, informal feedback from the French to the European level is consistent. Relations between the French regulatory bodies for media and the European Commission are reportedly cosy (Bahu-Leyser, 1993; Godard, 1995; Collins, 1994b; Trautmann, 1998). Proponents of French cultural policy have been successful at influencing European policies, particularly regarding the promotion of European production.[67] Content laws as governed by the CSA are relatively stringent in France, particularly regarding requirements for French content (Broadcasting and Cable, 1993).[68] This has been relatively significant for Europe. The 'French lobby' (Belluzzi, 1994) was successful in requiring that a majority of programming be of European origin in both the 1989 and 1997 TWF Directives. France enacted a more stringent requirement. The CSA requires a minimum of 60 per cent European works and a minimum of 40 per cent French productions. French music radio stations must broadcast a minimum of 40 per cent French music (50 per cent of which must be dedicated to 'new' French artists). EU media policy is thus very important to the French government. The French government requested the DG Culture portfolio in the year 1999, but was unsuccessful.

French regulation of broadcasting markets
Prior to 1986, France only permitted public service broadcasters. The public service channels were governed by a number of laws in France (in 1945, 1972, 1974 and 1982) (Guillou, 1988; Barendt, 1993; Kuhn, 1995).[69] Mostly these laws dealt with matters of content and funding. The 1982 Law on Audiovisual Communication (29 July 1982, also known as the Fillioud law) introduced some preliminary limited sector liberalisation. Private radio stations were allowed for the first time and public service television could be commissioned to private companies. Each licence was issued upon the discretion of France's first regulatory body for commercial broadcasting, the Haute Autorité de la Communication Audiovisuelle set up in 1982 (Bertrand, 1985; Robillard, 1995: 62). The regulatory body experienced many teething problems mainly resulting from challenges to its independence by political interference (Palmer and Sorbets, 1997).

Some years later, the 1986 Law on Freedom of Communication (No. 86-1067) brought in sector liberalisation with the licensing of commercial television stations (Barendt, 1993; Kuhn, 1995).[70] The first channel of the PSB, Télévision Française 1 (TF1) was privatised, a first in Europe. Liberalisation of the market required media ownership regulation. The 1986 law therefore laid down rules on media ownership (along with rules on licensing, pluralism, advertising, content and subsidies for audio-visual production). Ownership of a broadcasting company licensed for a national terrestrial television was limited to 25 per cent of the capital of voting rights. Special provisions on advertising were introduced, particularly in regard to the protection of children, a provision that eventually found its way into TWF.

The 1986 law established a new broadcasting regulatory body, replacing the Haute Autorité de la Communication Audiovisuelle with the Commisssion Nationale de la Communication et des Libertés. As the Commisssion Nationale de la Communication et des Libertés was again found to be overly prone to political influence, it was replaced by the Conseil Supérior de l'Audiovisuel (CSA) in 1988. The CSA has since been established as an independent regulatory body entrusted with powers to issue licences for private radio and television (terrestrial, cable and satellite). It is responsible for administering media ownership rules and regulating broadcasting content, advertising and the allocation of broadcasting subsidies. From 1986, private licences were given out on a case-by-case basis (Humphreys, 1996: 181).

The 1986 law included *cross-media* ownership rules. A terrestrial licence is denied to an owner with interests in more than two kinds of other media (e.g. newspapers, radio, cable) which reach prescribed ownership limits. Subsequent rapid growth in the broadcasting industry led to massive private sector lobbying for deregulation. Around the same time, the European Commission passed the 1989 TWF Act (which was approved in the Council of by Edouard Balladur, the then Minister of State, Minister of the Economy, Finance and Privatization). TWF required revision of France's 1986 broadcasting law.

The French government implemented TWF in its 1994 Broadcasting Law (No. 94-88). The 1994 law substantially loosens the 1986 ownership rules. The limits for ownership (by an individual or legal entity) were raised from 25 per cent to 49 per cent of the capital of voting rights of a broadcasting company. A further instrument was introduced in that ownership in a second company with a national broadcasting licence was set at 15 per cent of capital and voting rights, and ownership of a third to 5 per cent. TWF explicitly called for the permitting of satellite broadcasts from one member state to another. This meant the licensing of satellite stations at the national level. The 1994 French law set a limit for the ownership of satellite broadcasting companies at 50 per cent of the capital or voting rights. Foreign ownership in any French broadcasting company was limited to 20 per cent.

In its 1994 law, France introduced a new policy instrument: audience reach.[71] This was one of the policy instruments suggested (but discarded) in the 1993 Commission study on audience measurement (GAH, 1993: 101). Under the 1994 rules, the combined services of a media company (regional and local) were limited to an audience reach of 6 million viewers. Cable television was limited to an audience reach of 8 million viewers nationally or regionally (this would correspond roughly to 16 per cent of audience share). In contrast to these strict terrestrial rules, a company could own one satellite licence, but the number of channels and audience reach was not limited.[72] Within this framework of audience reach, the 1994 rules capped the number of terrestrial market players. A French company could only be granted one licence for a *national* terrestrial television station. Licences for *regional* and *local* terrestrial television are issued separated. A company may only be licensed for one *regional* television service (but can simultaneously own a number of *local* licences).

There is no limit to the number of radio networks a company can own, however the laws contain limits for audience reach which is determined by geographical area. Audience reach for a company radio network is set at 150 million for areas served by numerous radio networks (previously, this limit was 30 million in 1986). Cable radio broadcasting is limited to a combined audience reach of 8 million listeners.

Measures in the French 1994 law relating to cross-media ownership are limited. No company can be granted a broadcasting licence (for radio or television) if it already has either: an existing radio station reaching an audience reach of over 30 million, one or more licences for cable radio and/or cable television reaching an audience of over 6 million, one or more licences for a television service reaching an audience of over 4 million, or owns or controls one or more daily newspapers with a national circulation of over 20 per cent. This restriction applies both nationally and regionally.

In 1996, France enacted its Information Superhighway Law. The law authorised the licensing of trial digital and video-on-demand services. Articles 3 and 4 apply broadcasting laws No. 86-1064 and No. 94-88, but exempt video-on-demand services from Articles 27, 28, 28-1 and 70 of No. 86-1064 (relating to content). Licenses for trial digital television were awarded at the discretion of the CSA. In 1997, the French government drew up a revision of the 1994 Broadcasting Act. The CSA expressed dissatisfaction with the level of media concentration and a wish to return to the 1986 media ownership limit of 25 per cent (as opposed to the present level of 49 per cent) (Palmer and Sorbets, 1997). However the proposal never came to fruition, due particularly to a change in government in June of that year. In 2003, DTT licences were issued by the CSA.

In 2002, a campaign by teachers' unions and the press targeted the problem of the accessibility of pornography in France. A study carried out for the CSA by Mediamétrie found French audiences had access to 900 pornography films a month via satellite.[73] A survey found that that 89.6 per cent of boys aged 16 or 17 and 50 per cent of children under 11, had seen one or more pornographic films. The study also looked at the content of pornography which was found to be increasingly violent. It quoted sociological studies that linked the present increase in sexually violent crime by teenagers (also a problem in Italy) to exposure to such content. The claim is that adolescents reconstruct these acts. An opinion poll showed that 64 per cent of viewers were in favour of censorship. The French regulatory authority (CSA) targetted satellite channels broadcasting pornographic films. It drew up changes to national media law, evoking Article 22.1 of the TWF Directive, according to which broadcasts may not 'include any programmes which might seriously impair the physical, mental or moral development of minors, in particular programmes that involve pornography or gratuitous violence'. The CSA also proposed a modification of Article 15 of the Broadcasting law of 30 September 1986 to achieve an explicit ban of programmes that involve pornography or gratuitous violence. However, the CSA itself was doubtful that these proposals will be passed by Parliament, because it recognises that pornography is presently the most profitable sector in French broadcasting and it feared that if a law were passed media groups would simply base their headquarters abroad to bypass French content laws. It did not consider the British approach of criminalising the sale of set-top boxes, which side steps TWF provisions and thereby eludes jurisdiction of the ECJ. The CSA proposals were ultimately dropped when national (and international) attention began to focus on the personal reputation of the head of the regulatory authority (CSA), Dominique Baudis. In April 2003, national newspapers (led by Le Figaro) accused Dominique Baudis of recruiting a convicted serial killer (Patrice Alègre) to murder two prostitutes to prevent them from revealing details of sadomasochistic orgies organised for the élite of the city of Toulouse (where he was mayor). Following this press campaign, the CSA has not resumed proposals to curb the adult film industry.

French regulation of the press
France has not halted press concentration. The first French law to regulate ownership of the press was the Ordinance No. 45-1483 of June 1945[74] (Kuhn, 1995; Giullou, 1988: Humphreys, 1996). It forbade the ownership or control of more than one newspaper by any legal entity. The legal entity could not be of foreign origin. The law also required public access to company reports providing a complete financial breakdown. The legal provisions relating to ownership were however unsuccessful. Publishers largely disregarded the ownership limits and the French government did not enforce them (Palmer and Sorbets, 1997: 62–63).

France experienced quite a high level of concentration in the publishing industry (Kuhn, 1995, Humphreys, 1996). This remained unchecked by national legislation until a general competition law was introduced. From 1977, French companies were subject to the Concentration Control Law No. 77-806 of July. This general competition law, which was incorporated into the later 1986 Competition Ordinance No. 86-1243 (l'ordonnance no

86-1243). The Competition Advisory Board (Conseil de la Concurrence) was to monitor markets and report any legal digressions to the Ministry for Economic Affairs. The ministry then invited parties participating in a merger or acquisition to request voluntarily ministerial permission. It should be noted that the Competition Advisory Board is not a regulatory body and therefore not independent as such. Any decisions taken on anti-competitive behaviour are essentially made by the Minister for Economic Affairs. Since the November 1986 Press Law, general competition law has not ordinarily been utilised in connection with the press industry, as the market is now governed by specific ownership rules (see below). General competition rules can of course be employed if specific rules are not applied to a market concentration.

New rules affecting ownership of the press were included in the 1984 Transparency Law No. 84-937.[75] The law imposed limits on a publisher's circulation to 15 per cent of national dailies, 15 per cent of regional dailies or 10 per cent of the total circulation of national and regional dailies combined. A monitoring Committee on Press Transparency and Pluralism was set up accordingly (which was dismantled in 1986). Once again, however, the law was unsuccessful. The law's chief failing was that it could not be applied retroactively. Publishers exceeding circulation were not required to divest their interests. Large press groups made further newspaper acquisitions to the disapproval but not the prevention of both the Committee and Ministry for Economic Affairs.

This led the French government firstly to regulate the market status quo. The year 1986 saw the enactment of three new media laws: the August Press Law No. 86-897, the September Freedom of Communication Law No. 86-1067 (Loi no 86-1067 du 30 septembre 1986 Relative à la liberté de communication) and the November Press Law No. 86-1210 (Loi no 86-1210 du 27 novembre 1986. Complétant la loi no 86-897 du 1er août 1986 portant réforme du régime juridique de la presse et la loi no 86-1067 du 30 septembre 1986 relative à la liberté de communication). The November Press Law amends all previous laws. Articles from all three 1986 laws (86-897, 86-1067, 86-1210) are presently in use to regulate the press market.

The 1986 laws contain many rules relating to transparency and ownership. The media ownership rules laid out in the 1984 Law on Transparency were replaced with the 1986 Press Laws. The revised press ownership rules attempted to halt the progression of concentration in the press market by choosing limits that closely resembled the existing market status quo. According to Article 41, companies cannot acquire a new publication if the acquisition boosts their total daily circulation (of all the company's publications) to over 30 per cent nationally. It should be noted that this rule only applies to daily publications and not to weeklies (or other non-daily publications). This applies even if a company creates its own new publication, or experiences an increase in circulation of its existing publications.

In 1986 (single sector) ownership rules were introduced for the first time. In short, publishers were limited to a daily newspaper circulation of 10 per cent nationally if they own broadcasting interests. This limit was later raised to 20 per cent. Following the 1986 Press Law, there was no subsequent legislation of ownership of the press. However, both indirect and direct subsidisation of the sector continues in France. Directly, the state subsidies the news agency, Agence France Presse (AFP) which in turn directly subsidies newspapers and distribution networks. Indirectly, publishers receive lower corporate taxation rates, newspaper prices are fixed by the government and overseas sales of French newspapers are subsidised. In addition, journalists receive a number of subsidies e.g. for telephone bills and travel rebates and a 30 per cent reduction on income tax.

Conclusion

This chapter has shown the interplay between national and European media regulation. The European institutions have been driving policy convergence. The individual actions of these institutions have played a decisive role in shaping both the development of national media markets and the direction of national media policies. The TWF Directive mandated policy change through its implementation at national levels. The MTF and the ECJ required direct changes to national policies through their decisions.

Key overhauls of national media policies can be distinctly marked as occurring around the mid-1980s, the early 1990s and the mid-1990s. In the early 1990s, many countries had to allow for greater sector liberalisation than desired by their national governments, particularly the Netherlands and Spain. Other countries were committed to introducing laws for the first time, Italy and Luxembourg as cases in point. During the 1990s media laws were governed by decisions of the ECJ and MTF and influenced by Commission policy recommendations. The examples of the latter were instruments used to limit market expansion. Audience share was adopted in Germany and the UK in 1996 and was thereafter adopted in Ireland in 2001 and Romania in 2003. It is subsequently being considered in other countries. Audience reach was adopted in France. The 'convergence' initiative was embraced by Spain, Switzerland, Slovenia and the UK before actual enactment of the EC's 2002 regulatory framework for communications. Apart from the countries under examination in this chapter, media acts show increasing commonalties in Austria, Denmark, France, Greece, Holland, Luxembourg, Portugal and Sweden. In addition, national governments were shown to have disseminated their own policy recommendations using the EU as a platform for transfer. For example, France and Italy lobbied for EU content requirement to protect domestic production. The UK lobbied for changes to TWF to encompass its non-domestic satellite policy. Sweden was instrumental in lobbying for the protection of minors

(Krebber, 2001: 139). There is little doubt that policy convergence, through European-level action, is underway. The implementation of the new regulatory framework will of course mean further convergence across Europe.

Although the European institutions have been effective in steering national regulation, EC policy formation has not necessarily been democratic, nor has it represented a consistent approach. This considered, policy implementation has posed problems at the national level, as it has conflicted with traditional media regulation and national policy choices. As detailed in Chapter 4, EU media regulation has come into being as an outcome of an internal battle over competency within the European Commission. The same battles over competency are bound to arise with the new regulatory framework for communications, which is to have a great impact on national media legislation.

Notes

1 As shown in Chapters 2 to 6, this influence has been almost exclusively directed towards national broadcasting markets. The European institutions have been reluctant to directly intervene with national press markets. However, considering the effects of convergence and the extent of cross-media ownership, both press and broadcasting policies shall be addressed in this chapter.
2 Act 86-1067 of 30 September 1986 on the freedom of communication. Act 86-1210 of 27 November 1986; Amendment to Act 86-897 of 1 August 1986 regulating the press and Act 86-1067 of 30 September 1986 on the freedom of communication.
3 1987 Staatsvertrag über den Rundfunk im vereinten Deutschland.
4 Legge 25 February 1987 n. 67 – *recante disciplina delle imprese editrici e provvidenze per l'editoria.*
5 Ley 10/1988, 3 May, de Televisión Privada. B.O.E. núm. 108, 5 May 1988.
6 Loi n° 94-88, 1 February 1994. Modifiant la loi n° 88–1067, 30 September 1986 relative à la liberté de communication.
7 1991 Staatsvertrag über den Rundfunk im vereinten Deutschland.
8 Legge 6 August 1990, n. 223. Disciplina del sistema radiotelevisivo pubblico e privato.
9 Ley 25/1994 Televisión Sin Frontera, 12 July, amended by 22/1999, 7 June.
10 Loi no 96-299, 10 April 1996 relative aux expérimentations dans le domaine des technologies et services de l'information (1) J.O. Numero 86 11 April 1996 page 5569.
11 New Media Act No. 249. Legge, 1 July 1997, n. 249.
12 There are 15 state regulatory authorities as Berlin and Brandenburg share a regulatory body.
13 Bundesverfassungsgericht decision, 28 February 1961, Bundesverfassungsgericht decision, 27 July 1971, Bundesverfassungsgericht decision, 16 June 1981, Bundesverfassungsgericht decision, 4 November 1986 (establishing a 'dual system' of broadcasting), Bundesverfassungsgericht decision, 24 March 1987, Bundesverfassungsgericht decision, 5 February 1991, Bundesverfas-

sungsgericht decision, 10 June 1996, Bundesverfassungsgericht decision, 12 June 1997, Bundesverfassungsgericht decision, 22 April 1998.

14 This was the ruling of 16 June 1981 Bundesverfassungsgericht 57, 295 ff. See Robillard (1995: 10) Barendt (1993) and Lange and Van Loon (1990) for discussion.

15 For example, the German federal court specified that pluralist requirements (*Grundversorgung*) could be lessened for private broadcasters if they are heightened for public broadcasters.

16 Bundesverfassungsgericht decision 1/89, 22 March 1995.

17 The 1994 *MSG Media Service*, 1998 *Deutsche Telekom/Betaresearch*, 1998 *DF1/Premiere* and 1998 *Betaresearch/Bertelsmann/Kirch*.

18 Most of these are now available on the internet.

19 In 1997, a negative decision was made on the acquisition of Adolf Deil GmbH & Co. KG Druckerei and Verlag and Pirmasenser Zeitung by Tukan Verlagsgesellschaft GmbH Section 24 of GWB. A second negative decision stopped the acquisition of PSG-Postdienst Service GmbH by Axel Springer Verlag.

20 Law of 18 December 1991 updating the 1987 media law.

21 According to the 'Mediwet' (broadcasting act) of 1987, Staatsblad No. 249 of 4 June 1987.

22 No. 610, 9 October 1998 (No. 610) Telecommunicatiewet: houden regels inzake de telecommunicatie.

23 www.cvdm.nl/documents/mediaact.pdf.

24 1993 *BBC/BskyB/Football Association*, 1993 *British Telecom/MCI* and 1997 *British Telecom/MCI* (II).
Case No IV/M.856 (14 May 1997); 1997 *BskyB/British Digital Broadcasting* Case IV/M. 300.

25 JV.27, 22 March 2000.

26 These rules have of course been subject to circumvention by BSkyB as explained in Chapter 6.

27 The government in power directly makes appointments to the ITC. For this reason, its independence has been questioned. However, most appointments are drawn not from political parties, but from industry. As many ITC appointments traditionally came directly from ITV companies (pantouflage), the third channel has often been seen as self-regulated (Gibbons, 1997).

28 The informal correspondence is of interest considering the amount of time the Commission allows in such cases. The Commission sent a letter to the UK in November, 1992. The UK replied by letter in February 1993. The Commission then sent a reasoned opinion to the UK in September 1993, to which the UK responded by letter in January 1994.

29 Specifically, these are Articles 7(1) and (2), 8, 17(2), 18 and 20(3) of the Framework Directive (2002/21/EC); Article 5(1) of the Access Directive (2002/19/EC); and Article 7(3) of the Authorisation Directive.

30 Press rumours indicate that this is a political deal between Blair in order to gain Murdoch's support over UK entry into the Euro. This author is sceptical of these claims. If the UK broadcasting market is to be wholly owned by US operators, media support of the Euro is not expected to be high, even if the Murdoch newspapers do support it. In any case, there are already quite a number of US players in the British press and cable markets (Collins, 2003).

Rather the latest deregulatory move seems to reflect an attempt to solve a domestic problem. By allowing non-EU players into the market under the Communications Act, the UK is seeking to attract outside investment to rescue the bankrupt ITV companies and replace the failed venture in digital broadcasting (ITV Digital), thereby presenting potential competition to the satellite monopoly BSkyB.

31 Spain was established as a Parliamentarian Monarchy in Article 1.3 of the 1978 Spanish Constitution of 1978. Article 2 of the Constitution grants different powers to the central government and to the regions (called *autonomies*). Further powers have been granted in Constitutional Court decisions (STC 4/1981 [RTC 1981, 4], F3; STC 100/1984 [rtc 1984, 100] F2).

32 The Spanish regions have not lobbied the Commission individually regarding media policy in contrast to the German Länder (Blanco, and Vandenbulck, 1995) with the exception of Catalonia. Interestingly, Börzel found the same lack of Spanish regional lobbying of EC environmental policy (1999).

33 1988 Ley 10/88 de Televisión Privada.

34 1987 Ley 31/87 de telecomunicaciones.

35 1992 Ley de 35/92 Televisión Satélite.

36 1994 Ley 7/94 de Televisión Sin Fronteras.

37 'Spanish TV seeks new measurement', *Advertising Age*, 65, 14 (1994): 45.

38 1997 Ley 17/97 incorporation of the EC Directive 95/47/CE; and 1997 Ley 21/97 Reguladora de las Emisiones y Retransmisiones de Competiciones Deportivas.

39 Ley 16/97 amends Ley 17/97 with the changes mandated by the Commission.

40 Canal Satéllite Digital SL/Administracíon General del Estado.

41 Not all of them were of course in favour of media ownership rules, but on balance most were. Italian membership of the European Parliament's Committee on Culture, Youth, Education and the Media (CULT) at the time included: Monica Stefania Baldi (EPP), Umberto Bossi, Alessandro Fontana (EPP), Giancarlo Ligabue (EPP), Cristiana Muscardini, Carlo Ripa di Meana (EUL), Aldo Arroni (EPP), Roberto Barzanti (PES), Gerardo Bianco (EPP), Luciana Castellina (EUL), Marco Cellai, Maria Paola Colombo Svevo (EPP), Giacomo Leopardi (EPP), Luigi Moretti, Luisa Todini (EPP) and Luciano Vechhi (PEE).

42 Joined cases RTI, *Radio Torre, Rete A Srl, Vallau Italiana Promomarket Srl, Radio Italia Solo Musica Srl and Others* and *GETE Srl* v. *Ministero delle Poste e Telecomunicazioni.*

43 Kirch/Richemont/Telepiù Decision and Kirch/Richemont/ Multichoice / Telepiù.

44 Legge 14 April 1975, n. 103. Nuove Norme in Materia di Diffusione Radiofonica e televisiva.

45 Corte Constituzionale, Decision, 28 July 1976, n. 202.

46 Corte Consitucionale, Decision, 14 July 1988, n. 826.

47 Legge 6 August 1990, n. 223. Disciplina del sistema radiotelevisivo pubblico e privato.

48 The 1990 Act was updated in 1992 (Legge 17 December 1992 n. 408), 1993 (Legge 27 October 1993 n. 323), 1994 (Legge 1 March 1994 n. 153), and 1997 (Legge 1 July 1997, n. 249) following further constitutional court rulings.

49 These reflected definitions agreed within the Council of Europe.

50 Indirect subsidies are sometimes granted to broadcasters in the form of lower utility rates (telecommunications, electricity). Direct subsidies are given towards the cost of new agencies (up to 53 per cent of cost). Grants are provided for radio stations belonging to political parties.

51 This held after the first three years of a company's licence. For the first three years of broadcasting, a new company needed only guarantee that 4 per cent of its transmission time is of European origin. This was meant to encourage new entrants to the market.

52 Legge 27 October 1993 n. 323.

53 At the time, these were RAIuno, RAIdue, RAItre, *Retequattro*, *Canale 5*, *Italia 1*, Videomusic/TMC2, Telemontecarlo, Rete A, Telepiù 1, Telepiù 2, and Telepiù 3. Berlusconi owned exactly 3 of the 12 national channels which constituted 25 per cent.

54 Corte Constituzionale, Decision, 5.12.94, no. 420. See *Gazzetta Ufficiale*, special issue no. 51, 14 December 1994 for discussion.

55 Law No. 249 of 31 July 1997.

56 Legge 8 February 1948 n. 47, Disposizioni sulla stampa.

57 Legge 5 August 1981 n. 416 – *Disciplina delle imprese editrici e provvidenze per l'editoria.*

58 The 1981 Law also set out the rules on press subsidisation. Indirect subsidies are granted to publishers in the form of lower tax, transport, postal and telecommunications rates. This was due to the non-profitability of Italian newspapers at that time. Direct subsidies are given to the non-profit press, journalists unions, minority press and political party press. These subsidies are still in place today.

59 The Italian regions are considered to be: northwest (Piemonte, Valle d'Aosta, Lombardia, Liguria), the north-east (Trentino-Alto Adige, Veneto, Friuli-Venezia Giulia, Emilia-Romagna), central (Toscana, Umbria, Marche, Lazio, Abruzzo) and south (Molise, Campania, Puglia, Basilicata, Calabria, Sardegna, and Sicilia). Five of these regions (Valle d'Aosta, Trentino-Alto Adige, Friuli-Venezia Giulia, Sardegna, Sicilia) have special political autonomy for ethnic, historical and peripheral reasons.

60 Legge 25 February 1987 n. 67 – recante disciplina delle imprese editrici e provvidenze per l'editoria.

61 The 1987 also removed the 1981 rule which fixed newspaper sales prices.

62 Legge 10 October 1990 n. 287 – Norme per la tutela della concorrenza e del mercato.

63 Legge 10 October 1990 n. 287 – Norme per la tutela della concorrenza e del mercato.

64 The authority consists of 200 civil servants, but is headed by 5 members (one, a chairman), which are appointed jointly by the Speaker of Senate and Chamber of Deputies for seven-year non-renewable terms.

65 Legge 14 November 1995 n. 481, Art. 2 – Norme per la concorrenza e la regolazione dei servizi di pubblica utilità.

66 Istituzione delle Autorità di regolazione dei servizi di pubblica utilità.

67 This phenomena has existed in other policy areas (Cram and Drake, 1996).

68 Along with the requirements in broadcasting law, France enacted 'la loi Toubon' in 1994. The 1994 law forbids public bodies and companies engaged

in public activities to use an English expression where there is a French equivalent. It was passed as a direct reaction to the flood of US popular culture into
France. The law requires all advertising to be in French.

69   Further laws dealing solely with public service, and largely with problems of
     funding, were the 1989 Tasca and 1990 Lang laws.
70   The 1986 Law on Freedom of Communication was updated many times by
     amendments (Lois No. 86-1210, No. 87-588, 88-227, 89-25), decrees (décrets)
     and decisions (décisions). Each amendment to the law presented a step towards
     further liberalisation.
71   Article 15 of Law No. 94-88.
72   A television service, which is broadcast simultaneously by both terrestrial and
     satellite, is considered to be a single service and requires only one terrestrial
     licence.
73   www.csa.fr/actualite/dossiers/dossiers_detail.php?id=8864&chap=2094.
74   L'ordonnance no 45-1483 30 June 1945.
75   Loi no 77-806 du 19 Juillet 1977 relative au contrôle de la concentration
     économique et à la repression des ententes illicites et des abus de position
     dominante. Loi no 84-937, 23 October 1984.

8

Conclusion

It is clear from findings presented in this book that the EU institutions have not *viewed* the regulation of media markets as merely a correction of market inefficiency. Rather, they have taken on board considerations of the public interest, pluralism and democracy as shown by statements in competition decisions and the tightening of market measurements in the draft directive on media ownership. These approaches were derived from national rationales for legislation at the Member State level and democratic input from the European Parliament and interest groups as shown in Chapters 3 and 4. National laws were naturally a result of policy-making via democratic governance – i.e. ratification by national parliaments appointed by the electorate. However, the approach of the European institutions to the regulation of media markets *in terms of policy output* represents a fundamentally economic approach. This is due to legal constraints in the Treaties and the democratic weakness in the integral political structure of the European Union.

The 1989 TWF Directive, which liberalised broadcasting markets, was drafted in the spirit of the Single Market. Its ratification failed to take on board public interest amendments by the electorate (European Parliament) and reflected the preferences of Member State economic and trade Ministers voting in the Council which supported growth of national champions in home markets. Coming on the heels of the Single European Act the TWF Directive therefore established a framework for the creation of a 'single' audio-visual market through the legalisation of cross-border broadcasting. This, it was deemed, would strengthen the competitiveness of European media companies against competition in the international market. The Directive relied heavily upon technical arguments based upon internal market logic.

The application of TWF rode roughshod over national media laws which had over many decades developed to protect pluralist objectives. The ECJ ensured implementation of the liberalising TWF Directive by requiring changes to national media legislations. Chapter 2 showed how the ECJ further eroded national media legislation by *overriding* even minimum provisions enacted in the TWF to safeguard the public interest. In individual rulings, it enabled media companies to bypass national rules on media content, national content production and advertising, including rules prohibiting alcohol and tobacco advertising in France, banning children's advertising in Sweden and Norway and, in its decisions on the Italian market, TWF provisions on teleshopping and telepromotions.

The European Commission Draft Directive on media ownership began its life in the same mode as *TWF* – as an essentially liberalising Directive, set out to dismantle media ownership laws at national levels. The agenda was set by the 1993 Delors Paper on 'Growth, competitiveness' and employment and the 1994 Bangemann Paper on 'Europe and the global information society'. These White Papers provided political support and a deregulatory basis to the initiative by singling out the media sector as fertile ground for European capital growth and jobs.

However, this approach began to change. The first element of change came when the Commission provided a cultural opt-out in competition policy for media markets. This was Article 21(3) of the Merger Regulation which shielded national media laws designed to encourage 'plurality of the media' from EU competition law. The Commission's Merger Task Force recognised therewith the importance of media pluralism for assuring democratic goals. Chapters 3 and 7 showed that the Merger Task Force was not promoting the consolidation of national champions. Rather, it favoured the alliance of media groups across Member States (e.g. Canal Plus, CLT, News Corporation) than the support of national champions (e.g. Kirch, Mediaset and Prisa). Chapter 3 discussed how DG Competition in its decisions came to recognise the importance of pluralism in individual decisions. The second indication of change in the EC's approach was the recognition of the potential for public service broadcasters to protect pluralist goals. This came in the form the public service broadcasting protocol in the 1997 Amsterdam Treaty and DG Competition's special recognition of public service broadcasters in 1999. This was followed significantly by the 2000 Charter of Fundamental Rights of the European Union, Article 11(2) of which states, 'The freedom and pluralism of the media shall be respected'.

The ground-work, it seemed, was laid for a EU policy on media markets modelled on national approaches which regulated for the public interest goals of media plurality and social responsibility. This included protection of public service broadcasters and restriction of cross-media ownership. However, this was not to be. As shown, the failure of the *Ownership* Directive and the success of the *Convergence* Directive further embedded the EU's market-oriented approach.

The nature of the issue of the media ownership made it difficult for the Commission to produce a Draft Directive based upon market rationales. In seeking support for its initiative, the European Commission turned to policy solutions from smaller media companies, unions, journalists' federations, public service broadcasters and the European Parliament. The resulting 1997 Draft Directive on media ownership was much more restrictive than the original liberalising proposals suggested in 1992. This deemed the Directive politically infeasible.

Along this vein, political agreement over the revision of the *TWF* Directive was also dependent upon the exclusion of public interest considerations. Member State governments were not willing to take on board suggestions and amendments agreed upon by the majority of the European Parliament linked to democratic issues: content in programming, protection of minors against harmful programmes, stricter advertising rules, opt-outs for PSBs and restriction media ownership. Rather, national governments preferred a liberalising initiative which could override restrictive media laws enacted by national parliaments at home.

There remains the potential for the ECJ to make a progressive decision on media markets. As noted by Bulmer and Armstrong (1998), Court interpretations of Treaty provisions by the ECJ can be used as basis for EU policy-making. As explained in Chapter 2, the Protocol on public service broadcasting cannot itself be used to base policy upon, but a Court ruling interpreting the Protocol could be. The Court is not expected to make such a ruling considering its case history as it decided in five rulings that public service broadcasters should not be treated any differently from commercial broadcasters – thereby overruling European Commission competition law decisions. It is an unlikely outcome, not only because of Treaty restrictions, but also because the independence of European judges is under question. Judges are appointed by national governments and tend to act in the interest of their home country. However, in May 2003, the Court issued an opinion on the pending case *RTL Television* v. *Niedersächsische Landesmedienanstalt für privaten Rundfunk*, indicating that it may change its stance on advertising rules. This presents an opportunity for the Court to at least allow Member States to apply stricter rules for the protection of the public interest, rather than overruling them in the interest of the single market.

On balance, the empirical evidence presented in the book shows that media market regulation thus far has been unable to expand the boundaries of the EU as a regulatory state. Serious limits to EU policy-making persist which can be attributed directly to the democratic deficit of the EU (Ward, 2002). These will not be resolved without changes to the underlying make-up of the European institutions. The present trend towards the institutionalisation of 'soft' law and self-regulation represents further evasion of democratic processes.

This book contributes to the theoretical understanding of the EU. Caporaso (1996) and Scharpf (1996) have not seen much potential in EU regulatory policy for producing what is labelled 'positive' integration. In his article, 'Negative and positive integration in the political economy of European welfare states', Scharpf argues that EU regulatory policy is distinctly *negative* because it always leans towards to the liberalisation of markets and economic competition. This assumption is not disproved by empirical evidence presented in this book. Although, the European Commission has shown leanings towards 'positive' regulation (as defined by Scharpf), and the European Parliament has provided the EU with the potential, this has not been backed-up by political decision-makers in the Council of Ministers or the European Council.

According to Gormley (1985), regulatory policies of high complexity and high salience must be dealt with higher up or politically by heads of government. Due to the fact that it bridges the fundamental values of market freedom and pluralism, media market regulation can be defined as a policy area of high complexity and high salience. In Gormley's view of regulatory policy-making, this requires the highest-level political compromise. If a policy is to be formulated around public interest considerations, this must therefore come from the heads of Member States, possibly in the form of a change to the European Treaties.

The book's conclusion is therefore that EU media market regulation has provided *potential* for the expansion of the EU as a regulatory state, but thus far has lacked the political backing of Member State governments. Member State appointees to the Council of Ministers and Court of Justice are able to directly regulate national media markets while bypassing democratic input due to the weakness of the European Parliament. The European Commission meanwhile remains constrained by the Treaties to a reliance on economic arguments, which are unable to take on board public interest concerns. It is argued here that the EU has been unable to break away from this path, even in an area (media policy) which is of fundamental importance to democracy and of primary interest to the ordinary citizen.

A number of further opportunities present themselves in 2004: the creation of the European Constitution, EU enlargement under the Treaty of Nice, the intake of a new Commission and the on-going revision of the TWF Directive. A change in EU media policy could come if a clause for the protection of media pluralism were added to the newly emerging 'European Constitution'. The Draft Treaty establishing a Constitution for Europe, does include such provision.[1] It incorporates Article 11(2) of the EU Charter of Fundamental Rights. Article II-11 on freedom of expression and information states that 'The freedom and pluralism of the media shall be respected.' Cultural and audiovisual policy, however, remains an unanimity vote. The text of the draft Treaty was submitted on 18 July 2003 to the President of the European Council in Rome, Italian Prime Minister Silvio Berlusconi. Berlusconi was pushing for a final agreement at the 12–13 December Brussels Summit before it handed over the European Presidency to Ireland, but this was not forthcoming.

The European Union is to enlarge.[2] Much interest has been forming around the effect an enlarged Europe will have on the formation of advocacy coalitions and agenda-setting in the media field and ultimately the development of EU media policy. Of particular interest is the affect accession is to have on the EU's stance on public service broadcasting, TWF revision and trade in audio-visual services on the WTO platform. For example, the importance of the adoption of 'European' regulation (i.e. TWF) in accession countries is seen to strengthen the EU position in the WTO. As Johnson and Rollo (2001) explain:

> The US perceives EU cultural policies as protectionist and has mounted a concerted effort to prevent candidates from adopting EU policies ahead of membership. This is perhaps intended to enable the US to ask for compensation for reduced access to candidates' audio-visual markets, to the extent that the WTO General Agreement on Trade in Services permits that; or at least to gain some leverage over an EU policy on enlargement. (2001: 8)

In addition to TWF implementation, most accession states have broadcasting policies based upon European regulatory models, particularly the French model (Harcourt, 2003). Polish media law in particular very closely mirrors French regulatory models in both public and private broadcasting. In particular, the National Broadcasting Council was modeled 'after French practice . . . and was considered as properly safeguarding the independence of broadcasting by providing rules for a balanced political representation' (Kaminski, 2002). The French press ownership model of editors and journalists owning companies has been widely adopted in accession states, sometimes with discrepant results.

In June 2004 the European Parliament elections will take place and the European Council will appoint a new president of the European Commission for the period 2004–2010. On 1, November 2004, the new president and newly appointed Commissioners begin work. At this point, voting in the Council as provided for in the Treaty of Nice comes into effect. At this point, audio visual policy will be moved into the Information Society portfolio which the Luxembourg Commissioner Viviane Reding will preside over.

Challenges facing the regulatory framework for communications

Given its shaky democratic basis, the EU's regulatory framework for communications faces a number of legal and political challenges. Firstly, the efficiency of European regulation is in question. EU decision-making is slow paced and the result of compromise. Many initiatives prove technically complicated and difficult to implement and, by the time they are adopted, are outdated and oftentimes are overtaken by market solutions. Implementation remains one of the EU's biggest problems. At the same time, EU law, in particular competition law, is preventing Member State parliaments from regulating their own markets effectively.

Secondly, predictions of market and job growth have not shown promise. This presents a serious set-back to the European institutions, which have concentrated so heavily on the promise of communications industries to make up for the overseas flight of traditional industries, which have provided the majority of staple jobs until the present day. Thirdly, the necessity for specific market regulation is not going to go away. Competition policy alone does not provide enough markets players to ensure pluralism. Gateway bottlenecks have replaced the problem of spectrum scarcity, meaning that national governments are still faced with the dilemma of choosing one dominant market player over another. Fourthly, liberalisation of the communications market at the European level is presenting a threat to national regulation designed to promote democratic goals. As the EU has no democratic mandate, the fact that there has been no effort to counterbalance the negative effects of liberalisation (externalities) has produced serious concern. Although the European Parliament and a large number of interest groups have signaled the need for harmonisation in key areas, such as ownership regulation, there have been no attempts at coordination at the European level. The TWF provisions which were aimed at providing minimum protection for public viewing, such as the protection of minors and advertising restrictions, have been overturned by the ECJ or simply ignored by Member States without consequence. Large groups continue to dominate industrial fora, which dominate policy-making. This is even more the case since Member States introduced the institutionalisation of self-regulation in the Lisbon Council summit. The EU's concentration on capital investment has not necessarily produced the best result for democratic participation in Europe. Although access to diverse opinion in the media is generally understood to be a crucial component to democratic society, the EC regulatory framework for communication is seen to be eroding national mechanisms that guarantee plurality in media markets. Even if the Commission vision of a vast quantity of channels with interactive services were to be realised, this will not automatically provide media diversity, quality of programming output or even facilitate consumer choice. Media concentration by the same reasoning does not lead to a lowering in market prices or increased media diversity.

Efficiency
Academic examinations of EU policy argue that EU mandates often did not find the most efficient solutions to regulatory problems. The most cited examples of this in the media field have been the failed Directives that set standards for high definition and wide screen television (Collins, 1994b; Dai, Cawson and Holmes, 1996; Levy, 1999). By the time the MAC and HD-MAC standards had been adopted, the market had chosen different

standards or moved on to newer technology. This was probably more to do with the fact that the European Commission was interested in supporting European champions, as demonstrated by Dai, Cawson and Holmes (1996), than effective market regulation. Companies however act in global competitive markets. The European champion 'Philips' while developing HDTV in Europe was at the same time developing digital technology in the United States. The Commission's failure in this respect reflects the French failure to regulate its own market. The support of the national champion 'Canal Plus' to defend French culture in the world has largely backfired. The UK, in contrast, has taken the view that it does not really matter who owns the media as long as they are held accountable to the public interest through efficient regulatory requirements, e.g. those required of commercial operators, balanced by a strong PSB which sticks to its remit. Generally, the book has shown that state-owned companies have been shown to be more effective in reaching public policy goals (be it the production of European content or laying the 'last (cable) mile') than leaving it up to the market. European companies are acting in global markets and may, as with broadcasting groups in France or publishing groups in the Netherlands and Germany, one day decide to concentrate on markets other the European one.

It is precisely due to the failure of MAC and HD-MAC, that the Commission shied away from recommending standards in its 1995 Television Standards Directive for the digital television market. National governments attempted to enforce common standards at the national level, but, ironically, it was EU competition policy that permitted market operators to choose to compete with different systems than their competitors in each national market, as shown in Chapters 3 and 6. This represented a clear inconsistency in the EC approach. Member States originally preferred one digital platform for all their key national players and the use of a single encryption technology for set-top boxes. This was consistent with the (looser) regulatory framework recommended by DG Information Society and the recommendation in the EC 1995 TV Standards Directive. However, DG Competition mandated through its competition decisions, the establishment of at least two players in each national market and competition in the choice of encryption technologies at national levels.

When issuing licences for pay-television platforms in the mid 1990s, Member States initially preferred one tightly regulated consortium of all their key national players (e.g. Bertelsmann/Kirch/DeustchTelecom in Germany; Carlton/Granada/BskyB in the UK, RTL4/Veronica/Endemol in the Netherlands, Canal Plus España/Télefonica in Spain, etc.) rather than requiring each player to establish a separate platform. However, the EC competition directorate vetoed these choices in the interest of competition. The Commission mandated that there be multiple platforms at national levels. This policy was implemented to the avoidance of the imposition of must-carry rules and access requirements on single platforms, which would have required huge regulatory effort on the part of the EU institutions. The EC competition strategy did not work as dominant positions emerged over-time. Moreover, intense market competition weakened European parent companies (usually terrestrial television operators and publishing groups). Few of the major European players are presently in sound financial shape. The dilemma that the European institutions now face is that many European terrestrial and digital players are vulnerable to foreign (e.g. non-European) take-over. Europe already finds itself in a situation wherein initial investment in the new media markets of the early 90s (cable and satellite) largely came from established US corporations, such as AOL/Time Warner, Liberty, News Corporation, NTL, UPC and Viacom.

The Commission also let the market decide on standard setting. Companies, naturally, chose different systems. The cost was high for Europe, as the market could not function smoothly – once customers had bought an expensive set-top box, they were most likely to stick with that operator and could not easily migrate to another service, even if they wanted to. This meant decreased rather than increased consumer choice. Market players were forced to compete with technology rather than content. Competition led to market failure and concentration as detailed in Chapter 6. If Member States had been permitted (or even required) under EU law to impose a common standard, it may have created a level playing field for competition, greater consumer choice and lower technology costs for operators. The Commission did not have to choose the standard itself. The fact that the Commission in many cases supported the establishment of Canal Plus and the company's use of simulcrypt in many Member States, leads one to believe that the European Commission again was intent on the support of a European champion rather than establishing efficient market regulation. This is particularly because the alternative, multicrypt, is more compatible.

The Commission faces the same pitfalls with standards for Application Programming Interface (API) and Conditional Access (CA) systems. Under its 2002 regulatory 'framework' Directive, the Commission recommends, but does not impose, the DVB-MHP API standard for interoperability in interactive television. However, there has been little implementation of the MHP standard in European markets. The now-established market players simply do not wish to open markets to new entrants. As Arino points out the MHP system is also considered overly 'complex, with high processing requirements' and is considered by many market players 'not (to) offer any added value in comparison with existing market offerings' and is higher in cost (Arino, 2002). This is because MHP is a more advanced standard than existing standards, such as MediaHighway (Canal+) and OpenTV (BSkyB). Existing operators therefore have little incentive to migrate. The MHP standard has been endorsed by the European Broadcaster's Union (the

European association of public service broadcasters) and the Nordig Consortium (of Nordic broadcasters and communications operators in Denmark, Finland, Sweden, Norway and Iceland) has expressed a wish to migrate to MHP (Laven, 2002). This is because PSBs and operators in small markets would incur a high cost were they to produce separate set-top boxes. However, other API standards are more common in both the UK and the USA. In Europe, the standard 'Open TV', which is majority-owned by Liberty Media Corporation, is used by: Télévision Par Satellite (TPS) and Noos interactive services in France, BSkyB and British Interactive Broadcasting's (BIB) in the UK, Sweden's Telia, Denmark's Tele Danmark Kabel, Italy's Stream, Spain's Via Digital and the PrimaCom cable network in Germany. MediaHighway was developed and used by Canal Plus (shareholders in 2003 were Sun Microsystems, Sony, Sogecable and Thomson Multimedia). Betanova was developed by BetaResearch and is used by Premiere in Germany and Austria. Notwithstanding the potential pitfalls, there much is European pressure for systems using other API systems to migrate to MHP. Under the 2002 Framework Directive, the Commission reserves the right to make the agreed standard compulsory by 'all providers of digital interactive television services and . . . digital TV equipment' if Member States do not adopt it by July 2004. Thus, a further EU policy failure is in the cards. A better solution, as stated, would have been to allow Member States to impose their own standards and to attempt to influence (but not to mandate) national decision-making at this point. A better regulatory environment, not liberalisation, is more condutive to growth and competitiveness.

The push for traditional market operators to invest in new technologies has meant a high price for Europe. The argument that there would be complete convergence of all services (e.g. television, internet, radio) receivable in one 'entertainment centre' is far from becoming reality. Rather than substitutability, there exists distinct and complementary receiver systems, which require distinct and complementary policies and regulations. This does not mean a decrease in the regulatory challenges as regulation intervention could be needed any stage of the transmission: bundling, decoder technology, delivery system technology, scrambling, conditional access systems, common interfaces, APIs, EPGs, smart cards, etc.

Implementation
A greater problem confronting the Commission is lack of implementation by Member States. This was highlighted again in the 2000 White Paper on Governance followed by the 'Better lawmaking' action plan which undertook to 'legislate less but better' (CEC, 2002c). The Council of Ministers set up a working group to implement the plan. In parallel, the European Convention on institutional reform, established following the Laeken Declaration, set up a working group on the simplification of instruments and

procedures. The Working Group recommended to the European Convention that the EU concentrate on implementation and simplification of existing EU legislation rather than the production of new legislation.[3] This move is clearly a repeat of the measures taken following the 1992 the Edinburgh summit, but does not address the problem of implementation as such. The Commission continues to have weak monitoring mechanisms, and infringement procedures (according to Article 169 of the Treaty) are cumbersome. In 2003, the EC's biannual Scoreboard calculated that the record of existing Member States had worsened, with 559 outstanding cases of non-implementation.[4] The EC reports on TWF implementation show a high level of compliance but an independent assessment might indicate high compliance of some provisions and low compliance of others, such as advertising restrictions. The ECJ and the EC seem particularly preoccupied with the non-implementation of the provision on cross-border broadcasting and unconcerned with non-implementation of European quotas, advertising limits, minority protection, etc. The new regulatory framework for communications poses similar implementation problems. The framework is an essentially liberating one without the specification of balancing mechanisms. This reflects the way in which it was formed. Even though PSBs, consumer associations, etc. were able to insert an opt-out for national content requirements, the real test will be how the EU actually implements the Directives, particularly the ECJ.

A problem specific to media markets with respect to implementation is the traditional political ties of media groups. Politicians seem to believe that the media controls the minds of voters (even though there are many nuances, and this is oft times actually not the case).[5] Therefore, the choice of who controls the media market at national levels is politicised. Governments in power usually take a hands-on approach to the choice of instruments used to measure the market. Companies which succeed in market expansion are usually those closest to political parties in power. This is particularly the case in newspaper markets. New technologies, satellite and cable in the earlier years, were meant to put an end to spectrum scarcity and were seen as an opportunity to break political heavy handedness in broadcasting and create a genuine competitive market. However, national governments have often turned to conventional modes of control when choosing the national players, which now control gateway monopolies to new service platforms. The introduction of 'super regulators', as in the UK and Italy, have not solved this problem as final decision-making lies with government ministries. At the same time, as national governments did not relinquish media/cultural policy to the European level, the EC is unable to guarantee minimum standards for the protection of the public interest as it was viewed to be encroaching on cultural policy (exempt by subsidiarity). Enforcement of such provisions is virtually impossible as the EU institutions would be overstepping the borders mapped out by the Treaties. For their part, national parliaments are perhaps unwilling to extend qualified majority voting to Article 151 (on cultural policy), as they simply fear the power the EC would wield with the instrument.

Discourse

A second problem facing the European Commission is the validity of the discourse in which communications regulation is steeped – its predictions that liberalisation will encourage market investment and job growth (Kubicek, Herbert and Dutton, 1997). It is easy to observe that European Commission made a gross overestimate of sector growth in its White Papers. The present market slump and job losses in both new and traditional communications markets has laid the Commission bare to criticism that it used arguments of technological determinism and sector growth merely to justify sector liberalisation (Humphreys, 1996; Ward, 2003).

For their part, Member States have always preferred tightly regulated consortia of major national players rather than requiring each player to establish a separate platform. In order to promote competition, and perhaps to ensure pluralism as well, the EC has insisted that there be a number of platforms at national levels in new markets (particularly in digital satellite). As a result, many platforms failed due to existing market saturation. Companies have been unable to recoup investments, particularly in digital technology. In the past, companies willing to invest in new technology may have been aided or rewarded by governments, which would (in some way) compensate for losses. However, any government support would be blocked under EU state aid rules. Heavy losses and sometimes bankruptcy of pay television platforms across Europe (e.g. Canal Plus, Kirch, ITV Digital, Telepiù, Quiero, ViaDigital) has forced major sell-offs. US players are being invited in to pick up the pieces. Member States are reacting to this by attempting to push their original agenda forward within the European Council. This has been taken on board by the European Commission in its aforementioned eEurope initiative, which calls for greater public-private sector co-operation in the establishment of new markets.

The promise of job creation is also being questioned. Journalists' organisations and employee unions argue that new technologies, particularly e-initiatives such as those specified in the EU 'Information society project', and media concentration at national levels mean job loss not job production. The financial difficulties experienced by digital, satellite and cable companies in the late 1990s and early 2000s meant the liquidation of a number of European players and inevitable job losses in the newly created markets which were meant to provide job growth. New e-initiatives (such as e-learning, e-finance, etc.) threatens to replaces workers in service sectors and (in the case of e-learning) academia. This has been highlighted recently in the national press as call centers for everything from train enquiries to financial consultancy are being outsourced offshore.

Meanwhile, the media sector itself is highly volatile and remains a high-risk sector (shown in Chapter 6). This has a knock-on effect for pluralism. If technology and increased competition lead to cost cutting, this means not only staff lay-offs, but less investment in media content. Cost cutting is viewed to lead to a standardisation in media content, rather than diversification. The Council of Europe has argued that this can lead to a reduction in both the variation and amount of information sources (1996a). There is also the concern that media companies may sacrifice editorial independence in favour of producing profitability. Increased market competition inevitably means that companies are less likely and even unable to meet pluralist objectives even if they wanted to. Digression of one player (whether commercial or state-owned) in a given market (e.g. the evasion of advertising requirements or journalist codes) leads to digression by another if laws are not enforced (or are prevented from being enforced by European law). Companies gain market share over competitors by non-compliance.

For this reason, a stable regulatory environment is required, whether it is based on the older European model or the incoming US-imported model (of liberalisation, access, transparency and self-regulation). However, as demonstrated by the dangers of policy transfer in Eastern Europe (Harcourt, 2003), caution should be applied in the import of regulatory models. Europe has in place guarantees not only for restricting ownership, but guarantees protecting minority group representation and minority languages (including subsidisation in both press and broadcasting). It is important for minority groups to continue to have a voice in democratic processes, particularly given Europe's history. It should be noted that the USA has moved over time towards complete market liberalisation, including the recent removal of ownership rules. This liberal approach is increasingly applied to the regulation of content. Up until 1987, US broadcasters were answerable to the Fairness Doctrine, which called on broadcasters to promote internal diversity and provide equal time to political candidates. Since 1987, the Fairness Doctrine is no longer adhered to, due to a US Supreme Court ruling which ruled it unconstitutional.

Content production and distribution

The EU's policy of correcting the trade imbalance with the US in programme imports – one of the key reasons for EU legislation – is failing. As authors have pointed out, the audio-visual trade deficit is widening (Tongue, 1996; Ward, 2003: 106–9; Levy, 1999). European broadcasters rely heavily on US imports from the largest US content producers: Viacom, AOL-Time-Warner, Disney, Vivendi, MGM/UA, 20th Century Fox and Columbia Pictures. As it explained in Chapter 6, this is because US imports are inexpensive compared with European production. They are also time-savers. The US companies provide whole programming packages including scheduling and space for the insertion of commercial breaks. Packages are easy to purchase due to strong US distribution networks. By contrast, European, small and independent film producers rarely reach the small screen due to their comparatively higher cost and distribution difficulties at European and national levels.

The European Union has attempted to come to grips with the content problem through support mechanisms, namely the MEDIA programmes. MEDIA I programme (1990–95) provided direct support to European content production. MEDIA II (1996–2000) concentrated on training, the development of audiovisual projects and distribution. The funding for these programmes has been minute compared with subsidisation in other industries, with only 400 million Euro allocated to the most recent MEDIA Plus programme (2001–2005). The most recent MEDIA Plus programme spreads funding very thinly across five different funding areas: the focusing on the training of professionals; the development of production projects and companies; the distribution of cinematographic works and audiovisual programmes; the promotion of cinematographic works and audiovisual programmes; and support for cinematographic festivals. Under its presidency, the Italian government strongly supported these initiatives, due to the wish to preserve Italy's domestic film industry. However, problems of distribution, geographical rights and the promotion of European films have largely not been addressed.

European pay-television systems are under intense pressure to compete for sports rights. This has led to rocketing price increases in sports broadcasting rights, particularly for football. This in turn has contributed to the collapse of European pay platforms. The European Parliament highlighted the danger that consumers may have to pay in future to view international events, such as the Olympics, or significant national events. Therefore the 'Listed Events' was introduced in the 1997 TWF Directive which allows Member States to isolate certain events from exclusive rights contracts if they are considered to be of major importance for society. However, no effort to regulate the market has been made beyond national scrutiny of the purchasing of contracts.

Television, although the technology exists, is not becoming 'European', i.e. through simultaneous broadcast in many languages across Europe. This is too high a cost, as programming rights are restricted by geography. Generally, the norm for pan-European broadcasting are thematic channels for mainstream audiences or identification of niche audiences to boost profitability. Although an increasing number of satellites have 'European' footprints (Astra, Hot Bird, EuroBird, Sirius, Thor/ Intelsat, W1, AtlanticBird), pan-European broadcasting is dominated by US groups distributing their own content (e.g. the Bloomberg, CNBC, CNN International, Discovery, Fox Kids, MTV, National Geographic, Sky News, TV5, Universal Studios

Networks). Newer services, such as broadband, can offer little 'new' in terms of programming, as they are governed by the same rights agreements as broadcasters.[6] European channels are concentrating on niche programming channels, such as religious channels, adult film channels and shopping channels. In 2003, pan-European satellite services offered 188 chat channels, 80 teleshopping channels, 36 music channels, 35 religious stations, 13 fashion stations and seven (continuous broadcast) 'adult film' channels.

Hence, even though there is an increase in the number of channels, media concentration (and vertical integration of programme supply) may be preventing diversity rather than promoting it. In terms of pluralism, the greatest problem is undoubtedly distribution. Here, the European Union, with its concentration on the regulation of broadcasting platforms, has taken little action.

Media pluralism
The final problem is the fact that a number of national regulatory instruments used to protect the public interest are subject to erosion by cross-border broadcasting. Examples of these are restrictions on media ownership, minimum standards on media content, prohibition of pornography, limitation of television violence, bans on hatespeech and limits on advertising time. Some of these rules, such as limitations on advertising time, were harmonised by TWF which is flanked by an earlier 1984 Directive on misleading advertising.[7] But generally, the Directives set up minimum standards and the book has shown that EU institutions are not concerned with implementation. Media ownership and content are not regulated at the European level, as they are protected by subsidiarity. Antithetically, the majority of European democracies have considered strict regulation of the media industry, and in particular concentration, as important for assuring democratic representation. Limitations on media ownership has been viewed for political as well as historical reasons as a potential threat to democracy, freedom of speech and pluralist representation. The European Union's concentration on the exploitation of media markets for capital growth has sacrificed the wider goal of the protection of pluralism and therefore the protection of democracy in Europe. New forms of regulation, such as self-regulation, as compensating measures are regarded as weak instruments of control, as they are neither binding nor legally legitimate.

Notes

1 http://european-convention.eu.int/docs/Treaty/cv00850.en03.pdf.
2 On 1 May, the Accession Treaty enters into effect on which date the new EU members will become full members of the European Council and European Parliament. Each new Member State will appoint a European Commissioner (to be

approved not by the European Parliament, but by present Member States). Every new Member State will have one European Commissioner who will have the full right to vote within the Commission; however, the new Commissioners will not initially hold a portfolio. (Current portfolios will remain as at present and division of fields of activity will remain unchanged during the period of transition). In November 2004, a new Commission will be appointed by all Member States at which point Directorate Generals and Commissioner portfolios will be reorganised.

3   http://europa.eu.int/scadplus/leg/en/cig/g4000s.htm#s3.

4   There were, as of April 2003, 1530 Directives and 377 Regulations relating to the Single Market.

5   There are countless academic studies on the media and public opinion. Sociologists tend to argue that socialisation rather than the media is a key influence of public opinion formation. Further, different experiences in socialisation by individuals and groups effects media consumption. See the *International Journal of Public Opinion Research* for national case studies.

6   The only exception to this is PSB programming. The BBC is unwilling to broadcast via webcasting due to the profit made from selling its programming abroad. However, other European PSBs do webcast. Notably, Italy's RAI in particular is webcasting cultural, documentary and children's programmes via the internet.

7   Misleading Advertising Directive, 4. Council Directive 84/450/EEC of 10 September, 1984. OJ L 250/17.

Appendix 1: European Union legislation governing media markets, 1989–2004

Regulation 2004/139 on the control of concentrations between undertakings (Merger Regulation). *Official Journal of the European Communities* L 24, 29.01.2004.

Decision 2003/548/EC on the minimum set of leased lines with harmonised characteristics and associated standards referred to in Article 18 of the Universal Service Directive. *Official Journal of the European Communities* L 186, 25.07.2003.

Directive 2002/77/EC on competition in the markets for electronic communications networks and services (Liberalisation Directive). *Official Journal of the European Communities* L 249 of 17.09.2002.

Directive 2002/58/EC concerning the processing of personal data and the protection of privacy in the electronic communications sector (Data Protection Directive). *Official Journal of the European Communities* L 201 of 31.07.2002.

Decision 2002/627/EC establishing the European Regulators Group for Electronic Communications Networks and Services (European Regulators Group Decision). *Official Journal of the European Communities* L 200 of 30.7.2002.

Directive 2002/21/EC on a common regulatory framework for electronic communications networks and services (Framework Directive). *Official Journal of the European Communities* L 108 of 24.04.2002.

Directive 2002/22/EC on universal service and users' rights relating to electronic communications networks and services (Universal Service Directive). *Official Journal of the European Communities* L 108 of 24.04.2002.

Directive 2002/20/EC on the authorisation of electronic communications networks and services (Authorisation Directive). *Official Journal of the European Communities* L 108 of 24.04.2002.

Directive 2002/19/EC on access to, and interconnection of, electronic communications networks and associated facilities (Access Directive). *Official Journal of the European Communities* L 108 of 24.04.2002.

Decision 2002/622/EC on a regulatory framework for radio spectrum policy in the European Community (Radio Spectrum Decision). *Official Journal of the European Communities* L 108 of 24.04.2002.

Directive 2001/29/EC on the harmonisation of certain aspects of copyright and related rights in the information society. *Official Journal of the European Communities* L 167, 22.6.2001.

Regulation 2000/2887 on unbundled access to the local loop. *Official Journal of the European Communities* L 336 of 30.12.2000.

Directive 2000/31/EC on certain legal aspects of information society services, in particular electronic commerce in the Internal Market (Electronic Commerce Directive). *Official Journal of the European Communities* L 178 of 17.07.2000.

Directive 99/64/EC amending Directive 90/388/EEC in order to ensure that telecommunications networks and cable TV networks owned by a single operator are separate legal entities. *Official Journal of the European Communities* L 175 of 10.7.1999.

Directive 1999/5/EC on radio equipment and telecommunications terminal equipment (R&TTE). *Official Journal of the European Communities* L 91 of 07.04.1999.

Resolution concerning public service broadcasting. *Official Journal of the European Communities* C 30 of 05.02.1999.

Resolution on the consumer dimension of the information society. *Official Journal of the European Communities* C 023/1 of 28.01.1999.

Directive 98/84/EC on the legal protection of services based on, or consisting of, conditional access. *Official Journal of the European Communities* L 320 of 28.11.1998.

Recommendation 98/560/EC on the development of the competitiveness of the European audio-visual and information services industry by promoting national frameworks aimed at achieving a comparable and effective level of protection of minors and human dignity. *Official Journal of the European Communities* L 270 of 07.10.1998.

Directive 98/61/EC amending Directive 97/33/EC with regard to operator number portability and carrier pre-selection. *Official Journal of the European Communities* L 268 of 03.10.1998.

Directive 98/48/EC amending Directive 98/34/EC laying down a procedure for the provision of information in the field of technical standards and regulations. *Official Journal of the European Communities* L 217/18 of 05.8.1998.

Directive 98/43/EC on tobacco advertising. *Official Journal of the European Communities* L 213 of 30.07.1998 (annulled by Court of Justice case Case C-74/99).

Directive 97/55/EC amending Directive 84/450/EEC concerning misleading advertising so as to include comparative advertising. *Official Journal of the European Communities* L 194 of 10.07.1998.

Directive 98/10/EC on the application of open network provision (ONP) to voice telephony and on universal service for telecommunications in a competitive environment. *Official Journal of the European Communities* L 101 of 01.04.1998.

Corrigendum to Regulation 97/1310/EC amending Regulation (EEC) No 4064/89 on the control of concentrations between undertakings. *Official Journal of the European Communities* L 40 of 13.02.1998.

Directive 97/66/EC concerning the processing of personal data and the protection. *Official Journal of the European Communities* L 24 of 30.01.1998.

Directive 97/51/EC amending Council Directives 90/387/EEC and 92/44/EEC for the purpose of adaptation to a competitive environment in telecommunications. *Official Journal of the European Communities* L 295 of 29.10.1997.

Directive 97/36/EC amending Council Directive 89/552/EEC on the coordination of certain provisions laid down by law, regulation or administrative action in

Member States concerning the pursuit of television broadcasting activities (1997 Television Without Frontiers Directive). *Official Journal of the European Communities* L 202 of 30.07.1997.

Directive 97/33/EC on interconnection in Telecommunications with regard to ensuring universal service and interoperability through application of the principles of Open Network Provision (ONP). *Official Journal of the European Communities* L 199 of 26.07.1997.

Regulation 97/1310/EC amending Regulation (EEC) No 4064/89 on the control of concentrations between undertakings. *Official Journal of the European Communities* L 180 of 09.07.1997.

Directive 97/13/EC on a common framework for general authorizations and individual licences in the field of telecommunications services (Licensing Directive). *Official Journal of the European Communities* L 117 of 07.05.1997.

Directive 96/19/EC amending Directive 90/388/EEC with regard to the implementation of full competition in telecommunications markets (Full Competition Directive). *Official Journal of the European Communities* L 074 of 22.03.1996.

Directive 96/2/EC amending Directive 90/388/EEC with regard to mobile and personal communications. *Official Journal of the European Communities* L 020 of 26.01.1996.

Directive 95/46/EC on the protection of individuals with regard to the processing of personal data and on the free movement of such data. *Official Journal of the European Communities* L 281 23.11.1995.

Directive 95/47/EC on the use of standards for the transmission of television signals (Advanced Television Standards Directive). *Official Journal of the European Communities* L 281 of 23.11.1995.

Resolution on the image of women and men portrayed in advertising and the media. *Official Journal of the European Communities* C 296 of 10.11.1995.

Directive 95/51/EC amending Directive 90/388/EEC with regard to the abolition of the restrictions on the use of cable television networks for the provision of already liberalized telecommunications services. *Official Journal of the European Communities* L 256 of 26.10.1995.

Decision 94/800/EC concerning the conclusion on behalf of the European Community, as regards matters within its competence, of the agreements reached in the Uruguay Round multilateral negotiations (1986–1994). *Official Journal of the European Communities* L 336 of 23.12.1994.

Directive 94/46/EC amending Directive 88/301/EEC and Directive 90/388/EEC in particular with regard to satellite communications. *Official Journal of the European Communities* L 268 of 19.10.1994.

Agreement on the European Economic Area – Annex X – Audiovisual services – List provided for in Article 36 (2). *Official Journal of the European Communities* L 001 of 03.01.1994.

Directive 93/83/EEC on the coordination of certain rules concerning copyright and rights related to copyright applicable to satellite broadcasting and cable retransmission. *Official Journal of the European Communities* L 248 of 06.10.1993.

Resolution on the development of technology and standards in the field of advanced television services. *Official Journal of the European Communities* C 209 of 03.08.1993.

Directive 92/44/EEC of 5 June 1992 on the application of open network provision to leased lines. *Official Journal of the European Communities* L 165 of 19.06.1992.

Directive 92/38/EEC on the adoption of standards for satellite broadcasting of television signals. *Official Journal of the European Communities* L 137 of 20.05.1992.

Directive 91/287/EEC on the frequency band to be designated for the coordinated introduction of digital European cordless telecommunications (DECT) into the Community. *Official Journal of the European Communities* L 144 of 08.06.1991.

Directive 90/544/EEC on the frequency bands designated for the coordinated introduction of pan-European land-based public radio paging in the Community (ERMES Directive). *Official Journal of the European Communities* L 310 of 09.11.1990.

Directive 90/388/EEC on competition in the markets for telecommunications services (Services Directive). *Official Journal of the European Communities* L 192 of 24.07.1990.

Directive 90/387/EEC on the establishment of the internal market for telecommunications services through the implementation of open network provision (ONP Framework Directive). *Official Journal of the European Communities* L 192 of 24.07.1990.

Regulation 89/4064/EEC on the control of concentrations between undertakings (Merger Regulation). *Official Journal of the European Communities* L 395 of 30.12.1989.

Decision 89/630/EEC on the common action to be taken by the Member States with respect to the adoption of a single world-wide high-definition television production standard by the Plenary Assembly of the International Radio Consultative Committee (CCIR). *Official Journal of the European Communities* L 363 of 13.12.1989.

Directive 89/552/EEC on the coordination of certain provisions laid down by Law, Regulation or Administrative Action in Member States concerning the pursuit of television broadcasting activities (Television Without Frontiers Directive). *Official Journal of the European Communities* L 298 of 17.10.1989.

Decision 89/337/EEC on high-definition television. *Official Journal of the European Communities* L 142 of 25.05.1989.

Directive 86/529/EEC on the adoption of common technical specifications of the MAC/packet family of standards for direct satellite television broadcasting. *Official Journal of the European Communities* L 311 of 06.11.1986.

Directive 84/450/EEC relating to the approximation of the laws, regulations and administrative provisions of the Member States concerning misleading advertising. *Official Journal of the European Communities* L 250 of 19.09.1984.

Appendix 2: European Court of Justice and Court of First Instance cases, 1974–2003

Case C-245/01 *RTL Television GmbH* v. *Niedersächsische Landesmedienanstalt für privaten Rundfunk. Official Journal of the European Communities* C 304 of 23.10.2003.

Case C-304 Joined Cases T-346/02 and T-347/02 *Cableuropa SA and others* v. *Commission of the European Communities. Official Journal of the European Communities* C 304 of 13.12.2003.

Case T-346/02 *Cableuropa, S.A., Región de Murcia de Cable, S.A., Valencia de Cable, S.A., Mediterránea Sur Sistemas de Cable, S.A., y Mediterránea Norte Sistemas de Cable, S.A.* v. *Commission of the European Communities. Official Journal of the European Communities* C 19 of 25.01.2003.

Case C-390/99 *Canal Satélite Digital S.L.* v. *Administración General del Estado. Official Journal of the European Communities* C 6 of 08.01.2000.

Case C-308/99 *Télévision Française 1 SA (TF1)* v. *Commission of the European Communities supported by the French Republic. Official Journal of the European Communities* C 299 of 16.10.1999.

Case C-119/00 *Commission of the European Communities* v. *Grand-Duchy of Luxembourg. Official Journal of the European Communities* C 163 of 10.06.2000.

Case C-207/00 *Commission of the European Communities* v. *Italian Republic on Failure to transpose Directive 97/36/EC. Official Journal of the European Communities* C 211 of 22.07.2000.

Case T-206/99 *Métropole Télévision SA* v. *Commission of the European Communities. Official Journal of the European Communities* C 161 of 02.06.2001.

Case T-69/99 *Eurotica Rendez-Vous Television Danish Satellite TV (DSTV) A/S* v. *Commission of the European Communities. Official Journal of the European Communities* C 160 of 05.06.1999.

Case C-319/99 *Commission of the European Communities* v. *French Republic. Official Journal of the European Communities* C 299 of 16.10.1999.

Case No NN 88/98 *Financing of a 24-hour advertising-free news channel with licence fee by the BBC. Official Journal of the European Communities* C 78 of 18.3.2000.

Case E-8/97 *TV 1000 Sverige AB* v. *The Norwegian Government (represented by the Royal Ministry of Cultural Affairs). Official Journal of the European Communities* C 268 of 27.09.1998.

Case C-74/99 *Imperial Tobacco and Others*. Annulment of the EU Directive

98/43/EC of 6 July 1998 on advertising due to lack of EU legal competence. *Official Journal of the European Communities* C 74 of 15.5.1999.

Case T-46/97 *Sociedade Independente de Comunicação (SIC) SA* v. *Commission of the European Communities. Official Journal of the European Communities* C 176 of 24.06.2000.

Case C-212/98 *Commission of the European Communities* v. *Ireland. Official Journal of the European Communities* C 47 of 19.02.2000.

Case C-164/98 *D.I.R. International Film S.r.l.* v. *Others and the Commission of the European Communities. Official Journal of the European Communities* C 184 of 13.06.1998.

Case C-6/98 *Arbeitsgemeinschaft Deutscher Rundfunkanstalten (ARD)* v. *ProSieben Media AG. Official Journal of the European Communities* C 34 of 05.02.2000.

Case T-266/97 *Vlaamse Televisie Maatschappij NV* v. *Commission of the European Communities. Official Journal of the European Communities* C 281 of 02.10.1999.

Case 99/97 *Verein zur Förderung des Freien Wettbewerbs im Medienwesen* v. *TV Spielfilm Verlag GmbH*, preliminary ruling in Case C-135/97 *Verein zur Förderung des freien Wettbewerbs im Medienwesen* v. *MVF Magazin-Verlag am Fleetrand. Official Journal of the European Communities* C 94 of 28.3.1998.

Case C-56/96 *VT4 Ltd* v. *Vlaamse Gemeenschap.* European Court reports of 05.06.1997, page I-03143.

Case T-17/96 *Télévision Française 1 SA (TF1)* v. *Commission of the European Communities on Commission. Official Journal of the European Communities* C 265 of 18.09.1999.

Case T-95/96 *Gestevisión Telecinco SA* v. *Commission of the European Communities. Official Journal of the European Communities* C 340 of 07.11.1998.

Case T-221/95 *Endemol Entertainment Holding BV* v. *Commission of the European Communities. Official Journal of the European Communities* C 265 of 18.09.1999.

Case C-368/95 *Familiapress* v. *Bauer.* European Court reports of 26.06.1997, page I-03689.

Case C-34/95 *TV-Shop i Sverige AB (C-35/95) and (C-36/95) Konsumentombudsmannen (KO)* v. *De Agostini (Svenska) Förlag AB (C-34/95) and TV-Shop i Sverige AB (C-35/95 and C-36/95).* European Court reports of 09.07.1997, page I-03843.

Joined cases C-320/94, C-328/94, C-329/94, C-337/94, C-338/94 and C-339/94 *Radio Torre, Rete A Srl, Vallau Italiana Promomarket Srl, Radio Italia Solo Musica Srl and Others and GETE Srl* v. *Ministerio delle Poste e Telecomunicazioni.* European Court reports of 12.12.1994, page I-06471.

Case T-504/93 *Tiercé Ladbroke SA* v. *Commission of the European Communities.* European Court Reports of 12.06.1997, page II-0923.

Case C-14/96 *Criminal proceedings against Paul Denuit.* Reference for a preliminary ruling from the Tribunal de première instance de Bruxelles. European Court reports of 29.05.1997, page I-02785.

Joined cases T-528/93, T-542/93, T-543/93 and T-546/93 *Metropole Télévision SA and Reti Televisive Italiane SpA and Gestevisión Telecinco SA and Antena 3 de Televisión* v. *Commission of the European Communities.* European Court Reports of 11.07.1996, page II-0649.

Case T-52/96 R *Sogecable SA* v. *Commission of the European Communities.* European Court reports of 12.07.1996, page II-00797.

Joined cases C-34/95, C-35/95 and C-36/95 *Konsumentombudsmannen (KO)* v. *De Agostini (Svenska) Förlag AB* (C-34/95) and *TV-Shop i Sverige AB* (C-35/95 and C-36/95). European Court reports of 09.07.1997, page I-03843.

Case C-222/94 *Commission of the European Communities* v. *United Kingdom of Great Britain and Northern Ireland.* European Court reports of 10.09.1996, page I-04025.

Joined cases C-320/94, C-328/94, C-329/94, C-337/94, C-338/94 and C-339/94 *Reti Televisive Italiane SpA (RTI)* (C-320/94), *Radio Torre* (C-328/94), *Rete A Srl* (C-329/94), *Vallau Italiana Promomarket Srl* (C-337/94), *Radio Italia Solo Musica Srl and Others* (C-338/94) and *GETE Srl* (C-339/94) v. *Ministero delle Poste e Telecomunicazioni.* European Court reports of 12.12.1996, page I-06471.

Joined cases C-241/91 and C-242/91 *Radio Telefos Eireann (RTE) and Independent Television Publications Ltd* v. *Commission of the European Communities.* European Court reports of 06.04.1995, page I-00743.

Case C-23/93 *TV10 SA* v. *Commissariaat voor de Media.* European Court reports of 05.10.1994, page I-04795.

Case C-23/93 *Vereniging Veronica Omroep Organisatie* v. *Commissariaat voor de Media.* European Court reports of 07.10.1994, page I-04795.

Case C-327/93 *Red Hot Television.* Removed from the register on 29.03.1996.

Case C-23/93 *TV 10 SA* v. *Commissariaat voor de Media.* European Court reports of 05.10.1994, page I-04795.

Case T-543/93 *Gestevisión Telecinco SA* v. *Commission of the European Communities.* European Court reports of 14.12.1993, page II-1409.

Joined cases T-528/93, T-542/93, T-543/93 and T-546/93 *Metropole Télévision SA and Reti Televisive Italiane SpA and Gestevisión Telecinco SA and Antena 3 de Televisión* v. *Commission of the European Communities.* European Court reports of 11.07.1996, page II-0649.

Case C-98/92 *La Cinq* v. *European Commission.* European Court reports of 07.05.1992, page II-0001.

Case C-211/91 *European Communities* v. *Kingdom of Belgium.* European Court reports of 16.12.1992, page I-6757.

Case T-35/91 *Eurosport Consortium* v. *Commission of the European Communities.* European Court reports 28.11.1991, page II-01359.

Case T-44/90 *La Cinq* v. *European Commission.* European Court reports of 24.01.1992, page II-0001.

Case C-288/89 *Stichting Collectiev Antennevoorziening Gouda and Others* v. *Commissariaat voor de Media.* European Court reports of 25.07.1989, page I-04007.

Case 66/86 *Ahmed Saeed Flugreisen and Others* v. *Zentrale zur Bekämpfung unlauteren Wettbewerbs.* European Court reports of 11.04.1989, page 803.

Case C-260/89 *Elliniki Radiophonia Tilorassi – Anonimi Etairia* v. *Dimotiki Etairia Pliroforissis and Sotirios Kouvelas.* European Court reports of 31.07.1991, page 2925.

Case C-353/89 *Commission of the European Communities* v. *Kingdom of the Netherlands.* European Court reports of 25.07.1991, page I-4069.

Case T-76/89 *Independent Television Publications Ltd* v. *Commission of the European Communities.* European Court reports of 10.07.1991, page II-00575.

Joined cases C-241/91 P AND C-242/91 P *Radio Telefos Eireann (RTE) and Independent Television Publications Ltd* v. *Commission of the European Communities.* European Court reports of 06.04.1995, I-0743.

Case C-352/85 *Bond van Adverteerders and others* v. *The Netherlands.* European Court reports of 26.04.1988, page I-2085.

Case T-70/89 *The British Broadcasting Corporation and BBC Enterprises Limited* v. *Commission of the European Communities.* European Court reports 10.07.1991, page II-00535.

Case C-77/89 *R Radio Telefis Eireann* v. *Commission of the European Communities.* European Court reports of 11.05.1989, page I-01141.

Case T-30/89 *Hilti* v. *Commission.* European Court reports of 12.12.1989, page II-01439.

Case T-83/91 *Tetra Pak International SA* v. *Commission.* European Court reports of 06.10.1991, page II-00755.

Case T-76/89 *Independent Television Publications Ltd* v. *Commission of the European Communities.* European Court reports of 10.07.1991, page II-0575.

Case T-70/89 *The British Broadcasting Corporation and BBC Enterprises Limited* v. *Commission of the European Communities.* European Court reports of 10.07.1991, page II-0535.

Case C-352/85 *Bond van Adverteerders and others* v. *The Netherlands.* European Court reports of 26.04.1988, page I-02085.

Case C-163/84 *Hauptzollamt Hannover* v. *Telefunken Fernseh und Rundfunk GmbH.* European Court reports of 07.10.1985, page 03299.

Case C-311/84 *Telemarketing* v. *CLT 1985 abuse of dominant position.* European Court reports of 03.10.1985, page 03261.

Case C-298/83 *Comité des industries cinématographiques des Communautés européennes (CICCE)* v. *Commission of the European Communities.* European Court reports 28.03.1985, page 01105.

Case C-262/81 *Coditel SA and others* v. *Cinè Vog and others (Coditel II).* European Court reports of 06.10.1982, page 03381.

Case C-126/80 *Maria Salonia* v. *Giorgio Poidomani and Franca Baglieri, née Giglio.* European Court reports of 16.06.1981, page 01563.

Case C-262/81 *Coditel SA, Compagnie Generale pour la Diffusion de la Television and others* v. *CineVog Films SA and others.* European Court reports of 06.10.1982, page 03381.

Case C-52/79 *Procureur du Roi* v. *Marc J.V.C. Debauve and others 1980 the discrimination of broadcasting signals due to national origin.* European Court reports of 18.03.1980, page 00833.

Case C-33/74, *Johannes Henricus Maria van Binsbergen* v. *Bestuur van de Bedrijfsvereniging voor de Metaalnijverheid.* European Court reports of 03.12.1974, page 01299.

Case C-155/73 *Tribunale civile e penale di Biella.* European Court reports of 30.04.1974, page 00409.

Appendix 3: Directorate General for Competition cases, 1989–2004

Case M.2978 *Lagardere/NaTexis/VUP*. Press release IP/04/15. 07.01.2004. Non-opposition.

Case COMP/M.2876 *Newscorp/Telepiù*. Press release IP/03/478. 02.04.2003. Non-opposition.

Case M.2978 *Lagardere/NaTexis/VUP*. Press release IP/03/808. 05.06.2003. Non-opposition.

Case M.3303 *GE/Vivendi/Universal Entertainment*. 19.12.2003. Non-opposition.

Case M.3240 *Liberty Media/QVC*. 25.08.2003. Non-opposition.

Case 38287 *Telenor +/Canal+/Canal Digital*. Press release IP/04/2. 29.12.2003 Antitrust: Exemption.

Case COMP/C2/38.287 *Telenor/Canal+/Canal Digital*. *Official Journal of the European Communities* C 149 of 26.6.2003. Non-opposition.

Case M.3085 *Schroders Ventures Ltd/Premiere*. *Official Journal of the European Communities* C 32 of 21.02.2003. Non-opposition.

Case M.3031 *Burda/HDP/Catherine Nemo*. *Official Journal of the European Communities* C 47 of 27.02.2003. Non-opposition.

Case M.2995 *Apax Europe/Goldman Sachs/Providence/Telekom Cable/JV*. *Official Journal of the European Communities* C 52 of 06.03.2003. Non-opposition.

Case M.2995 *Mediaset/Telecinco/Publiespañ*. *Official Journal of the European Communities* C 100 of 26.04.2003. Non-opposition.

Case M.3183 *Holtzbrink/Networxs/WeltBild/Tonline Venture/Berteslmann Online*. *Official Journal of the European Communities* C 155 of 03.07.2003. Non-opposition.

Case M.3162 *Hearst/De Telegraaf/Tijdschriften/JV*. *Official Journal of the European Communities* C 204 of 29.08.2003. Non-opposition.

Case 37398 UEFA. *Official Journal of the European Communities* L 291 of 08.11.2003. Antitrust: Exemption.

Case M.3197 *Candover/Cinven/Bertelsmann Springer*. *Official Journal of the European Communities* C 207 of 03.09.2003. Non-opposition.

Case M.3223 *ONEX/Kieft/Neue FilmPalast*. *Official Journal of the European Communities* C 199 of 23.08.2003. Non-opposition.

Case JV.48 *Vodafone/Vivendi/Canal Plus*. *Official Journal of the European Communities* C 118 of 20.05.2003. Non-opposition.

Case M.2616 *Deutsche Bank/TDC/JV. Official Journal of the European Communities* C 51 of 26.02.2002. Non-opposition.

Case JV.57 *TPS. Official Journal of the European Communities* C 137 of 08.06.2002. Non-opposition.

Case M.2766. *Vivendi Universal/Hachette/Multithematiques. Official Journal of the European Communities* C 154 of 28.06.2002. Non-opposition.

Case M.2723 *RTL/ProsiebenSat1/VG Media. Official Journal of the European Communities* C 201 of 24.08.2002. Non-opposition.

Case 37219 *Banghalter & de Homem Christo/SACEM.* 12.08.2002. Rejection of complaint.

Case M.2845 *Sogecable/CanalSatélite/Vía Digital.* 14.08.2002 Non-opposition.

Case M.2550 *Mezzo/Muzzik. Official Journal of the European Communities* C 21 of 24.01.2002. Non-opposition.

Case N. 548/01 *Aid to local television stations in the Frenchspeaking community in Belgium. Official Journal of the European Communities* C 150 of 22.06.2002. Non-opposition.

Case M.2883 *Bertelsmann/Zomba. Official Journal of the European Communities* C 223 of 19.09.2002. Non-opposition.

Case M.2925 *Charterhouse/DCD/Telediffusion de France SA. Official Journal of the European Communities* C 327of 28.12.2002. Non-opposition.

Case M.2783 *Mediatrade/Endemol/JV. Official Journal of the European Communities* C 320 of 20.12.2002. Non-opposition.

Case M.3018 *Candover/Cinven/KAP. Official Journal of the European Communities* C 327 of 28.12.2002. Non-opposition.

Case COMP/C2/38.464 *TF1/Eurosport SA/Consortium Eurosport. Official Journal of the European Communities* C 218 of 14.09.2002. Non-opposition.

Case IV/M.1978 *Telecom Italia/News Television/Stream. Official Journal of the European Communities* C 066 of 15.03.2002. Non-opposition.

Case COMP/M.2996 *RTL/CNN/Time Warner/N-TV. Official Journal of the European Communities* C 245 of 11.10.2002. Non-opposition.

Case COMP/38.089 *Télèvision Francáise 1 and Mètropole. Official Journal of the European Communities* C 103 of 03.04.2001. Non-opposition.

Case IV/M.2300 *YLE/TDF/Digita/JV. Official Journal of the European Communities* C 272 of 27.09.2001. Non-opposition

Case IV/M.2407 *Bertelsmann/RTL Group. Official Journal of the European Communities* C 291 of 17.10.2001. Non-opposition.

Case IV/M.2437 *NEC/Toshiba. Official Journal of the European Communities* C 189 of 05.07.2001. Non-opposition.

Case M.2222 *UGC/Liberty Media. Official Journal of the European Communities* C 172 of 16.06.2001. Non-opposition.

Case M.2407 *Bertlesmann/RTL. Official Journal of the European Communities* C 291 of 17.10.2001. Non-opposition.

Case M.2483 *Group Canal+/RTL/GJCD/JV.* Not published in the *Official Journal.* Press release IP/01/1579. 13.11.2001. Non-opposition.

Case M.2471 *Accenture/Lagardere/JV. Official Journal of the European Communities* C 327 of 22.11.2001. Non-opposition.

Case M.2487 *Bertelsmann/Arnoldo Mondadori/JV. Official Journal of the European Communities* C 279 of 03.10.2001. Non-opposition.

Case M.2572 *Time/IPC. Official Journal of the European Communities* C 321 of 16.11.2001. Non-opposition.
Case IV/M.2480 *Thomson/Carlton/JV. Official Journal of the European Communities* 238 of 24.08.2001. Non-opposition.
Case IV/M.2124 *ISP/ESPN/GLOBOSAT. Official Journal of the European Communities* C 190 of 06.07.2001. Non-opposition.
Case IV/M.2155 *Schmid/MOBILCOM. Official Journal of the European Communities* C 130 of 01.05.2001. Non-opposition.
Case IV/M.2643 *Blackstone/CDPQ/DeTeKS/BW. Official Journal of the European Communities* 358 of 15.12.2001. Non-opposition.
Case IV/M.2211 *Universal Studio Networks/De Facto 829 (NTL)/Studio Channel Ltd. Official Journal of the European Communities* 363 of 19.12.2001. Non-opposition.
Case IV/M.1958 *Bertelsmann/GBL/Pearson TV. Official Journal of the European Communities* C 180 of 26.06.2001. Non-opposition.
Case IV/M.1958 *Bertelsmann/Kooperativa Förbundet/BOL.* Nordic *Official Journal of the European Communities* C 212 of 25.07.2000. Non-opposition.
Case JV.40 *Canal+/Lagardere/Canal Satellite. Official Journal of the European Communities* C 002 of 05.01.2001. Non-opposition.
Case M.2165 *Gruner + Jahr/Publigroupe/G+J Medien. Official Journal of the European Communities* C 196 of 12.07.2001. Non-opposition.
Case M.2211 *Universal Studio Networsk/De Facto 829 (NTL)/Studio Channel Ltd. Official Journal of the European Communities* C 363 of 19.12.2001. Non-opposition.
Case M.2336 *Thomson Multimedia/Technicolor. Official Journal of the European Communities* C 206 of 24.07.2001. Non-opposition.
Case 37576 *UEFA's broadcasting regulations. Official Journal of the European Communities* L 171 of 26.06.2001. Opposition.
Case M.1943 *Telefonica/Endemol. Official Journal of the European Communities* C 235 of 17.08.2000. Non-opposition.
Case M.2147 *VNU/Hearst/Stratosera. Official Journal of the European Communities* C 16 of 18.01.2001. Non-opposition.
Case IV/M.1889 *CLT-UFA/Canal Plus/Vox. Official Journal of the European Communities* C 134 of 13.05.2000. Non-opposition.
Case JV.30 *BVI television (Europe)/SPE Euromovies Investments/Europe Movieco Partners. Official Journal of the European Communities* C 95 of 04.04.2000. Non-opposition.
Case JV.39 *Bertelsmann/Planeta/NEB. Official Journal of the European Communities* C 125 of 04.05.2000. Non-opposition.
Case IV/32.150 *Eurovision. Official Journal of the European Communities* L 151 of 24.06.2000.
Case IV/M.0037 *BSkyB/KirchPayTV. Official Journal of the European Communities* C 110 of 15.04.2000. Non-opposition.
Case IV/M.1972 *Granada/Compass. Official Journal of the European Communities* C 237 of 19.08.2000. Non-opposition.
Case IV/M.2026 *Clear Channel Communications/SFX Entertainment. Official Journal of the European Communities* C 366 of 20.12.2000. Non-opposition.

Case JV.37 *BSkyB/KirchPayTV*. *Official Journal of the European Communities* C 07. 21.03.2000. Non-opposition.

Case JV.46 *Blackstone/CDPQ Kabel NordrheinWestfalen*. *Official Journal of the European Communities* C 66 of 20.06.2000. Non-opposition.

Case JV.5 *CEGETAL/Canal +/AOL/Bertelsmann*. *Official Journal of the European Communities* C 24 of 28.01.2000. Non-opposition.

Case NN-88/98 *Financing of a 24-hour advertising-free news channel with licence fee by BBC*. *Official Journal of the European Communities* C 78 of 18.03.2000. Non-opposition.

Case COMP/M.2652 *Callahan Invest/Kabel Baden-Württemberg*. *Official Journal of the European Communities* C 395 of 02.08.2000. Non-opposition.

Case IV/M.2050 *Vivendi/Canal Plus/Seagram*. *Official Journal of the European Communities* C 311 of 13.10.2000. Non-opposition.

Case NN 140/98 *Capital increase and other support measures in favour of RAI Text*. *Official Journal of the European Communities* C 351 of 04.12.1999.

Case M.1701 *Gruner+Jahr/Dekra/Faircar*. *Official Journal of the European Communities* C 24 of 24.11.1999. Non-opposition.

Case NN-70/98 *State Aid to Public Broadcasting Channels 'KinderKanal' and 'Phoenix'*. *Official Journal of the European Communities* C 238 of 21.08.1999. Non-opposition.

Case JV.33 *Hearst/VNU*. *Official Journal of the European Communities* C 143 of 16.05.2001. Non-opposition.

Case COMP/JV.27 *Microsoft/Liberty Media/Telewest*. *Official Journal of the European Communities* C 342 of 30.11.1999. Proposal withdrawn.

Case IV/M.1529 *Havas Advertising/Media Planning*. *Official Journal of the European Communities* C 190 of 07.07.1999. Non-opposition.

Case IV/M.1401 *Recoletos/UNEDISA*. *Official Journal of the European Communities* C 4064 of 01.02.1999. Non-opposition.

Case IV/M.1574 *Kirch/Mediaset*. *Official Journal of the European Communities* C 255 of 08.09.1999. Non-opposition.

Case IV/M.1327 *NC/Canal Plus/CDPQ/Bank America*. *Official Journal of the European Communities* C 233 of 14.08.1999. Non-opposition.

Case IV/JV.16 *Bertelsmann/VIAG/Game Channel*. *Official Journal of the European Communities* C 186 of 20.05.1999. Non-opposition.

Case IV/M.1529 *Havas Advertising/Media Planning*. *Official Journal of the European Communities* C 190 of 10.06.1999. Non-opposition.

Case 36237 *TPS*. *Official Journal of the European Communities* L 90 of 02.04.1999. Antitrust exemption.

Case IV/M.1459 *Bertelsmann/Havas/BOL*. *Official Journal of the European Communities* C 176 of 06.05.1999. Non opposition.

Case IV/M.1407 *Bertelsmann/Mondadori*. *Official Journal of the European Communities* C 145 of 22.04.1999. Non-opposition.

Case IV/M.1455 *Gruner+Jahr/Financial Times/JV*. *Official Journal of the European Communities* C 247 of 20.04.1999. Non-opposition.

Case IV/M.1377 *Bertelsmann/Wissenschaftsverlag Springer*. *Official Journal of the European Communities* C 122 04.05.1999. Non-opposition.

Case IV/M.1275 *Havas/Bertelsmann/Doyma*. *Official Journal of the European Communities* C 139 of 19.05.1999. Non-opposition.

Case IV/M. 476 *Telia/Telenor/Schibsted. Official Journal of the European Communities* C 220/09 of 31.07.1999. Non-opposition.

Case IV/M.993 *Bertelsmann/Kirch/Premiere. Official Journal of the European Communities* L 53 of 27.02.1999. Opposition.

Case IV/M.1027. *Deutsche Telekom/BetaResearch. Official Journal of the European Communities* L 53 of 27.02.1999. Opposition.

Case 36539 *British Interactive Broadcasting. Official Journal of the European Communities* L of 06.12.1999. Antitrust: exemption.

Case IV/M.999 *CLT-UFA/Havas Intermédiation. Official Journal of the European Communities* C 39 of 06.02.1998. Non-opposition.

Case IV/M. 1072 *Bertelsmann/Burda/Futurekids. Official Journal of the European Communities* C 116 of 16.04.1998. Non-opposition.

Case IV/M.1040 *Wolters Kluwer/Reed Elsevier. Official Journal of the European Communities* C 13 of 17.01.1998. Case dropped after Commission objection.

Case No M.1219 *Seagram/Polygram. Official Journal of the European Communities* C 309 of 09.10.1998. Non-opposition.

Case IV/M.1091 *Cableuropa/Spainco/CTC. Official Journal of the European Communities* C 97 of 31.3.1998. Non-opposition.

Case IV/M.1022 *Cable i Televisio de Catalunya (CTC). Official Journal of the European Communities* C 101 of 03.04.1998. Non-opposition.

Case IV/M.939 *Bankamerica/General Electric/Cableuropa. Official Journal of the European Communities* C 235 of 2.8.1997. Non-opposition.

Case IV/M.973 *Bertelsmann/Burda Hos Lifeline. Official Journal of the European Communities* C 360 of 26.11.1997. Non-opposition.

Case No IV/M.972 *Bertelsmann/Burda/Springer Hos MM. Official Journal of the European Communities* C 360 of 26.11.1997. Non-opposition.

Case No IV/M.856 *British Telecom/MCI (II). Official Journal of the European Communities* C 336 of 08.12.1997. Non-opposition, but abandoned.

Case No IV/M.866 *CEREOL/ SAT. Official Journal of the European Communities* C 146 of 14.05.1997. Non-opposition.

Case No IV/M 827 *DBKOM. Official Journal of the European Communities* C 168 of 03.06.1997. Non-opposition.

Case IV/M.878 *RTL 7. Official Journal of the European Communities* C 122 of 01.07.1997. Non-opposition.

Case IV/M.826 *ESPN/Star. Official Journal of the European Communities* C 386 of 11.11.1996. Non-opposition

Case No IV/M.0779 *Bertelsmann/CLT (Ufa). Official Journal of the European Communities* C 364 of 04.12.1996. Non-opposition

Case No IV/M.810 *N-TV. Official Journal of the European Communities* C 366/05 of 05.12.1996. Non-opposition.

Case IV/M.553 *RTL/Veronica. Official Journal of the European Communities* L 649, 17.07.1996. Opposition.

Case IV/M.717 *Viacom/Bear Stearns. Official Journal of the European Communities* C 132 of 04.05.1996. Non-opposition.

Case IV/M.0709 *Telefónica/Canal Plus/Cablevisión. Official Journal of the European Communities* C 228 of 07.08.1996. Opposition.

Case IV/M.673 *Channel Five. Official Journal of the European Communities* C 57 of 27.02.1996. Non-opposition.

Case IV/M.595 *British Telecomm/VIAG. Official Journal of the European Communities* C 15 of 20.01.1996. Non-opposition.

Case No IV/M.655 *Canal/UFA/MDO. Official Journal of the European Communities* C 15 of 20.01.1995. Non-opposition.

Case IV/M.544 *Unisource/Telefónica. Official Journal of the European Communities* C 13 of 06.11.1996. Non-opposition.

Case No IV/M.604 *Albacom (BT/BNL). Official Journal of the European Communities* C 278 of 24.10.1995. Non-opposition.

Case IV/M.553 *RTL/Veronica/Endemol. Official Journal of the European Communities* C 294 of 19.11.1996. Opposition.

Case No.IV/M.618 *Cable&Wireless/Vebacom. Official Journal of the European Communities* C 231 of 16.08.1995. Non-opposition.

Case IV/M.490 *Nordic Satellite Distribution. Official Journal of the European Communities* C 53 of 19.07.1995. Opposition.

Case 4064/89 *Seagram/MCA. Official Journal of the European Communities* C 149 of 16.06.1995. Non-opposition.

Case IV/M.584 *Kirch/Richemont/Multichoice/Telepiù. Official Journal of the European Communities* C 129 of 16.06.1995. Non-opposition.

Case IV/M.566 *CLT/Disney/Super RTL. Official Journal of the European Communities* C 144 of 10.06.1995. Non-opposition.

Case IV/M.579 *Blockbuster/Burda. Official Journal of the European Communities* C 129 of 25.05.1995. Non-opposition.

Case IV/M.538. *Omnitel/Burda. Official Journal of the European Communities* C 96 of 20.04.1995. Non-opposition.

Case IV/M.561 *Securicor/Datatrak. Official Journal of the European Communities* C 82 of 20.03.1995. Non-opposition.

Case IV/M.525 *Vox (II). Official Journal of the European Communities* C 57 of 07.03.1995. Non-opposition.

Case IV/M.469 *MSG Media Service. Official Journal of the European Communities* L 364 of 09.11.1994. Opposition.

Case IV/M.489 *Bertelsmann/News International/Vox Decision. Official Journal of the European Communities* C 274 of 01.10.1994. Non-opposition.

Case IV/M.410 *Kirch/Richemont/Telepiù Decision. Official Journal of the European Communities* C 225 of 13.08.1994. Non-opposition.

Case IV/M.353 *British Telecom/MCI. Official Journal of the European Communities* C 259 of 27.08.1993. Non-opposition.

Case IV/M.425 *BS/BT. Official Journal of the European Communities* C 134 of 17.05.1994. Non-opposition.

Case IV/M.423 *Newspaper Publishing. Official Journal of the European Communities* C 85 of 22.03.1994. Non-opposition.

Case IV/32.150 *EBU/Eurovision Decision. Official Journal of the European Communities* L 179 of 22.07.1993. Exemption (overturned by ECJ).

Case IV/33 *Tiercé Ladbroke SA. Official Journal of the European Communities* C 699 of 24.06.1993. Opposition (upheld by ECJ).

Case IV/33.145 and IV/33.245 *BBC/BSkyB/Football Association. Official Journal of the European Communities* C 94 of 03.04.1993. Non-opposition.

Case IV/M.176. *Sunrise Television Decision. Official Journal of the European Communities* C 18 of 24.01.1994. Non-opposition.

Case IV/M.133 *Ericsson/Kolbe. Official Journal of the European Communities* C 27 of 22.01.1992. Non-opposition.

Case IV/M.110 *ABC/Generale des Eaux/Canal+/WH Smith. Official Journal of the European Communities* C 244 of 10.09.1991. Non-opposition.

Case IV/32.524 *Screensport/EBU. Official Journal of the European Communities* L 063 of 09.03.1991. Opposition.

Case Iv/M037 *Matsushita/MCA. Official Journal of the European Communities* C 10 of 18.1.1991. Non-opposition.

Case IV/30.566. *UIP Decision. Official Journal of the European Communities* L 226 of 12.07.1989. Non-opposition.

Case IV/31.731. *ARD/Metro Goldwyn Meyer. Official Journal of the European Communities* L 284 of 03.10.1989. Non-opposition.

Appendix 4: Treaties of the European Union

2003 Draft Treaty establishing a Constitution for Europe. *Official Journal of the European Communities* C 169 of 18.07.2003.

2001 Treaty establishing the European Community (the Treaty of Nice). *Official Journal of the European Communities* C 80 of 10.03.2001.

1997 Treaty of Amsterdam: Consolidated Version of the Treaty Establishing the European Community. *Official Journal of the European Communities* C 340 of 10.11.1997.

1992 Treaty on European Union (Treaty of Maastricht). *Official Journal of the European Communities* C 191 of 29.07.1992.

1987 Single European Act. *Official Journal of the European Communities* L 169 of 29.06.1987.

1957 Treaty establishing the European Economic Community (Treaty of Rome).

Appendix 5: European Commission Questionnaires

Questionnaire No I concerning a possible initiative on media ownership

Pluralism and media concentration in the internal market
QUESTION 1: The Commission would welcome the views of interested parties regarding the needs for action, and in particular on:
- any cases where the Community dimension or media activity has meant that restrictions on media ownership imposed for the purpose of maintaining pluralism have become ineffective, for example because they circumvented or because of transparency problems; the existence of restrictions or restrictive effects other than those identified here:
- practical instances where ownership questions restrictions have actually impeded the activity of economic operators in the sector;
- the sectors and activities which are especially affected by restrictions on ownership (for example is the press subject to restrictive effects not only in respect of multimedia aspects but also In respect of monomedia aspects?)

QUESTION 2: The Commission would welcome the views of interested parties on whether the needs identified of sufficient importance, in the light of community objectives, to require action in the media industry and, if when such action should be taken.

QUESTION 3: The Commission would welcome he views of interested parties on the effectiveness, in the light Community objectives, of action which would be taken solely at Member State level.

QUESTION 4: The Commission would welcome the views of interested parties on the content of a possible harmonisation instrument as envisaged above, and in particular on the two variants for its scope on the use real audience as a basis for setting thresholds, on the demarcation of distribution areas, on any other references, and on ways of defining the concept of controller.

QUESTION 5: The Commission would welcome the views of interested parties on the desirability of action to promote transparency which would be separate from a harmonisation instrument.

QUESTION 6: The Commission would welcome the views of interested parties on the desirability of setting up a body with competence for media concentration.

QUESTION 7: The Commission would welcome the views of interested parties on each of these foreseeable options.

Complementary questionnaire (II)

Relating to the green paper 'pluralism and media concentration in the internal market: an assessment of the need for community action' of 23 December 1992 (COM (92) 480 final)

QUESTION A. New technologies

A.1 Identify the new technologies or those under expansion which will effect the market (distinguishing namely between those which, from the point of view of the consumer, will replace existing technology and those which will be of a more complementary nature giving details of the expected time scale for implementation of these technologies).

A.2 What economic impacts will be foreseeable at the Community level, in particular on the market structure and on the strategy of operators within the internal market? This evaluation will not have to be all encompassing but should be carried out on a technology by technology basis. It is important to give precise information about the access costs to these technologies, in particular for the consumer and the operators.

A.3 What impacts will be foreseeable on the national statutory arena in regard to media ownership? Does current national legislation covering media ownership permit, or, on the contrary, limit, the development of these new technologies (explain the effect of any limitations)?

A.4 To what degree could the new technologies develop conditions for the granting of authorisations or licences applicable to television or radio operators? In particular, which conditions, besides those relating to pluralism, could be envisaged?

QUESTION B. Potential development of national legislations

B.1 Are you aware of any proposals for new anti-concentration rules, in the Member States, specific to the media? What is their origin and objective?

B.2 Would you welcome a change in the applicable regulatory framework?

B.3 What factors could change the national regulatory framework in the future (new broadcaster authorisations, case law developments, political debates, ineffectiveness of national rules, over-stringent rules, etc.)?

B.4 How long did it take to draw up the current regulations and were you involved in this process?

B.5 Could these possible changes accentuate or attenuate the regulatory disparity between the Member States of the Community?

QUESTION C. Possible use of the audience criterion

C.1 Given that a criterion of potential audience (like the population covered by a satellite footprint) would be too restrictive, what type of audience measurement might be utilised in particular for multimedia and monomedia concentration of radio and television enterprises (for example, 'audience share' for television, 'daily share' for radio, number of dailies sold for newspapers)?

C.2 With reference to criteria used in national arenas, namely the number of channels will the audience criterion offer more opportunities to access the market, namely for thematic channels (by reason of their weak audience)?

C.3 What might the necessary conditions be to make a system using thresholds based on audience levels workable (compatibility, comparability, equivalence, etc.?) Is it possible to have a single audience criteria applicable to multimedia or is it necessary to have several distinct criteria applicable to each media or combinations of media?

C.4 Might it be deemed necessary to have complementary criteria such as, for example, that of language of the media, that of the type of radio station or TV channel concerned, that of the number of licenses granted at the same time, etc. . . . ?

C.5 Should the fixing of thresholds leave a discretion to the Member States to set stricter limits for operators established on their territory?

QUESTION D. Possible use of the media control criterion

D.1 Is it necessary to go further than existing company law to define media control in specific rules?

D.2 what comments can be made on the definitions used for media controllers in current national regulations?

D.3 What elements should a definition contain bearing in mind the objectives of effectiveness, adaptability to the Community framework, and compatibility with existing systems as well as the economic and technological effects that could result?

Questionnaire No III concerning a possible initiative on media ownership

Pluralism and media concentration in the internal market
QUESTION A. The need for Community action

A.1 Can you comment (giving practical examples etc.) on the analysis of the need for a Community initiative set out in the communication?

A.2 Have you any specific comments to make on the analyses presented in Part III.A. of the communication or the impact of establishing a set of Community ground rules?

QUESTION B. Scope of a possible initiative

B.1 Are new interactive services already covered by the national rules on media ownership that concern you? (if so please describe the relevant provisions).

B.2 If not, is any draft regulation under consideration or is the possibility of applying rules on media ownership to interactive services under discussion?

B.3 Should a possible Community initiative cover new interactive services? If so, why?

B.4 Should a possible Community initiative cover concentration between press enterprises? (Please give reasons).

B.5 Would it not be sufficient to apply (national or Community) competition law, with specific notification thresholds where appropriate?

B.6 If concentration between press enterprises were to be covered, what type of publication should be included (e.g. all daily press, the daily newspapers, magazines)?

B.7 Should public channels be fully or partly subject to the same conditions governing access to media ownership as private channels? (please give reasons).

B.8 Could certain channels be excluded on the basis of the programmes they broadcast (specialised, general-interest, news-only, etc.) or other criteria such as the language in which they are broadcast?

B.9 Do the specific rules and regulations on media ownership which are designed to safeguard pluralism and which concern you cover operators (in the production, distribution, cable distribution, etc. sectors) outside the traditional media (television, radio and newspapers)?

B.10 Would be necessity for rules on pluralism (not competition rules) to cover non-media enterprises or vertical integration itself? If so, why?

QUESTION C. Principles underpinning the internal market

C.1 Could the place establishment of a media enterprise be used to determine which State is responsible for supervising it and which law it is governed by (jusridiction criteria)?

C.2 If it were decided to opt for Community harmonisation, which type of harmonisation should be chosen; complete or minimum?

QUESTION D. Conditions governing access to media ownership to be included in a possible initiative

D.1 Are there, in the Member States which concerns you any new rules (dating from after the December 1992 Green Paper), planned measures or discussions on the conditions governing access to media ownership thought necessary in order to safeguard pluralism? If so, what is the approach taken: tighten the limits, relaxing or liberalising the regime to take account of new technologies, increasing effectiveness, etc.?

D.2 What is your assessment (effectiveness, implementation suitability for the information society, etc.) of the criteria used in existing or planned rules and regulations on pluralism with a view to limiting media concentration (limitation of the holding that can be acquired in the capital of any one television channel; limitation of the number of channels; limitation by reference to the public served; limitation by reference to market share; etc.)

D.3 What type of conditions and what type of criteria should be used in a possible Community initiative on media ownership in order to safeguard pluralism? (Please give reasons).

D.4 On what analysis (of the impact on pluralism and of the economic impact) do you base your appraisal of the conditions and criteria? (Please present the analytical method).

QUESTION E. Criteria for defining the media controller

E.1 Please describe briefly the definition(s) of media controller used in die rules on access to media ownership that concern you. You are welcome to comment or the analysis made in the study

E.2 Should a possible Community initiative define de facto control or it be confined to de jure control? Where appropriate, how could de facto control be defined in a possible Community initiative?

E.3 Please comment on the tour criteria identified in the study: ownership links, links with employees, financial links and contractual links (supply, distribution, etc.).

E.4 How should these criteria be spelt out, in particular the criterion of contractual links which should make it possible to cover cases of vertical integration?

E.5 If several criteria were to be used for identifying the media controller(s), what should the relationship between them:

- criteria to be ranked by order of importance, or some criteria having subsidiary status;
- criteria to be applied cumulatively without any order of precedence;
- assessment on a case-by-case basis at the discretion of the national authorities

E.6 To what extent do you consider that the vertical integration of functions such as broadcasting and conditional access will affect pluralism as well as competition?

E.7 Should family links be taken into account in identifying the media controller? If so, how: up to what degree? Should a link constitute merely am indication or a presumption? Under what circumstances should the presumption be dropped or be deemed irreputable?

E.8 Should a change of media controller he subject to prior authorisation or merely to notification?

QUESTION F. Criterion of actual audience

F.1 Could the audience criterion be used for the purposes of safeguarding pluralism to measure the level of media concentration? Please comment on the attached study on the feasibility of using audience measurement

F.2 What conditions would have to be satisfied for it to be feasible louse the audience criterion?

F.3 Should the audience criterion be used in conjunction with other additional criteria (number of channels, revenue, restrictions on holdings, etc.)? If so, why?

F.4 Within the area in which the channel is broadcast, should it not be possible to waive application of the thresholds where they are exceeded only in a small or sparsely populated area? If so, on what basis should such an area be defined: size or population?

F.5 What reference period should be taken for audience measurements (e.g. the most recent twelve-month period for which data are available)?

F.6 What type on audience measurement should be used? What is your opinion on the types of measurement envisaged in the conclusions of the study;

- monomedia television concentration: Audience share.-share of total TV viewing time;
- monomedia radio concentration: Listenership share: share of daily average reach-the average number of listeners listening to a station at least once a day:
- monomedia newspaper concentration (if the case arises): Circulation share share of daily average number of copies of each issue circulated the public;
- multimedia concentration: Daily average contact (radio = listenership share; TV = day average reach (the average number of viewers viewing a channel at least once a day: newspapers = daily average readership (the daily average number of readers per issue)?

F.7 Should there be a single overall multimedia limit or several cumulative limits according to the type of concentration (monomedia television/monomedia radio/multimedia)

F.8 Should a distinction be drawn between the type of channel concerned (specialised, general-interest, news-only etc.)?

F.9 To what extent could multi-channel television broadcasting be taken into account?

F.10 Should the types of measurement (mentioned in question F.6) be found and spelt out in the Directive and, if so, to what extent?

F.11 What could be the thresholds above which a media concentration could be limited in the interests of pluralism? (Please specify the type of criteria and the reasoning on which you base these thresholds).

F.12 On what analysis (of the pact on pluralism and of the economic impact) do you base your view of these thresholds? (Please present the method of analysis).

F.13 What effect should exceeding these thresholds have (prohibition of the concentration, presumption against it, further examination of the case, flexibility in other respects etc)?

QUESTION G. Disqualified persons

G.1 What are the rules restricting or preventing the access of certain persons to media ownership in the Member State(s) which concern you?

G.2 What types or categories of person should be denied access to media ownership by a possible Community initiative and why?

QUESTION H. Transparency and exchange of information

H.1 For what types of information should disclosure to the competent authorities be made mandatory?

H.2 What types of information should be confidential?

H.3 How could the direct exchange of information between the national authorities be organised and facilitated?

H.4 Should information on operators who have been granted an authorisation or licence be systematically published?

QUESTION I

I.1 What advantages could a European committee offer compared with a situation where only the national authorities were involved and co-operated directly with each other? Now could such a committee ensure that possible initiative was applied more effectively?

I.2 What could be the composition and terms of reference of a European committee?

I.3 How could the independence of such a committee be ensured?

QUESTION J. Type of Community Instrument

J.1 What type of legal instrument should be chosen for a possible Community initiative: a Directive, a regulation, a recommendation or any other type of measure (please specify)?

References

Agence Europe (1996a), 'Commission policy debate on Wednesday on concentrations and pluralism in the media-European Directive or a simple recommendation', 02.09.1996.

Agence Europe (1996b), 'Commission proposes approving before summer break its proposal on concentration of media, setting ceilings for audience shares in order to safeguard pluralism', 18.07.1996.

Agence Europe (1996c), 'Commission policy debate on concentration', 29.07.1996.

Agence Europe (1996d), 'Mr Monti to continue examination of initiatives to be taken on mergers and pluralism-opinions differ at Commission', 05.09.1996.

Agence Europe (1996e), 'Council explains its rejection of parliaments amendments to its common position on Television Without Frontiers', 17.09.1996.

Agence Europe (1996f), 'Concern of European publishers over the draft directive on concentrations and pluralism', 02.09.1996.

Agence Europe (1997a), 'Commission discusses draft directive on ownership of media in the single market', 03–4.03.97.

Agence Europe (1997b), 'European Commission gives itself more time to study the issue of media ownership', 21.03.1997.

Allen, D. (1996), 'Competition policy: policing the single market', in H. Wallace and W. Wallace (eds), *Policy-Making in the European Union*, Oxford: Oxford University Press, pp. 158–83.

Arino, M. (2002), 'The role of regulation in emerging markets: standard setting and interoperatility in interactive television', EUI Working Group on Media Law and Policy, Florence, 18 December.

Bahu-Leyser, D. (1993), 'Mass media policy', in Francois-Georges Dreyfus, Jacques Morizet and Max Peyrard (eds), *France and EC Membership Evaluated*, London: Pinter Press, pp. 232–44.

Bangemann, M. (1997), Speech at the Geneva Telecom Interactive 'A new world order for global communications', Conference organised by the International Telecommunication Union (ITU), 08.09.1997.

Barendt, E. (1993), *Broadcasting Law: A Comparative Study*, Oxford: Clarendon Press.

Belluzzi, M. (1994), 'Cultural protection as a rationale for legislation: the French language law of 1994 and the European trend toward integration in the face of increasing US influence', *Dickens Journal of International Law*, 14, pp. 127–39.

Beltrame, F. (1996), 'Harmonising media ownership rules: problems and prospects', *Utilities Law Review*, 5:7, pp. 182–75.

——(1997), 'A socio-legal analysis of the European legislative initiative on pluralism and media concentration in the Internal market', PhD thesis, Università degli studi di Milano.

Bertrand, C.J. (1985), 'Cable television in France', in Ralph M. Negrine (ed.), *Cable Television and the Future of Broadcasting*, York: St Martin's Press, pp. 134–63.

Blanco, S. and J. Vandenbulck (1995), 'Regions v. states and cultures in the EC media policy debate: regional broadcasting in Belgium and Spain', *Media, Culture and Society*, 17, pp. 239–51.

Blumler, J. (1992), *Television and the Public Interest Vulnerable Values in West European Broadcasting*, London: Sage.

Bomberg, E. and J. Peterson (1999), *Decision-making in the European Union: Towards a Framework for Analysis*, London: Macmillan Press.

Booz-Allen & Hamilton (1989), 'Strategic partnerships as a way forward in European broadcasting', by I. Hughes, A. Mierzwa and G. Morgan, London: Booz-Allen & Hamilton.

——(1990), 'Television ownership and control in the nineties', London: Booz-Allen & Hamilton.

——(1992), 'Study on pluralism and concentration in media – economic evaluation', Brussels, 6 February commissioned by the Commission of the European Communities, DG III-F-5.

Börzel, T. (1999), 'Towards convergence in Europe? Institutional adaptation to Europeanization in Germany and Spain', *Journal of Common Market Studies*, 37:4, pp. 573–96.

Bowler, S. and D. Farrell (1995), 'The organizing of the EP committees specialization and co-ordination', *British Journal of Political Science*, 25, pp. 219–43.

Brealey, M. (1994), 'European community competition policy', *Journal of Common Market Studies*, 32:4, pp. 278.

Brenner, J.L. (1993), *Competition Policy and a Changing Broadcasting Industry*, Paris: OECD.

British Media Industry Group (BMIG) (1995), *A New Approach to Cross-Media Ownership*, London.

Broadcasting and Cable (1993), 'French quotas', *Broadcasting and Cable*, 123:36, pp. 28.

Bromley, M. (1999), 'The UK market', *European Journalist Center newsletter*, May.

——(2001), 'The British media landscape', *European Journalist Center newsletter*, www.ejc.nl/jr/emland/uk.html.

Bulmer, S. (1994), 'Institutions and policy change in the European communities: the case of merger control', *Public Administration*, 72:3, pp. 423–44.

Bulmer, S. and K. Armstrong (1998), *The Governance of the Single European Market*, Manchester: Manchester University Press.

Bundgaard, Bente (1990), 'The big players in Europe', IFJ Information Sheet, June.

Butterworth's Merger Control Review (1995), 'Article 8 decisions: Nordic Satellite Distribution – Case No.IV/M490', *Buttersorth's Merger Control Review*, 5:3, pp. 12–15.

Caiger, A. (1997), 'Guide to United Kingdom and European Union competition policy', *Entertainment Law Review*, 22:1, pp. 96–7.

Caporaso, J. (1996), 'The European Union and forms of state: Westphalian, regulatory or post-modern?', *Journal of Common Market Studies*, 34:1, pp. 29–52.

Carat Crystal and Bird & Bird (2002), 'Study on the development of new advertising techniques for DG Culture', Brussels, 21.05.2002.

CEC (Commission of the European Communities)

——(1978a), 'Untersuchung zur Konzentrationsentwicklung in Presse und Verlagswesen der Bundesrepublik Deutschland. Evolution Concentration and Competition Series'. Luxembourg, Office for Official Publications of the EC. 1978.

——(1978b), 'A Study of the Evolution of Concentration in the press and General Publishing Industry of the United Kingdom, Evolution Concentration and Competition Series'. Luxembourg, Office for Official Publications of the EC. 1978.

——(1983), 'Realities and tendencies in European television: perspectives and options'. COM (83) 299 final. Brussels.

——(1984), 'Television Without Frontiers: Green Paper on the Establishment of the Common Market for Broadcasting, Especially by Satellite and Cable'. COM (84) 300. Brussels, May 1984.

——(1985), 'White Paper on completing the internal market: from the Commission to the European Council'. COM(85) 310. Milan, 28-29.06.1985.

——(1989), 'Satellite Broadcasting in Europe and the New Technologies'. Prepared for DG VI by G. Locksley. Brussels. May.

——(1990), 'Communication to the Council and European Parliament on audiovisual policy'. COM(90) 78. Brussels, 21.02.90.

——(1992a), 'Pluralism and media concentration in the internal market' Green Paper, COM(92) 480. Brussels, 23.12.1992.

——(1992b), 'The operation of the Community's internal market after 1992. Follow-up to the Sutherland Report'. SEC(92) 2277 final. 02.12.1992.

——(1992c), 'Report on the internal market after 1992. Meeting the challenge. From the High Level Group on the Operation of Internal Market. (Sutherland Report). November 1992.

——(1993a), 'Growth, competitiveness and employment: the challenges and ways forward into the 21st Century'. White Paper, COM (93) 700 final. Brussels, 05.12.1993.

——(1993b), 'Follow-up to the Sutherland Report: legislative consolidation to enhance the transparency of Community law in the area of the internal market'. COM(93)361 final. 16.12.1993.

——(1993c), 'Communication on the handling of urgent situations in the context of implementation of Community rules. Follow-up to the Sutherland Report'. COM(93)430 final. 16.12.1993.

——(1994a), 'Follow-up to the consultation process relating to the Green Paper on 'Pluralism and media concentration in the internal market – an assessment of the need for community action'. COM (94) 353. Brussels, 05.10.1994.

——(1994b), 'Compilation of submissions to the first and second Commission questionnaire on media ownership'. Working document of Directorate-General for the Internal Market no. XV/9555/94. Brussels, 1994.

——(1994c), 'Resolution on a framework for Community policy on digital video broadcasting'. *Official Journal of the European Communities* C 181 of 02.07.1994.

——(1994d), 'La Transparence dans le contrôle des médias'. Report submitted to the European Commission by the European Institute for the Media. Düsseldorf 1994.

——(1994e), 'Europe and the global information society, Recommendations to the European Council. Report by the High Level Group on the Information Society' (Bangemann Report). Brussels, May 1994.

——(1994f), 'Europe's way to the information society: An action plan'. COM (94) 347 Final. Brussels, 19.7.1994.

——(1995a), 'Proposal for a Directive amending Council Directive 89/552/EEC on the coordination of certain provisions laid down by law, regulation or administrative action in Member States concerning the pursuit of television broadcasting activities'. COM (95) 86. *Official Journal of the European Communities* C 185 of 19.07.1995.

——(1995b), 'Agreement between the Government of the United States of America and the Commission of the European Communities regarding the application of their competition laws'. *Official Journal of the European Communities* L 132 of 15.06.1995.

——(1996a), 'Report on building the European information society for us all. First reflections of the High Level Group of Experts'. Interim Report. Directorate-General for employment, industrial relations and social affairs (V), Unit V/B/4. 01.04.1996.

——(1996b), 'Communication on the implications of the information society for European Union policies: Preparing the next steps'. COM (96) 395. Brussels, 14.07.1996.

——(1996c), 'Report on competition rules in the culture sector'. Directorate-General for Competition (IV), 01.09.1996.

——(1996d), 'Draft Proposal for a Directive on Media Pluralism'. Directorate-General for the Internal Market (XV), Brussels, July.

——(1996e), 'Note on the Status of Work on the Regulatory Implications of the Convergence Between Telecommunications and Audiovisual Sectors'. Brussels, November.

——(1996f), 'Green Paper on Commercial Communications in the Internal Market'. COM (96) 192. Brussels, April.

——(1997a), 'The convergence of the telecommunications, media and information technology sectors, and the implications for regulation', Green Paper, COM (1997) 623. Brussels, 03.12.1997.

——(1997b), 'Proposal for a Directive on "Media ownership in the internal market"', Working document of Directorate-General for the Internal Market (XV). Brussels, 01.02.1997.

——(1997c), 'Second report on the application of Directive 89/552/EEC "Television without frontiers"'. COM (97) 523. Brussels, 21.0.1997.

——(1997d), 'Action plan for the Single Market', COM (97)1. Brussels, 04.06.1997.

——(1997e), 'Building the European information society for us all. Final Policy Report of the High-Level Expert Group'. HC240.9 I55E87. Brussels, April.

——(1998a), 'Report on job opportunities in the information society. Exploiting the potential of the information revolution'. COM (1998) 590. Brussels, 25.11.1998.

——(1998b), 'Report on the digital age: European audiovisual policy'. From the High Level Group on Audiovisual Policy, chaired by Commissioner Marcelino Oreja. Brussels, 26.10.1998.

——(1998c), 'Study on the comparative overview of current regulatory environment in telecommunications and broadcasting sectors: Annex I: Study on adapting the EU telecommunications regulatory framework to the developing multimedia environment conducted for the European Commission' (Directorate-General XIII) by Squire, Sanders & Dempsey L.L.P. Brussels, 01.01.1998.

——(1999a), 'Communication from the Commission towards a new framework for electronic communications infrastructure and associated services – the 1999 communications review'. COM (1999) 539, Brussels, 01.11.1999.

——(1999b), 'Communication from the Commission on the convergence of the telecommunications, media and information technology sectors, and the implications for regulation: results of the public consultation of the Green Paper'. COM (1999) 108. Brussels, 14.12.1999.

——(1999c), 'Communication on principles and guidelines for the Community's audiovisual policy in the digital age'. COM (1999) 657. Brussels, 14.12.1999.

——(1999d), 'Annex to Council Decision No. 276/1999/EC adopting a multiannual Community Action Plan on promoting safer use of the Internet by combating illegal and harmful content on global networks'. *Official Journal of the European Communities* C 33 of 06.02.1999.

——(1999e), 'Decision on state aid financing of a 24 hour news channel out of the licence fee by the BBC'. SG (99) D/10201.

——(1999f), 'Resolution concerning public service broadcasting'. *Official Journal of the European Communities* C 30 of 05.02.1999.

——(2000), 'Pluralism and concentration in the media in the age of globalisation and digital convergence', Economic and Social Committee. Rapporteur: Joël Decaillon. Brussels, 29.03.2000.

——(2001a), 'Communication on the application of state aid rules to public service broadcasting'. COM (2001) 320 *Official Journal of the European Communities* C 320/5 of 15.11.2001.

——(2001b), 'White Paper on European governance', COM (2001) 428 *Official Journal of the European Communities* C 287 of 12.10.2001.

——(2001c), 'Communication on services of general interest in Europe', COM (2000) 580. Brussels, 17.10.2000.

——(2002a), 'The 2003 regulatory framework for electronic communications and services – Implications for broadcasting', Working Document of the Open Network Provision Committee. Directorate-General Information Society. Brussels, 14.06.2002.

——(2002b), 'eEurope 2005: An information society for all'. Presented to the Seville European Council of 21/22 June 2002. COM(2002) 263. Brussels, 28.5.2002.

——(2002c), 'European Governance: Better-lawmaking'. COM(2002) 275. Brussels, 05.06.2002.

——(2003a), 'Communication on the future of European regulatory audiovisual policy'. COM (2003) 784. Brussels, 15.12.2003.

——(2003b), 'Conclusions 2003/C13/01 of the Council on the Television Without Frontiers Directive'. *Official Journal of the European Communities* C 13 of 18.01.2003.

——(2003c), 'Fourth report on the application of Directive 89/552/EEC Television Without Frontiers'. COM(2002) 778. Brussels, 06.01.2003.

——(2003d), 'Green Paper on Services of general interest'. COM (2003) 270. Brussels, May 2003.

——(2003e), 'Towards, an international instrument on cultural diversity. Communication from the Commission to the Council and the European Parliament. COM (2003) 520. Brussels, 27.08.2003.

——(2004), 'White Paper on Services of general interest'. COM (2004) 374. Brussels. 12 May 2004.

Chalaby, J.K. (2002), 'Transnational television in Europe: the role of pan-European channels', European Journal of Communication, 17:2, pp. 183–203.

Chalmers, D. (1998), European Union Law, London: Ashgate.

Chrocziel, P. and J. Dieselhorst (1996), 'Multimedia legislation in Germany: what is "broadcasting?"', Computer and Telecommunications Law Review, 2:5, pp. 194–97.

Cini, M. and L. McGowen (1999), Competition Policy in the European Union, London: Macmillan.

Collins, R (1994b), Broadcasting and Audio-visual Policy in the European Single Market, London: John Libby.

——(1994a), 'Unity in diversity? The European single market in broadcasting and the audiovisual, 1982–92', Journal of Common Market Studies, 32:1, pp. 89–102.

——(1998), From satellite to Single Market: New Communication Technology and European Public Service Television, London: Routledge.

——(2003), 'Enter the Grecian horse? Regulation of foreign ownership of the media in the UK', Policy Studies, 24:1, pp. 17–31.

Collins, R. and C. Murroni (1996), New Media, New Policies: Media and Communications Strategy for the Future, London: Sage.

Common Market Law Review (CMLR) (1995), 'Case C-23/93', Common Market Law Review, 32:5, pp. 1257–76.

Communications and Information Technology (CIT) (2001), The Media Map of Western Europe, London: CIT.

Competition Policy Newsletter (2000), Number 3, Brussels: European Commission, October.

Congdon, T., A. Graham, D. Green and B. Robinson (1995), The Cross Media Revolution: Ownership and Control, London: John Libbey.

Council of Europe (1997), 'Report on media concentrations and pluralism in Europe', Secretariat Memorandum prepared by the Directorate of Human Rights, MM-CM 6, Strasbourg, January.

Crabit, E. (1995), 'Medienpluralismus und konzentration. 10 Fragen und Antworten zu den Arbeiten der Kommission', IRIS, pp. 12–14.

Crabit, E. and J. Bergevin (1995), 'Le cadre réglementaire des services de la société de l'information: Laboratoire pour un nouveau droit du marché intérieur?', Revue du Marché Unique Européen, 1, pp. 17–74.

Cram, L. (2001), 'Governance "to go": domestic actors, institutions and the boundaries of the possible', Journal of Common Market Studies, 39:4, pp. 595–618.

Cram, L. and H. Drake (1996), 'French leadership in the European context', American Political Science Association conference, San Francisco.

Craufurd Smith, R. (2002), 'State support for public service broadcasting: the position under European Community law', *European Public Law*, 8, p. 107.

——(2003), 'European Community audiovisual policy and reform of the "Television Without Frontiers Directive"', *European Current Law*, May.

Curran, J. and J. Seaton (1997), *Power without responsibility: the press and broadcasting in Britain*, London: Routledge.

Dai, X., A. Cawson and P. Holmes (1996), 'The rise and fall of high-definition TV: the impact of European technology policy', *Journal of Common Market Studies*, 34:2, pp. 149–66.

Dammeyer, A. (1996), 'Europa muß mehr Verantwortung für eine soziale und pluralistische Mediengesellschaft übernehmen', Public speech by the German Minister for Federal and European Affairs, European Parliament, Brussels.

Davies, S. and D. Hall (1999), 'Corruption and whistle-blowing: a back-ground note for TUAC', Public Services International Research Unit, London.

Davis, A. (1997), 'European Union: Commission priorities for consumer policy', *Consumer Law Journal*, 5:1, pp. 105–11.

Dehousse, R. (1998), *The European Court of Justice: The Politics of Judicial Integration*, Basingstoke: Macmillan.

De La Porte, Caroline (2002), 'Is the open method of coordination appropriate for organising activities at European level in sensitive policy areas?', *European Law Journal*, 8:1, pp. 38–58.

Della Sala, Vince and Amie Kreppel (1998), 'Dancing without a lead: legislative decrees in Italy', in Matthew Shugart and John Carey (eds), *Executive Decree Authority*, Cambridge: Cambridge University Press.

Dellarte, P. (1996), *Oltre Il Villaggio Globale*, London: Electra.

de Mateo, R. (1997), 'Regulation of the Media in Spain, in B.S. Ostergaard (ed.), *The Media in Western Europe*, London: Sage.

De Mendivil, A.A. (1995), 'Spain: broadcasting', *Computer and Telecommunications Law Review*, 1:6, pp. 145–6.

Dempsey, J. (1996), 'Survey – Europe's most respected companies: conflict of cultures for media giant', *Financial Times*, 18 September.

Department of National Heritage (DNH) (1996a), *Terrestrial Digital Broadcasting: An Explanatory Guide to the Provisions introduced by the Broadcasting Act*, London: DNH.

——(1996b), *Media Ownership Regulation: An Explanatory Guide to the Provisions in the Broadcasting Acts 1990 and 1996*, London: DNH.

De Witte, B. (1995), 'The European content requirement in the EC Television Directive – five years after', *The Yearbook of Media and Entertainment Law*, pp. 101–27.

Dieter, W. (1997), 'Position on the subject of "Commission and national competence – a debate"', Paper presented at the Future of Merger Control in Europe conference, Committee C (Antitrust and Trade Law) of the International Bar Association, European University Institute, Florence, 26 September.

Doyle, G. (2002), *Media Ownership: The Economics and Politics of Convergence and Concentration in the UK and European Media*, London: Sage Publications.

Drake, H. (1997), 'The European Commission and the politics of legitimacy in the EU', in N. Nugent (ed.), *At the Heart of the Union: Studies of the European Commission*, London: Macmillan, pp. 226–44.

Earnst & Young (2002), *M&A Trends in the European Publishing Industry*, London: Earnst & Young.

Eberlein, B. (2004), 'Formal and informal governance in Single Market regulation', in Thomas Christiansen and Simona Piattoni (eds), *Informal Governance in the European Union*, Cheltenham: Edward Elgar.

Economic and Social Committee (1993), 'Opinion on the Commission Green Paper action', *Official Journal of the European Communities* C 304.

——(1995), 'Opinion on Follow-up to the consultation process relating to the Green Paper on pluralism and media concentration in the internal market-an assessment for Community action', *Official Journal of the European Communities* C 110 of 02.05.1995.

——(1998), 'Opinion on Commission draft Directive amending Directive 90/388/EEC', *Official Journal of the European Communities* C 407 of 28.12.1998.

——(2000), 'Pluralism and concentration in the media in the age of globalisation and digital convergence', Rapporteur: Joël Decaillon, Brussels, 29.03.2000.

EP (European Parliament)

——(1980a), 'The threat to freedom of speech and media pluralism through the commercialisation of the New Media'. Document 1-422/80. September 1980.

——(1980b), 'Proposal for a European television area'. Document 1-409/80. September 1980.

——(1982), 'Report on radio and television broadcasting in the European Community on behalf of the Committee on Youth, Culture, Education, Information and Sport (The Hahn Report). Document 1-1013/81. 23.02.1982.

——(1984), 'Resolution on report on radio and television broadcasting in the European Community (The Hahn Resolution). *Official Journal of the European Communities* C 87 of 05.04.1982.

——(1985), 'Resolution on the economic aspects of the common market for broadcasting'. Document A2-102/85. *Official Journal of the European Communities* C 300 of 30.09.1985.

——(1986), 'Resolution on the Fifteenth Report of the CEC on competition policy'. Document A2-10/86. 14.11.1986.

——(1987), 'Resolution on the Sixteenth Report of the CEC on competition policy'. Document A2-223/87.

——(1988), 'Barzanti Report PEDOC A2-246/87'. *Official Journal of the European Communities* C 110 of 27.04.1988.

——(1990a), 'Resolution on the draft Commission directive amending Directive 90/388/EEC in order to ensure that telecommunications networks and cable TV networks owned by a single operator are separate legal entities'.

——(1990b), 'Resolution on media takeovers and mergers'. *Official Journal of the European Communities* C 68 of 15.02.1990.

——(1990c), 'Albor motion for resolution on concentration of information'. Document B3-455/90.

——(1990d), 'Ferri motion for resolution on anti-trust legislation for the media'. Document B3-842/90.

——(1991a), 'Titley and others motion for resolution on importance of diversity in the media'. Document B3-894/91.

—— (1991b), 'Titley and others motion for resolution on tendency towards the concentration of ownership in the media industry'. Document B3-895/92.

—— (1991c), 'Ortega motion for resolution on local television in Europe'. Document. B3-721/91.

—— (1991d), 'Motion for Resolution on media concentration and the organization of the "Fourth Estate"'. B3 – 0220/91.

—— (1992a), 'Resolution on media concentration and pluralism of information'. *Official Journal of the European Communities* C 282 of 16.09.1992.

—— (1992b), 'Resolution on media concentration and diversity of opinions'. *Official Journal of the European Communities* C 284 of 02.11.1992.

—— (1993a), 'Resolution on freedom of expression, freedom of the press and freedom of information'. *Official Journal of the European Communities* C 20 of 24.01.1994.

—— (1993b), 'Renewal of United International Pictures exemption'. *Official Journal of the European Communities* C 329 of 19.11.1993.

—— (1994a), 'Resolution on Concentration of the media and pluralism'. *Official Journal of the European Communities* C 323 of 21.11.1994.

—— (1994b), 'Resolution on the Commission Green Paper "Pluralism and Media Concentration in the Internal Market"'. Document A3-0435/93. *Official Journal of the European Communities* C 44/177 of 14.02.1994.

—— (1995a), 'Resolution on pluralism and media concentration'. *Official Journal of the European Communities* C 166 of 15.06.1995.

—— (1995b), 'Resolution on the communication from the Commission "Green Paper on the liberalization of telecommunications infrastructure and cable television networks"'. *Official Journal of the European Communities* C 109 of 01.05.1995.

—— (1995c), 'Resolution on the G7 conference on the information society'. *Official Journal of the European Communities* C 56 of 06.05.1995.

—— (1996a), 'Pluralism and Media Ownership – A Study of the Commission's Proposal'. Document NW/CT. 20.10.1996.

—— (1996b), 'Motion for a resolution: the future of public service television in a multi-channel digital age' (Carol Tongue Report). Document A4-0243/96.

—— (1998), 'Resolution on the draft Commission directive amending Directive 90/388/EEC in order to ensure that telecommunications networks and cable TV networks owned by a single operator are separate legal entities'. Document A4-0487/98. *Official Journal of the European Communities* C 150, 28.05.1999.

—— (2001), 'Resolution on the third report on the application of Directive 89/552/EEC 'Television without Frontiers'. COM 2001. Document A5-0286/2001. *Official Journal of the European Communities* C 87 11.04.2002.

—— (2002), 'European Parliament resolution on media concentration'. Provisional Document P5_TA-PROV2002/0554.

—— (2003a), 'Provisional draft report on the Communication from the Commission to the Council, the European Parliament and the European Economic and Social Committee on a Comprehensive EU Policy Against Corruption'. Committee on Citizens' Freedoms and Rights, Justice and Home Affairs. (2003/2154(INI)). Rapporteur: Francesco Rutelli. 02.09.2003.

—— (2003b), 'Provisional draft report on the application of Directive 89/552/EEC "Television without Frontiers"'. Committee on Culture, Youth, Education, the Media and Sport Document A5-0251/2003. Rapporteur: Roy Perry. 05.05.2003.

——(2004), 'Possible breach of expression and information rights in the EU and Italy, Article 11(2), Charter of Fundamental Rights. Document 339.618/PR. April 2004.

European Audio-visual Observatory (1997), *Statistical Yearbook on the Media*, Strasbourg: European Audio-visual Observatory.

——(2002), *Statistical Yearbook on the Media*, Strasbourg: European Audio-visual Observatory.

European Institute for the Media (EIM) (1993), *Media Concentration in Europe: Commercial Enterprise and the Public Interest*, Düsseldorf: European Institute for the Media.

——(1994), *La Transparence dans le contrôle des médias*, Düsseldorf: European Institute for the Media.

——(1995), 'Bericht über die Entwicklung der Meinungsvielfalt und der Konzentration im privaten Rundfunk gemäß § 21, Abs. 6, Staatsvertrag über den Rundfunk im vereinten Deutschland', *Die Sicherung der Meinungsvielfalt. Die Landesmedienanstalten*, Berlin: Vistas, pp. 127–220.

European Council (2002), European Council, Presidency Conclusions, Barcelona, March.

European Report (1995a), 'Broadcasting: Oreja calms US fears without making concessions', *European Report*, 2044.

——(1995b), 'Media concentration directive in the pipeline', *European Report*, 2071.

——(1996a), 'Information Society Forum presents its recommendations', *European Report*, 2132.

——(1996b), 'Broadcasting: European Parliament rejects television quotas', *European Report*, 2175.

——(1996c), 'MEPs urge "Tougher" television Directive', *European Report*, 2172.

——(1996d), 'Restricting mergers to protect pluralism', *European Report*, 2151.

——(1996e), 'Commission reveals strategy', *European Report*, 2152.

——(1996f), 'Commission divided on draft Directive on Media Ownership', *European Report*, 2154.

European Union (2000), 'Charter of Fundamental Rights European Union', *Official Journal of the European Communities* C 364/3, 18.12.2000.

European Voice (1997), 'Media industry awaits Monti's second coming', *European Voice*, 3–9 April.

Fenoulhet, T.R. 'The regulatory dynamics of the information society', in A. Dumort and J. Dryden (eds), *The Economics of the Information Society*, Luxembourg: Office for Official Publications of the European Communities and OECD, pp. 20–30.

Fine, F.L. (1997), 'Recent developments in EC Merger Control', Future of Merger Control in Europe conference, European University Institute, Florence, September.

Fraser, M.W. (1996), 'Television', in H. Kassim and A. Menon (eds), *The European Union and National Industrial Policy*, London: Routledge, pp. 153–77.

Froehlinger, M. (1993), 'EG Wettbewerbsecht und Fernsehen', *Rundfunk und Fernsehen*, 41, pp. 59–65.

Frohn, R. (1996), 'Land-Bund-Europa: Überholtes Kimpetenzgerangel? Der Rundfunk in der globalen Multimediawelt von morgen', speech to public service conference by the Nordrhein-Westfalen Staatsekretär, October.

Fuller, C. (1995), 'Media ownership rules: a quarrelsome subject in Europe', *Broadcasting and Cable*, 7:3, pp. 16–17.

Gagliardi, A. (1994),'Legal aspects of the Italian broadcasting system-a state of flux', *Copyright World*, 52, pp. 35–49.

Garrett, L.L. (1994), 'Commerce versus culture: the battle between the United Sates and the European Union over audiovisual trade policies', *North Carolina Journal of International Law and Commercial Regulation*, 19, pp. 553–77.

General Agreement on Tariffs and Trade. Multilateral Trade Negotiations Final Act Embodying the Results of the Uruguay Round of Trade Negotiations, Art. xxix (2) (b), 15 April: 33 1.L.M.1125.

Gibbons, T. (1997), *Regulating the Media*, London: Sweet & Maxwell.

—— (2003), 'Control over technical bottlenecks – a case for media ownership law?', Vertical Limits – New Challenges for Media Regulation, Observatory/IviR/EMR Workshop, Amsterdam, September.

Glencross, D. (1991), 'Independent Television Commission: the reform of Broadcasting Regulation', in C. Veljanovski (ed.), *Regulators and the Market: An Assessment of the Growth of Regulation in the UK*, London: Institute of Economic Affairs, pp. 141–51.

Godard, F. (1995), 'France takes reins of EU as European co-production slides; with culture politics on legislative burner, stricter content quotas sought', *Broadcasting and Cable*, 125:4, p. 98.

Goodhall, Alexander, & O'Hare (GAH) (1993), 'Audience measurement in the EC', Report for Directorate-General for the Internal Market (XV), European Commission, September.

—— (1994), 'Feasibility of using audience measures to assess pluralism', position paper prepared for Directorate-General for the Internal Market (XV), European Commission, November.

Goldstein, A.E. and G. Nicoletti (1995), 'Corporate governance in Italy', *OECD Observer*, March/April, pp. 47–9.

Gormley, W.T. (1985), 'Regulatory issue-networks in a federal system', *Polity*, 18, pp. 595–620.

Graham, C. (1996), 'Reform of United Kingdom competition policy', *Utilities Law Review*, 7:4, pp. 128–31.

Grisold, A. (1996), 'Press concentration and media policy in small countries', *European Journal of Communication*, 11:4, pp. 485–509.

Guillou, B. (1991), *Expanding Abroad: The Canal Plus Experience*, 5th International Marketing Satellite Conference, London.

—— (1988), *La régulation de la télévision*, Paris: La Documentation Française.

Gustafsson, K.E. and L. Weibull (1997), 'European newspaper readership: structure and development', *Communications*, 22:3, pp. 249–73.

Hall, D. (1998), 'Restructuring and privatization in the public utilities – Europe', in De Luca, L. (ed.), *Labour and Social Dimensions of Privatization and Restruc-*

turing (public utilities: water, gas and electricity), Geneva: International Labour Office, pp. 109–51.

Hancher, L. (1999), Case C7/97, *Oscar Bronner GmbH & Co. KG v. Mediaprint ZeitungsundZeitschriftenverlag GmbH & Co. KG, Mediaprint Zeitungsvertriebsgesellschaft mbH & Co. KG and Mediaprint Anzeigengesellschaft mbH & Co. KG*, Judgment of the Sixth Chamber, 26 November 1998, *Common Market Law Review*, 36: 1289–307.

Harcourt, A. (1996), 'Regulating for media concentration: the emerging policy of the European Union', *Utilities Law Review*, 5:7, pp. 202–10.

——(2003), 'The regulation of media markets in selected accession states in Central and Eastern Europe', *European Law Journal*, 8:2, pp. 316–40.

Hayward, J. (1995), *Industrial Enterprise and European Integration: From National to International Champions in Western Europe*, Oxford: Oxford University Press.

Heritier, A. (2001), 'Overt and cover institutionalization', in Stone Sweet, A.W. Sandholts and N. Fligstein (eds), *The Institutionalization of Europe*, Oxford: Oxford University Press, pp. 56–70.

Herkströter, D. (1994), 'Die Entwicklung der Landesmediengesetze', *Rundfunk und Fernsehen*, 42, pp. 60–81.

Herold, A. (2003), 'European public film support within the WTO framework', *IRIS. Legal Observations*, June, Strasbourg: European Audiovisual Observatory.

Herman, E.S. and N. Chomsky (2002), *Manufacturing Consent: The Political Economy of the Mass Media*, New York: Pantheon Books.

Hills, Jill and Maria Michalis (2000), 'Restructuring regulation: technological convergence and European telecommunications and broadcasting markets', *Review of International Political Economy*, 7:3, pp. 434–64.

Hirsch, M. and V. Petersen (1992), 'Regulation of media at the European level', in K. Siune and W. Truetschler (eds), *Dynamics of Media Policy: Broadcasting and Electronic Media in Western Europe*, London: Sage Publications, pp. 42–56.

Holtz-Bacha, C. (1991), 'From public monopoly to a dual broadcasting system in Germany', *European Journal of Communication*, 6, pp. 223–40.

Hooper, J., J. Cassy and M. Milner (2002), 'Investors take Kirch's fate to the wire', *Guardian*, 4 April.

Hopewell, J. (1996), 'The reign in Spain: new regime faced with thorny media problems', *Variety*, 362:10, pp. 41.

Humphreys, P. (1994), *Media and Media Policy in Germany: The Press and Broadcasting Since 1945*, New York: Berg German History-Media Publisher.

——(1996), *Mass Media Policy in Western Europe*, Manchester: Manchester University Press.

——(1997), 'Power and control in the new media', ECPR workshop New Media and Political Communication, Bern, February.

——(1998), 'The goal of pluralism and the ownership rules for private broadcasting in Germany: re-regulation or de-regulation?', *Cardozo Arts and Entertainment Law Journal*, 16:2–3, pp. 527–55.

Humphreys, P. and M. Lang (1998), 'Regulating for media pluralism and the pitfalls of Standortpolitik in a federal political system: a study of the re-regulation of German broadcasting ownership rules', *German Politics*, 7:2, pp. 176–201.

Information Infrastructure Task Force, US Department of Commerce (1993), *The National Information Infrastructure: Agenda for Action*, 15 September.

IPTS (2000), 'Employment outlook and occupational change in the media content industries (2000–2005)', Scenarios and background note, IPTS, Seville.

Isofides, P. (1997), 'Methods of measuring media concentration', *Media, Culture and Society*, 19, pp. 643–63.

Istituto di Economia dei Media (1998), '*L'industra della comunicazione in Italia*', Torino: Fondazione Rosselli.

Johnson, Debra and Nicole McCormick (1996), 'Canal+ gets green light in Germany', *Broadcasting and Cable*, 126:35, p. 69.

Johnson, M. and J. Rollo (2001), 'EU enlargement and commercial policy: enlargement and the making of commercial policy', Sussex European Institute Working Paper.

Jones, C. (1999), 'The evolution of media regulation in the US: pluralism and commercial broadcasting', Paper presented to the Programme in Comparative Media Law and Policy, University of Oxford University, 16 June.

Jones, T. (1996), 'Opinion split over media ownership', *European Voice*, 05.09.1996.

——(1997), 'Commission trio united over media ownership', *European Voice*, 27.02.1997.

Jordan, G. and J. Richardson (1979), *Governing Under Pressure: The Policy Process in a Post-parliamentary Democracy*, Oxford: Blackwell.

Kagan (2003), *Media Mergers and Acquistions*, London: Kagan.

Kaminski, I. (2002), 'Western media standards and their applicability in the new democracies – non-constitutional issues', Open Society Initiative, Budapest.

Kies, R. (2002), 'E-voting and the formation of public opinion', EUI Working Group on Media Law and Policy, November.

Kleinsteuber, H. (1997), 'Federal Republic of Germany (FRG)', in Bernt Stubbe Østergard (ed.), *The Media in Western Europe: The Euromedia Handbook*, London: Sage, pp. 7–97.

Kleinsteuber, H. and B. Thomaß (2002), 'The German media landscape', European Journalism Centre, www.ecj.nl.

KMPG (1996), 'Public policy issues arising from telecommunications and audiovisual convergence', Commission of the European Communities, Brussels.

Knill, C. and D. Lehmkuhl (1999), 'How Europe matters', European Integration online Papers (EioP), 3:7.

Kon, S. (1996), *Competition Law and the Audio Visual Industry*, London: S.J. Berwin & Co.

Korthals Altes, W.F. (1993), 'European law: a case study of changes in national broadcasting', *Cardozo Arts and Entertainment Review*, 11, pp. 313–35.

Koss, S. (1984), *The Rise and Fall of the Political Press in Britain*, London: Hamish Hamilton.

Krebber, D. (2001), *Europeanisation of Regulatory Television Policy*, Baden-Baden: Nomos Verlagsgesellschaft.

Kubicek, H., W. Dutton and R. Williams (eds) (1997), *The Social Shaping of Information Superhighways: European and American Roads to the Information Society*, Frankfurt: Campus Verlag.

Kuhn, M. (1998), 'How can Europe benefit from the Digital Revolution?', Speech given by the President of Polygram Filmed Entertainment to the European Audiovisual Conference, Birmingham, 6–8 April.

Kuhn, R. (1995), *The Media in France*, London: Routledge.

Ladeur, K.H. (1995), 'Unternehmensverfassung und Rundfunkverfassung', in W. Hoffmann-Riem and T. Vesting (eds), *Perspektiven der Informationsgesellschaft*, Baden-Baden: Nomos, pp. 172–89.

Lane, D. (1997), 'Prodi delays reform of TV regulation', *Financial Times*, 29 August.

Lang, J.T. (1997a), 'Media, multimedia and European Community Antitrust Law', Directorate-General for Competition (IV), European Commission.

Lang, Matthias (1997b), 'Entering the digital age: the promise of pluralism and the danger of monopoly control', ECPR-Workshop, 'New media and political communication', March.

Lange, A. and S. Newman-Baudais (2003), 'The fragmented universe of film distribution companies in Europe', Paper at the workshop 'Distribution of European films' during the Ministerial Seminar of the Ministers of Culture of the European Union on 'The circulation of European works of art inside the European Union: support mechanisms and new technologies', Venice, 28–31 August.

Lange, A. and A. Van Loon (1990), 'Multimedia concentration regulation in Europe', Montpellier, IDATE and Amsterdam, Institute for Information Law.

Laven, P. (2002), 'Technical standards (MHP)', Co-regulation of the Media in Europe Workshop, Organised by OBS, IViR, EMR, European University Institute, Florence, 6 and 7 September.

Leibfried, S. and P. Pierson (1996), 'Social policy', in H. Wallace and W. Wallace (eds), *Policy-Making in the European Union*, pp. 185–207.

Leonard, Tom (2003), 'Tessa Jowell's millionaire husband in fraud inquiry', *Daily Telegraph*, 8 February.

Levy, D.A. (1997), 'Regulating digital broadcasting in Europe: the limits of policy convergence', *West European Politics*, 20:4, pp. 24–42.

—— (1999), *Europe's Digital Revolution: Broadcasting Regulation, the EU and the Nation States*, London: Routledge.

Llorens-Maluquer, C. (1998), 'European responses to bottlenecks in digital pay-TV', *Cardozo Arts and Entertainment Law Journal*, 16:2, pp. 425–49.

Majone, G.D. (1992), 'Regulatory federalism in the European Community', *Environment and Planning Policy C: Government and Policy*, 10, pp. 299–316.

—— (1993), 'The European Community between social policy and social regulation', *Journal of Common Market Studies*, 31:2, pp. 153–70.

—— (1994), 'The rise of the regulatory state in Europe', *West European Politics*, 17:3, pp. 77–101.

—— (1996), *Regulating Europe*, London: Routledge.

—— (2000), 'The credibility crisis of community regulation', *Journal of Common Market Studies*, 38:3, pp. 299–316.

Mancini, P. (1999), 'New frontiers in political professionalization', *Political Communication*, 16:3, pp. 231–45.

McGowan, L. and S. Wilks (1995), 'The first supranational policy in the EU: competition policy', *European Journal of Political Research*, 28, pp. 141–69.

McKenna, A. (2000), 'Emerging issues surrounding the convergence of the telecommunications, broadcasting and information technology sectors', *Information and Communications Technology Law*, 9:2, pp. 103–27.

McQuail, D. (1994), *Mass Communications Theory*, London: Sage.

Mastroianni, R. (1999), 'La revisione della direttiva "televisione senza frontiere"', *Diritto delle radiodiffusioni e delle telecomunicazioni*, 1, pp. 185–95.

——(2000), 'Case C6/98, *Arbeitsgemeinschaft Deutscher Rundfunkanstalten (ARD)* v. *PRO Sieben Media AG*, Judgement of the Court (Sixth Chamber) of 28 October 1999', *Common Market Law Review*, 37, pp. 1445–64.

Mazzoleni, M. (1999), 'The Italian market', *European Journalist Center newsletter*, May.

Michalis, M. (1999), 'European Union broadcasting and telecoms: towards a convergent regulatory regime?', *European Journal of Communication*, 14:2, pp. 147–71.

Moran, M. and T. Prosser (1994), *Privatization and Regulatory Change in Europe*, London: Oxford University Press.

MUDIA (2002), *The European Multimedia News Landscape*, Madrid: Institute for Prospective Technological Stuides (IPTS).

Murdock, G. (2000), 'Digital futures: European television in the age of convergence', in Wieten *et al.* (eds), *Television Across Europe: A Comparative Introduction*, London: Sage, pp. 35–57.

Murschetz, P. (1998), 'State support of the daily press in Europe: a critical appraisal. Austria, France, Norway and Sweden Compared', *European Journal of Communication*, 13:3, pp. 291–313.

Natalicchi, G. (2002), *Wiring Europe: reshaping the European telecommunications regime*, Boulder, CO: Rowman & Littlefield.

National Economic Research Associates (NERA) (1995), *Media Market Shares*, August, London: DNH.

New Media Markets (1994), 'RTL chief attacks audience-share plan', *New Media Markets*, 12:27, pp. 6–7.

——(1995), 'German regulators at odds over ownership plan', *New Media Markets*, 13:37, pp. 8–10.

Noam, E. (1995), 'Electronics and the dim future of the universities', *Science*, 270.

——(1998), 'Will books become the dumb medium?', *Educom Review Sequence*, 33 (March/April).

Norris, P. (2000), *A Virtuous Circle: Political Communications in Post-Industrial Democracies*, Cambridge: Cambridge University Press.

OECD (1992a), *Telecommunications and Broadcasting: Convergence or Collision?* Paris: OECD.

——(1992b), *Convergence between Communications Technologies: Case Studies from North America and Western Europe*, Paris: OECD.

——(1993), *Competition Policy and a Changing Broadcast Industry*, Paris: OECD.

OECD (1998), 'The role of telecommunication and information services polices', Background Paper for the OECD Ottawa Ministerial Conference A Borderless World: Realising the Potential of Global Electronic Commerce, Ottawa, Canada, 7–9 October.

OECD and DG XIII of the European Commission (1997), 'The regulatory dynamics of the information society in the economics of the information society', Paris: OECD.

Ostergaard, B.S. (1997), *The Media in Western Europe*, London: Sage.

Palmer, M. and C. Sorbets (1997), 'France', in Bernt Stubbe Østergard (ed.), *The Media in Western Europe: The Euromedia Handbook'*, London: Sage, pp. 57–73.

Palzer, C. (2003), 'European provisions for the establishment of co-regulation frameworks', Co-regulation of the Media in Europe Workshop, organised by OBS, IViR, EMR, European University Institute, Florence, 6 and 7 September.

Picard, R. (2002), 'Assessing audience performance of public service broadcasters', *European Journal of Communication*, 17:2, pp. 227–47.

Poll, G. (1996), 'Germany: new TV ownership regulations', *International Media Law*, 14:8, pp. 63.

Radaelli, C. (1997), *The Politics of Corporate Taxation in the European Union*, London: Routledge.

——(2003), 'The open method of coordination: a new governance architecture for the European Union?', Swedish Institute for European Policy Studies, Stockholm, April.

Ridder, C.M. (1996), 'Germany', in *Media Ownership and Control in the Age of Convergence*, London: International Institute of Communications.

Robillard, S. (1995), *Television in Europe: Regulatory Bodies Status, Functions and Powers in 35 European Countries*, London: Libbey.

Robins, K. and D. Morley (1992), 'Euroculture: Communications, community and identity in Europe', Cardozo Arts & Entertainment Law Journal, 11: 387.

Rhodes, R. (1988), *Beyond Westminster and Whitehall*, London: Routledge.

Röper, H. (2002), 'Formationen deutscher Medienmultis 2002: Entwicklungen und Strategien der größten deutschen Medienunternehmen', *Medienperspektiven*, 9: 406–32.

Sanchez-Tabernero, A. *et al.* (1993), *Media Concentration in Europe: Commercial Enterprise and the Public Interest*, Düsseldorf: European Institute for the Media.

Satori, C. (1996), 'The media in Italy', in Weymouth and Lamizet, *Markets and Myths: Forces for Change in the Media of Western Europe*, pp. 134–70.

Scharpf, F. (1996), 'Negative and positive integration in the political economy of European welfare states', in G. Marks *et al.* (eds), *Governance in the European Union*, London: Sage, pp. 15–39.

——(1997), *Games Real Actors Can Play*, Boulder, Co: Westview.

Scheuer, A. and M. Knopp (2003), '"Digital television glossary": vertical limits', New Challenges for Media Regulation Observatory/IviR/EMR Workshop, Amsterdam, September.

Schlesinger, P. (1995), 'The cross media ownership debate', Stirling: Stirling Media Research Institute.

Schoof, J. and K. Brown (1995), 'Information highways and media politics in the European Union', *Telecommunications*, 19. pp. 325–38.

Scott, J. and D.M. Trubek (2002), 'Mind the gap: law and new approaches to governance in the European Union', *European Law Journal*, 8:1, pp. 1–18.

Shapiro, M. (1980), *Courts: A Comparative and Political Analysis*, Chicago: University of Chicago Press.

Shew, W. (1989), *Measures of Media Concentration* (commissioned by News International), Washington, DC: American Enterprise Institute.

——(1994), *UK Media Concentration* (commissioned by News International), Director of Economic Studies, Arthur Andersen Economic Consulting, London.

Snoddy, R. (1997), 'UK: EU raises doubts on digital TV licence bid', *Financial Times*, 4 June.

Sparks, C. (1995), 'Concentration and market entry in the UK national daily press', *European Journal of Communication*, 10:2, pp. 179–206.

Stone Sweet, A., W. Sandholts and N. Fligstein (eds) (2001), *The Institutionalization of Europe*, Oxford: Oxford University Press.

Suarez Lozano, J.A. (1996), 'The 93/83/EEC Directive is incorporated in the Spanish legal system through the 28/1995 Law', *Entertainment Law Review*, 7:2, pp. 93–4.

Thatcher, M. (1999), *Politics of Telecommunications*, Oxford: Oxford University Press.

Tongue, C. (1996a), 'Pluralism and media ownership – a study of the Commission's (Summer 1996) Proposal', European Parliament, Brussels.

——(1996b), 'From a letter to all European Commissioners', October.

Trautmann, C. (1998), Speech given by the French Minister for Culture at the European Audiovisual Conference, Birmingham, 6–8 April.

Trubek, D. and J. Mosher (2002), 'New governance, employment policy and the European social model', in J. Zeitlin and D.M. Trubeck (eds), *Governing Work and Welfare in a New Economy: European and American Experiments*, Oxford: Oxford University Press, pp. 59–87.

Tucker, E. (1994), 'EU launches debate on new rules for IT', *Financial Times*, 23 September.

——(1995), 'Dutch television venture blocked', *Financial Times*, 21 September.

——(1997), 'EU media initiative bogged down', *Financial Times*, 13 March.

——(1998), 'Europe's paper mountain', *Financial Times*, 11 February.

Tucker, E. and H. Carnegy (1995), 'Ban on Nordic satellite TV joint venture', *Financial Times*, 20 July.

Ungerer, H. (1996), 'EC Competition law in the telecommunications, media and information technology sectors', *Fordham International Law Journal*, pp. 844–1177.

Ungerer, H. (2002), 'Media in Europe: media and the EU competition law', Conference on the Media in Poland by the Polish Confederation of Private Employers, Bristol Hotel, Warsaw, 13 February.

Venturelli, S. (1998), *Liberalizing the European Media: Politics, Regulation, and the Public Sphere*, Oxford: Oxford University Press.

Vilches, L. (1996), 'The media in Spain', in Weymouth and Lamizet, *Markets and Myths: Forces for Change in the Media of Western Europe*, pp. 173–99.

Volcansek, M. (1992b), 'The European Court of Justice: supranational policy making', *West European Politics: Special Issue – Judicial Politics and Policy Making in Western Europe*, 15, pp. 109–21.

Voorhoof, D. (1995), 'The Netherlands TV10-case and the judgment of the European Court of Justice: ECJ, 5 October 1994, C-23/93', *Journal of Media Law and Practice*, 16:2, p. 67.

Voltmer, K. (2000), 'Structures of diversity of press and broadcasting systems: the institutional context of public communication in Western democracies', WZB working paper. March.

Wallace, H. (1996), 'Politics and policy in the EU: the challenge of governance', in W. Wallace and H. Wallace (eds), *Policy-Making in the European Union*, Oxford: Oxford University Press, pp. 3–36.

Ward, David (2003), *The European Union Democratic Deficit and the Public Sphere: An Evaluation of EU Media Policy*, Amsterdam: IOS Press, p. 164.

Wall Street Journal (1997), 'The EU should leave media rules to Member States', 25 March.

Wattel, P. (1995), 'Case C-23/93, *TV 10 SA* v. *Commissariaat voor de Media*, judgment of 5 October 1994; circumvention of national law; abuse of Community law?', *Common Market Law Review*, 32:5, pp. 1257–70.

Weiler, J.H.H. (1994), 'A quiet revolution: the ECJ and its interlocutors', *Comparative Political Studies*, 26, pp. 510–34.

Wessels, W. and W. Weidenfeld (1997), *Europe from A to Z: Guide to European Integration*, Brussels: Institut für Europäische Politik.

Weymouth, A. and B. Lamizet (eds) (1996), *Markets and Myths: Forces for Change in the Media of Western Europe*, London: Longman.

Williams, G. (2002), *European Media Ownership: Threats on the Horizon*, Maastricht, European Journalism Centre, www.ejc.nl.

Wincott, D. (1993), 'The Treaty of Maastricht: an adequate constitution for the European Union?', EPPI Occasional Paper, 6.

—— (2001), 'Looking forward or harking back? The Commission and the reform of governance in the EU', *Journal of Common Market Studies*, 39:5, pp. 897–911.

Wolf, D. (1997), 'Position on the subject of "Commission and National Competence – A Debate"', Future of Merger Control in Europe conference, European University Institute, Florence, 26 September.

Ward, D. (2003), 'State aid or band aid? An evaluation of the European Commission's approach to public service broadcasting', *Media Culture and Society*, 25:2, pp. 233–47.

World Bank (2001), 'Media', *World Development Report 2002: Building Institutions for Markets*, New York: Oxford University Press.

Ypsilanti, Dimitri (1997), Speech on Convergence at The Aftermath of Liberalisation: Multi-level Governance in the Regulation of Telecommunications Workshop. Organised by the EUI Working Group on Telecommunications and the Information Society, European University Institute, Florence, 14 November.

Zampetti, A.B. (2003), 'WTO rules in the audio-visual sector', Hamburgisches Welt-Wirtschafts Archiv (HWWA), Hamburg Institute of International Economics, no. 229.

Zenith (2002), *Annual World Press Trends*, London: Zenith.

Index